Polish Music since Szymanowski

This book looks at Polish music since 1937 and its interaction with political and cultural turmoil. In Part One, the author places musical developments in the context of the socio-political upheavals of inter-war Poland, Nazi occupation, and the rise and fall of the Stalinist policy of socialist realism (1948–54). Part Two investigates the nature of the 'thaw' between 1954 and 1959, focussing on the role of the 'Warsaw Autumn' Festival. Part Three discusses how composers reacted to the onset of serialism by establishing increasingly individual voices in the 1960s. In addition to a discussion of 'sonorism' (from Penderecki to Szalonek), the author considers how different generations responded to the modernist aesthetic (Bacewicz and Lutosławski, Baird and Serocki, Górecki and Krauze). Part Four views Polish music since the early 1970s, including the recurring issue of national identity, as well as the arrival of a talented new generation and its ironic, postmodern slant on the past.

ADRIAN THOMAS is Professor of Music at Cardiff University and is a specialist in Polish music. He is the author of monographs on Bacewicz (1985) and Górecki (1997). He also contributed over fifty entries on post-war Polish composers to *The New Grove Dictionary of Music and Musicians* (2001). He is currently writing a study of Lutosławski's Cello Concerto as well as carrying out further research into socialist realism and Polish music in the post-war decade.

Music in the 20th Century

GENERAL EDITOR   Arnold Whittall

This series offers a wide perspective on music and musical life in the twentieth century. Books included range from historical and biographical studies concentrating particularly on the context and circumstances in which composers were writing, to analytical and critical studies concerned with the nature of musical language and questions of compositional process. The importance given to context will also be reflected in studies dealing with, for example, the patronage, publishing, and promotion of new music, and in accounts of the musical life of particular countries.

Recent titles

The music of John Cage
James Pritchett

The music of Ruth Crawford Seeger
Joseph Straus

The music of Conlon Nancarrow
Kyle Gann

The Stravinsky legacy
Jonathan Cross

Experimental music: Cage and beyond
Michael Nyman

The BBC and ultra-modern music, 1922–1936
Jennifer Doctor

The music of Harrison Birtwistle
Robert Adlington

Four musical minimalists: La Monte Young, Terry Riley, Steve Reich, Philip Glass
Keith Potter

Fauré and French musical aesthetics
Carlo Caballero

The music of Toru Takemitsu
Peter Burt

The music and thought of Michael Tippett: modern times and metaphysics
David Clarke

Serial music, serial aesthetics: compositional theory in post-war Europe
M. J. Grant

Britten's musical language
Philip Rupprecht

Music and ideology in Cold War Europe
Mark Carroll

Polish music since Szymanowski
Adrian Thomas

Polish Music since Szymanowski

Adrian Thomas

CAMBRIDGE
UNIVERSITY PRESS

PUBLISHED BY THE PRESS SYNDICATE OF THE UNIVERSITY OF CAMBRIDGE
The Pitt Building, Trumpington Street, Cambridge, United Kingdom

CAMBRIDGE UNIVERSITY PRESS
The Edinburgh Building, Cambridge, CB2 2RU, UK
40 West 20th Street, New York, NY 10011–4211, USA
477 Williamstown Road, Port Melbourne, VIC 3207, Australia
Ruiz de Alarcón 13, 28014 Madrid, Spain
Dock House, The Waterfront, Cape Town 8001, South Africa

http://www.cambridge.org

First published 2005

Printed in the United Kingdom at the University Press, Cambridge

Typeface Minion 10.5/13.5 pt.   *System* LATEX 2$_\varepsilon$ [TB]

A catalogue record for this book is available from the British Library

Library of Congress Cataloguing in Publication data
Thomas, Adrian, 1947–
Polish music since Szymanowski / Adrian Thomas.
       p.   cm. – (Music in the twentieth century ; 19)
Includes bibliographical references (p. 354) and index.
ISBN 0-521-58284-9
1. Music – Poland – 20th century – History and criticism.   I. Title.   II. Series.
ML297.5.T47   2004
780′.9438′0904 – dc21   2003055134

ISBN 0 521 58284 9 hardback

in memory of my parents

Let all streams springing from universal art mingle freely with ours; may they impregnate, differentiate and transform it in accordance with its particular attributes. We ought not to lose organic connection with universal culture, because it is only on such a plane that a truly great, living art, including nationalistic music, can flourish.

Karol Szymanowski, 'On Contemporary Musical Opinion in Poland' (1920), in Alistair Wightman (trans. and ed.), *Szymanowski on Music* (London: Toccata Press, 1999), p. 93

Contents

Musical examples

Table

Preface

In the late 1960s, I encountered two pieces of post-war Polish music: a score and recording of Lutosławski's *Trois poèmes d'Henri Michaux* and a recording of Górecki's *Refrain*. To someone being schooled in Western avant-garde modernism, their impact was immediate, not least because they managed to be both contemporary and communicative as well as sounding totally different from current Western European music. When I visited my first 'Warsaw Autumn' festival in 1970 and spent a short period of study in Kraków on a British Council grant, I discovered that this combination was characteristic of most Polish music of the time. As more scores came to my attention, I began to realise how complex were the cultural and political currents in Polish post-war music. This book is therefore an attempt to encompass those aspects that seem to me to have been central in shaping Polish music of the past sixty years or so.

I have not aimed to be comprehensive. Without resorting to long lists of composers and their works, this would have been well nigh impossible. It would also have been counterproductive, because so few of their names and titles, let alone the music itself, are known outside Poland. I hope that the many composers on whose imaginative and invigorating work I have not elaborated will forgive my concentration on what, for want of a better word, is my personal 'canon'. Over the years, many individual pieces have caught my ear, especially at the annual 'Warsaw Autumn' festival, yet it remains a fact that only a few Polish composers have international reputations. It is therefore inevitable that they should be central to any survey of post-war Polish music. In the 1960s, it was Penderecki and Lutosławski who became especially prominent; in some European countries, notably West Germany, a few other composers were also known, such as Serocki, Baird and Górecki. Only in the 1990s, however, did the music of Górecki rival that of Penderecki and Lutosławski internationally, while the profiles of Baird and Serocki faded (they both died in their fifties in 1981). There is, therefore, a revisionist ambition for this volume, which attempts to broaden the discussion in order to contextualise the music of Lutosławski, Penderecki and Górecki, counterpointing it with that of other Polish composers whose music is also worthy of attention yet which today often languishes on shelves, even in Poland.

Polish music has experienced amazing peaks and troughs in the almost seven decades since the death of Szymanowski, Poland's best-known composer of the first half of the twentieth century. The book is geared to these main turning points. The music covered in Part I, 'The captive muse', for example, is viewed through the lens of overpowering military and political circumstances. It is therefore as concerned with polemics as it is with music. It attempts to reveal how Polish composers reacted to the pressures of the Second World War and the period of socialist realism that followed in the post-war decade. 'Facing west' charts the volte-face of Polish musical culture in the second half of the 1950s as composers engaged with the Western avant-garde; particular acknowledgment is made to the pivotal role of the 'Warsaw Autumn' festival, which began in 1956. Part III, 'The search for individual identity', which covers the 1960s, is a series of composer profiles with detailed discussion of the most significant compositional issues. In some cases, the time-frame has been extended into the 1970s: Lutosławski and Penderecki's music is taken to the mid-1970s, when each showed a shift in emphasis, while the output of Baird and Serocki is considered up to the end of the decade. In their several ways, these twenty or so composers represent the range of individuality in the 1960s; they also helped, to a greater or lesser degree, to create the phenomenon often referred to as the 'Polish School' or sonorism. These profiles are therefore intended to chart the mix of distinctiveness and commonality that each composer developed. Parts IV and V are primarily concerned with developments since the early and mid-1970s, with particular emphases on the significance of continuing modernist ideals, of secular and sacred Polish traditions in the shaping of post-sonoristic idioms, and of the compositional concerns of the post-war generation of Polish composers, including elements of postmodernism and experimentalism.

This canvas is large and the range of works deserving of discussion is enormous. Bearing in mind, however, that much of the repertoire is unfamiliar outside Poland, I have tried, wherever possible, to cite and discuss works that have been published and/or recorded commercially. Fortunately, for several decades after the war, Poland's primary publishing firm, PWM, was led by a determined editorial team headed by Tadeusz Ochlewski and Mieczysław Tomaszewski. They promoted a vast array of music with innovative layouts and cover designs. Unfortunately, access to these materials outside Poland, apart from those few composers with Western publishers such as Boosey & Hawkes, Chester Music and Schott, has always been haphazard. With regard to CD recordings, certain composers have had wide Western releases (initially with reissues of Polskie Nagrania LP recordings on Olympia, more recently with new performances issued by companies like Argo, Decca, Deutsche Grammophon, Elektra Nonesuch, EMI, Naxos, ProViva and Wergo). Most works, however, have been recorded only on the limited-issue 'chronicle' LPs, cassette tapes and CDs of performances at 'Warsaw Autumn' festivals. And while these never had wide distribution, they are often the only way to hear music by lesser-known composers as well as that by composers as high-profile as Bacewicz, Baird and Serocki whose commercial CD catalogues are woefully incomplete. Regrettably, gaining access to materials outside Poland is still difficult. Some centres do exist – such as the Central European Music Research Centre at Cardiff University (UK) and the Polish Music Center in Los Angeles (USA) – and Polish Cultural Institutes in different countries may also have conduits to recordings, scores and books.

The number of people who have enhanced my understanding of Polish music over many years is legion and I owe them all a great deal. Many composers have discussed their music with me and donated recordings and copies of unpublished scores. Just as importantly, those involved in the promotion and dissemination of Polish music have been unfailingly helpful: Mieczysław Tomaszewski, Leszek Polony, Andrzej Kosowski and their colleagues at PWM, Elżbieta Markowska, Bohdan Mazurek and Józef Patkowski at Polish Radio, Kazimierz Nowacki, Stanisław Czopowicz and Iza Hilmi at the Library of the Polish Composers' Union (ZKP), and Jolanta Bilińska and her successors at the 'Warsaw Autumn' Festival Office at ZKP. Elżbieta Szczepańska and Michał Kubicki have been a constant support over many years and without their help and advice my task would have been much more daunting. I have also, I hope, learned much from my non-Polish friends and colleagues, including Jim Samson, John Casken, Martina Homma, Charles Bodman Rae and Steven Stucky. The unreserved academic support and research funding from The Queen's University of Belfast since the early 1970s, and latterly from Cardiff University, have been crucial factors. I would also like to thank the UK Arts and Humanities Research Board, whose financial support in 2001–3 contributed to the research for Part I.

In bringing this book to its final shape, I have benefited hugely from the sage counsels and eagle eyes of several people who read part or all of the typescript: Beata Bolesławska, Anwar Ibrahim, Michał Kubicki, Nicholas Reyland and the series editor Arnold Whittall, who also witnessed my initial fascination with the music of Lutosławski and Górecki. I have been bolstered by the patient encouragement of Penny Souster, and Michael Downes and Paul Watt have assisted enormously in the final stages of production. Any remaining errors of fact or perception are mine alone; I simply hope that what follows will spur readers to investigate this often extraordinary period of European music in new and divergent ways.

Adrian Thomas
Cardiff–London, Easter 2003

Acknowledgements

The following examples are reproduced by kind permission of Polskie Wydawnictwo Muzyczne (Polish Music Publishers) PWM, Kraków: 1.1, 1.2, 2.1, 2.2, 3.1, 4.1, 4.2, 5.1, 5.3 – 5.6, 7.1–7.4, 7.7, 8.1–8.14, 9.1, 9.11–9.16, 10.1–10.4, 11.1–11.7, 12.4, 12.5, 13.1–13.4, 15.1–15.5, 15.8.

The following are reproduced by permission of Boosey and Hawkes Music Publishers Ltd:

Example 2.3 from *Tragic Overture* © Copyright 1959, Example 3.2 from *Lullaby* © Copyright 1956, Examples 3.3 and 3.4 from *Nocturne* © Copyright 1956, Example 3.5 from *Sinfonia Rustica* © Copyright 1957 and Example 5.2 from *Sinfonia Elegiaca* (Symphony of Peace) © Copyright 1972 by Hawkes & Son (London) Ltd.

Example 9.13 from *Old Polish Music* © Copyright 1988 and Examples 13.3 and 13.4 from *Already it is Dusk*, Op. 62 © Copyright 1989 by Boosey & Hawkes Music Publishers Ltd. for the world except Poland, Albania, Bulgaria, China, the former Yugoslavia, Cuba, North Korea, Vietnam, Romania, Hungary, the former Czechoslovakia, and the former USSR.

The following are reproduced by permission of Chester Music, London: Example 5.6 from *Little Suite* © Copyright 1953 and Example 8.6 from *Trois poèmes d'Henri Michaux* © Copyright 1963, 1991 by Polskie Wydawnictwo Muzyczne, Kraków, Poland. Transferred to Chester Music Limited. © Copyright Chester Music Limited for the World excluding Poland, Albania, Bulgaria, China, the territories of former Czechoslovakia, the territories of former Yugoslavia, Cuba, North Korea, Vietnam, Rumania, Hungary, and the whole territory of the former USSR. All Rights Reserved. Reprinted by permission.

Example 7.7 from *Five Pieces* © Copyright 1985 by Polskie Wydawnictwo Muzyczne, Kraków, Poland. Transferred 2000 to Chester Music Limited. © Copyright 2000 Chester Music Limited for the World excluding Poland, Albania, Bulgaria, China, the territories of former Yugoslavia, Cuba, North Korea, Vietnam, Rumania, Hungary, the territories of former Czechoslovakia and the former USSR. All Rights Reserved. Reprinted by permission.

Examples 8.3 and 8.4 from *Epiphany Music* © Copyright 1964 and Example 8.5 from *Sinfonia breve* © Copyright 1968 by Edition Wilhelm

the former territories of Czechoslovakia, Yugoslavia and Union of Soviet Socialist Republics.

Examples 9.2 and 9.7 from *Dimensions of Time and Silence* and Examples 9.3 and 9.5 from *Anaklasis* © by Moeck Verlag, Celle, Germany, for all countries with the exception of Poland, © by Schott Musik International, Mainz, Germany.

Example 9.9 from *Dies Irae* © by Moeck Verlag, Celle, Germany, for all countries with the exception of Poland, Albania, Bulgaria, Hungary, Rumania, Chinese People's Republic, Cuba, North Korea, and the former territories of Czechoslovakia, Yugoslavia and Union of Soviet Socialist Republics, © by Schott Musik International, Mainz, Germany.

Example 15.5 from *Sonata* © by Moeck Verlag, Celle, Germany, for all countries with the exception of Poland, Albania, Bulgaria, Hungary, Rumania, Chinese People's Republic, Cuba, North Korea, and the former territories of Czechoslovakia, Yugoslavia and Union of Soviet Socialist Republics.

The following are reproduced by kind permission of Schott & Co. Limited, London:

Examples 9.2 and 9.7 from *Dimensions of Time and Silence* and Examples 9.3 and 9.5 from *Anaklasis*, Example 9.9 from *Dies Irae*, Example 9.10 from *Magnificat*, Examples 11.8 and 11.9 from Violin Concerto no.1, Examples 11.10 and 11.11 from Cello Concerto no.2, Examples 11.12 and 11.13 from String Trio, Example 11.14 from Symphony no.5 and Examples 12.2 and 12.3 from *Polish Requiem*.

Example 9.14 from *Aarhus Music* © 1971 by Seesaw Music Corp, New York. Reprinted by permission.

The following are reproduced by kind permission of Edition Modern, Munich:

Example 10.3 from *Piece for Orchestra no.1* and Example 10.5 from *Homophony*.

Example 11.3 is reproduced by kind permission of Edition Pro Nova, Sonoton Music, Munich

Example 15.7 from *Only Beatrice* is reproduced by kind permission of the author.

Every effort has been made to obtain permission to use copyright materials; the publishers apologise for any omissions and would welcome these being brought to their attention.

Abbreviations

AK   Armia Krajowa (Home Army)
ISCM   International Society for Contemporary Music
PWM   Polskie Wydawnictwo Muzyczne (Polish Music Publishers)
PZPR   Polska Zjednoczona Partia Robotnicza (Polish United Workers' Party)
WOSPR   Wielka Orkiestra Symfoniczna Polskiego Radia (Great Symphony Orchestra of Polish Radio)
ZKP   Związek Kompozytorów Polskich (Polish Composers' Union)

PART I

The captive muse

1 Szymanowski and his legacy

In May 1935, Karol Szymanowski reached the Latvian capital, Riga, as part of what turned out to be his last major concert tour. Although the performance of his *Symphonie concertante* for piano and orchestra (1932) failed to materialise, he did accompany his sister, the soprano Stanisława Szymanowska, and the violinist Wacław Niemczyk in two recitals of his songs and chamber music. Coincidentally, the twenty-two-year-old Witold Lutosławski was also in Riga to perform his Piano Sonata (1934) as part of a student exchange concert. Tantalisingly, this was to be the one and only meeting between two of the major figures in twentieth-century Polish music.[1] Lutosławski later recalled: 'Szymanowski was extremely kind to our small group. He came to our concert, we walked around the town together and accompanied him to Radio Riga . . . After our concert, Wacław Niemczyk told me: "Karol liked your Sonata very much; however he wouldn't say it to you."'[2]

Two years later, on Easter Sunday, 29 March 1937, Szymanowski died aged fifty-four in a Swiss sanatorium, the victim of long-term tuberculosis. For some time, Szymanowski had felt neglected in Poland. As he wrote from his rented home, 'Atma', in the Tatra mountain resort of Zakopane in 1934:

> Polish officialdom (the Government) repeatedly refuses to recognise me.
> They do so only when I am needed for propaganda purposes, as it is
> impossible even for them to deny that amongst creative artists (not virtuosi)
> I alone (and not solely amongst composers but in other fields as well) have
> already acquired some reputation abroad . . . The fact is, they care nothing for
> me here, and that I could die without anyone lifting a finger.
>
> My funeral will be a different story. I am convinced it will be splendid.
> People here love the funeral processions of great men.[3]

His prediction was correct. The ceremonies began in Warsaw (Lutosławski recalled that 'the performance of the Stabat Mater during Szymanowski's funeral celebrations, in the Holy Cross Church, was for me a truly unique experience which I even find difficult to describe'[4]) and ended in Kraków, where he was laid to rest in the crypt of the Pauline church on Skałka, alongside other Polish luminaries such as the playwright, poet and painter, Stanisław Wyspiański (1869–1907). Barely a month later, the memorial concert in Warsaw's Philharmonic Hall – which included the Third

Symphony (1916) and Second Violin Concerto (1933) – was virtually empty.[5]

Lutosławski's funeral in 1994 was in marked contrast to the pomp that attended Szymanowski's last journey. Every effort was made to keep it low-key, only a hundred or so mourners marking the interment of his ashes in Warsaw's Powązki Cemetery in an area where other Polish composers and musicians are also buried. There was a palpable sense that his death on 7 February quietly but firmly marked the end of an era as significant to Polish music in the second half of the twentieth century as Szymanowski's had been in the first half. And yet Krzysztof Penderecki (b. 1933), arguably the best-known composer of the next generation, reportedly eulogised Lutosławski as having been the greatest Polish composer since Chopin, effectively relegating Szymanowski to the second rank. While his may have been an isolated opinion, it nevertheless questioned the commonly held view that Szymanowski was the first worthy Polish heir to Chopin. But, as Szymanowski's letter of 1934 indicates, his position in Polish musical life was never comfortable and the reception of his own compositions and progressive ideas was frequently hostile or indifferent – he was more likely to be feted on his trips abroad, be it in Prague, Paris, New York or Riga.

Szymanowski was essentially an outsider. His life up to 1919 was spent mostly far from Warsaw, at the family home in Tymoszówka in Ukraine (which up to the end of the First World War was part of the Russian-controlled sector of Poland). A period of study in Warsaw (1901–5) was followed by prolonged stays in Vienna and a number of journeys to Italy, Sicily and North Africa (1911–14), as well as to Paris and London shortly before the outbreak of war in 1914. In the early years of the twentieth century, Szymanowski's detachment from Warsaw's sluggish musical establishment provided the impetus to attempt a re-energisation of the city's musical life on a number of occasions, the first of which occurred at the conclusion of his studies. With a few contemporaries, he formed a group called 'Young Poland in Music' ('Młoda Polska w muzyce'). It was modelled on the fin-de-siècle movement in literature and the visual arts, 'Young Poland', which had flourished in Kraków with Wyspiański as its leading light. The other members of 'Young Poland in Music' were the composers Ludomir Różycki (1884–1953), Apolinary Szeluto (1884–1966) and Grzegorz Fitelberg (1879–1953); Fitelberg, however, rapidly changed tack and developed into one of Poland's leading conductors and advocates of new music (he became sufficiently well known to be chosen to conduct the premiere of Stravinsky's *Mavra* in Paris in 1922). Mieczysław Karłowicz (1876–1909), whose symphonic poems displayed the most advanced musical idiom among young Polish composers, maintained a loose association with the group, but he died in an avalanche in the Tatra Mountains before he could achieve his full potential.

The group's inaugural concert in Warsaw on 6 February 1906 included Różycki's symphonic poem after Wyspiański, *Bolesław the Bold* (1906), Szymanowski's *Variations on a Polish Folk Theme* for piano (1904) and his *Concert Overture* (1905), with its clear indebtedness to Richard Strauss's *Don Juan*. Strauss was regarded, alongside Wagner and Reger (and also, in Szymanowski's case, the Russian composer Scriabin), as a central model for the regeneration of Polish music. With the lack of publishing outlets in Warsaw, the group established its own company under aristocratic patronage in Berlin and the members variously furthered their studies both there and in Dresden, Leipzig and Vienna. They had no joint manifesto, however, and soon went their separate ways, Szeluto into virtual obscurity and Różycki into increasingly conservative compositional idioms. The mantle of responsibility for reinvigorating Polish composition fell therefore onto the shoulders of Szymanowski and Fitelberg.

Szymanowski's wanderlust in the years preceding the First World War opened up completely new vistas, notably the music of Debussy and Ravel as well as Stravinsky, whom he met in London in 1914. Among the new works he heard in these years were *Pelléas et Mélisande*, *Daphnis et Chloé*, *Petrushka* and *Le chant du rossignol*: 'Stravinsky (of Russian Ballets fame) is a genius – I am terribly excited by him and as a consequence I am beginning to hate the Germans.'[6] Equally powerful was the impact of Mediterranean culture, which led to his first 'Arabic' work, *Love Songs of Hafiz* for voice and piano (1911), and which culminated in the evocative Sicilian story of the opera *King Roger* (1918–24). These outside influences, combined with the continuing influence of Scriabin, only served to emphasise his otherness within the Polish context, especially as late nineteenth-century Germanic idioms were beginning to take a hold amongst his compatriots. With the enforced isolation and disruption during the war and the outbreak of the Russian Revolution in 1917, the works of Szymanowski's middle period – *Myths* for violin and piano (1915), Third Symphony, First Violin Concerto (1916), First String Quartet (1917) – remained hidden from public view. These pieces have long been regarded as among his finest achievements. They demonstrate his ability to meld high romanticism with the subtle harmonic shadings and instrumental textures of recent French music (Stravinsky's influence at this point was less marked than in the 1920s). Perhaps most significantly, he seemed to have shed the structural formalities of earlier symphonic works, such as the Second Symphony (1910), and developed a wondrously seductive developmental process that was both static and mobile. Not unsurprisingly, this potent filtering of Strauss and Scriabin through the prism of Debussy, Ravel and early Stravinsky proved to be peculiarly personal and one that in the event had few resonances for other Polish composers.

For the remaining twenty years of his life, Szymanowski continued to follow an independent compositional path, with the crucial proviso that from 1921 onwards, starting with the song-cycle *Wordsongs* (*Słopiewnie*), he once more refiltered his innate expressive sensuousness through a prism, this time that of indigenous Polish music. Certainly, there is an element of a novel exoticism here, but Szymanowski's purpose was clear: to provide musical leadership in the creation of a specifically Polish identity for the newly emergent nation (at the end of the war Poland had become independent for the first time in over a hundred years). An important by-product of this shift was Szymanowski's renewed attempt to find common ground with Polish audiences; his wartime compositions had been lukewarmly received in Warsaw in 1919. By writing his set of twenty Mazurkas for piano (1926) he signalled his links with a genre synonymous with Chopin, although their rough-hewn harmonic language is far removed from that of his predecessor. The Stabat Mater (1926) connected with older Polish choral and sacred traditions, while the ballet-pantomime *Mountain Robbers* (*Harnasie*, 1923–31) was the most vivid example of his fascination with, and absorption in, the song and dance idioms of the *góralski* (highlander) folk traditions of the Tatras. *Mountain Robbers* may be seen as the most overt Polish tribute to the example of Stravinsky's *Petrushka*, *The Rite of Spring* and *Les noces*. Younger composers were more intrigued by Stravinsky's music from the Octet onwards, and this move towards a pared-down, cooler expressive palette is also reflected in Szymanowski's last orchestral works, the *Symphonie concertante* and the Second Violin Concerto.

Given the new social-political context within Poland, it seems extraordinary that, once more, Szymanowski was acting more or less alone in drawing so intensively on his native traditions. None of his near-contemporaries was half as interested in defining afresh the nature of Polishness in music. As examples of a forgotten generation, whose copious oeuvre of the interwar period has almost totally disappeared from the Polish repertoire, three figures stand out: Witold Maliszewski (1873–1939), a former student of Rimsky-Korsakov (and teacher of Lutosławski) who remained true to his Russian training, later incorporating some Polish folk influences; Eugeniusz Morawski (1876–1948), whose music was partly influenced by French impressionism (he studied composition and painting in Paris); and Piotr Rytel (1884–1970), more notorious for his anti-Semitism and newspaper criticism unsympathetic to Szymanowski than for the post-Wagnerian flavour of much of his music. A renewal of interest in the output of this generation may yet unearth compositional achievements to set against those of Szymanowski, but at this distance in time it seems an unlikely prospect.

One of the striking aspects of Szymanowski's life at the end of the 1920s was his willingness to take on the daunting task of improving the Warsaw Conservatoire (1927–9); for two further years he was Rector of its successor, the Warsaw Academy of Music (1930–2). He revitalised the teaching staff, not without resistance and resentment, and most accounts credit Szymanowski with leading tertiary music education in Poland into the modern world, even though it gave him less time to compose.[7] His public utterances on music education are, in essence, a defence of his progressive reforms and reinforce his image as an inspirational figure for musical patriotism. In his rectorial address of 1930, he called for the attainment of a 'consistently high artistic standard of national culture, with its own special colour and expression, which not only illuminates and moulds the spiritual character of a nation, but also shines far beyond the frontiers of the state as a visible, indestructible symbol of its creative strength'.[8]

Szymanowski's adoption of a public profile, initiated in musical terms in 1906 with the formation of 'Young Poland in Music', took a much more polemical turn with his articles of the 1920s, beginning with the first of several attacks on the entrenched conservatism of Polish musical life, 'On Contemporary Musical Opinion in Poland' (c.1925–6). His critical spats with Rytel and others show his determination to stand his ground, even though he clearly felt that he was often in a minority of one. More fascinating is the totality of his rejection of German music ('the art of yesterday') – and, by implication, strong elements of his own pre-war beliefs. Like most Poles, he abhorred Schoenberg, although the extent of his acquaintance with the music remains uncertain and he was capable of a relatively measured assessment of the German tradition.[9] When Szymanowski turns to non-German music, he can still be critical: his idolisation of Stravinsky (1924)[10] and Ravel (1925)[11] is balanced by a sharply etched discussion (1924) of Les Six ('I have not abandoned hope for the future well-being of Milhaud, Auric and Poulenc'[12]) and of Satie ('that old immoralist and *farceur*'[13]).

Szymanowski writes with the greatest fervour on ethnic music. His much-quoted essay 'On Highland Music' (1924), for example, is a passionate appeal to save what he perceived as the rapidly eroding highlander culture around Zakopane. Elsewhere, his championing of Chopin is strikingly eloquent. Even when responding to an article by Bartók on the origins of folk music (1925), he cannot resist setting the argument within the German context, asserting that

> Thanks to its mighty breadth and its continuing irreplaceable value, the great century-and-a-half (from Bach to Wagner), while not ceasing to be, in the noblest sense of the word, a 'nationalistic' expression of the Germanic spirit, thrust upon all of us an obligatory aesthetic canon and universal ideal of such weight that it crushed individual upsurges of creativity to evolve in their own way (Chopin), and became in fact the *international* musical ideal.[14]

The juxtaposition between the German tradition and the lone voice of Chopin is a recurring theme, as in his unsentimental essay of 1923:

> . . . great music can be based on foundations other than those of the ever-shrinking circles of German 'emotionalism'. That liberation must rest first upon the elevation of the artistic qualities of ethno-musical traits of other national groupings. This involves not only 'formal' qualities, but the very 'spirit' of the music, its deepest substance. This process has already been accomplished in France and Russia, and what an enormous role Chopin's music played in this process! . . . I should like the 'transformation of values' which Chopin initiated a century ago to become at last an accomplished fact in Poland.[15]

Szymanowski 'reads' Chopin in contemporary terms and this filter deliberately reinforced Szymanowski's own experience. There is a palpable sense of Szymanowski struggling to achieve not only Poland's musical identity but also his own, and his was not to be the last such creative struggle in twentieth-century Polish music.

The 'transformation of values' in the newly independent Poland was an uphill task. On a material level, progress was patchy. Polish Radio began broadcasts in 1926, but few new scores found publishing outlets in Poland itself. Concert life, however, certainly had its crowning moments. While it is true to say that Warsaw continued to be the main musical centre, Kraków, Poznań and Lwów also had successful professional operatic productions and concert seasons (Honegger's *Le roi David* and Janáček's *Jenůfa* received their Polish premieres in Poznań in 1926). In Warsaw, there were Polish premieres of Wagner's *Tristan und Isolde* (1921) and *Siegfried* (1925), Ravel's *L'heure espagnole* (1925), Strauss's *Salome* (1931) and Křenek's *Jonny spielt auf* (1934). Ballet productions were created for Stravinsky's *The Firebird* and *Petrushka* (1922) and Ravel's *Daphnis et Chloé* (1926). New orchestral repertoire included, although not to universal acclaim, Schoenberg's *Verklärte Nacht* in 1922 and the First Chamber Symphony a year later. Polish premieres of other contemporary pieces included Prokofiev's 'Classical' Symphony (1923), Weill's Violin Concerto (1927), Shostakovich's First Symphony (1929), Berg's Three Orchestral Pieces (1930), Bartók's

Third String Quartet (1931) and Hindemith's *Mathis der Maler* (1937).

Nor was Warsaw off the map in terms of international performers. It welcomed, especially in the 1930s, conductors such as Kleiber, Horenstein, Krauss, Mitropoulos, Klemperer (*Petrushka*, 1934), Walter, Furtwängler, Markevich and Ansermet (Berg's Violin Concerto and Stravinsky's *Jeu de cartes*, 1938). Instrumental virtuosi included Schnabel, Arrau, Heifetz, Serkin, Gieseking and Kempff, alongside Polish players such as Huberman, Kochański, Szeryng, Haendel and Balsam.[16]

Arguably the most riveting occasions for Polish audiences were the visits of composer-performers. Milhaud and Poulenc came to Poland in 1922 and Prokofiev played his Third Piano Concerto and a solo recital in Warsaw in 1925, the first of several visits over the next decade. Stravinsky played his Concerto for Piano and Winds in 1924, Ravel came to Warsaw to hear Marguerite Long play his G major Concerto in 1932, Hindemith played his Konzertmusik for viola and orchestra in the same year, and Rachmaninov performed his Second Piano Concerto and *Rhapsody on a Theme of Paganini* in 1936. The strangest event was the brief visit of the American composer Henry Cowell, who gave a recital of his experimental piano music in March 1926. In April 1939, Warsaw was also the venue for the annual festival of the International Society for Contemporary Music (ISCM), when Polish audiences had the opportunity to hear a wide range of new music from across Europe, although the planned visit of Webern to the festival did not materialise.

The spasmodic appearance of new foreign works on Polish concert programmes, coupled with an educational environment at tertiary level which did not begin to cater properly for composers until the late 1920s, provoked the younger generation, like the 'Young Poland in Music' composers before them, to look further afield for stimulus. This time, however, with Szymanowski's active encouragement, up-and-coming composers went to Paris rather than Berlin. The reasons for this were several. France, and particularly Paris, had long been a magnet for Polish artists. The insurrection against the Russians in 1830–1 led not only to Chopin's enforced exile in France but also to that of many literary figures as part of the so-called 'Great Emigration'. Szymanowski's own espousal of French musical idioms as an alternative to the pre-war dominance of German symphonism was also a factor. But the overwhelming attraction appears to have been the freshness, vivacity and aesthetic clarity of new French music, of Jean Cocteau and 'Les Six', of Stravinsky and neo-classicism.

In 1926, a group of Polish music students in Paris formed the 'Association des Jeunes Musiciens Polonais à Paris', which mounted concerts of Polish music (including performances of pre-twentieth-century works) and acted as a focal point for the younger generation. Like many of their American contemporaries, most of the composers among them had come to study with Nadia Boulanger, although some went to Paul Dukas, Albert Roussel and Charles Koechlin. In the period up to 1939, well over a hundred composers and performers became members of the Association. Most returned to Poland at the end of their studies and played a part in Polish musical life during and after the Second World War. Of these, Stanisław Wiechowicz (1893–1963), Tadeusz Szeligowski (1896–1963), Jan Maklakiewicz (1899–1954), Bolesław Woytowicz (1899–1980), Piotr Perkowski (1901–90), Zygmunt Mycielski (1907–87) and Grażyna Bacewicz (1909–69) warrant closer inspection. Both Wiechowicz's *The Hop* (*Chmiel*, 1926), a popular dance stylisation of a well-known wedding song, and Szeligowski's *Green Songs* (*Pieśni zielone*, 1930), whose harmonic language and treatment of thematic material have strong links with Szymanowski, separately reinterpret their Polish roots. Maklakiewicz, whose music was also influenced by Szymanowski's example, showed evidence of stronger archaistic tendencies (*Cello Concerto on Gregorian Themes*, 1928) and an interest in oriental culture (*Japanese Songs*, 1930). Perkowski's insouciant Sinfonietta (1932), closer to Poulenc than Stravinsky, is less overtly Polish in tone; in complete contrast, Woytowicz's *Poème funèbre* (1935) is unusual not only for its dark-hued language, but also for being an isolated example, at the time, of a piece with a direct relation to an historical event, namely the death of the charismatic inter-war Polish leader, Marshal Piłsudski. Chamber music was an active element in the 1930s and included Woytowicz's First String Quartet (1932), Bacewicz's Wind Quintet (1932) and Mycielski's Piano Trio (1934).

For some other Polish composers, life abroad proved too alluring. Among those who remained in France were Aleksander Tansman (1897–1986), one of the first to arrive in Paris after the end of the First World War (he became a French citizen in 1938), and Antoni Szałowski (1907–73). Tansman was a rare example of a Polish emigré who established a successful international compositional career. His inter-war music is characterised by strong jazz and neo-classical idioms (the Second Piano Concerto, 1927, shows a kinship with Gershwin, Ravel and Poulenc), as well as wistful references to Polish folklore. Of particular interest are the string quartets (nos. 2–4, 1922–35), whose combination of lyricism and vigour anticipates Bacewicz's quartets. Fate has been less kind to other emigré composers, whose music remains comparatively unknown.[17] Szałowski, for example, is remembered mainly for his Overture (1936), which is a particularly vivacious example of a common Polish approach to neo-classical procedures. It eschews the hard-edged radicalism of Stravinsky's gestural and motivic dislocation in favour of a more traditional thematic continuum, a tendency which was eventually to reach its apogee in Lutosławski's Concerto for Orchestra (1950–4).

There remained a number of composers who, for various reasons, did not participate in the general traffic between Poland and France. Some chose to study elsewhere: Czesław Marek (1891–1985), Józef Koffler (1896–c.1943–4) and Andrzej Panufnik (1914–91) preferred Vienna; Jerzy Fitelberg (1903–51), son of the conductor, went first to Berlin, where he studied with Franz Schreker, before succumbing to the lure of Paris. Bolesław Szabelski (1896–1979), Roman Palester (1907–89) and Lutosławski were educated only in Poland, although Palester visited Paris in 1936 and Lutosławski planned to study there but was thwarted by the start of the Second World War. Marek's contact with Poland after settling in Switzerland in 1932 was negligible, and Jerzy Fitelberg further distanced himself by moving from Paris to New York in 1940. Panufnik's graduate studies abroad (1937–9) were particularly interesting in view of his later career. He concentrated on conducting (with Felix Weingartner in Vienna and Philippe Gaubert in Paris) as well as taking the opportunity to hear new pieces (in Paris, for example, he heard Berg's *Lyric Suite* and Bartók's *Sonata for Two Pianos and Percussion*). More tellingly, he devoted many hours to studying the music of the Second Viennese School: 'With passion and enthusiasm, I read virtually all the printed scores, played them on the piano, analysed them in detail and contemplated them long and deeply. The composer to whom I felt closest was Webern.'[18]

From this group of composers, Palester and Koffler came to be regarded in the 1930s as two of the most significant. Each had several works performed at ISCM festivals and each was committed to the goal of regenerating Polish music through stretching its horizons (in this sense, Szymanowski was an inspirational figure, though more for his stand on musical principles than in terms of style). Of his *Symphonic Music* (1930), performed at the ISCM Festival in London a year later, Palester later averred that 'in this score there was not a trace of Szymanowski, just a little Stravinsky and mostly Hindemith'.[19] His knowledge of contemporary European music was broad – when his folk-inspired *Dance from Osmołoda* (1932) was performed at the ISCM Festival in Barcelona in 1936, he was able to hear Berg's Violin Concerto and Bartók's Fifth String Quartet. Palester rapidly became an energetic activist for new music, especially in the SKP (Polish Composers' Association) from 1932, playing a significant part in the organisation of the 1939 ISCM Festival in Warsaw and Kraków, and writing trenchant articles.[20]

Koffler was even more prominent as an educationalist and as polemicist for new music, notwithstanding his geographical location in Lwów, on Poland's eastern borders. His position was particularly isolated because his was the lone Polish voice advocating the music of the Second Viennese School. He had met Berg during his studies in Vienna (1920–3), although his training did not include contact with Schoenberg (he studied composition with Hermann Graedener, conducting with Weingartner, and musicology with Guido Adler). He took it upon himself to analyse Schoenberg's early twelve-note works before making his first technical forays in works such as *Quinze variations d'après une suite de douze tons* (1927), which he dedicated and sent to Schoenberg. In fact, Schoenberg's initial alliance of the series to eighteenth-century structures and gestures, as in the Suite for Piano op. 25, was to endure in Koffler's own search for a balance between twelve-note thematicism and neo-classical gestures and procedures.

Koffler's expressive intent was closer to that of Schoenberg and Berg than to Webern's aesthetic, as is evident in both his outstanding String Trio (1928) and the cantata *Love* (*Miłość*, (1931), a setting of part of St Paul's First Letter to the Corinthians (Ex. 1.1). Both works were presented at the 1931 ISCM Festival in Oxford and London. After the 1934 ISCM Festival in Carlsbad, for which he was a juror, Koffler made sure that, even if Polish audiences were unlikely to hear any of the new pieces played there, they would at least be aware of the existence of Schoenberg's Variations for Orchestra, Berg's Suite from *Lulu* and Webern's Concerto for Nine Instruments.[21] As a rare Polish symphonist in the 1930s, Koffler broke new ground in scoring his Third Symphony (*c*.1935) for wind and percussion. More significantly, the Symphony reveals a further moderation of the underlying twelve-note technique by motivic and pitch repetitions and by the use of tonally centred harmonic-textural blocking which brings to mind composers as varied as early Stravinsky, Hindemith and Debussy (Maciej Gołąb has memorably described the opening Adagio as a 'pulsating plasma'[22]). But the strongest impression is of a masterful ability, like that of Berg, to unite disparate material into a persuasive musical argument.

Between 1936 and 1938, the Polish periodical *Muzyka* published a series of profiles of contemporary Polish composers. Altogether, eight were featured: Michał Kondracki (1902–84), Koffler, Palester, Maklakiewicz, Woytowicz, Tadeusz Kassern (1904–57), Jerzy Fitelberg and Szałowski. Today, little of the music of these composers is available in performance, recording or print, so it is hard to assess their true significance both then and now. Notwithstanding their various achievements – and the music of Koffler and Palester has recently been well served by Polish musicology – these

Example 1.1. Koffler, *Love* (*Miłość*, 1931), first song (Adagio), bb. 14–22.

composers, either individually or as a group, have not dispelled the impression that Szymanowski *was* Polish music in the 1920s and 1930s, an impression which persists by default. Certainly he towered internationally above his compatriots, but *Muzyka*'s selection remains an eloquent statement of the gulf between the perception of Polish music at the time of Szymanowski's death and that which developed after the Second World War. Nevertheless, it is apparent that in the 1930s Szymanowski, notwithstanding his position as a figurehead for the younger generation of composers, became increasingly marginalised. His enforced absence abroad because of continuing ill health was further exacerbated by concert tours undertaken to keep himself

Example 1.2. Malawski, Variations (1938), fugue (Allegro Moderato), bb. 6–10.

and his dependants financially solvent. Furthermore, the polemical argument for change was taken over by the likes of Palester and Koffler, and the increasing vitality of these and other young composers provided a different aesthetic standpoint.

In the two and a half years between Szymanowski's death and the start of the Second World War, some members of the younger generation gave cause for optimism for a revitalised Polish musical culture. On the one hand, Szymanowski's musical language was alluded to in Lutosławski's Symphonic Variations (1938) and further developed in two post-romantic tributes: Mycielski's *Lamento di Tristano* (1937) and Szeligowski's *Epitaph on the Death of Karol Szymanowski* (1937). The music of his own pupil, Szabelski, was also indebted to his teacher (his Second Symphony, 1929–32, uses the same folk sources employed by Szymanowski in Stabat Mater and *Mountain Robbers*).[23] It is likewise perfectly understandable that new pieces, particularly by composers who did not study abroad, should also be dependent on the leading foreign contemporary figures whose music had featured on Polish concert platforms – Debussy, Ravel, Honegger, Stravinsky, Prokofiev and Hindemith. The gestural vocabulary and timbral world of Stravinsky's early ballets, for example, were clearly influential on Szabelski's orchestral *Study* (1938) and on Lutosławski's Symphonic Variations, although there is a substantial aesthetic gap between Szabelski's hearty epigonism and the subtler discourse of Lutosławski's score.

The contemporaneous orchestral Variations by Artur Malawski (1904–57) makes an interesting comparison with Lutosławski's set. Both operate within the Brahmsian variational tradition, concluding with fugal sections. Lutosławski's assured mastery of orchestration, crisp articulation, symphonic structure and tonal direction anticipates many features of later masterpieces, including the Concerto for Orchestra and *Funeral Music* (1954–8). Malawski's set of ten variations and fugue is less sophisticated orchestrally and closer to Hindemith in its extensive counterpoint and harmonic rationale. The folk origins of its theme are more explicit than Lutosławski's, and yet the motivic development frequently denies a clear tonal basis, preferring instead to explore the total chromatic, as is demonstrated by the repeated twelve-note chord before the fugue and in the fugue subject itself (Ex. 1.2). In this sense, albeit informally, Malawski aligns himself with dodecaphonic experimentation. Generally speaking, most young Polish composers active in 1939, while still feeling their way within a European context, were of a mind to explore rather than entrench. This attitude, whilst marginalising Szymanowski and his music, was in accordance with his overriding vision for the future of Polish music.

2   The Second World War

With Hitler's invasion on 1 September 1939, Poland's two decades of independence came to an abrupt halt. Over six million Poles lost their lives during the Second World War – almost twenty per cent of the population. Quite apart from the terror of everyday life, with its street seizures and summary executions, the ghettoisation and persecution of the Jewish population and the ruthless murder and deprivation carried out in the concentration camps, any expression of Polishness could prove fatal. Polish institutions and organisations were liquidated by the occupying Nazi forces. An early signal of German intent was a summons to leading academics of the Jagiellonian University in Kraków to attend a meeting on 6 November 1939: the 183 professors who turned up were immediately imprisoned and sent to the Sachsenhausen concentration camp.

The Germans were determined to eradicate the Polish nation, although they can hardly have been surprised that, as already shown by nineteenth-century insurrections against occupying powers, Poles should now demonstrate equally incredible and sometimes foolhardy bravery in defending their nationhood. A Polish resistance movement, known as the Home Army (AK – 'Armia Krajowa'), was immediately mobilised and Poles created for themselves 'a State within a State'.[1] As Adam Zamoyski relates:

> The life of the nation was lived in hiding. For a period of six years, education at every level was carried on secretly in indescribable conditions. Bombs were manufactured, plays were staged and books were published under the nose of the Germans, and hardly a national holiday passed without the Polish national anthem and *God Save the King* being broadcast all over the city [Warsaw] through the official German megaphone system. The whole spectrum of activities was carried out with an efficiency and wit that tend to obscure the difficulties and dangers involved. Torture, concentration camp and death awaited anyone on whom German suspicion fell.[2]

Nor must it be forgotten that large parts of Eastern Poland, including Lwów, where Koffler was based, were occupied by Soviet forces shortly after the start of the Second World War; there, too, Polish lives were endangered and severe restrictions imposed on Polish national identity.

In the German occupied territories, which included Warsaw and Kraków, extensive underground musical activities sprang up: 'In late 1939 and early 1940, a fairly stable basis for musical life [in Warsaw] was organised in the form of an underground Union of Musicians which set up six committees dealing with concerts, education, reconstruction of the Philharmonic Hall, reconstruction of the Opera House, musical publications and the musical repertoire for resistance groups.'[3] A few organisations were approved by the Nazi authorities, notably a school of music set up in Warsaw by the composer and noted teacher, Kazimierz Sikorski (1895–1986). As far as the Germans were concerned, the school trained orchestral musicians, but it secretly taught other subjects, such as theory, composition and conducting: 'Graduates were granted two diplomas: an official one confirming the completion of a course at the Staatliche Musikschule (State School of Music) and the illegal underground diploma of the Warsaw Conservatoire.'[4] Among its 'secret' graduates were the composers Andrzej Dobrowolski (1921–90) and Kazimierz Serocki (1922–81) and the composer, later conductor, Jan Krenz (b. 1926).

Music-making was also largely forced underground, with many concerts taking place in private homes. The fifth anniversary of Szymanowski's death (1942) was marked by such a recital, which was introduced in dramatic terms by his cousin, Jarosław Iwaszkiewicz: 'We gather here in secrecy, like the first Christians in the catacombs, secretly to celebrate the memories of our great artists. And the more we have faith in our past, so we must now conceal our cults. The secret cults of our great people must burst into flame as the great fire of a true culture.'[5] The private recital to mark the seventh anniversary of Szymanowski's death included a two-piano performance of his *Symphonie concertante*.[6] A few months later, the recital's master of ceremonies, the young composer Roman Padlewski (1915–44), died a hero's death in the Warsaw Uprising.[7] Even during the turbulent two months of the Uprising, it appears that Polish musicians still managed to organise several dozen concerts.[8]

There were also occasional opportunities for larger-scale performances, normally clandestine or as part of a charity event. Among the orchestral works composed and performed in Warsaw during the war were the Divertimento (1940) by Witold Rudziński (1913–2004) and Panufnik's *Tragic Overture* (1942); Koffler's *Festive Overture* (c.1940) was performed in Lwów in 1941. The repertoire of new chamber music was understandably larger. Some pieces were premiered in private homes and many more were heard in artists' cafés, which served as the only public venues for musicians to perform on a regular basis. Constantin Regamey (1907–82), the Swiss composer who was educated in Warsaw between the wars and because of family ties stayed in Poland until the end of 1944, performed, like Lutosławski and Panufnik, as a café pianist:

> Life was now totally surrealistic in Poland, where the black market was king. One way of earning money was provided by the cafés; because the town had been destroyed by shelling, there was no coal; we warmed up in public establishments, which were full, and exchanged political gossip. Musicians, conservatory professors, suddenly out of work, knuckled down to playing tangos and slow foxtrots in just such cafés; others became cloakroom attendants. This type of work became the principal support for many an intellectual and teacher.[9]

Even so, such venues were by no means safe havens. In Warsaw, Regamey, Panufnik and Lutosławski were lucky on occasion to escape arrest in lightning raids, whereas well over a hundred people who had the misfortune to be in the 'Artists' Club' ('Dom Plastyków') in Kraków on 10 April 1942 were sent to nearby Auschwitz, where nearly all perished.

In Warsaw, Woytowicz opened his 'Art Gallery' ('Galeria Sztuki'), with a two-hundred-seat capacity; even more renowned was 'Art and Fashion' ('Sztuka i Moda'), where over 1300 concerts took place on a daily basis during the war.[10] The Lutosławski–Panufnik duet developed its repertoire of some two hundred light-music arrangements here. But the cafés were also places where serious music could be heard (including the most enduring Polish work of these years, Lutosławski's *Variations on a Theme of Paganini* for two pianos, 1941). The best of Polish artists took part: singers like Ewa Bandrowska-Turska, Ada Sari and Adam Didur, violinists like Eugenia Umińska, Irena Dubiska and Wacław Niemczyk, pianists of the calibre of Zbigniew Drzewiecki, Jan Ekier and Jerzy Lefeld. Woytowicz, who gave up composition for the duration of the war, performed several cycles of the complete Beethoven piano sonatas.

Many Polish musicians lost their lives.[11] Casualities included Marian Neuteich (1906–43), composer, cellist and founder of the Polish Radio String Quartet, who died in the Warsaw Ghetto, and two other members of the same quartet, one dying in prison, the other in a public street execution. Undoubtedly one of the most tragic losses was that of Koffler, the details of whose fate subsequent to the arrival of the Germans in Lwów in 1941 remain uncertain. Like many other Jews, he and his family were forced to find refuge where they could in order to avoid the ghettos, and the greatest likelihood is that they were shot dead by the Germans somewhere in south-eastern Poland in 1943–4.[12]

Koffler's experiences after 1939 once again isolated him from the generality of Polish musical life. His *Festive Overture*, Fourth Symphony (1940) and *Ukrainian Sketches* for string quartet (before 1941) were composed not under Nazi control but within the socialist-realist context that followed on from the Soviet annexation of eastern Poland in September 1939. In March 1940, Koffler's pre-war Second Symphony (1933) was the object of critical discussion about its relevance to the new Soviet art. And although Koffler was probably justified in having felt neglected in pre-war Poland, the sub-missive tone of his comparison of past and present circumstances in 1940 is in striking contrast to the combative and independent critical stance he took on musical issues before the war:

> It was hard to live and work in 'pre-war Lwów', hard for all musicians, hard for me too. The city's musical culture went from bad to worse. There was no permanent opera nor symphony orchestra. There were only masses of unemployed, hungry musicians . . . The Warsaw Philharmonic and Polish Radio ignored me as a composer . . .
>
> Then, however, came the unforgettable autumn of 1939, when the Red Army arrived – and everything changed. I was given the possibility to live and work like a free and happy man, I was able to realise my creative plans, something which previously I could not even dream of doing . . . My colleagues and I are eagerly working on composition, musicology and research . . . We are certain that our creative activity will always be supported by our party and government, by the whole of Soviet society, for whose benefit we work.[13]

Koffler's apologia is a sorry indication of his plight and prescient of the situation in which his compatriots would find themselves barely a decade later in post-war Poland.

The *Festive Overture* was commissioned to celebrate the first anniversary of the Soviet arrival in Lwów, but no score survives. There is still a dodecaphonic basis to the Fourth Symphony, but one that continues the moderating process observed in the Third Symphony. In fact, Gołąb sees the Fourth as evidence of a longer-range synthesis:

> Koffler's remaining links with the inspirational circle of the Viennese School became increasingly tenuous. By the end of the 1930s, the historical provenance of this inspiration was changing: it was not the experimentally treated dodecaphony or 'analytical' instrumentation of the scores of Schönberg and Webern from the 1920s and 30s that were the object of inspiration, but rather the traditional, post-romantic *gestus* of earlier Viennese compositions from around 1910, over which was laid the neo-classical experience of a composer who was entangled until the end of his creative path in the selective synthesis of the initially antithetical musical traditions of his time.[14]

Example 2.1. Padlewski, Sonata for solo violin (1941), opening.

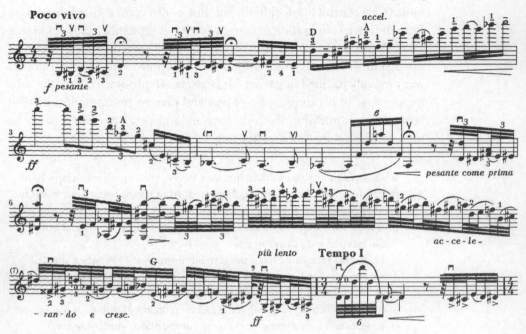

Koffler's distancing from the more experimental aspects of Viennese dode-caphony may be seen both as a personal creative evolution and as latterly enforced by circumstances beyond his control. Although both the Symphony and the *Ukrainian Sketches* still have a high dissonance quotient, the latter work is openly more tonal and, in its use of indigenous melodies, recalls his pre-twelve-note *40 Polish Folk Songs* (1925). It is easy, in retrospect, to see Koffler's abiding devotion to neo-classical gestures as a negative regression from some putative, Second Viennese norm, but there are strong arguments for viewing the technical as well as the aesthetic character of his music as progressive in its synthesis. Its freedom from dogma certainly finds parallels in the wartime music of both Padlewski and Regamey.

Padlewski's small output includes the Sonata for solo violin (1941) and a String Quartet (1942), both performed during the war. The Sonata is a dra-matic, almost wilful exploration of free atonality within modified classical structures and it marked him out as one of the most promising composers of the generation that included Lutosławski and Panufnik (Ex. 2.1). At the start of the war, Regamey, like Padlewski, had not yet made a compositional impact on Polish music. In fact, Regamey was self-taught as a composer; his profession was as a multilingual specialist in oriental culture, as a philoso-pher and as a forward-thinking music critic. By the time of his fortunate escape to Switzerland at the end of 1944, he had fully engaged in the country's musical and intellectual life, not least through the unparalleled success of the clandestine performances of his *Persian Songs* (*Pieśni perskie*, 1942), in an initial version for baritone and two pianos, and the Quintet for clarinet, bassoon, violin, cello and piano (1944).

The texts for the *Persian Songs* are from the *Rubáiyát of Omar Khayyám*; Regamey's selection emphasises the enigma of *la condition humaine*, and ends, not surprisingly in the circumstances, on a subdued note:

> Notre venue ici-bas, notre mort, à quoi bon?
> Quelle est la gloire des sages et de ceux qui croient?
> Ou sont les cimes de notre folle espérance?
> Poudre, poudre, tout n'est que poudre et retourne à la poudre.

As in Maklakiewicz's pre-war *Japanese Songs*, there are a few traces of orientalisms in the musical language, although Regamey drew more extensively upon the example of heightened lyricism to be found in the music of Szymanowski (the songs, *King Roger*), Berg (*Wozzeck*), Ravel (*Shéhérazade*) and Scriabin. His approach to the seven songs in the cycle ranges from the epigrammatic (the dramatic ariosos of the first two songs) to the sensuous (no. 3, with its Bergian B natural pedal point). In the fourth song, 'quasi una danza', he recalls the parodistic swagger in the martial rhythms of Prokofiev, Berg and Weill, while Berg's post-romantic idiom is a strong influence on no. 6, whose evocation of 'le vide et la noir' is a bleak descendant of Szymanowski's Third Symphony, 'Song of the Night', also composed in wartime. One of the most interesting features of this exceptionally imaginative work is the richness of its pitch organisation, which ranges from modality to bitonality and atonality. In the fifth song, he makes a brief foray into twelve-note composition, although this shift in technical focus is blended, like all the other elements, into the overridingly ecstatic tone of the cycle.

Regamey's other wartime work, the Quintet, extended his expertise in twelve-note writing. Like the *Persian Songs* earlier, it caused quite a stir at its premiere on 6 June 1944, as Lutosławski later recalled:

> It immediately created a sensation in Warsaw's musical circles and then throughout Poland. One realised that one was faced with a work that was perfectly constructed, extremely refined and, furthermore, totally independent of what had hitherto constituted style and method in the Polish musical milieu of the thirties and forties. No wonder: it really was the first work composed in Poland on the basis of dodecaphonic technique. (To be sure, the first Polish dodecaphonist was Józef Koffler, who was living in Lwów at the time; his activities, however, were virtually unknown in Warsaw.) On its

own, the technique [Regamey] used would not have been enough to make this work so sensational. There were other contributory factors: above all one must highlight the composer's extraordinary imagination as well as his very personal treatment of Schoenberg's methods . . . 'You will find nothing like it in the whole of Polish chamber music,' one member of the quintet told me after the concert. This phrase, one might add, remains valid even if we eliminate the word 'Polish'.[15]

Notwithstanding Lutosławski's Warsaw-centric view of Koffler (typical of the time), his comments leave no doubt as to the impact of Regamey's Quintet. Above all, it is a virtuoso score of symphonic proportions, lasting some thirty-five minutes. The flair and creative freedom with which he moulds his ideas is, as Lutosławski says, quite unlike anything else in Poland at the time. Certainly, the rondo finale has the strong rhythmic drive associated with French neo-classicism, but the work's ancestry lies more in late nineteenth-century and early twentieth-century models, in the impassioned Piano Quintet of Liszt's Polish pupil, Juliusz Zarębski (1854–85), as well as in Schoenberg's First Chamber Symphony. And there are many moments when Regamey approaches the sound world of Messiaen's *Quatuor pour la fin du temps*, composed in a Silesian labour camp three years earlier. This, of course, is coincidental, but the two works share the same instrumentation, with the addition of a bassoon in Regamey's Quintet. The resemblance between the delicate use of tremoli and semi-resonant piano chords in the fifth variation of the opening movement and textures in Messiaen's Quartet is uncanny, as is Regamey's use of major triads as luminous resolution points in the prevailing bitonal discourse.

Regamey's 'very personal manner' in utilising the twelve-note technique has parallels in Koffler's earlier example, mainly in its use of the concept of twelve-note thematicism. But Regamey's approach is even more flexible than Koffler's, as Alicja Jarzębska has outlined.[16] In the opening movement, he creates a forty-six-note theme that is the direct source for the nine subsequent variations. But he feels at liberty to nip and tuck this theme to suit different compositional demands, whether melodic or harmonic. In the central 'Intermezzo romantico', Regamey returns to the more conventional twelve-note model, but again branches out on his own by using three distinct rows, typically separated instrumentally between melody and accompaniment (Ex. 2.2). Here, too, the breadth of his harmonic language allows for more conventional by-products, such as diatonic triads.

If Koffler and Regamey and, to a looser extent, Padlewski explored new methods of pitch organisation as an adjunct to traditional thematic phrasing and development, Panufnik focused early on in his career on a more

Example 2.2. Regamey, Quintet (1944), 'Intermezzo romantico' (Lento), second section.

selective motivic coherence. This radicality is particularly apparent in the *Tragic Overture*, performed in Warsaw in 1943.[17] Built from a single four-note cell, its interval content is clearly derived from the twelve-note manipulations he observed when analysing Webern's scores in Vienna in 1937: 'He seemed to me the most original of the three [Schoenberg, Berg and Webern], and I was attracted towards the exquisite crystal-like structures he built with such precision.'[18] Panufnik, who at one point considered studying with Webern, saw the apparent imbalance between the Austrian's technical perfection and emotional expression as a creative barrier: 'I threw my dodecaphonic sketches into my waste-paper basket, and concluded that I should never again try to borrow methods from other composers.'[19]

Example 2.3. Panufnik, *Tragic Overture* (1942, reconstructed 1945), fig. 34
($\downarrow = c.100$).

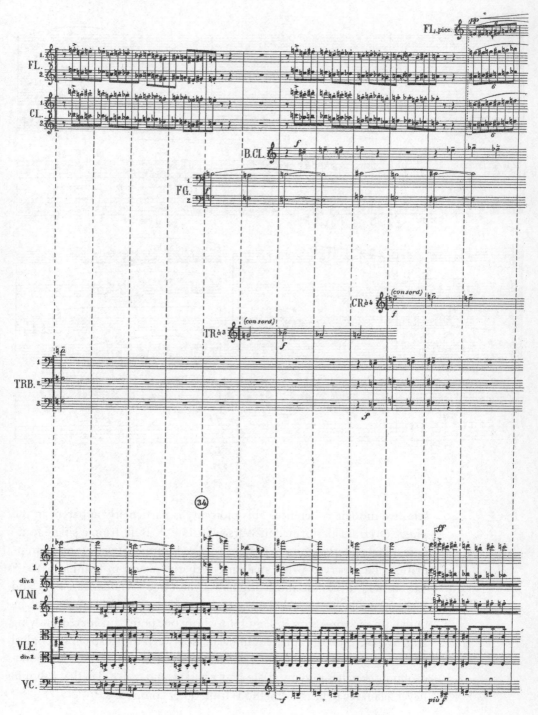

The *Tragic Overture* is a significant work for a number of reasons. Panufnik had discovered a concise way of combining the total chromatic, employing overlapping chains of the four-note motif, with a range of diatonic formations (including parallel dominant sevenths and a major-minor melodic idea), culminating in a final chord whose eleven pitches derive from interlocked major and minor triads. Furthermore, he gave himself rhythmic and expressive breathing space in the overall sonata structure by setting the pervasive quaver pulsations against 'second subject' counter-melodies proceeding at a slower rate of change. The textural and registral layering is most obviously engineered by processes of augmentation and diminution of the four-note motif, which Stephen Walsh memorably describes as one 'which twists in on itself like a coursed hare'[20] (Ex. 2.3).

While most Polish compositions written during the Second World War had an oblique relationship to the context in which they were written (Lutosławski's *Paganini Variations* or Szeligowski's Piano Concerto, 1941), Panufnik's *Tragic Overture* is one of the few surviving works explicitly to reflect the war. Its occasional onomatopoeic effects are, however, overwhelmed by the insistent pounding of the four-note motif. It is surely no coincidence that the quaver rhythm of this motif is identical to that of the opening of Beethoven's Fifth Symphony, which was used by the BBC as its wartime call signal (in Morse code it represents 'V' for 'Victory'). But the connection with Beethoven's first movement gains more substance in the proposal that Panufnik's overture has deeper parallels, melodically and structurally, than simply a pervading rhythmic motif.[21] Whatever Panufnik's conscious intent, there is no denying that he was setting out on a quite new and distinctive path, one which, with the deaths of Koffler and Padlewski, and the departure of Regamey, was to place him in the vanguard of Polish music after the war.

3 Post-war reconstruction

In many ways, it is astonishing that Polish musicians were able to achieve so much under Nazi oppression. Despite the loss of many scores written both during and before the war, most devastatingly during the Warsaw Uprising in 1944, many substantial pieces survived or, notably in the case of Panufnik, were reconstructed from memory. Some works, of course, had to wait until after 1944 to be performed. Thanks to detailed forward planning by the Polish musical underground during the war, institutions were rapidly established in 1945, including Polish Radio, radio and concert orchestras in various cities, the Polish Composers' Union (ZKP), and the Polish Music Publishers (PWM) in Kraków. Music schools and conservatories soon followed. In contrast to the wholesale destruction of Warsaw, Kraków had survived virtually unscathed and therefore had the facilities to provide the focus for the nation's musical activities. One of the first events was a Festival of Contemporary Polish Music at the beginning of September 1945. In the opening concert, exactly six years to the day from the Nazi invasion, the newly formed Kraków Philharmonic Orchestra premiered Bacewicz's Overture (1943) and Palester's Second Symphony (1942). Bacewicz's Overture shows how she was distancing herself from Parisian chic and developing a particularly vigorous slant on neo-classicism, while still maintaining an essentially diatonic idiom and strong adherence to the tonic key. She also tellingly incorporates the rhythmic 'V' for 'Victory' motif into the symphonic argument, although it has a less pervasive role than in Panufnik's *Tragic Overture*. Like Panufnik's work, its dark, low tones and aggressive moto perpetuo invoke, intentionally or subconsciously, the mood of determined resistance characteristic of occupied Poland. A more clear-cut and substantive example of a 'war' composition than either of these overtures is Woytowicz's Second Symphony, 'Warsaw' (1945), dedicated to his brother 'Andrzej, killed in the Warsaw Uprising'. Its first movement replaces the customary sonata-allegro with an extended lament, the scherzo quotes from the 1831 revolutionary song 'Song of Warsaw' ('Warszawianka'), and the original coda of the finale was a version of Woytowicz's own wartime underground song.

Already in 1945 distinctions were being drawn between the music of the past and music of the future. One of Poland's most trenchant writers and critics, Stefan Kisielewski (1911–91), who was also a composer of witty, neo-classical pieces, reported on the Festival in Kraków. As far as he was concerned, Bacewicz's Overture, grouped along with music by Perkowski, Szeligowski and others, was fixed in the past represented by the French School. He was more interested in other new compositions, which included Palester's Second Symphony:

> The second group of festival pieces was made up of works 'looking to the future' – in the real avant-garde sense of the word, driving a path into as yet unknown thickets of genuinely new music. This is the aspiration for a new monumentality, for constructional grandeur, enclosing an emotional charge yet clearly centred in the contemporary – not just having experiments in mind, but rather wanting to re-establish themselves and to justify their own existence not only in 'the new thrills' desired by the impressionists or even in the folk period of Stravinsky but more in the creation of a new emotionality and grandeur.[1]

Kisielewski seems to be voicing a desire for the grand design as a liberation from the confines of the war, as a vehicle for a new expressiveness, and, by implication, as a musical component of the nation's task in rebuilding itself materially and psychologically. He also appears to be calling for a line to be drawn under the foreign compositional trends prevalent in inter-war Poland, requiring composers to look for new avenues (it is perhaps significant that nowhere in his article does he mention the Second Viennese School).

Palester's Second Symphony met Kisielewski's criteria (Ex. 3.1). It is a full-blooded four-movement work in the tradition of Brahms, with cyclic cross-references and a double fugue for its finale. Unlike Bacewicz's Overture, the symphony displays a high level of dissonance, evolving quasi-tonal structures and a densely orchestrated musical argument. At its Paris premiere in 1946, it raised doubts in Nadia Boulanger's mind as to Palester's willingness to be concise and self-critical.[2] Certainly the symphony is characterised by exuberant contrapuntal layering and instrumental doublings, but for Kisielewski it was a positive work, reminiscent of the architectural grandeur of Roussel.

It is worth considering the strands of French music that proved to be most enduring in Polish music after 1939. Commentaries of the time were at least as likely to mention Roussel and Honegger as the more lightweight Parisian composers of the inter-war years. On the one hand, the first movement of Szeligowski's effervescent Piano Concerto owes much to Poulenc's rhythmic élan and humorous spirit. Nevertheless, it is the more robust neo-classicism of Roussel and Honegger that is closer to the Polish experience. Even before

Example 3.1. Palester, Second Symphony (1942), opening.

Example 3.1. (*cont.*)

the war, Honegger was a name to conjure with in Poland: he was accorded a monographic concert in Warsaw in January 1933 which included the *Mouvement symphonique no. 2, 'Rugby'* (Fitelberg had premiered *Mouvement symphonique no. 1, 'Pacific 231'* in Warsaw in 1924), the Piano Concertino and First Symphony. Roussel's music, however, was far less known in Poland, although Lutosławski recalled the impact on him of the Polish premiere of Roussel's Third Symphony in the early 1930s and of a recording he heard during the war:

> It made a strong impression on me . . . the richness of harmony in Debussy's and Ravel's music had a strong influence on me; but I was never happy because it was used for suites or ballets or some symphonic poems, but never for more serious forms like symphonies. Roussel's symphonies, especially the Third, filled that gap. He used the richness of the French world of harmony . . . in a form which makes us think about Brahms. He is a sort of French Brahms of the twentieth century.[3]

Lutosławski's First Symphony (1941–7), like Palester's Second, is a product of the war years and eschews programmatic associations. In aligning themselves with the symphonic lineage of Roussel–Brahms–Beethoven, both works demonstrate the irrelevance of Szymanowski's symphonic legacy, whose three mature symphonies displayed a healthy disregard for the genre's classical tradition. Szymanowski's elliptical Second Symphony, for example, has but two movements, the second of which combines slow movement and scherzo in a set of variations, followed by a climactic fugue functioning as a finale. His Third Symphony is a large-scale, uninterrupted ternary design in which the central section approximates to a scherzo, while the Fourth, the *Symphonie concertante*, follows the traditional three-movement structure of a concerto. The symphony as a genre in Poland had had virtually no pedigree in the nineteenth century, so Szymanowski had had to follow his own instincts. His immediate successors, virtually without exception, reverted to a conservative four-movement pattern although, like Szymanowski's Second Symphony, several concluded with a fugue or double fugue, as do the second symphonies by Woytowicz and Palester.

Lutosławski's goal appears to have been to work painstakingly through the technical and expressive challenges of a full symphony for the first time, independent of Szymanowski. It was his first major piece since the pre-war Symphonic Variations and understandably, given its protracted realisation, it is something of a stylistic patchwork. There is evidence of Roussel's influence in the structural tautness; Steven Stucky further indicates that Lutosławski modelled the finale 'directly on the large sonatina form (i.e. sonata without development) which Brahms chose for the finales of his first and third symphonies'.[4] Yet while certain musical ideas, such as the rhythmic build-up to the recapitulation in the first movement, are reminiscent of the sturdiness of Roussel's Third Symphony, in terms of sound world it is other composers who are more likely to come to mind. Bartók lies behind the second movement, Poco adagio, especially in its central section recalling the Hungarian's 'night music' (from fig. 44); it also contains traces of Prokofiev's jaunty sense of the grotesque. Stravinsky's ballet score, *The Firebird*, is strongly felt in the third movement, Allegretto misterioso, a somewhat leaner relative not only of 'Kashchei's Dance' but also the vein of waltz reminiscences found in Ravel. Elsewhere, particularly in the 'big tunes' of the outer and slow movements, a broader, more romantic character is in evidence, one which anticipates the music of Lutosławski's final decade. In the light of his subsequent scores, the orchestral flair and the ingenuity of his metrical flexibility are particularly noteworthy, and both contribute to his unerring sense of symphonic drama. And yet the symphony has an unsettled, wary character, as if in its nervous energy it is looking back over the shoulder both at its various musical sources and at the times in which it was conceived. It has maintained its position as arguably the most cogently argued Polish symphony of the post-war decade, although it is understandable that Lutosławski later came to regard it as a dead end in his search for an individual language.

If some composers were still finding their feet in the post-war years, others were re-establishing their contacts abroad. Several concerts were organised in Paris, notably an orchestral showcase in December 1946, when Fitelberg conducted Lutosławski's Symphonic Variations, Palester's Second Symphony and Szymanowski's *Mountain Robbers*. Fitelberg went on to conduct Palester's Symphony in The Hague and Rome in 1947. Panufnik's *Nocturne* (1947) was premiered a year later in Paris, as was his *Polish Suite* in 1949 (the latter was commissioned by UNESCO to commemorate the hundredth anniversary of Chopin's death and was later retitled *Hommage à Chopin*). The ISCM festivals, which had given Koffler and Palester much needed foreign exposure before 1939, were now even more important at this time of recovery. At the 1946 Festival in London, Palester's Violin Concerto (1941) was conducted by Fitelberg, while Panufnik's *Five Polish Peasant Songs* (*Pięć pieśni ludowych*, 1940) was conducted by the composer. In Copenhagen in 1947, Panufnik conducted the Bassoon Concerto (1944) by Michal Spisak (1914–65) and Lutosławski attended as a representative of the ZKP, as he did in Amsterdam a year later. In 1948 in Holland, Palester's Third String Quartet (1944) was joined by Panufnik's *Lullaby* (*Kołysanka*, 1947) and Malawski's Symphonic Studies (1947). A highlight of the 1949 Festival in Palermo, attended by Panufnik, was a performance of Szymanowski's opera *King Roger*, which is set in twelfth-century Sicily.

It becomes evident that Palester and Panufnik quickly came to be regarded in these immediate post-war years as the most significant Polish composers, as if the creative initiative had been passed into their hands. Neither Perkowski nor Woytowicz, for example, fully roused themselves compositionally after 1945; Wiechowicz concentrated on strengthening the amateur choral movement as both conductor and composer, while Mycielski played a crucial role organisationally and polemically rather than compositionally. In contrast, during the immediate post-war years Palester's music was performed not only in major European cities but also in New York. But it was Panufnik who was breaking really new compositional ground and fulfilling the promise of the *Tragic Overture*. 1947 was an astonishingly fertile year for him: he composed *Circle of Fifths* (*Krąg kwintowy*) for piano, *Nocturne* for orchestra, *Lullaby* for twenty-nine strings and two harps, and a Divertimento for strings based on string trios by Feliks Janiewicz (1762–1848). A year later he completed the first of his acknowledged ten symphonies, *Sinfonia rustica*.

What quickly becomes apparent is Panufnik's ability to develop an individual musical language. This was characterised above all by a distinctive clarity – clarity of technique and expression, of timbre, harmony, motif and structure. There is still a residue of Webern's influence in this regard, but also now an acknowledgement of Debussy's textural sensitivity and of Bartók's rhythmic and motivic detailing and coincidentally of the type of *plein-air* neo-classicism which Copland developed in the 1930s and 40s after his own studies in Europe.

In *Circle of Fifths*, Panufnik set himself a deliberately restricted task, and the schematicism is apparent. Prefaced by a Preludium, there is a sequence of alternating Interludes (slow, soft, *una corda*) and Studies (fast, loud, *tre corde*), the cycle beginning on C sharp and moving through the traditional circle of fifths until A flat is reached in the Postludium. Each of the twelve short movements is a variation on a hidden 'theme', which is embellished, excerpted or registrally displaced. The scalic and arpeggiated features of this spectral idea lends the set an air of general understatement, in comparison to the high thematic profiles of previous circle-of-fifths models by Bach and Chopin. There is a heavy reliance on underlying scalic sequences, with exploration of symmetry (the palindrome of no. 4) and shared features in contiguous movements (a repeated rhythmic underlay in nos. 4 and 5, jazz harmony in nos. 9 and 10). No. 8 is perhaps the most forward-looking, in that it consists of transposed repetitions of a twelve-note arpeggiation comprising the three diminished-seventh chords stacked on top of each other at a tone's distance. Although Panufnik never varies the intervallic make-up of the arpeggiation (except at the final 'cadence'), it is the first example of focussed harmonic partitioning in Polish music and is a forerunner of the twelve-note spread arpeggios of the fourth of Serocki's *Suite of Preludes* (1952) and, more obviously, of Lutosławski's harmonic exploration begun in his *Five Songs* (*Pięć pieśni*, 1957). There were other incidental forays into twelve-note collections during these years, including the double-bass pizzicato at the start of the third movement of Lutosławski's First Symphony, and they demonstrated at least an awareness of the concept of non-diatonic pitch structures even if they remained far removed in technique and spirit from serial developments in Western Europe.

Schematic presentation of material is more apparent in *Lullaby*, which in effect is an extended 'interlude'. Here the layering of musical ideas is the *raison d'être* and, notwithstanding the essentially abstract rather than figurative nature of Panufnik's craft, was suggested, as so often in his music, by a sentimental extra-musical stimulus. On one of his visits abroad, Panufnik found himself at night on Waterloo Bridge in London:

> The river's flow and the night sky over a misty city prompted the idea of music on three planes: a pulsating rhythm of harps to correspond to the gentle, uninterrupted flow of the river; a group of solo instruments, some moving in quarter tones, for the drifting clouds; and above, like the moon which was also looking down on Poland, the song of a Polish peasant, based almost entirely on the pentatonic scale and played by a succession of solo string instruments: violin, then viola, then cello.[5]

Whereas the melodic foundation of *Circle of Fifths* remained obscured, the 'song of a Polish peasant' in *Lullaby* is stated openly four times, moving down from high violin to cello in four octave-displaced stages. Its classic ABB folk phrase structure and A major tonality remain unaltered. Panufnik envelopes it in a *con sordino* skein of overlapping ideas, which includes a triadic ostinato (I–V–II–V), an artificial-harmonic pedal point on the tonic, and quarter-tone, chromatic and arpeggic movement added at each successive stage of the structure. The quarter tones, unlike Hába's contemporaneous work in Czechoslovakia, are decorative: they and the glissandos (which Panufnik omitted from the score in its 1955 revision) never occur on the downbeat.

Example 3.2. Panufnik, *Lullaby* (*Kołysanka*, 1947), fig. 6.

Instead they fill in between notes of the A major scale which can be a semitone, minor third, perfect fourth or octave apart. Panufnik takes great care to
differentiate this skein by dynamic layering, simple polymetric divisions and
a range of playing techniques (Ex. 3.2). The experimental nature of *Lullaby*
gives it curiosity value, although the use of register and textural density to
determine structural progress was to have consequences in his later music.
More significantly was the notoriety the work achieved in Poland in the late
1940s: no one else was abandoning traditional procedures as radically as
this. The actual sound world Panufnik created in *Lullaby* is more edgy and
less sweetly beguiling than its programmatic origins or the look of the score
might suggest.

This is not an observation that could be made of the most substantial work
of 1947, *Nocturne* (another, though less specific evocation of the night). It
is comparatively relaxed in tone and execution, preferring organic growth
to mechanical processes. Although it has an overall arch structure, only the
outer edges are obviously concerned with mirror imaging. The unusual feature which marks off these sections – a twelve-note ladder of alternating
perfect fifths and diminished fifths, played by the piano – again anticipates Lutosławski's harmonic arsenal from the late 1950s onwards. There
is a totally confident handling of a range of harmonic idioms. On occasion, Panufnik seems to be recalling Fauré and Debussy, although any such
resonances are filtered through his own sensibility. As in the more robust
Tragic Overture, triadic elements are often only partially in focus and dominant harmony sequences are mixed with his own fingerprint of combined
major-minor harmony; its archetypal format consists of an inverted major
triad with flattened third placed melodically above, as in bar 3 of Ex. 3.3.
Panufnik's acute awareness of orchestral sonority is most clearly demonstrated by the work's opening. At the time, its quiet boldness must have
been astonishing (although it was premiered in Paris in 1948, it was not
heard in Poland until early 1949, even though it had won the Szymanowski
Competition in Kraków in 1947). There is little sense of pulse and the material which is revealed with the greatest delicacy is minimal, depending for
its impact on single gestures (Ex. 3.4): a tamburo piccolo roll, a 'pause', a
suspended cymbal struck with a timpani stick, a second 'pause'; the same
pattern is then repeated, this time with added viola and cello harmonics –
an upper F creating a minor ninth with a lower E, then the two moving each
a semitone closer, upper E with lower F. This non-melodic, non-triadic,
barely harmonic language, combined with the subtlest of unpitched percussion, is light years from Palester or Lutosławski at the time; it unwittingly anticipates the turnaround in Polish music a decade and more later,

Example 3.3. Panufnik, *Nocturne* (1947, rev. 1955), fig. 7.

when timbre and texture came to dominate the thinking of many of his compatriots.

As yet, Panufnik had not essayed a larger symphonic structure since his two wartime symphonies. He had reconstructed the First Symphony (1939) at the end of the war but destroyed the score after a performance in 1945 in Kraków; Mycielski's description of the piece indicates quite strongly that the symphony's opening bore a striking resemblance to the start of the later *Nocturne*.[6] If in fact the pieces are related, that would indicate that Panufnik's radical rethink of his musical language began much earlier than hitherto thought. The appearance of *Sinfonia rustica* (1948) was a major event. It won the ZKP's Chopin Competition prize in April and was premiered in May 1949. As the title suggests, the symphony turns again to Polish folk culture, although more in the line of the clean-cut, bitter-sweet settings of the wartime *Five Polish Peasant Songs* than the artifice of *Lullaby*, even though the slow movement draws on the compositional experience of the latter work. The external impulse on this occasion was Panufnik's fascination with the patterns of the semi-abstract, palindromic paper-cuts made by Polish peasants (he returned to this same source for his Third String Quartet, 1990). The symmetrical structure of these paper-cuts is paralleled by the the work's platform layout, echoing Bartók's *Music for Strings, Percussion and Celesta* by placing the two string orchestras on either side of the central

Example 3.4. Panufnik, *Nocturne* (1947, rev. 1955), opening.

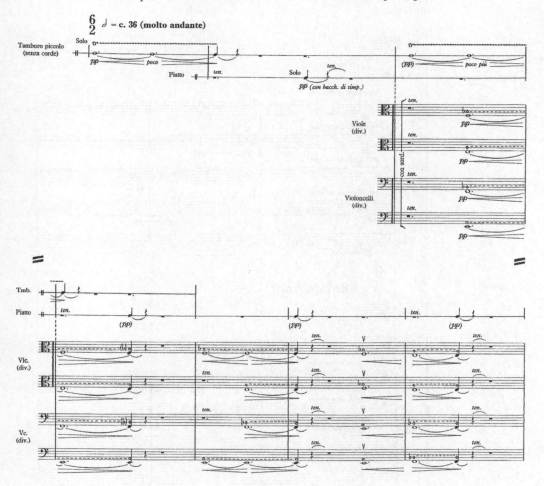

body of eight wind instruments. Panufnik's score is one of his most relaxed, with an easy-going charm and artful freshness that distinguish it from its worthy contemporaries. Folk tunes from northern Poland are presented as themes with inventive layered accompaniments in a classically designed symphonic format, the diatonic context decorated with piquant chromatic and major-minor conjunctions. Quixotically, when he revised the work for Western publication in 1955, Panufnik excised the most abstract and forward-looking texture, the introduction to the slow movement (Ex. 3.5). In the opening twenty bars, he picks out a folk tune in the lower strings by overlapping successive *sf* > *p* entries, traces of which still appear at the end of the movement in the later revision.

Example 3.5. Panufnik, *Sinfonia rustica* (1948), original opening of third movement.

In all these works, Panufnik was cutting a lonely path through Kisielewski's 'unknown thickets'. But he avoided monumentality and conventional musical discourse, concentrating on textural matters and allusion rather than on declamation. In combining a cool classicism with folk materials, he was seemingly providing a new model of Polishness, a timely successor to Szymanowski's pre-war example. But Panufnik was to become but one of many victims to circumstances largely beyond his control, circumstances which once again brought extra-musical forces to bear upon the creative thinking and output of Polish composers.

Example 3.5. (*cont.*)

4   Socialist realism I: its onset and genres

The need for communal effort after the Second World War was not peculiar to Poland – in the United Kingdom, for example, Churchill was replaced by Attlee and a Labour government which brought in the National Health Service and nationalised a number of industries. In Poland, the need for a strong infrastructure was paramount, not least because the Eastern territories, including Lwów, had been retained by the Soviet Union, and in compensation Poland had gained western lands from the Germans, including the city of Wrocław (formerly Breslau). The establishment of the PWM music publishers, the ZKP, Polish Radio, and of orchestras and music schools in major cities provided an early and enduring framework for the common good of post-war music. Creatively, there was initially a fair degree of independence in the arts and, finance permitting, opportunities to travel or study abroad. As in the inter-war years, Paris was the prime focus for musicians: Panufnik, as musical director of the Warsaw Philharmonic, went there in 1946 to purchase scores and parts (music by Debussy, Ravel, Roussel and Messiaen), as well as fulfilling conducting engagements in the next few years in Berlin, London and Zurich. In 1947, both Serocki and Stanisław Skrowaczewski (b. 1923) began composition studies with Boulanger.

Nevertheless, for the vast majority of composers there was no alternative but to make the best of the opportunities available within Poland. A number of them worked at some point for PWM in Kraków, including Kisielewski, Malawski, Mycielski, Palester and Panufnik. In fact, Panufnik was responsible for inventing the now universally acknowledged score layout where pages are left blank of all but the active playing parts (Witold Rudziński recalls that the original wartime manuscript of Panufnik's *Tragic Overture* was already laid out in this way, with no wasted empty staves).[1] Other composers worked at Polish Radio – Lutosławski started in 1945 as a music reporter and quickly moved to writing incidental music for radio plays and poetry programmes. Some were professional performers – Bacewicz concertised as a solo violinist until the early 1950s – while many were closely involved in tertiary-level music education, notably Sikorski, Szeligowski and Wiechowicz.

And yet in 1945 there lurked intimations of a new ideology, especially from those who had had contact with Soviet culture during the war. In the first issue of the periodical *Ruch Muzyczny* (*Musical Movement*), Rudziński sent out a message which, although it may have been perfectly reasonable in the circumstances, sowed the seeds for a hard-line government cultural policy a few years later:

> The new post-war reality makes its own demands on us. The masses, hitherto deprived of opportunities in the sphere of culture, are now coming forward for their share. The modern Polish composer goes to meet them, knows them and wants to sacrifice his many personal desires in order to co-ordinate his work with the most vital needs of a Polish culture regenerating itself after such unbearable devastation. He realises, however, that the composer's position of honour – writing and working for the masses – at the same time entails being concerned for high artistic standards in society's wishes. It equally means a responsibility to posterity for the manner and degree to which people's spontaneous drive for culture is put into effect.
>
> From the point of view of the composer as an individual, it is necessary to ensure the greatest possible creative freedom, artistic means and trends, coupled with the unrestrained right of artistic criticism. These are the two cardinal assumptions, from which there can be no departure, be it for reasons of personal dignity or concern for the free and natural development of compositional talents.
>
> New tasks call for new means . . . The sooner good music reaches the peasant and the worker, the sooner we can look into the future with absolute certainty, confident that the great riches of Polish culture will get into the proper hands.[2]

Part of the creative realignment was the utilisation of folk songs and dances, the birthright of the people. But whereas Hungarian children enjoyed the inestimable heritage of Kodály's educational activities and the wide repertoire he created, Poland had had no such figure before the war. With the dearth of printed musical material, Lutosławski was one of many who responded voluntarily to the need, writing his *Folk Melodies* for piano (1945), *20 Polish Carols* for voice and piano (1946), and numerous children's songs. But by the late 1940s such innocent activity was not enough, just as Panufnik's incorporation of folk songs into his concert works did not make them immune to criticism.

The catalyst for change took place in Moscow, at the Conference of Musicians at the Central Committee of the All-Union Communist Party.[3] This three-day conference in January 1948 witnessed the haranguing of composers by the Party's prime cultural ideologue, Andrei Zhdanov, and the humiliation of Shostakovich and Prokofiev. Its transcripts give a good idea of the level of musical argument and the atmosphere in which it was conducted. The conference's primary aim was to bring errant composers to book, to rein in their individuality, a process that had begun before the war but was deemed in the late 1940s to have slipped. The goal was music for the masses – 'socialist realism' – and an end to (Western-inspired) abstraction and experimentation, which was dubbed 'formalism'. The Stalinist definition of art – 'socialist in content and national in form' – became the watchword, especially elsewhere in the Eastern bloc. And Zhdanov's death seven months later did not interrupt this policy, which was enthusiastically promulgated by his successor, Tikhon Khrennikov.

Despite the fact that Poland had greater contact with the West immediately after 1945, no one remained in doubt for long that the upheavals of the war had left Poland within the Soviet sphere of influence, alongside other 'Eastern' European countries. Churchill's famous speech in Fulton, Missouri, on 5 March 1946 had already acknowledged the new reality:

> From Stettin [Szczecin] in the Baltic to Trieste in the Adriatic an iron curtain has descended across the Continent. Behind that line lie all the capitals of the ancient states of Central and Eastern Europe . . . and all are subject, in one form or other, not only to Soviet influence but to a very high and, in many cases, increasing measure of control from Moscow.[4]

One of the early signs of this influence was the Soviet manipulation of the World Congress of Intellectuals for Peace, which was organised by a joint French–Polish committee (members included Iwaszkiewicz, Le Corbusier, Léger and Barrault) and was held in the newly Polish city of Wrocław (25–8 August 1948). Left-leaning delegates from the West included writers (Eluard, Julian Huxley, Quasimodo and Sartre) and visual artists (Picasso); Panufnik agreed, albeit reluctantly, to lead the Polish delegation. A number of foreign delegates, including Huxley, walked out of the Congress after the Soviet writer Ilya Ehrenburg attacked Western authors: 'if hyenas could use fountain pens, and jackals could use typewriters, they would write like T. S. Eliot'.[5]

Polish arguments for and against socialist realism took a more serious although impassioned tone, avoiding hysterical invective. The temperature was steadily raised in 1948, and *Ruch Muzyczny* is a fair barometer. Its first two issues in 1948 had included extensive articles on atonalism by the composer Roman Haubenstock (1919–94), who had studied with Koffler before the war. Although not illustrated by musical examples, his elucidation of the evolution, aesthetics and techniques of the Second Viennese School (with references also to Křenek and Hába), from free atonality to twelve-note principles, gave both composers and the flexing muscles of the Polish Ministry of Culture much to think about.[6] By the end of the year, polemical articles by Khrennikov, the Polish musicologist Józef Chomiński (1906–94) and the Polish Deputy Minister of Culture, Włodzimierz Sokorski (1908–99), extolled the virtues of socialist realism, while Kisielewski engaged in one of his many acts of guerrilla warfare against the new dogma.[7] Sokorski continued the pressure into 1949, several times invoking the importance of Polish folk culture, and he was joined in argument by Mycielski. But *Ruch Muzyczny*'s continuing support for new music – including a graph-based analysis of part of Panufnik's *Lullaby*[8] – enraged the authorities, who compelled the magazine to publish a Soviet article accusing Schoenberg of being the 'liquidator of music'.[9] *Ruch Muzyczny* was itself liquidated after the next issue in December 1949.

But the magazine had fulfilled one outstandingly useful function in October that year. It devoted almost thirty pages to detailed coverage of a composers' conference in Łagów Lubuski, in western Poland, between 5–8 August 1949.[10] This document is as significant for an understanding of the development of Polish socialist realism as Zhdanov's actions eighteen months earlier were in the Soviet context. But it is clear from the outset that the Polish authorities were intent on persuasion rather than browbeating. Instead of the formal urban surroundings used in Moscow in deepest winter, the Polish Ministry of Culture chose a picturesque medieval castle in a rural setting at the height of summer. It was a wily move, and an almost unreal sense of reasoned discussion pervades much of the conference proceedings. In fact, despite a strong suspicion that many speakers were hedging their bets, there are many instances of outspokenness, as the debate struggled to come to grips with the concept and practicalities of the realist/formalist divide. And although the conference was attended by less than half of the membership of the ZKP (notable absentees included Bacewicz, Kisielewski and Panufnik), most of the significant composers were there, even if some, like Lutosławski, said barely a word. The generation who had studied in Paris with Boulanger was best represented: Alfred Gradstein (1904–54), Maklakiewicz, Mycielski, Perkowski, Rudziński, Sikorski and Woytowicz. Others included Jan Ekier (b. 1913), Palester, Szabelski and Zbigniew Turski (1908–79), while composers of the youngest generation, then still in their twenties, were represented by Tadeusz Baird (1928–81), Krenz and Serocki. Also in evidence were the musicologists Chomiński and Zofia Lissa (1908–80). Three concerts of new Polish orchestral music were given by the Poznań Philharmonic Orchestra under its young conductor, Stanisław Wisłocki, as well as a recital of piano miniatures and songs, the latter accompanied by their composers, Gradstein and Lutosławski.

Ruch Muzyczny's coverage of the Łagów conference was prefaced by an editorial and articles by Sokorski and Mycielski. The editorial encapsulated the general tenor of socialism in the arts: 'The contents of works created in the socialist epoch must be free of pessimism, nihilism, catastrophism and escapism. And that is because the socialist epoch brings with it greatness, certainty and joy.'[11] Sokorski's resumé of the conference, 'Towards Socialist Realism in Music',[12] lays into Western culture along traditional Stalinist lines:

> Over the past half-century we have witnessed, among intellectuals and artists still clinging to old world ideology, a characteristic helplessness when faced with the necessity to capture the objective truth of the new epoch. This is the consequence of the collapse of the capitalist system, which has led to the decline of all previous aesthetic notions. In the visual arts, this means notions of mass, colour and symmetry, in music the notions of tonality, harmony and the unity of content and form, or the equivalent notions in other fields of art.
> . . . The initially deep and thrilling pessimism of Stravinsky, Debussy, Ravel or here Szymanowski is transformed, as the crisis in the system measurably deepens, into formalistic juggling, into a burlesque of dodecaphonists, into a snobbish cultivation of discordant jazz.[13]

The links between political systems and the state of health of their artistic outpourings is a familiar feature of Stalinist thinking, and Sokorski was no exception in seeing America as the main enemy of the socialist new order. His antagonism towards jazz is largely politically inspired (both Stalin and Hitler had problems with it), but his antagonism here may have been directed less towards music of the swing era than to the recent development of bebop. Fifty years after this conference, it is possible to see some perspicacious observations in Sokorski's diatribe, notably the ways in which it is now admitted that the United States blatantly used its arts (especially film, popular music and abstract painting) as cultural-political weapons in its fight for the soul of a deeply divided post-war Europe:

> To eliminate life's emotions and to confine the aesthetic feeling of music to what Clive Bell called 'the abstract significance of form', this was the task American and Western European composers set themselves over the past fifty years. It was obvious right from the start that this kind of music would be completely devoid of any national or folk character, that it was inevitably heading towards a soulless cosmopolitanism, with the added consequence that it was doomed to fall under the dictate of the musical deformities of American jazz.
> Small wonder, then, that American imperialism is today making use of formalistic, cosmopolitan, anti-national and non-humanistic music as one of the principal means of influencing the human psyche, of blunting its ethical and aesthetic sensitivity, of destroying folk and national musical trends with a

view to overcoming other nations in their struggle for freedom, social justice and the new constructive and clearly delineated order of the socialist system.

The issue of formalism and cosmopolitanism in music is therefore of interest to us not only as an artistic phenomenon, not even only as a political phenomenon, but as a specific form of the penetration of political nihilism and hopelessness of the so-called pan-American culture into the sphere of music.[14]

And while Sokorski named names and certain musical parameters, it was left to Mycielski, then the President of the ZKP, to try emolliently to provide an all-embracing definition of socialist realism, in the only passage in *Ruch Muzyczny*'s coverage to be printed in bold:

> The Polish Composers' Union conceives of musical realism as an expression of the strivings of society and adopts an anti-formalistic stance. The composer is not an individual separated from society but one thanks to whom, through artistic expression, a musical work possesses an emotional content which can move the broad masses. Cosmopolitan language, being indifferent to manifestations of national style, is rejected. The composer is to create Polish music, though that does not mean folk quotations but music whose melodic contour, rhythm, form, harmonies and overall atmosphere add up to features that make it possible to distinguish a given work as belonging to or developing further the creative elements characteristic of the Polish musical school.[15]

Mycielski's words, echoing those of Rudziński four years earlier, stress the primacy of national over personal identity. Szymanowski's definition of Polishness was no longer relevant, and new, clearly simpler ways were to be sought. As ever, it was easier to damn a work's negative, formalist qualities than to pinpoint its positive, realist attributes. And this was not least because the confrontation between the two concepts proceeded from a reactionary standpoint: composers felt compelled to deconstruct in order to create, and unsurprisingly this caused enormous problems.

One of the ways in which the ZKP, at the behest of the Ministry of Culture, tried to assist matters in the early 1950s was to hold listening sessions (*przesłuchanie*, otherwise translated as auditions, vetting panels, interrogations – they were all of these). The concerts at Łagów and the discussions from the floor provided an early example of such occasions, and it is in the transcripts of these listening sessions that the measure of the problem can be seen. Several participants were forthright in their criticism of the new extra-musical, socio-political dimension. Perkowski, for example, said on the first day that 'the question of formalism and realism is plainly a political issue'.[16]

Others, especially the trio of youngsters – Baird, Krenz and Serocki – were more willing to take on board the new ideology. Krenz provided one of the few poetic moments, when he alluded to the epilogue of the most famous nineteenth-century Polish epic poem, *Pan Tadeusz*, by Chopin's contemporary, Adam Mickiewicz: 'There are surely no composers so stubborn that they would sincerely recoil from having their pieces [performed] "under the thatch".'[17] But Baird later wondered

> in what kind of musical language is the composer supposed to reach the listener: the old or the new? Meanwhile, from his own experience, coll[eague] Baird can give examples of peasants not understanding very simple and valuable contemporary works (by Szeligowski and Wiechowicz) while workers on another occasion (at a concert for leading workers) did not even understand Chopin.[18]

Baird's juvenile Sinfonietta in C major (1949) was one of the conference's great successes, but even then its simplistic harmonic and thematic character as well as its four-square phrasing must have seemed to discerning ears to be the result of an artistic calculation that the lowest common denominator was the route to success. One short-lived consequence was the formation by Baird, Krenz and Serocki of 'Group '49' ('Grupa '49'), whose aim, as Serocki put it, was to create 'a bright and simple music, allowing for an emotional experience'.[19] The question of musical language was crucial, and discussions of several other orchestral works brought matters to a head.

Panufnik's *Nocturne*, performed in his absence, had a mixed reception. Sokorski attempted, in words of both praise and censure, to seal the discussion: '*Nocturne* is a work of great calibre, very characteristic of the composer's musical style. However, the means of expression employed in this piece, bordering on the non-musical sphere, are judged by Min[ister] Sokorski as formalistic.' Woytowicz had some reservations, but stood up to Sokorski: '*Nocturne* is for him most difficult in this respect [accessibility], yet it is a work with a great future and a sure success in the making.' Szeligowski applauded Panufnik's 'dynamic logic'.[20] But undoubtedly it was its experimental, semi-abstract character, emphasised at the expense of overt expressiveness, which proved its downfall in these circumstances.

The work which received the most critical attention was Turski's three-movement Second Symphony 'Olympic' (1948), which had been entered, together with Bacewicz's *Olympic Cantata* (1948), for the international arts competition that ran alongside the first post-war Olympic Games in London that year. Turski's Symphony won first prize, but just a year later, at Łagów, it was lambasted by Sokorski as a piece which in its content is incompatible with the spirit of our time. True, one can detect an emotional content, but it is the emotion of someone who is lost, in this case in the terrible period of the occupation . . . The piece terrifies and confuses the listener . . . its language is formalistic through and through.[21]

Lissa, who was the most powerful Polish musical figure in the application of Marxist ideology in the late 1940s and early 1950s, succinctly summarised the party line on Turski's Symphony (of which only the second and third movements were played at the conference): 'It has to be stated openly that this Symphony is incapable of "mobilising" our man.'[22]

'The listener' and 'our man' were, of course, the embodiment of the masses, the worker and the peasant. But if the composers and musicians present at Łagów felt intimidated, some showed commendable courage in supporting Turski's Symphony:

> When coll[eague] Perkowski first heard the Symphony on the radio, it
> seemed to him grey and gloomy. After this performance he has to change his
> mind. Even though the language of the piece is totally alien to him, the whole
> work makes a staggering impression . . . it is one of the most outstanding
> works of recent times.[23]

> [Wisłocki] had worked on the 'Olympic' Symphony with great pleasure,
> mainly because he liked its emotional content. He pointed to its elaborate,
> very beautiful and smooth cantilena in the middle movement and described
> the last movement as 'thrilling'. He has no doubts that the work would score
> further successes.[24]

> The 'Olympic' Symphony is the best proof that it is not only tonal music that
> can be logical, for this is a piece in which one cannot find consonances. The
> final E major triad, when juxtaposed with the remaining dissonances, itself
> seems to be a dissonance. (Ekier)[25]

As the discussion proceeded, the view that Turski's Symphony did not fit the present-day need for optimism was reinforced by Rudziński, who evidently disliked the finale:

> Regarding the third movement, he upholds his reservations because he
> considers it emotionally repulsive . . . Even if the whole piece seems too
> sinister (including the third movement), we must remember that it has its
> origins in the terrible years of occupation and may be treated as an historical
> document of obsolete times.[26]

Rudziński was not alone in implicitly locating it alongside other works (recent symphonies by Lutosławski, Palester and Woytowicz) which had been definitively shaped by the war.

The most reasonable, if in the end unsuccessful, attempt to ward off the harshest criticisms of the Symphony came from Ekier:

> Coll[eague] Ekier judges that it is still difficult today to achieve a situation in which the experience of the composer and the listener will be emotionally on the same level. Perhaps in five or ten years' time, coll[eague] Turski's musical language will become understandable to every musical listener. That is why one should not make too hasty conclusions about the formalism of the 'Olympic' Symphony. This is particularly because we have become accustomed to differentiate between formalism and realism as between black and white, forgetting that there are shades of grey. So inasmuch as coll[eague] Turski's Symphony, like other pieces, conveys the times of cosmic tragedy, let us not pass such categorical judgements and, if we do, let us supplement them with a question mark.[27]

On the last day of the conference, Turski replied to the welter of comments, but first put a question to the Deputy Minister of Culture:

> He says that he makes his statement conditional, however, on the kind of response he gets from the Minister to the question: did the cited judgements refer to the Symphony or to himself as the composer?
>
> Min[ister] Sokorski answers that the judgements referred solely to the piece.
>
> Coll[eague] Turski expresses his appreciation . . . and states that he does not wish to defend his piece. He takes the opportunity, however, to explain a few points. It was his intention when composing the Symphony to conclude it with optimistic accents. Judging by the majority of people's comments, he had not been successful in this. Such remarks are valuable to him because they will allow him in the future to avoid the means of expression employed in that piece to express a similar, i.e. optimistic content. Nevertheless, the composer expresses his doubts whether one can draw conclusions about the intention of a composer from, for example, the intonation of a cry, whether this is a cry of terror or joy, surprise or fear, etc. His own experience tells him that this is not possible. That is why he is inclined to ascribe listeners' reactions to his piece solely to the misunderstanding of his intentions. While stressing that the statements of the musicologists Dr Lissa and Dr Chomiński were particularly useful to him, the composer contested coll[eague] Chomiński's view that the instrumentation of his Symphony has features of a musical post-romanticism. According to the composer, more evident is the influence of impressionism or of the school of Rimsky-Korsakov.[28]

Notwithstanding the evidence of these reactions to Turski's Symphony which line up on either side of the realist/formalist divide, there are some more technical clues in the above comments which facilitate a closer understanding of both the symphony and its reception and which, in the process, provide some basis for a broader comprehension of the compositional problems under Polish socialist realism.

The 'Olympic' Symphony, with its three *attacca* movements rather than the traditional four, has an unusual sense of symphonic consequence. Its sense of unease is initiated by a swirling eleven-pitch ostinato (Ex. 4.1), a loose counterpart to the taut twelve-note equivalent in the third movement of Lutosławski's First Symphony. Having established a clearly defined and spacious sonata exposition (an introduction and two subject groups), Turski dispenses with a development and closes the movement with a tense, quasi-developmental amalgamation of themes from the exposition. He seems to be suggesting by engineering this collapse that the symphonic argument is incomplete. The central movement, Larghetto, provides an important respite from, rather than an answer to, the thematic and structural questions posed by the first movement. This is where he most closely approaches impressionism, filtered as it were through Szymanowski's experience of Debussy and Ravel. Its 'beautiful and smooth cantilena' is seductively couched in sustained chords and flickers of orchestral colours before achieving a rich and resonant apotheosis (Ex. 4.2). The finale was clearly intended as the main resolution of the first movement, at admittedly less than a third of its temporal length. Successive themes from the first movement are extensively remodelled: the symphony's opening ostinato becomes a dance in 3/8, while the double theme of the Allegro is split into a grotesque march on E flat clarinet and a brass fanfare. The shadow of Prokofiev hangs rather lugubriously over the proceedings, and Turski's strivings for an optimistic conclusion are effortful. In socialist-realist terms, he cannot quite shake off the dark-hued tone established at the outset. Even so, the symphony deserves more than just a place in the history books, if only for its unorthodox formal design and confidently dissonant idiom.[29]

Turski was the main victim of Łagów; his treatment and the system of listening sessions were to provide a context for new Polish music for the next five years. Lutosławski's First Symphony was banned just over a month later, following a walk-out of Soviet jurors during its performance in the opening concert of the 4th Chopin Piano Competition in Warsaw. Sokorski reputedly said after the concert in the artists' room: 'A composer like Lutosławski should be thrown under a tram.'[30] Panufnik's *Sinfonia rustica* was banned in 1950, when Sokorski declared during a visit to Warsaw by Khrennikov: '*Sinfonia rustica* has ceased to exist.'[31]

Example 4.1. Turski, Second Symphony 'Olympic' (1948), first movement, opening.

Tucked away in the concert of songs and children's pieces at Łagów were several examples of a genre apparently new to most Polish composers, the mass song. This was another import from the USSR (alongside the cantata), where it fulfilled the function of encouraging the Soviet worker and peasant to greater achievements at times of material and national crisis. In itself, this was a perfectly worthy concept, and we have only to think of shanties,

Example 4.2. Turski, Second Symphony 'Olympic' (1948), central movement, bb. 315–17.

scouting songs and wartime popular songs to realise that the 'mass' song was a familiar outlet for propaganda throughout Europe and elsewhere. In fact, a number of composers had willingly contributed notable examples of uplifting songs to the cause of the Polish underground movement during the war, Panufnik's *Warsaw Children* (*Warszawskie dzieci*) and Lutosławski's *Iron March* (*Żelazny marsz*) among them. Some are common-time marches, others are based on folk tunes and rhythms in 3/4 or 6/8. Their general idiom is necessarily straightforward, although occasionally, as in the whole-tone melodic and harmonic deformations of Lutosławski's *An Open Space Before Us* (*Przed nami przestrzeń otwarta*), composers stretched the genre to encompass experimental ideas.

The socialist mass song was, however, a completely different matter. The element of political 'persuasion' from the Ministry of Culture, acting on behalf of the Party, was anathema to most Polish composers, and it was in the sphere of the mass song and the cantata that socialist propaganda had the most direct impact on them. At Łagów, a couple of songs by Gradstein were performed, but in fact the concept of the socialist mass song had been introduced to Poland two years earlier in an article by Lissa, who was Vice-Director of the Department of Music at the Ministry of Culture.[32] Further coverage followed in the musical and literary press, and in 1948 there were several attempts to realise Lissa's vision. In March, over thirty writers and composers met under the auspices of the Ministry of Culture to discuss implementing her policy on mass songs;[33] in April, the Ministry in conjunction with Polish Radio organised a mass-song competition with substantial prize money. The required parameters were to become standard:

> Songs should be written in stanza form, with clear-cut rhythms and an easily memorable refrain. The melody must be tonal and suitable for general amateur performance, while the accompaniment must be harmonically transparent and not overly complicated. It is desirable that songs should rely on Polish folk themes or be written in the style of Polish patriotic, revolutionary or soldiers' songs, etc. Songs with a dance-jazz character will not be considered.[34]

The competition attracted over four hundred entries, and the genre was up and running, although most examples written over the next seven years were more the result of individual commissions than competitions. The results, of course, were highly variable, and were often linked to the subgenres that emerged. Some of the most desultory examples, which although strongly promoted never achieved general popularity, were those linked to openly political events. Panufnik, for example, wrote four such songs, though only two have survived. The first won a closed mass-song competition in 1948 to celebrate the formation of the PZPR – Polish United Workers' Party (note the absence of the word 'Communist', a deliberate Polish decision not to alienate wide sections of the population). Panufnik submitted three songs, one of which – *Song of the United Party* (*Pieśń Zjednoczonej Partii*) – is a simplistic common-time march on which little compositional care was lavished. It nonetheless has more character than *New Time* (*Nowy czas*), which he composed for the Second PZPR Congress in 1954.

Some mass songs were connected with the military, and here the links with the USSR are more in evidence. A volume of soldiers' songs – published in October 1953, seven months after Stalin's death – opens with *Stalin is with Us* (*Stalin z nami*), by Maklakiewicz.[35] It is followed by songs to the PZPR leader, Bolesław Bierut, and to the Soviet-born Marshal Konstantin Rokossovsky, who became the Polish Minister of Defence in 1949. But as the volume progresses, the tone becomes less political. Songs concentrate instead on the soldier's fight for freedom, such as Lutosławski's *Road to Victory* (*Zwycięska droga*, c.1950–2), as well as on stories about sweethearts and fond memories of country life laced with memories of war and struggle, such as Serocki's *Katy* (*Kasia*, 1951) and *Rowan Song* (*Jarzębinowa pieśń*). Lutosławski's three soldiers' songs (1953, but not published until 1954) are high-class examples of popular songs, based on folk dance rhythms such as the krakowiak and resolutely eschewing conventional march rhythms. In fact, where Panufnik's handful of mass songs are bluntly disinterested, there is a strong sense in Lutosławski's ten examples from 1950–3 that he took some trouble to give them musical integrity. Nowhere is this more apparent than in the only one not to be published, *Comrade* (*Towarzysz*, 1952), to a text by one of Poland's foremost poets, Stanisław Wygodzki. Its metric, melodic and harmonic expressiveness realises the palpable humanity of the text in a way unmatched by any other political or soldier's song of the period.[36]

The Polish authorities were too canny to think that political texts and martial music were enough to encourage greater social effort and cohesion. So there was a marked trend to appeal to the sense of nationhood, to the desire for peace, to young people and their organisations, and to the rebuilding of the countryside, industry, and Warsaw. The tone ranges from the solemn – Gradstein's *Polish Song of Peace* (*Polska pieśń pokoju*, 1952) written for the National Congress in the Struggle for Peace – to the popular, like *Red Bus* (*Czerwony autobus*, 1952) by Władysław Szpilman (1911–2000). One of the most popular forms at the popular end of the market was the waltz. The best known of these – Gradstein's *On the Right a Bridge*,

On the Left a Bridge (*Na prawo most, na lewo most*, 1950) – celebrated the rebuilding of communications across the Vistula River in Warsaw. Other waltzes marked the painstaking restoration of Warsaw's Old Town, systematically destroyed by the Nazis at the end of the war. Szpilman's *Like the Young Old Town* (*Jak młode Stare Miasto*, 1951) is a well-known example and was included in Poland's first colour feature film, *Adventure in Mariensztat* (*Przygoda na Mariensztacie*, 1953), a gentle, though inevitably propagandist comedy lauding a picturesque development on the river plain near Warsaw's Old Town.[37]

While the mass song was a pliable tool in the hands of the state commissioners – and could sometimes seem to have no socio-political dimension whatever – the other Soviet import, the cantata, was more overtly polemical. As a consequence, fewer Polish composers felt able to contribute. Some examples – like Lutosławski's recently rediscovered *Hail to Warsaw!* (*Warszawie-Sława!*, c.1950) – are so small in scale as to be more like an extended mass song. Few cantatas are longer than fifteen minutes and so do not begin to match up to the Soviet examples held up to them as models by the Ministry of Culture (Shostakovich's *Song of the Forests*, 1949, was often cited). But it was here that obeisance to the USSR was most blatant. Five Polish cantatas were written in praise of Stalin: the first was penned by Rytel, the pre-war scourge of Szymanowski, and Gradstein wrote the best known, *A Word about Stalin* (*Słowo o Stalina*, 1951). Contributors to the non-Stalin cantata included Krenz, whose *Conversation of Two Cities* (*Rozmowa dwóch miast*, 1950) opens with comradely greetings exchanged between Warsaw and Moscow, and Skrowaczewski, who composed *Cantata about Peace* (1951). Like Krenz, Skrowaczewski soon forsook a compositional career and made his name as a conductor. A latecomer was Baird's *Ballad of the Soldier's Cup* (*Ballada o żolnierskim kubku*, 1954). It has to be said that little of lasting musical value was produced in these cantatas. They are so dominated by the occasional nature of the projects that few manage to develop either a musical argument or a consistent style. Among the more risible features is the way in which both Krenz and Skrowaczewski conclude their cantatas with earnest Baroque fugues of embarrassing pomposity and gaucheness, possibly in emulation of the earlier fashion for culminating fugal movements in Polish symphonies. Arguably the most successful Polish cantata, from a musical point of view, was Szeligowski's *Charter of Hearts* (*Karta serc*, 1952), written for the proclamation of the new constitution for People's Poland. For this occasion, Szeligowski composed a rousing quasi-operatic scena which owed as much to the genre of the late-romantic French cantata as to his burgeoning activities as a composer of opera.

The Polish cantata was aesthetically – and sometimes morally – the most problematic of socialist-realist genres. While mass songs were not intended to play a foreground or ceremonial role in the State's self-aggrandisement, that was the primary function of the cantata. And this ceremonial aspect, alongside other features of what Mieczysław Tomaszewski has perceptively dubbed 'panegyric music', led to some agonising compositional decisions:

> We have to consider the price . . . which the composer pays for writing a work within a system which is openly or crypto-totalitarian . . . in Poland this was never the price of life or the fundamental threat to one's existence, with the exception of the obvious case if one wanted to write a cantata about the crimes of communism or an elegy to the heroes of the Home Army . . . Undoubtedly, however, the 'price' differed greatly. We might suggest different gradations, as follows:
>
> – 'holy peace' ['święty spokój', a Polish idiom for peace and quiet]
> – the possibility of pursuing one's profession
> – the possibilities for one's development
> – favourable attitude and recognition
> – receiving of special favours, material well-being
> – a brilliant career.[38]

Many propaganda works were written under some kind of duress – it was one way that a composer could 'pursue his profession'. Tomaszewski recounts that Rytel's cantata to Stalin had a deliberate motive: 'In the immediate postwar years of the so-called silent terror, the first cantata to Stalin was obviously written as some sort of expiation, almost in self-defence, by the pre-war critic of "bolshevism in music".'[39] And it has long been assumed that Lutosławski's mass songs were part of his plan to stay on the right side of the authorities – his family, for example, had had connections with prominent people in the wartime underground AK, whose members were ruthlessly rooted out by the Polish communist militia after the war. Perhaps his *Hail to Warsaw!* was also part of this tactic.

Lutosławski always maintained that he had to earn a living (as did his colleagues, of course):

> . . . the fact is that I have never resorted to compromise. The only thing for which I can reproach myself is the circumstance that I have written several 'mass songs' . . . In short, I selected some texts, in which there were no political implications whatsoever, and composed a few songs – alas, what's done is done.[40]

Lutosławski was being disingenuous. All but one of his mass songs (the folk-style *I Would Marry* – *Wyszłabym ja*, 1950) have overt connections with the military, with youth organisations or the rebuilding of Poland. Two songs – *New Foundry* (*Nowa Huta*) and *The Most Beautiful Dream* (*Najpiękniejszy sen*), both dating from 1950 – are about the development of the heavy industry complex outside Kraków. But Lutosławski was doing nothing more reprehensible than most other composers.

It comes as a shock, however, to find that he composed an outright political work in 1949. In a handwritten letter of 8 April 1950, concerning pieces which might be performed at the 1951 Festival of Polish Music, Lutosławski cited two already written works, the second of which was called *A July Garland* (*Lipcowy wieniec*): 'A triptych for solo baritone, men's choir and symphony orchestra entitled A JULY GARLAND (a piece written to words by K. I. Gałczyński, on the occasion of the 5th anniversary of the July Manifesto), duration c. 10'.[41] That Lutosławski should have written a piece celebrating the manifesto declaration of the Soviet-backed Polish Communist Party issued in Lublin on 22 July 1944 is a matter of considerable astonishment. Although no trace of the full score has appeared, let alone of a complete performance, an annotated set of parts has recently been found in the library of the House of the Polish Army.

22 July 1949 was, of course, less than two weeks before the Łagów conference. The date of the July manifesto subsequently became the date that marked the establishment of People's Poland. Important events, such as the completion of major civil engineering projects, were programmed to celebrate its anniversary: most notoriously, the Palace of Culture and Science – Stalin's 'gift' to the Polish people which still dominates the skyline of Warsaw – was opened on this date in 1955.

The Party issued a commemorative tome for 22 July 1949 that was both a congratulatory chronicle of the past five years as well as a coded warning to those who were not wholeheartedly supportive of the PZPR and its socialist programme. In the chapter on the arts, the musical community is criticised for lagging behind in the promotion of socialist-realist values, especially in several exhortatory paragraphs devoted specifically to 'New Composers':

> As a result of pre-war conditions, in which there was no interest in our indigenous culture, composers turned to Western European centres. It is here that the source lies for the habit of measuring achievements by using the criteria of formalist West-European music, in which the surrendering to the influences of formalism's harmful and degenerate aesthetic is inherent.
>
> The struggle against formalism in music is transforming the content of contemporary music in a process which is spontaneous and not in any way automatic. Aware of the momentous significance of the current

transformations, and moved by their pathos, composers are making strenuous efforts to find in our creativity a mode of expression which will be in harmony with our epoch. In the process of crystallisation, the influence of the achievements of the music of the USSR and the struggle of Soviet composers for socialist realism in music are of great significance.

The contemporary generation of Polish composers has two simultaneous duties to perform: to raise the level of Polish musical creativity, in which Szymanowski has stood alone over the past few decades, as well as to find a new style by overcoming formalistic Western influences by employing the methods of socialist realism.

This is not an easy task considering the lack of competent and ideologically prepared music critics. And yet the attempt has been made. This attempt, supported by talents of exceptional potential, finds expression in the creation of new musical forms which answer the needs of the mass listener, such as the cantata, mass song, opera and ballet, or in ever stronger links with indigenous musical traditions and in an ever stronger emphasis on the aspects of content and ideology.

That is why, even though there have yet been no definitive achievements, the fact that music has embarked on this questing road allows one to believe that at some point in the development of music a moment will come when a music is born which expresses the greatness of our revolutionary transformations.[42]

While the early 1950s were to see Polish composers fulfilling a number of obligations for the mass song, cantata and opera, the longed-for 'moment' was elusive. Certainly, the authorities made as much fuss as they could about Poland's first socialist-realist opera, Szeligowski's *The Scholars' Revolt* (*Bunt żaków*, 1951).[43] Its plot – based on real events in Kraków in 1549 during the reign of King Zygmunt II August (he appears briefly in the opera) – fulfilled socialist demands by having a Polish subject and by revolving around an oppressed community (university students) fighting through collective action against injustice from the bourgeoisie (the townspeople). Its success lay in the prime role given to the chorus and to a timely amalgamation of nineteenth-century idioms (including Wagnerian leitmotivic procedures and Mussorgskian treatment of recitative and folk melodies) with a modally inflected language that was designed to incorporate familiar tunes from the Polish Renaissance. The antique flavour, which Szeligowski stretched to incorporate Baroque counterpoint, also proved popular with other composers (Baird, Krenz, Panufnik) in their accommodation of socialist realism. The overall impression, however, is that *The Scholars' Revolt* is a rather primitive and unadventurous scion of the works of Poland's nineteenth-century operatic master, Stanisław Moniuszko (1819–72). But it remains one of the most accurate resumés of Polish socialist-realist ideals in music. Paralleling Aleksander Ford's film biopic of Chopin, *Chopin's Youth* (*Młodość Chopina*, 1952), which sets the composer in the mêlée of the Paris commune and barricades of the 1830s, Szeligowski's Renaissance students are depicted as fervent republicans, closing the opera with the cry 'Long live the Polish Republic!' set to a well-known fifteenth-century student tune from carnival time, *Breve Regnum*.

But try as it might, the Ministry of Culture found that composers were persistently reluctant to create 'new forms', especially large-scale opera, and when they did, as in their cantatas, the results were generally undistinguished. Composers remained drawn to less programmatic, less polemical genres – symphonic, chamber and solo instrumental music – and it is in these areas that their creative dilemmas as well as the range of solutions attempted reveal a depth of artistry and stylistic tolerance that was largely precluded in their text-bound music. And the one undoubted 'moment' of quality in the socialist-realist period came only towards its end, and moreover in a work far removed from an overt programme: Lutosławski's Concerto for Orchestra.

5 Socialist realism II: concert music

In the early 1950s, no one in Poland had any reason to think that the Stalinist policy of socialist realism would ever be changed: the pattern of Soviet-inspired governmental interference in the creative arts seemed there to stay. 'Przesłuchanie' were a prime controlling mechanism throughout 1950–2 and, despite financial blandishments in the form of commissions, especially for the socialist-realist showcase Festival of Polish Music in 1951 (and its follow-up four years later), nothing could hide the fact that musical life was closely steered and monitored by the Party and its cultural agencies. That was the main reason why Palester, who had spent more time in Paris than in Poland since 1947, eventually decided to remain in France and was struck off the list of members of the ZKP in April 1951. A month later, Czesław Miłosz – who went on to become one of Poland's foremost writers and winner of the Nobel Prize for literature in 1980 – quit his diplomatic post as Polish cultural attaché in Paris and went into exile. In both cases, their work was banned for the foreseeable future in Poland, and they deliberately did themselves no favours by attacking the PZPR and its policies both on air and in print. Palester broadcast for many years from 1952 on the Polish-language section of Radio Free Europe and went into print in the Polish expatriate press in Paris.[1] In *The Captive Mind*, the most perceptive account of Polish socialist realism in literature, Miłosz examined four literary case studies as well as the general situation of the creative artist in Poland: 'Instead of writing the dissonant music of former days, they composed marches and odes. Instead of painting abstractions as before, they turned out socially useful pictures. But since they could not rid themselves completely of their former personalities, they became schizophrenics.'[2]

As will be discussed later as one of four case studies of composers in the years 1949–55, the clearest musical example of creative schizophrenia was Panufnik, who was himself struck from the ZKP after fleeing Poland in 1954. Whereas Miłosz, writing in 1951–2, disguised the identities of his four case studies of Polish authors by using the first four letters of the Greek alphabet as codenames,[3] the Polish composers discussed below now need no such protection. The work of 'Group '49', Panufnik, Bacewicz and Lutosławski highlights the principal trends and issues faced by all Polish composers during this high-watermark period. To a greater or lesser extent, Mycielski, Perkowski and Turski experienced similar problems. Kisielewski, a vocal opponent of socialist realism, suffered many setbacks, as for less obvious reasons did Malawski, whereas Szabelski kept his own counsel in Katowice, away from the centres of debate and controversy in Warsaw and Kraków.

What emerges is a picture of considerable variety of genre and style, of composers who chose quite different paths through the socialist-realist thicket. Many favoured large-scale orchestral works, especially the symphony, a genre that had emerged as being of major interest to Polish composers only in the 1940s, though the increase may also have stemmed from the heavy promotion of Soviet music in post-war Poland. Many leaned on eighteenth-century forms and idioms; some resorted to arrangements of old Polish music. While large-scale rhetoric dominated the orchestral sphere, those who chose to utilise Poland's folk tradition – and they were surprisingly few, given the many exhortations to do so – found opportunities to sidestep much of the bombast and create music with greater character and distinctiveness. These composers, like Bacewicz, Lutosławski and Serocki, were also those who found it easiest to support their larger commissions with small-scale works, also customarily based on Polish folk materials. Each composer made compositional choices and was from moment to moment open or resistant to coercion and criticism. Each resolved such pressures in different ways, both within and outside the arena of propaganda music. That the concert music of the early 1950s was as varied as it was suggests that Polish composers were more alert to the range of potential responses to the overarching socialist-realist aesthetic than has often been acknowledged.

Group '49

For the three members of 'Group '49' – Baird, Krenz and Serocki – the strain was ostensibly less than that experienced by those who had established a compositional voice prior to 1947. The press tried to build them up as a cohesive group: they were the 'talents of exceptional potential', the young stars of the socialist future. As Serocki had said at Łagów: 'The youngest generation does not have to carry baggage from the past . . . they have no ingrained habits to discard.'[4] And they seem to have suffered less from post-compositional censure by their peers than did older composers. The case of Krenz is salutary. Five months after the Łagów conference, in January 1950, Krenz conducted the Warsaw Philharmonic Orchestra in a programme devoted to 'Group '49'. The programme included his earliest major composition, the First Symphony (1947–9), Serocki's *Four Folk Dances* (1949) and Baird's Piano Concerto (1949), with Serocki as soloist. Krenz had admired Panufnik's music since hearing the premiere of *Tragic*

Overture as a teenager during the war, so it is not surprising that the Symphony cleaves in some measure to the abstract, carefully wrought schemata in Panufnik's compositions of the late 1940s. Its opening movement, for example, uses an almost fully chromatic sequence of three-note pitch groupings in both harmonic and melodic guise. The Symphony also explores a range of ostinati and polyrhythmic heterophony. That this appears to have been acceptable when Panufnik's own music was under critical scrutiny is worth noting; furthermore, Krenz does not appear to have been deterred from testing boundaries in subsequent pieces. 'Lullaby' and 'Elegy', the first and third of the four movements in his *Suite of Nocturnes* (1950), draw on Panufnik's night pieces while the more dissonant chording and textures of 'Elegy' also belong to the same world as Turski's banned Second Symphony. The colouristic ideas and folk-based motifs of *Rhapsody* (1952) – scored for string orchestra with obbligato roles for xylophone, tam-tam, timpani and celesta – also attest to Krenz's understanding of the textural and thematic breakthroughs in Panufnik's recent works, whether they were in or out of favour.

Regrettably, Krenz was also compelled by circumstances to provide tamer music for popular consumption. His response was symptomatic. At one end of the spectrum, he made relatively straight arrangements of old Polish music to fulfil the demand for the re-establishment of a purely Polish (i.e., non-Western) culture. His *Suite of Dances* (1953) is for its time a remarkably sensitive orchestration of short pieces from the famous sixteenth-century lute tablature of Jan z Lublina. Panufnik had more or less started this trend with his Divertimento for strings on themes by Janiewicz, followed by *Old Polish Suite* for strings (1950) and, less persuasively, by *Gothic Concerto* (1951, rev. as *Concerto in modo antico*, 1955). If such arrangements were a convenient escape route from facing contemporary compositional issues, a less satisfactory one was that of pastiche. In *Classical Serenade* for small orchestra (1950), Krenz composed a spotless though unexceptional eighteenth-century fake which cleverly wove into its first movement a section marked 'Alla Polacca' (cf. also Baird's looser *Overture in Old Style*, 1949). A third route was that of quasi-pastiche. The most enduring examples occur in Baird's music: the Renaissance-inspired *Colas Breugnon* for flute and strings (1951), *Three Songs to Italian Texts* (1952), written to celebrate the five-hundredth anniversary of the birth of Leonardo da Vinci, and his rather later settings of Shakespeare in *Four Love Sonnets* (*Cztery sonety miłosne*, 1956).

While the compositional careers of Baird and Serocki flourished, Krenz the composer virtually disappeared from view in 1953 apart from his work as a film composer. The reason was practical: several Polish composers developed secondary careers as performers. Serocki had a brief period as a concert pianist, while Bacewicz had been continuing a twin path as violinist and composer since the 1930s. Panufnik had combined conducting with composition, and no doubt Krenz had this career pattern in mind in the early 1950s. In 1953, however, he succeeded Grzegorz Fitelberg, the doyen of Polish conductors and Szymanowski's friend and champion, as the director of the Great Symphony Orchestra of Polish Radio (WOSPR) and, in his turn, became one of the great champions of Polish music, not least the compositions of his erstwhile colleagues in 'Group '49'.

It would be unfair to promote the favourable reception accorded Baird's Sinfonietta at Łagów as giving the work anything other than historical significance. His Piano Concerto, also written in 1949, is a richer prospect. On the one hand, like a number of other piano works of the time – Bacewicz's Piano Concerto (1949) and Second Piano Sonata (1952), Serocki's Piano Concerto 'Romantic' (1950) and Krenz's Concertino for piano and orchestra (1952) – Baird's Piano Concerto lies in the shadow of Szymanowski's *Symphonie concertante*, especially in the use of the *oberek* or *mazurek* (a fast 3/8 or 3/4) for the finale. His lyrical tendencies, however, come to the fore in the slow movement 'in modo d'una canzona rustica'. Its pervasive use of a 7/4 metric pattern, like Krenz's use of five-bar phrases in the *oberek* finale of his Concertino, indicates that composers did not feel so constrained that they could not explore non-standard patterns of metre or phrasing.[5]

Baird's three large-scale pieces of the early 1950s – First Symphony (1950), Second Symphony 'Quasi una fantasia' (1952) and Concerto for Orchestra (1953) – chart the struggle between his natural subtlety and the extrovert qualities expected in such symphonic outlets. The First Symphony is an extended, five-movement successor to the Sinfonietta, but the work strives awkwardly in its attempt at symphonic coherence. Its often forceful character is carried over into the Concerto for Orchestra, where the socialist-realist search for order and stability is realised in a particularly blunt and uncompromising way. The opening 'Grave e fugato' has all the monumentality of Stalinist rhetoric (the fugato is especially solemn) and is followed by a muscle-bound gigue. Even the 'Recitativo e arioso' makes heavy weather of an essentially Shostakovichian idiom. The final 'Toccata e hymne' is a grandiose and virtually monothematic apotheosis, producing one of the clearest Polish examples in the post-war decade of marshalled optimism. Not surprisingly, the Concerto for Orchestra, alongside other overblown orchestral pieces of the early 1950s, has become an historical relic. And yet it was still possible for one critic in 1956 to hail it and other works for their supposed independence from socialist dogma and as models for a new Polish music:

> Baird's Concerto has a particular significance for modern Polish music. It belongs to those still rather few pieces, like Lutosławski's Concerto for Orchestra, Szabelski's Third Symphony and Malawski's Second Symphony, which break the magic circle of the mass song, the panegyric cantata and the symphony with a happy ending [z happy endem]. More pieces like these and undoubtedly before long we will correct the embarrassing backwardness of recent years and make really up-to-date art in our music.[6]

Baird's Second Symphony, however, is less justifiably forgotten. On the structural level, he breaks the traditional mould by having just three movements – Largo, Allegro, and Allegro ma non troppo – and the Largo accentuates this unconventionality by lasting for over half the duration of the Symphony (cf. the proportions of Turski's Second Symphony). And it is the Largo which commands attention, for it is here that the 'fantasia' element operates. Its elegiac lyricism is evident from the opening bars in which a clarinet melody is unfurled over sustained strings, an uncanny foreshadowing of the start of Lutosławski's Fourth Symphony four decades later. Baird's mastery of introspective expression, and his decision to let it dominate the Symphony at the outset, was unusual, not to say daring (only Skrowaczewski in the third section of his *Cantata about Peace* achieves a comparably elevated tone). Regrettably, but not exceptionally for the time, the faster movements disappoint and fail to mesh with the inspiration of the Largo. Perhaps unsurprisingly, it was accused of formalism after its premiere in February 1953.[7]

Serocki's response to socialist realism took a number of paths. He was a prolific author of music for voice, including mass and soldiers' songs, a cantata *Warsaw Bricklayer* (*Warszawski murarz*, 1951) and two symphonies (1952, 1953), the second of which, for soprano and baritone soloists, chorus and orchestra, is subtitled 'Symphony of Songs'. Its four movements, with texts on country life (including a wedding song, lullaby, and farming song), form a picturesque cantata sequence echoing the folk-based music of both Stravinsky and Szymanowski. The tone is one of gentle lyricism, enlivened by the wedding-song scherzo (based on the *oberek*) and by bold twists to the underlying modal idiom. Furthermore, Serocki's highly developed sense of metrical flexibility is put to particularly expressive use in the word-setting. It is one of the most accomplished Polish vocal-instrumental works of the period (a cantata in all but name), mainly because it largely sidesteps current ideology and in an evocative and stylistically consistent way gives voice to the ingrained Polish sentiment for the countryside, however conservative and rose-tinted that may be.

Serocki's powerful symphonic talent is heard to best advantage in the 'heroic struggle' of the First Symphony. Unlike Krenz and Baird, Serocki found a consistent stylistic voice and rapidly developed complete confidence in his handling of symphonic structure. While there are debts to Hindemith and Turski and the almost obligatory rhetorical chorales, he demonstrates a special flair for music in fast tempi and metric inventiveness throughout the symphony, welding his multifarious ideas into a convincingly incisive argument. And he begins to stretch the boundaries of the socialist-realist dictates by including highly chromatic passages in the outer movements. He had become acquainted with twelve-note techniques when he came across the writings of René Leibowitz during his studies with Boulanger in Paris in 1947–8, and his inclusion of such material formed part of the spasmodic dalliance with twelve-note pitch groupings in the music of several Polish composers in the late 1940s and early 1950s (though none approached the stylistic concepts of the Second Viennese School at this stage). But Serocki was rather more overt than the others, and later neo-classically driven works, such as *Suite of Preludes* and the dynamic Piano Sonata (1955), provide a range of concrete examples. The fourth prelude, for example, uses the over-tone series as the initial skeletal basis for twelve-note arpeggic patterns, suggesting that he knew the opening of Berg's Violin Concerto. The Suite as a whole also testifies to Serocki's interest in jazz (Ex. 5.1), an idiom likewise officially denounced at the time by the authorities. The Sonata, which was written three years later and lies chronologically on the brink of the new creative freedoms allowed from 1956 onwards, has a number of freewheeling explorations: the second subject of the first movement, for example, develops twelve-note chains in simple two-part counterpoint. Ancillary to these works are Serocki's widely performed and more straightforwardly neo-classical pieces for trombone, including the Concerto (1953) and Sonatina (1954).

Krenz, Baird and Serocki were only a loose compositional alliance. Krenz and Baird struggled stylistically more than Serocki, and Krenz changed career after a few years. But both Baird and Serocki, notwithstanding the original aesthetic precepts of Łagów and 'Group '49', fairly quickly established individual musical characters which were to be maintained in their experimental music after 1956. Like most composers who had been active in the early 1950s, neither Baird nor Serocki was later keen for much of their music of that time to remain in the public domain, but at a distance of several decades it is possible to evaluate their achievements more dispassionately. Although

Example 5.1. Serocki, *Suite of Preludes* (1952), no. 2, opening.

some of their output was uneven, there is sufficient evidence to warrant the reinstatement of those works in which either they created a persuasive musical argument in the socialist-realist context or explored beyond what was apparently possible. This latter point is important, because it demonstrates that they, and others, did not passively acquiesce in the Ministry of Culture's plans.

Panufnik

The case of Panufnik is both complex and unique in post-war Polish music. His battle to follow his own creative impulses was complicated by personal and public factors, not least his increasing inability to solve his compositional dilemmas. He resolved the conflict in dramatic fashion by taking an opportunity in July 1954 to flee to the West, where he took up residence in England. As a refugee from communism, he followed in the footsteps of Palester and Miłosz; his name was expunged from the ZKP and censors ensured that he went virtually unmentioned in Poland until his music was heard there again in 1977. Both Baird and Serocki, as Panufnik's guarantors in Warsaw, suffered short-term career setbacks as a result of Panufnik's action.

On the surface, this is a clear-cut case of a composer deciding that he could no longer endure artistic restrictions under socialist realism in People's Poland. And yet his situation was quite different from that of Palester, who saw the signs of repression early on and took advantage of his alternative base in Paris to avoid the compromises all creative artists in Poland were being forced to make. Miłosz was more obviously involved in politics, as he represented Poland in a full posting at the Paris embassy. Panufnik was nominally free of any ties with the Party; nonetheless, he allowed himself, to a degree unlike other Polish composers, to be used extensively by the PZPR as the presentable face of Polish music and culture.[8] In Tomaszewski's terms, Panufnik did more than simply seek 'holy peace'; in fact, peace and quiet deserted him the more he was enmeshed in the system and the more he enjoyed 'special favours, material well-being' if not 'a brilliant career'.

In his later autobiography, Panufnik stressed his total abhorrence of his situation and of the Party (although he clearly felt some respect and even affection for both Sokorski and Lissa), emphasising that all such activities were carried out against his will. With family difficulties and tragedies to cope with, the early 1950s were undoubtedly psychologically difficult years, but he nevertheless enjoyed material privileges unavailable to his fellow composers; his commission fees were always at the top end of the scale and, more significantly in view of his subsequent escape, he was able, in his capacity as a conductor or as a representative of the ZKP, to travel abroad occasionally, both to other communist countries and to Western Europe. Such trips were exceedingly rare amongst other musicians, but they inevitably reminded him of the more conducive artistic atmosphere and living conditions in the West. After the initial flurry of press excitement on his arrival in London, he found to his chagrin that the exchange was not guaranteed to be for the better. He pointedly commented: 'I had leapt from my Polish position of No. One to No One at All in England.'[9]

In terms purely of his musical productivity and critical success between 1949 and 1954, however, Panufnik's leading position in Poland was questionable. His output, aside from his arrangements of old Polish music, was restricted to just a few pieces: four published mass songs, a score for the propagandist film *We Pledge* (*Ślubujemy*, 1952), *Symphony of Peace* (*Symfonia pokoju*, 1951), *Heroic Overture* (*Uwertura bohaterska*, 1952) and an educational Wind Quintet for flute, oboe, two clarinets and bassoon (1953). When he left Poland, he abandoned unfulfilled commissions for a *Lyric Symphony*, a *Ceremonial Overture* to celebrate the tenth anniversary of People's Poland, and a *Ballade* for string quartet.[10] The whole sorry story suggests an increasing creative impotence in the glare of public expectation.

The composition and reception of the *Symphony of Peace* is indicative both of Panufnik's acceptance of his pre-eminent role in Polish musical culture in the early 1950s and of the sometimes uncomfortable critical attention his new compositions received as a result of his position. Panufnik claimed in his autobiography that he unwittingly suggested in Moscow, when part of a high-level cultural Polish delegation to the USSR in late May and early June 1950, that he 'hoped to begin a new symphony, probably a *Symphony of Peace*. No sooner had I uttered those words than I bitterly regretted them. But my Russian colleagues sighed audibly with relief: at last someone in Poland was taking up an ideologically important subject!'[11] And, sure enough, Panufnik's remark was left to haunt him until (and after) he conducted the premiere on 25 May 1951 in Warsaw as part of the Festival of Polish Music. But the impression Panufnik gives that he capitulated to pressure to provide an ideologically based work is unconvincing. He had already requested, on 21 April 1950, a subvention to enable him to write a *Revolutionary Symphony* ('In connection with the proposed Festival of Polish Music, I would like to compose a great symphonic piece entitled REVOLUTIONARY SYMPHONY'[12]), a proposal with considerable ideological overtones. He evidently abandoned it in favour of the *Symphony of Peace*. His changed decision may have been influenced by both political and social pressure, as the peace issue came to the fore both nationally and internationally as a result of the Stockholm Appeal in 1950. Panufnik's coerced involvement in this arena continued through his presence at a number of peace congresses between 1950 and 1952; several compositions after 1954, however, testify to an abiding and voluntary commitment to peace.

Panufnik's *Symphony of Peace* rapidly assumed the status of prime cultural icon for Polish socialist realism, notwithstanding some critical reservations on aspects of its compositional and ideological effectiveness. It was performed in the USSR and GDR in 1951–2 and broadcast across Europe from Kraków in May 1954. In February 1955, seven months after he left Poland, it was given its American premiere in Detroit in a performance conducted by Stokowski and attended by the composer. Ironically, it was then broadcast back to Poland by the CIA-funded Voice of America.[13] Panufnik subsequently salvaged virtually all but the closing mass hymn to create his *Symfonia elegiaca* (1957), implying that he stood by the vast majority of the music of *Symphony of Peace*, its political context notwithstanding.

Example 5.2. Panufnik, *Symphony of Peace* (1951), opening.

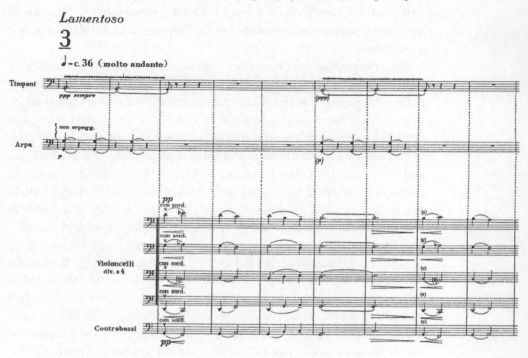

It is not surprising that the work had a puzzled reception in Poland. Most critics praised it, but its musical language – typically elegant, predominantly lyrical in the outer movements and quasi-militaristic in the central 'Drammatico' – was criticised for traces of church modality and for a certain passivity in its attempt to rally the masses to the cause of peace (Ex. 5.2). And even though Panufnik intended the closing hymn to peace, to a text by Iwaszkiewicz, to be an 'extended and symphonic mass song',[14] its melodic and structural stiffness is in marked contrast to the rest of the symphony. It might also be observed that the language of the first movement in particular formed part of the compositional continuum between Panufnik's music of the late 1940s and his music from 1960 onwards, suggesting that he was largely immune, consciously or subconsciously, to the more obvious stylistic demands of socialist realism. The closest he came to socialist-realist rhetoric was in *Heroic Overture*, whose first version (1950) was withdrawn after its much-criticised premiere, and replaced in 1952, when it won the Olympic Games prize in Helsinki, four years after Turski's ill-fated 'Olympic' Symphony had received the same accolade in London.[15]

There may have been many reasons why Panufnik failed to adapt compositionally to the socialist-realist ethos. His folk-based pieces of the late

1940s – *Lullaby, Sinfonia rustica* and *Polish Suite* – all came in for criticism and in his last four years in Poland he never revisited the folk sources which, for many other composers, offered clear possibilities for connecting with the masses. His mass songs, including the coda to *Symphony of Peace*, are among the least inspired and most unbending Polish examples of the genre. Unlike Lutosławski, who turned himself to a range of tasks (incidental and radio music, children's songs etc.), or Bacewicz, with her other career as violinist and pianist, Panufnik seemed to have fewer artistic options. In the early 1950s, he had no permanent conducting position in Poland, which would have tempered his material and creative problems. It was, therefore, a stroke of exceptional good luck and planning by his friends abroad that he was able to escape Poland when he did.

Bacewicz

If Panufnik's case history demonstrates his inability to balance his private compositional impulses with the system's public demands, Grażyna Bacewicz managed with apparent ease to fulfil her role as both performer and composer. She was a popular and highly regarded performer: as a violinist, in 1952 she premiered her Fourth Violin Concerto (1951) and Fifth Violin Sonata (1951), while in 1953 she gave the premiere of her Second Piano Sonata, arguably the most significant Polish work for solo piano in the post-war decade, not least because it updated the robust Szymanowskian approach to Polish folk traditions, especially in the *oberek* rhythms of the finale. Her prodigious output between 1948 and 1955 included five solo concertos, three symphonies and the Partita (1955), a piano quintet, two string quartets, three violin sonatas and numerous small folk-dance pieces used as encores in her violin recitals, a ballet, a cantata and the work which remains most securely in the repertoire, the Concerto for String Orchestra (1948).

The Concerto for String Orchestra has become the standard-bearer for Polish neo-classicism, not least because of its persuasive reinterpretation of the Baroque concerto grosso (Ex. 5.3). At the same time, there is no slavish following of traditional procedures, as the unusual balance of thematic areas in the first movement demonstrates. The buoyant final 6/8 Vivo is an early example of an idiom that recurred in many of her later finales. But it is in the central Andante that Bacewicz's technical and expressive mastery is most enduring (Ex. 5.4). The opening violin ostinato, with its characteristic melody anchored to pivot notes, shimmers in its combination of sul ponticello, con sordino, ordinario and tremolo. Its build-up to the first climax, along with the developing melody in the lower strings,

Example 5.3. Bacewicz, Concerto for String Orchestra (1948), first movement, opening.

provokes an intense, introspective examination of the main material. The entire work exudes creative optimism which, unlike many of her compatriots, she managed to maintain to a large degree in the dark years that lay ahead. Almost uniquely, she seems to have completely avoided any obvious creative-political compromises.[16] Most noticeable, aside from the encore pieces, is the almost complete absence of descriptive titles

Example 5.4. Bacewicz, Concerto for String Orchestra (1948), second movement, opening.

relating to folk music or Polish regeneration, let alone more obvious political issues.

Bacewicz's language remained rooted in her pre-war musical experiences in Paris and she was able to utilise her essentially neo-classical idiom, enriched with folk inflections, in steering an overtly non-programmatic path through the minefield of socialist realism. Sometimes, however, she did veer towards the prevailing ethos, most evidently in the symphonies. From the somewhat elliptical melodic, harmonic and structural processes in the Second Symphony (1951), Bacewicz developed a more focused rhetoric in the Third Symphony the following year. With its clear motivic identity, harmonic rationale and symphonic breadth, it develops from lugubrious tenseness in the opening movement to the optimal release of the finale. That is to be expected in the climate of the times, but Bacewicz's individual touches along the way make the Third Symphony something above the ordinary. The subtle ways in which the main motivic fragment informs or finds parallels in later themes, such as the folk-inspired idea in the trio section of the scherzo, is evidence of careful compositional craft of a traditional kind. There are also links with contemporary composers, as in the finale, where Bacewicz emulates Shostakovich in areas of sparse orchestration or Roussel in the robustness of the rhythmic momentum. But neither this symphony nor its successor (1953), with its more exploratory use of shifting metres (first movement) and tentative feints at twelve-note pitch sequences (finale), gives as much evidence of Bacewicz's distinctiveness as either her concertos, especially the Fifth Violin Concerto (1954), with its strong Szymanowskian overtones, or more particularly her chamber music.

In the post-war decade, Bacewicz maintained the repertoire of Polish instrumental chamber music almost single-handedly. There are no other string quartets of note apart from Woytowicz's Second (1953), no quintets apart from a few for wind instruments, with only Malawski's Piano Trio (1953), Serocki's *Suite for Four Trombones* (1953) and a few sonatas or duos by other composers having stood the test of time.[17] Bacewicz's dedication to chamber music is remarkable, especially given the lack of encouragement for genres which had little propaganda value and the dearth of players in a position to devote themselves to chamber music.[18] One of Bacewicz's achievements stood out from the others: her Fourth String Quartet (1951) won the Concours International pour Quatuor à Cordes in Liège that same year, and her success was much vaunted in the Polish press as evidence of the international quality, and direction, of current Polish music.

Where the Third Quartet (1947) has an insouciant ease and a clearly traditional tonal structure (features shared by its near-contemporary, the Concerto for String Orchestra), the Fourth is a fascinating example of Bacewicz's ability to maintain her own stylistic identity and absolute mastery of writing for strings while at the same time moving some way towards accommodating aspects of current cultural thinking, such as the incorporation of folk-style melodies. What she characteristically does not do is look for the lowest common denominator nor for the most obvious sequence of musical ideas. In the first movement, for example, the first subject (a simple four-square folk theme, imaginatively couched first in canon and then in rich passing chromaticism) has all the appearance of a traditional second subject after the intense introductory Andante (Ex. 5.5). The profile of the actual second subject is also subdued, almost neutral, and the way in which both subjects are intercut with strong-willed chordal ideas suggests a further attempt to disrupt mainstream structural conventions for expressive ends. Indeed, each of the quartet's three movements is moulded in ways that indicate that she was determined to shape the musical material and its destination, current expectations notwithstanding. This approach is nowhere clearer than in the Fifth Quartet (1955), whose quest for motivic cohesion and *Dürchführung* is remarkable for its time. This impressive quartet is the culmination of several years of intense compositional activity in which Bacewicz grasped the necessity of developing her own complex but approachable voice, regardless of attempts by politicians to persuade composers to reach out to the masses with music that was more direct and less challenging. She had the craft, flexibility and willpower to survive.

Lutosławski

The same qualities were demonstrated by Lutosławski, although his strategies were different. While Panufnik and Bacewicz had their performing activities as a 'second string', Lutosławski rarely took to the concert platform or podium. Instead, he had a staff job at Polish Radio, composing music for the radio and theatre. Additionally, he contributed significantly in the sphere of 'functional' music, through his many songs for children. He was by no means the only composer to do so: it was a useful foil against any criticism of distance from the political prerogatives. Of the six composers discussed in this section, Lutosławski was the most assiduous in drawing sustenance from folk music – 'music that remains doctrinally neutral yet meets with approval'[19] – and this must have been a conscious decision for self-defence as a way of partially sidestepping ministerial pressure. Apart from the quixotic *Overture for Strings* (1949), whose experimental air was soon stifled, all of Lutosławski's concert pieces of this period are based directly on folk sources, and several have descriptive titles to match: *Little Suite* (*Mała suita*, 1950), *Silesian Triptych* (*Tryptyk śląski*, 1951), *Bucolics* (1952), Concerto for Orchestra and *Dance Preludes* (1954). While Bacewicz co-opted folk-style melodies and dance forms into some works, weaving them into what was otherwise a style largely independent of folk music, Lutosławski developed his music closely on the basis of a compositional analysis of folk melodies. He astutely avoided making his folk arrangements sound too precious or delicate, a criticism which had been levelled at Panufnik's *Polish Suite* (Panufnik's use of vocalise and the ethereal atmosphere were described by

Example 5.5. Bacewicz, Fourth String Quartet (1951), first movement, figs. 4–6.

some colleagues in 1950 as 'a characteristic escape from expressiveness' and 'soulless'[20]).

Lutosławski's treatment of folk song in the first half of the 1950s has closer parallels in Panufnik's earlier *Five Polish Peasant Songs* and his own *Folk Melodies*. This is especially evident in *A Straw Chain* (*Słomkowy łańcuszek*, 1951), with its straightforward transcriptions, occasional harmonic pungency and 'outdoor' woodwind instrumentation. *Silesian Triptych* is conceived on a broader canvas, with deft orchestral accompaniments and interludes, melodic repetitions and extensions, closer in spirit to Canteloube's inter-war *Chants d'Auvergne* than to Serocki's 'Symphony of Songs'. When using folk melodies without text, Lutosławski gives his imagination a much freer rein. He is less inclined to use the folk material in straight quotation and more as a source for motivic development as well as an opportunity for ingenious explorations in polymetre and non-diatonic scales and harmony. The modestly titled *Little Suite* – which lies at the light-music end of the spectrum – is, in fact, a highly effective advertisement for the use of folk tunes in an orchestral context (and it duly received approbation in the Party-controlled musicological press).[21] Its orchestral clarity and precision are unique for the time, when other composers (apart from Krenz) were more inclined to big-boned orchestral thickening, with chamber textures and

Example 5.5. (*cont.*)

solos a rare commodity. The opening 'Shepherd's Pipe' ('Fujarka') encapsulates the vivacity of this approach (Ex. 5.6). The main melody belongs to
the same idiom of the decorated triad as the melody in Chopin's Mazurka
op. 68/3. Lutosławski's keen ear and sense of creative artifice led him to
score it for just piccolo, side drum and strings. He added to the interest by
overlapping three-bar piccolo phrasing with a four-bar string pattern whose
harmony accumulates an extra pitch-class on each repetition, ending up on
a second inversion of a dominant eleventh. The effect is of gentle bucolic
improvisation, helped rather than hindered by a few two-bar pauses for the
piccolo and side drum. That this exquisitely engineered subtlety should then
be met by a pounding Stravinskian figure on strings, bassoons and horns
demonstrates Lutosławski's innate understanding of the power of strongly

Example 5.6. Lutosławski, *Little Suite* (*Mała suita*, 1950), first movement 'Fujarka', opening.

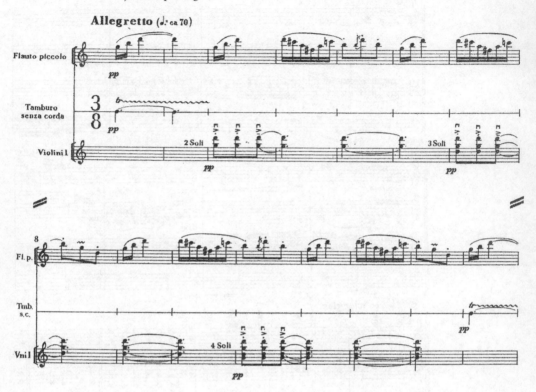

contrasted ideas. *Little Suite* has few pretensions to large-scale symphonic dialogue, but it served as an extremely useful work-out for Lutosławski's timbral palette and techniques for extrapolating symphonic motifs from folk music.

The experience ultimately bore fruit in his only other substantial orchestral work of the period, the Concerto for Orchestra, begun in 1950. His modest original intention was a sequel to *Little Suite* for the re-established Warsaw Philharmonic. It emerged as a work of some thirty minutes' duration, completed at the start of August 1954 (less than three weeks after Panufnik's escape to England) and premiered in November that same year. Even had the work been seen as a qualified success, there can be little doubt that both it and its composer, in the light of recent events and the fact that 1954 marked the tenth anniversary of People's Poland, would have been hailed as national treasures. As it was, the imagination, scale and socialist-realist relevance of the Concerto for Orchestra were recognised immediately;[22] it has since proved to be one of Lutosławski's most popular pieces both in Poland and abroad. It was not the first post-war Polish Concerto for Orchestra; that had been Baird's, premiered in May 1954. But whereas Baird's work was a four-movement symphony in all but name, Lutosławski's turned out to be a major reconfiguration of the structural possibilities in a multi-movement orchestral piece. It had three movements – 'Intrada', 'Capriccio notturno e Arioso', and a 'Passacaglia' leading directly into a 'Toccata e Corale' – whose macrostructural end-weighting was to become a dominant feature of his music from the early 1960s onwards. Of course, a triumphant conclusion was *de rigeur* for socialist-realist music, and the Concerto for Orchestra obliges,[23] more in passing than as an ideological decision. But the cultural-political context inevitably conditions any broad-based historical interpretation of the work's impact.

Its panache and character are undoubted. There are, however, not many obvious parallels of instrumental virtuosity with the best-known previous Concerto for Orchestra, by Bartók (1943), although the delicacy and wit of the 'Capriccio notturno' (including its unusual percussion fade-out) is highly memorable. So too is the more monumental accretion and reduction of motivic layers in the arch-shaped 'Intrada' (shades of both Bartók and Britten's *Sinfonia da Requiem*, 1940). Elsewhere, the rhetoric is remarkably close to the grandiosity of other contemporary Polish pieces (for example, the 'Arioso', the climax of the 'Passacaglia', and the conclusion). It is also a significant example of the widespread Polish trend in the early 1950s for using eighteenth-century genres as compositional crutches (cf. the four movements of Baird's Concerto for Orchestra).[24] In an age of uncertainty, proven formal devices from the distant past were very useful, even if only as safety blankets, their implementation in 1950s Poland being quite distinct from inter-war neo-classicism elsewhere. Lutosławski's genius was not to make heavy weather of these archaic resources. Where Baird's concluding 'hymne' is a leaden, dutiful apotheosis of a main theme, Lutosławski's 'Corale' (a device possibly modelled on Bartók's example) is new material, introduced into the finale as a moment of reflection before becoming part of the rousing conclusion. More tellingly, Lutosławski saw the potential for combining eighteenth-century frameworks with the motivic possibilities of Polish folk music:

> The concerto for orchestra differs from the rest of my 'folkloric' compositions in that it treats folklore material as 'rough stuff' for a large baroque-like construction. In my *Folk Melodies*, *Little Suite*, *Silesian Triptych*, and other works of that type, song (or dance) was being stylized somehow or other, which is not the case in the Concerto, although it contains not only those folk themes which have been found by musicologists, but also quite a number of

folk motifs overlooked by them. It is a neo-baroque composition, in a sense. The opening Intrada is played *détaché* à la Bach and Handel. There are Passacaglia, Toccata, Capriccio. But all these baroque genres are folklore-tinctured, which results in fairly novel patterns – I don't know of any other instance of such a 'bond' between baroque and folklore.[25]

Lutosławski ensures a wide range of expressive possibilities by treating this 'rough stuff' to differing degrees (Lutosławski found his material in the published collections of the nineteenth-century ethnographer Oskar Kolberg). The theme of the 'Passacaglia', for example, remains very close to its source, while that of the 'Arioso', as demonstrated by Stucky, has been more conspicuously developed.[26]

The most artful refashioning of folk tunes is in the 'Intrada': Lutosławski remains remarkably faithful to the Kolberg originals, at the same realising acutely their potential for organic development, contrapuntal compatibility and structural contrast. In the outer sections, for example, the main theme and its counterpoints maintain their original 3/8 metre, two-by-two-bar phrasing and rhythmic character, and Lutosławski undoubtedly chose them also because they shared similar rhythmic and cadential patterns, notably in the second bar of each phrase. There is therefore an easy flow between one theme and the next, enlivened by gentle chromatic contradictions: in the first instance when all are present (bb.16–23, led off by the second violins), the common modality is spiced by the close succession of G natural by G sharp in the counterpoint while the theme contradicts this sharpening, as on its previous two statements, with a flattening musica ficta interpretation of its highest note (here, a naturalised F sharp).

Lutosławski's attention to detail is the key to his achievement. The 'Intrada' is built on small fragments, rather than long-breathed melodies, enabling the composer, as Stucky puts it, 'to be master, not slave, of folklore'.[27] Lutosławski goes further by characterising his themes in ways totally at variance with their original folk texts. His developmental outlook is also evident in telling details. In the opening section of the 'Intrada', for example, the main theme is marked 'aggressivo', its counterpoints unmarked. On the return of the section, the theme is characterised as 'dolce, poco espress.', and the counterpoints as 'indifferente'.

Macro-structural concerns are also carefully developed. It can be no accident that both the first two movements seem preparatory to the third (what Stucky would later call end-accented form),[28] both being straightforward ternary structures with evanescent conclusions. Indeed, it is possible to see the 'Passacaglia' as being, at least in part, a third 'preparation' because, for all its developmental construction (an overlapping 'chain' of eighteen

statements of the passacaglia theme with fewer variations), the upward
migration of the passacaglia is a reminder of a parallel registral shift in
the outer sections of the 'Intrada';[29] as such, it is too contained in its formal
design to achieve developmental release by itself.[30] In that sense, the Concerto for Orchestra may be deemed to have four movements (as posited by
James Harley),[31] in which the structural interplay of toccata and chorale of
the finale proper has a stronger dynamic impact, not least in liberating the
passacaglia theme from its straitjacket and thrusting it into the foreground
as the main propellant of the 'Toccata'. The treatment of this particular
folk theme, including its transformation from duple to triple metre, amply
illustrates Lutosławski's concept of his unique bonding of the baroque and
folklore. The folk-tincturing is more than skin-deep, however, and gives the
Concerto for Orchestra a compelling energy and freshness which a reliance
on eighteenth-century practices alone would not have provided. Whether
Stucky is right in saying that this stylistic amalgam is 'modern enough and
personal enough to burst the bounds of *socrealizm*'[32] is a matter for debate,
because from the wider Polish context it could equally be argued that the
Concerto for Orchestra is definitively a creature of its time as well as, miracu-
lously, a transcendence of it. At the time, its materials, goal-directed structure
and clear expressive idiom epitomised many of the ideals of socialist realism,
and had this cultural policy persisted it might well have spawned numerous
imitators of its intelligent design and exceptional imagination.

PART II

Facing west

6 The 'Warsaw Autumn'

Within a year of Stalin's death, there were flickering signs of moderation in Polish culture. The eleventh session of the Council of Culture and Art (15–16 April 1954) was one turning point. Mycielski, for example, raised the issue of conflict between artistic truth and ideology:

> Crusading art is art against the established order of things . . . On the other hand the art of an ideology, which has triumphed and reached power, must fight in another way . . . But then we – in order not to damage the building, in order not to give our foes material for their propaganda . . . – we place on the writer a kind of bridle so that he either resigns, or becomes cynical, or falls silent, or writes apologetic or panegyric works. He does not, however, present living truth, as he sees and feels it . . .[1]

According to Panufnik, Sokorski (who had been promoted to head the Ministry of Culture a while earlier) had allowed the impression to develop before the Council met that there might be some changes in the air.[2] At one point in his speech, Sokorski admitted that '[the] underestimation of form . . . the relinquishing of innovations . . . are conducive . . . to trivial, unaesthetic works . . . Socialist realism is neither a definite artistic school, nor a definite style, nor a recipe.'[3] There was little argument on that score, but elsewhere in his speech Sokorski dashed any hope of real change and reiterated the standard Party position. The general tone of retrenchment precluded any obvious or immediate weakening of state control over the arts, and this appears to have been one of the last straws for Panufnik, who defected less than three months later.

Lissa also deliberated in public, at the ZKP Congress in April 1954. She had just given a paper on the formation of a national style in Polish music at the International Musicological Congress in Paris (the first time since the war that Poland had been represented). She utilised a particularly negative passage from Honegger's recently published autobiography, *Je suis compositeur*, to bolster the East–West divide, retorting: 'None of our composers writes "atomic" symphonies or "concrete" music, or "electronic", or quartets "for the end of the world" [sic].'[4] While acknowledging that there had been organisational mistakes in the early 1950s at the Ministry of Culture and Art (where she maintained her senior position), and berating the ZKP for weak management, she reiterated the existing policy: 'We follow the same road as the USSR, the road leading to a socialist society.'[5] In one of the more unexpected passages, she attacked young composers, including those submitting works to join the Youth Circle of the ZKP:

> Hence the sometimes aimless, zigzagging path of our young and even younger composers, especially members of the Youth Circle. This state of affairs is plainly visible in their student works. The experiments of our young ones, with whom I meet to look through their pieces, ranges wildly from dodecaphony and Stravinskiada to banal nineteenth-century epigonism.[6]

Quite apart from reinforcing Lissa's role in monitoring the output of composers, this indicates that Serocki's *Suite of Preludes*, composed two years earlier, was not an isolated instance of a young composer testing the boundaries of the acceptable.[7] The fact, however, that by April 1954 student composers were putting forward 'experimental' pieces for assessment by Lissa and, presumably, their professors indicates that, at this level at least, stylistic norms were being openly challenged, thus antedating the conventionally understood watershed of 1956.

The Party leadership had activated discussions at the Council of Culture and Art partly, it would seem, because composers and other artists were becoming less malleable.[8] Indeed, despite the Party's attempts to shore up its central control, the history of the years between Stalin's death and the Polish confrontation with Stalin's successor, Khrushchev, in Warsaw in October 1956 is one of increasing dissent both within and outside the Party. It was a slow, piecemeal process, with no guaranteed outcome (for an outline of some of the cultural events which have since come to symbolise these changes, see Appendix 1). At the time of Panufnik's defection, for example, it had seemed that the policy of socialist realism would not be rescinded. And yet Panufnik had felt unusually emboldened to stand up for Turski's Second Symphony in a newspaper interview given a few weeks before he left Poland: 'For me, for example, the fact of the complete withdrawal from the concert platform of Turski's "Olympic" Symphony, which won the Gold Medal at the 1948 Olympics in London, is mystifying. I can see no formalism there.'[9] It was because of such small, but daring acts that the political edifice began to crumble.

In the field of music, the authorities tried to bolster their position in 1954 in several ways. There was a further effort to resuscitate the mass song, the output of which had declined rapidly since its highpoint in 1950–1: songs were commissioned and written for the Second Party Congress in March that year (Panufnik's *New Time* was one of twelve published to mark the

occasion). But there was little enthusiasm either for these politicised examples or for the genre itself. Whereas Polish Radio's listing magazine *Radio
i Świat* (Radio and the World) had frequently published the words and
music of mass songs in the early 1950s, these were gradually replaced from
1954 onwards by songs in more popular dance idioms (foxtrots, waltzes
and tangos) as well as occasional appearances of songs from the West
(Kern's 'Ol' Man River', Gershwin's 'Summertime' and 'I Got Plenty o Nut-
tin', Yves Montand's 'C'est si bon' and Donaldson's 'Hawaiian Lullaby').
By Christmas 1956, the magazine felt comfortable with printing a Polish
Christmas carol, with broadcasts of traditional Christmas music for the first
time since 1947.

In the field of concert music, composers were commissioned to write
pieces to celebrate the tenth anniversary of People's Poland (1944–54) and a
successor to the 1951 Festival of Polish Music was organised. This took place
in the first months of 1955. It was a more modest affair than its predecessor
and came in for criticism for its lack of imagination and audience appeal. In
effect, its concept was being overtaken by events and by the sense of change
in Polish life and culture. The second festival's relative failure has often been
cited as a root cause of the emergence of the festival which was to launch and
lead Polish music into a new era, the 'Warsaw Autumn'. In fact, as Cynthia
Bylander has shown, the verifiable origins of this breakthrough in October
1956 stretch as far back as the summer of 1954, around the time of Panufnik's
defection.[10]

The ZKP had elected a new Presidium in April 1954, led by Kazimierz
Sikorski, whose status as the foremost composition teacher in Poland dated
back to his heroic efforts during the Second World War. His vice-presidents
were two of his recent students, Baird and Serocki. The youthfulness of
the new Presidium was reinforced by the inclusion of Dobrowolski and
Włodzimierz Kotoński (b. 1923), both in their early thirties; in its short,
fifteen-month period of office, this team turned out to be the catalyst for
musical change in Poland. Initial contacts with government were made in
mid-1954, and outline approval for an international music festival was given
at the very highest level before the second Festival of Polish Music began in
January 1955. By June 1955, the ZKP was able to announce that the 'Warsaw
Autumn' festival would take place in 1956. Neither Baird nor Serocki, who
have since been largely credited with founding the 'Warsaw Autumn', was
re-elected to the Presidium in June 1955, although the evidence suggests
that they remained closely involved in the realisation of the project, which
materialised between 10–21 October 1956. The driving force behind the
'Warsaw Autumn' was composers' overwhelming sense of cultural isolation
and their wish to break the provincial nature of Polish music, underlined

as it had been since the late 1940s by propaganda prerogatives. For the composers, a genuine international exchange was sought, although the idea that Poland could show off its wares was more fundamental in the eyes of the Party. The ZKP tried to cover all viewpoints in its foreword to the Festival programme book:

> Thanks to the current Festival, foreign musicians will have the opportunity for the broad study of outstanding works of contemporary Polish music, while composers of 'the Polish school', which can boast fine successes in the international arena, will gain valuable opportunities for comparison between their successes and those of composers from other countries.
>
> We hope that this, the first collation conceived on such a scale on Polish territory of many trends of contemporary musical creativity, will give participants in the Festival the opportunity for free and frank exchange of experience and opinion, contributing to the tightening of sincere bonds of cultural community between artists taking part in the Festival.[11]

In earlier days such fine words would have rung hollow, but at this juncture they signified a seismic shift in cultural resources and practice. The results were limited, compared to subsequent years (the next 'Warsaw Autumn' was in 1958, and thereafter the festival was planned on an annual basis), as an analysis of the performers and repertoire reveals.

There were more foreign concerts (eleven) than Polish (eight), with appearances from behind the Iron Curtain of the State Symphony Orchestra from Moscow and the State Philharmonics from Brno and Bucharest (two concerts apiece), alongside the Tatrai Quartet from Budapest. The West was represented by ensembles from two centres with long-standing historical ties with Poland. There were two concerts each by the Vienna Symphony Orchestra (with Alfred Brendel and Michael Gielen) and the ORTF from Paris (conducted by Jean Martinon), as well as a recital by the Paris-based Parrenin Quartet. Polish performances were led by the front-rank orchestras: the National Philharmonic from Warsaw (opening and closing concerts), two concerts each by WOSPR and the Silesian Philharmonic, both from Katowice (then still known as Stalinogród), and the Polish Radio Choir and Orchestra from Kraków.

The repertoire of the first 'Warsaw Autumn' is indicative of the isolation of the preceding seventeen years (see Appendix 2 for a full list of pieces). If certain oddities in a festival of contemporary music are ignored (such as the inclusion of symphonies by Brahms and Tchaikousky), it immediately becomes apparent that, for the organisers of the 1956 festival, 'contemporary' meant European music from 1900 onwards (there was no American music at this first festival). Of the foreign repertoire, certain trends stand out, including a continuing interest in French music, with stalwarts such as Auric, Honegger, Messiaen and Ravel, plus the Polish premieres of works by Dutilleux, Jolivet and Milhaud (significantly, the most feted guest at the festival was Boulanger). There was an initial foray into the hitherto demonised repertoire of twelve-note composition, with Polish premieres of Berg's *Lyric Suite* and Schoenberg's Piano Concerto and a few pieces by lesser-known members of the younger generation of serialists (Apostel and Martinet, for example, but no Boulez or Nono). There was a fairly predictable range of Soviet music (Khachaturian, Miaskovsky, Prokofiev and Shostakovich) and a smattering of works by composers from elsewhere within the Soviet bloc.

Most notable, however, was the concerted attempt to reinstate Bartók and Stravinsky. Whereas Bartók was represented by three pieces, notably the Concerto for Orchestra and the Polish premiere of his Fifth String Quartet, Stravinsky received six performances, concentrating on the ballet scores for Diaghilev: *Fireworks, The Firebird* (suite), *Petrushka* (suite), *The Rite of Spring, Jeu de cartes* and *Ebony Concerto*. Of these, only the last was announced as a Polish premiere, although Lutosławski for one maintained that *The Rite of Spring* had not previously been performed in Poland. It would be a mistake, however, to assume that the first 'Warsaw Autumn' was entirely responsible for this breakthrough to the West. In fact, the rehabilitation of Stravinsky had begun during the 1955–6 season of the National Philharmonic in Warsaw, which included *Petrushka* and *Symphony of Psalms*, along with Berg's Violin Concerto and Hindemith's *Mathis der Maler*. The Kraków Philharmonic, under its progressive young conductor Bohdan Wodiczko, had begun to test the boundaries of cultural control even earlier by programming Bartók's *Sonata for Two Pianos and Percussion* in January 1953 and his Third Piano Concerto and Viola Concerto during the 1953–4 season. Perhaps most impressively, the Kraków Philharmonic gave the Polish premiere in 1953–4 of Messiaen's 'Symphonic Fragment' (almost certainly *Les offrandes oubliées*), thereby anticipating the performance at the first 'Warsaw Autumn' more than two years later.[12]

Polish Radio had also been playing its part (it had broadcast Lutosławski's First Symphony, reportedly banned in 1949, on 23 August 1954), although it really came into its own as an active partner of the 'Warsaw Autumn', and this partnership continues to this day. Its roster of live and delayed relays from the first festival was substantial, and at the end of the festival its listings magazine even printed a short unsigned article on serialism, with musical examples.[13] When broadcasts of electronic music and *musique concrète* began in December 1956, there were no means of production in

Poland. That situation was remedied in November 1957, when Polish Radio against all financial odds established the first electronic music facility in Eastern Europe; its Experimental Studio was headed by Józef Patkowski, a young musicologist and lecturer in acoustics.[14] In fact, it was only the sixth such studio, following closely on the heels of centres in Paris (1948), New York (1951), Cologne (1951), Tokyo (1953) and Milan (1953). As a signal of creative intent, this remarkably swift development was scarcely less powerful than the first 'Warsaw Autumn'.

The repertoire of Polish music at the first 'Warsaw Autumn' is revealing. Only one work received its first performance (Baird's *Cassazione*, 1956), although several others (such as Malawski's Second Symphony 'Dramatic', 1955 and Serocki's Sinfonietta, 1956) had been premiered earlier in 1956. There is just a suggestion, therefore, that the repertoire committee had not quite rid itself of the notion of vetting works in advance (there would be many more world premieres of Polish pieces at the festival from 1958 onwards). The Polish repertoire was characterised, like the two Festivals of Polish Music in 1951 and 1955, by its concern to contextualise modern pieces. Two works by Szymanowski framed the entire festival – Stabat Mater and the Third Symphony. There was a wide selection of recent Polish pieces, most of them couched in neo-classical terms or drawing on eighteenth-century forms, sometimes also reliant on folklore (Bacewicz, Lutosławski, Sikorski, Szabelski). Some grittier works, like Woytowicz's Second Symphony, with its basis in the composer's wartime experiences, were also included. There were even pieces by emigré Polish composers (the neo-classical Spisak and Szałowski), but there was no space for the most recent absentee, Panufnik, who would not feature in a 'Warsaw Autumn' programme until the Polish premiere of *Universal Prayer* (1969) in 1977.[15]

The sense that the Polish contribution was primarily a retrospective on the post-war decade is hard to avoid (quite a few pieces performed in 1956 had already been aired at the 1955 Festival of Polish Music, some even in 1951). Given recent political circumstances and the desire to show off 'the Polish school', this is understandable, not least because few of the post-war Polish pieces had been performed outside Eastern Europe. So, while Lutosławski's Concerto for Orchestra and Bacewicz's music, for example, were highlighted, there was also considerable interest in those pieces written since 1955. These were Baird's *Cassazione*, Dobrowolski's First Symphony (1955), Malawski's Second Symphony, and Serocki's Sinfonietta. Of these, Dobrowolski's Symphony has never been recorded or published, though the brief programme note suggests a work in the mould of mid-1950s Polish symphonies, with its traditional classical forms and with the outer movements containing substantial fugal sections.[16] Malawski's Symphony is likewise reliant on classical structures, though after the third movement, Scherzo, he places two movements, an Intermezzo 'in free form' and a Capriccio acting as a short epilogue.

Reception of these new pieces was by no means uniform. In a characteristically informed critique of the festival, Mycielski indicated that Polish musicians were aware of what was happening abroad, even if they lacked direct experience:

> The festival did not show the newest musical trends which currently exist in the West . . . There is a group of young people which is absolutely burning to hear the mysterious Nono, Boulez or Stockhausen, to hear the experiments of P. Schaeffer's *musique concrète* or the latest German attempts in electronic music . . . Not only concrete or electronic experiments, but also pointillism, the decomposition of music, i.e. lines, motifs, rhythms (their continuity), into the primary elements, are unknown to us . . . Poland has not yet passed through the stage of dodecaphony and of pieces constructed on an ordered series of notes. We will either skip these stages or produce something of our own which will to some degree answer the real needs of our creators.[17]

The repertoire of the next four 'Warsaw Autumn' festivals (1958–61) clearly charts the process of informing Polish audiences and composers of what was happening in the West (Appendix 3). With regard to non-Polish compositions, there was still a considerable process of catching up (first 'appearances' included Webern in 1958 and Varèse in 1959). There was also an astonishing acceleration towards a genuinely contemporary repertoire, with almost all of the foreign pieces receiving their Polish premieres. In the most ground-breaking concert in 1958, David Tudor played piano music by both the American and European avant-garde (Cage, Nilsson, Stockhausen and Wolff) and Stockhausen introduced a programme of electronic music (pieces by Berio, Eimert, Ligeti, Maderna, Pousseur and his own *Gesang der Jünglinge*). By 1959, the shift of balance to music of the 1950s was more noticeable, with the new repertoire not wholly confined to visiting Western virtuosi but embedded in programmes given by Polish performers. Pierre Schaeffer followed Stockhausen's example the previous year and introduced a programme of *musique concrète* pieces (Ferrari, Mâche, Philippot, Schaeffer, Henry and Xenakis). Severino Gazzelloni and Marcelle Mercenier gave a flute and piano recital (Berio, Boulez, Henze, Messiaen, Pousseur and Varèse), the Parrenin Quartet performed Boulez, while Polish orchestras performed recent pieces by Amy, Dallapiccola, Hindemith, Nono and Regamey. In 1960, the Parrenin Quartet, on its third visit to the festival, introduced Carter's music to Poland and the NHK Symphony Orchestra provided the unprecedented exoticism of Japanese repertoire. By 1961, the festival had fully established its avant-garde credentials with regular appearances of the latest Western offerings on its programmes.[18]

By the same token, there were far fewer Polish 'classics' and an almost immediate focus on what Polish composers had just written, with the festival's Polish repertoire growing from twenty-five per cent in 1958 to thirty per cent in 1961 and the number of world premieres increasing exponentially. Among the notable events were the first performances in 1958 of Baird's *Four Essays*, Kotoński's *Chamber Music* and *Epitaph* (*Epitafium*) by Henryk Mikołaj Górecki (b. 1933), alongside performances of Lutosławski's *Funeral Music* and Serocki's *Heart of the Night* (*Serce nocy*) and *Musica concertante*. In 1959, there were premieres of Bacewicz's *Music for Strings, Trumpets and Percussion*, Baird's *Espressioni varianti*, Górecki's First Symphony '1959' and Szabelski's *Improvisations*; Penderecki made his first appearance at this festival with *Strophes*. The 1960 and 1961 festivals continued the parade of new Polish compositions, which by this stage were beginning to show fascinating glimpses of innovative creative personalities. Among the highlights in 1960 were Bacewicz's Sixth String Quartet, Górecki's *Scontri*, Kotoński's *Study on One Cymbal Stroke* (*Etiuda na jedno uderzenie w talerz*), Lutosławski's *Five Songs*, Penderecki's *Dimensions of Time and Silence* (*Wymiary czasu i ciszy*), *Tertium datur* by Bogusław Schaeffer (b. 1929), Serocki's *Episodes*, Szabelski's *Sonnets* and radio operas by Bacewicz and Zbigniew Wiszniewski (b. 1922). The 1961 festival was distinguished above all by the premieres of the full, revised version of Lutosławski's *Venetian Games* (*Gry weneckie*) and Penderecki's *Threnody for the Victims of Hiroshima* (*Tren ofiarom Hiroshimy*).

These developments drew the attention of foreign music critics, publishers and promoters, such as Peter Heyworth from the *Observer*, Paul Moor of the *New York Times* and Otto Tomek from WDR, Cologne, and such contacts proved crucial for the Poles and their international ambitions. The festival also attracted visits from major foreign composers, such as Evangelisti, Hába, Nono and Stockhausen (1958), Pierre Schaeffer and Shostakovich (1959), Britten and Nono (1961) and Cardew, Carter, Donatoni and Xenakis (1962). And, despite continuing tight controls on foreign travel by Polish citizens, professional visits to the West were now possible. In 1957, for example, Dobrowolski, Wojciech Kilar (b. 1932), Kotoński, Krenz and Serocki were among a group of Polish composers who attended the annual Internationale Ferienkurse für Neue Musik in Darmstadt.[19] Lutosławski's foreign travels had begun two years earlier: he had visited festivals in Helsinki and Salzburg in 1955–6, but more importantly he became involved in the ISCM following Poland's readmission to the organisation in 1957. Along with Bacewicz, he attended the 1958 ISCM festival in Strasbourg and was appointed to the jury of the 1959 festival in Rome.[20] Of the youngest generation, Penderecki first went abroad in 1959, when he spent two months in Italy as part of the prize for scooping the top three awards, with *Psalms of David* (1958), *Emanations* (1958) and *Strophes* (1959), at the Second ZKP Young Composers' Competition. Górecki won the same competition the following year, with *Monologhi*. His case illustrates the problems of obtaining a foreign-travel permit. His wish to use the prize to study with Nono in Italy was thwarted when he was refused a passport, so instead he travelled to Paris for three months at the end of 1961 where he encountered Western culture and society for the first time. Such limited opportunities for broadening musical horizons reinforced the centrality of the 'Warsaw Autumn' throughout the 1960s for the exchange of music and ideas, not only for Polish composers but for all musicians intrigued by this extraordinary interface between East and West.

7 Engaging with the avant-garde

Inevitably, this upsurge in activity and creative enthusiasm, even if it was to a large extent concentrated on ten days each year in Warsaw, filtered right through Polish musical life, to composers, performers and those involved in higher education; there was a strong feeling of liberation and anticipation.[1] When the ZKP held its ninth General Assembly six months after the first 'Warsaw Autumn', in March 1957 (it had been two years since the previous meeting), Lutosławski spoke for most of its membership when he said:

> So our assembly, for the first time in a very long while, is taking place in an atmosphere of true creative freedom. No one here will persecute anyone for so-called formalism, no one will prevent anyone from expressing his aesthetic opinions, regardless of what individual composers represent.
>
> When today, from the perspective of eight and a half years, I look back on the notorious conference in Łagów in 1949, when the frontal attack on Polish musical creativity began, I go cold just remembering that dreadful experience . . . We all know that it was the work of people to whom the very idea of beauty is totally foreign, people for whom music is of no interest unless there is some tale or legend attached.
>
> The period of which I speak may not have lasted long, because it actually passed a couple of years ago, but it was nevertheless long enough to have visited tremendous damage on our music. The psyche of a creative artist is an extremely delicate and precise instrument. So the attack on that instrument and the attempt to subdue it caused not a few of us moments of severe depression. Being completely cut off from what was happening in the arts in the West likewise played no small role in that dismal experiment to which we were subjected.
>
> Have we shaken ourselves free of this state of dejection? Do we have enough enthusiasm for new creative explorations? Certainly, yes. But even so our situation is far from easy. Before each of us stands the problem of finding our place in the tumult represented by the arts of our time . . . Not all of us have a clear view on what is happening in this music, where it is going. I believe, however, that it is only a question of time, that not only will we reach a clear view on the situation but also that we will play a positive and not insignificant role in it.[2]

Charting the range of compositional responses to this 'tumult' in the first few years after 1956 offers a rare opportunity to examine creative responses to external stimuli following a period of cultural repression.

There can have hardly have been a greater shock to composers fed on folk music and eighteenth-century cast-offs than confronting not only the twelve-note music of Schoenberg, Berg and Webern, but also the live and electronic music of Stockhausen, Berio, Boulez, Nono and Maderna (the concepts and aleatory world of Cage did not impinge until 1960). General access to scores, let alone recordings, of these and other Western composers who were of the same generation as Baird, Kotoński, Schaeffer and Serocki, was virtually non-existent, unless surreptitious raids were made on publishers' exhibition stands at the 'Warsaw Autumn'. Unsurprisingly, different generations reacted differently and it is reasonable to assess their initial responses in three groups: (a) those composers born before the First World War and educated between the wars, (b) those composers born in the newly independent Poland of the 1920s whose tertiary education was completed by the mid-1950s, and (c) the youngest generation, born in the late 1920s and early 1930s, whose tertiary education took place during the second half of the 1950s.

In some ways, the first group is the most intriguing because by 1956 they had already had considerable compositional exposure. This generation included Szeligowski, Wiechowicz, Kazimierz Sikorski, Perkowski, Woytowicz, Mycielski, Kisielewski and Bacewicz, all of whom had studied in Paris between the wars, plus three composers whose studies were confined to Warsaw: Turski, Szabelski, and Lutosławski. Most of the group had had works performed abroad in the years immediately after the Second World War (in Paris or at ISCM festivals) and all had endured what Lutosławski described as the 'dreadful experience' of socialist realism. The response of this generation was the most mixed. There were those for whom artistic freedom came too late or who could not raise much enthusiasm for 'new creative explorations'. At sixty, Szeligowski, for one, was too entrenched to change; he followed up the success of his socialist-realist opera, *The Scholar's Revolt*, with several more works for the stage, including a science-fiction opera about cybernetics, *Theodore Gentleman* (1960). Wiechowicz followed his well-defined path of idiomatic choral music, though his introspective anti-war cantata, *Letter to Marc Chagall* (1961), the first Polish work dedicated to victims of the Nazi concentration camps, is the only one of his works not to be based on folklore.

Of those who focussed on instrumental repertoire, Kazimierz Sikorski continued to concentrate on the genres of the concerto (*Polyphonic Concerto* for bassoon and orchestra, 1965) and symphony (Symphony no. 6, 1983), maintaining his essentially neo-classical outlook. Likewise Perkowski remained faithful to his pre-war roots, notably in the intense post-Szymanowskian idiom of the Second Violin Concerto (1960), though by the time of the Cello Concerto (1974) some of the impressionist aspects of his language had been tinged by more recent colouristic experiments. Woytowicz's Third Symphony for piano and orchestra (1963), apart from being generically and in some measure linguistically indebted to Szymanowski's *Symphonie concertante*, is an artful example of a composer trying to create a rapprochement between competing impulses. Progressing in a series of nine short and highly contrasted sections shaped in an arch form, Woytowicz's Symphony combines lyrical and colouristic application of twelve-note ideas with neo-classical gestures in a way unmatched by any of his contemporaries. Occasionally Mycielski came close, but despite including some twelve-note elements, he could not substantially shed either his neo-classical background or the folklore which had so effectively informed his First Symphony (1951). In the four later symphonies (1961–77), as well as choral music, his voice was one of sombre and considered reflection. The neo-classicism of Kisielewski, on the other hand, was characterised by wit and self-awareness, and these attributes subsequently led him to incorporate ironic allusions to the avant-garde in works such as *Meetings in the Desert* (*Spotkania na pustyni*, 1969). As critics, both Mycielski and Kisielewski stayed abreast of new ideas, but neither was especially comfortable in the new climate as composers, and few of their works made much impact after the mid-1950s. Turski never really recovered from his mauling at Łagów in 1949 and, though he continued composing into the 1970s, his music remained on the sidelines.

The reactions of the two most able of the older generation, Bacewicz and Lutosławski, is particularly fascinating. Neither was prepared to ditch the past without long and careful thought. Lutosławski frequently commented on his sense of isolation from what may be termed the new hegemony – other composers seemed to be willing to exchange *socrealizm* for serialism without much care for their own reflections and intuitions. Of course, Bacewicz and Lutosławski had distinguished themselves by finding an individual compositional modus vivendi under both Nazi censorship and Stalinist dogma. They had a strong sense of their own character and believed, in the face of a third challenge, that they could forge their own way forward.

Since her Fifth String Quartet, Bacewicz had reduced her prodigious rate of production, creating among large-scale works only the Partita, Ten Concert Studies for piano (1956), Symphonic Variations and the unreleased Sixth Violin Concerto (both 1957). Her first major public statement was *Music for Strings, Trumpets and Percussion* (1958). There was little pretence that this broke new ground in terms of Bacewicz's overall stylistic goals; her particular brand of neo-classicism still held good and the title's allusion to Bartók implied no more than had Lutosławski's Concerto for Orchestra.

More tellingly, Bacewicz was assessing her position by looking back at her most successful post-war piece, the Concerto for String Orchestra, and, ten years on, reinterpreting it under new conditions. Once she had done this, she was able to move on to new challenges in the 1960s.

Music for Strings, Trumpets and Percussion prolonged her neo-Baroque tendencies by maintaining the three-movement format of its predecessor, reusing eighteenth-century figuration and reinforcing its concept as a concerto grosso by adding new instrumental colours to the string base. A new harmonic astringency is evident. The opening section of the first movement, for example, is built on dissonant combinations of tritones which build to a climactic twelve-note chord (this is a coincidental parallel with Lutosławski's main harmonic preoccupation). It is no surprise, in the light of previous works, that this movement takes an individual slant on traditional first-movement form.[3] Despite the eighteenth-century backbone, the emphasis on developmental processes leads to many shifting perspectives as the movement unfolds. This feature also dominates the central Adagio (Ex. 7.1), which emerges as a troubled, almost emaciated shadow of its predecessor in the Concerto for String Orchestra. The opening violin ostinato is intervallically constrained (tight semitonal motion around D natural) and texturally attenuated (sul tasto). The melodic idea in the lower strings is likewise lacking in aura. Where Bacewicz had already challenged preconceptions in the central Andante of the Concerto by marginalising the recapitulation, here she drops it altogether. The reduction of the admittedly minimal material which began the Adagio to almost featureless clusters of trills, marked 'con sord' and 'sul tasto', creates an open-ended design in which the music simply evaporates. What in 1948 had been sumptuous and confident, in 1958 became desolate and uncertain. It was no less powerful for that, but it did indicate that she had not yet fully faced up to the challenges of the new.

Lutosławski also produced a major work in 1958, his *Funeral Music* for strings, which did engage in a particular way with twelve-note techniques as well as reiterating his strong links with Bartók. Like his Concerto for Orchestra, this memorial tribute was four years in the making. Most striking is Lutosławski's mastery of structural evolution, the dramatic import of every moment carefully judged. Despite its power and originality, it remains something of an anomaly in his post-1956 output, looking backwards in style and outlook but simultaneously exploring the linear possibilities of a twelve-note row. Lutosławski used to react sharply when commentators persisted in linking *Funeral Music* to serialism. He did not want, under any circumstances, to be associated with the ethos of the Second Viennese School. At the time of the premiere in March 1958, he commented:

Example 7.1. Bacewicz, *Music for Strings, Trumpets and Percussion* (1958), second movement, opening.

What I have developed in this piece is a set of means which allow me to move in a certain sense within the confines of twelve tones, naturally outside the tonal system and dodecaphony. It is for me the beginning of a new period; it is the result of long experience. I attempted to create a set of procedures which will become my property. And this is the first (and certainly not the last) word uttered in the new language.[4]

Lutosławski, typically clear-sighted, was staking out his territory, even if the future would not so straightforwardly match his expectations.

His scores and sketches, however, as Martina Homma has shown with regard to later works,[5] reveal how indebted he was at times to basic twelve-note techniques, including hexachordal complementarity. In *Funeral Music*, the principal twelve-note idea is treated canonically and in different transpositions, but Lutosławski's focus on just two linear intervals, the tritone and semitone, masks the technical underpinning, giving it the guise of an almost tonal sequence. The authority with which he treats his material – for example, the way he guides it inexorably towards the heterophonic repetitions of the climax on B and F naturals – is irresistible; in terms of both compositional style and technique, as well as symphonism, it is closely linked to earlier orchestral pieces. The momentum of the central 'Metamorphoses' towards its culmination is met in an unexpected way. The 'Apogee' consists of a procession of twelve-note chords which concertina inwards onto the single note which initiates the recapitulation of the initial twelve-note theme. It is in chords such as these, which verticalise all the twelve pitch classes, that Lutosławski found the key to his future development. He had already explored in *Five Songs* (1957) various ways of organising such chords, such as partitioning the twelve pitch classes into three identically patterned four-note groups (nos. 2 and 4) or into four augmented triads. He had also investigated asymmetrical vertical arrangements, such as white- and black-note arpeggiation (no. 1). Indeed, *Five Songs* was in many ways to prove more relevant to later developments than *Funeral Music*, even though only the latter has maintained a position in concert repertoires at home and abroad. Not for the first time in these years, a composer looked both backwards and forwards as he tried to determine how his musical language might develop. And the rhythmic-metric stiffness of Lutosławski's next composition, the Three Postludes (1958–60), is witness to the fact that, without further stimulus from outside his own workshop, he might have been thwarted in his ambition to create his new language, of finding his place in the tumult.

The 'middle generation' group of composers had fewer qualms about outside influences. By and large, it was quicker off the mark, although some, like Juliusz Łuciuk (b. 1927), Krystyna Moszumańska-Nazar (b. 1924) and Witold Szalonek (1927–2001), did not make a decisive move until the 1960s. The group included Baird, Dobrowolski, Kotoński, Schaeffer and Serocki. They were no longer the youngest generation and several of them had accumulated some socialist-realist 'baggage'. There were some immediate solutions to this dilemma. Dobrowolski, for example, drew on Hindemith in his Wind Trio (first performed in June 1956) while Baird's *Cassazione*, which he worked on from mid-1955 to mid-1956, still essentially inhabited the world of his orchestral works from earlier in the 1950s, notwithstanding its greater tolerance of dissonance and elementary use of a twelve-note series as an ad hoc motivic resource. His Divertimento (1956) for woodwind quartet

Example 7.2. Baird, Divertimento (1956), second movement 'Duetto', opening.

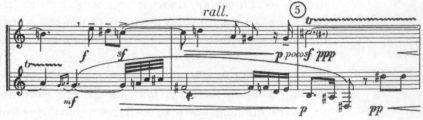

is more clearly neo-classical (its five movements have titles like 'Capriccio', 'Arietta', 'Quasi valse' and 'Marcia') and closer in orthodoxy to Schoenberg's early twelve-note chamber pieces. The second movement, 'Duetto', gives evidence of Baird's potential for expressive rhythmic flexibility (Ex. 7.2). His innate lyricism, already observed in his works of the socialist-realist years, began to flower anew in the String Quartet (1957), where the influence of Berg is paramount. Each of these last two works is based on more than one series: the Divertimento has a different series for each movement, and several of them show clear evidence that Baird was conscious of hexachordal complementarity in their construction, even if this feature did not play a prominent part in their deployment. In the Quartet, the finale utilises the series elaborated in the first movement as well as a permutation of a second series from the central movement.

Serocki was more cautious with regard to twelve-note technique. Both his Piano Sonata and Sinfonietta for double string orchestra show that any passing interest in twelve-note ideas is totally subservient to an overwhelming neo-classical drive. Indeed, in the Sinfonietta, arguably the most successful Polish composition of 1956, triadic, quartal or octatonic configurations are more keenly sensed than twelve-note ideas (there are strong hints of Bartók, especially in the finale). But with his next two pieces, Serocki tackled new compositional issues more directly. Both *Heart of the Night* and *Eyes of the Air* (*Oczy powietrza*, 1957) are song-cycles to texts by front-rank Polish poets (Konstanty Ildefons Gałczyński and Julian Przyboś respectively).

Heart of the Night originated as a cycle for baritone and orchestra, and its extensive pitched percussion section (xylophone, glockenspiel, marimba, vibraphone plus mandolin, guitar, celesta, piano and two harps) is not only the first example of extended timbral interests in Polish scores but also an indication of significant future developments in Serocki's work. The vocal line is lyrically sustained in a mildly old-fashioned way, enlivened by a degree of registral disjunction and moments of *Sprechstimme*. As to pitch organisation, Serocki shares Baird's preference at this stage for multiple series (the baritone enunciates a new row on his first entry in each of the five songs) and for a degree of freedom in terms of repetition and note order. The centrality of the twelve-note pitch organisation and its almost permanent state of metrical volatility ensure that there is no slipping back into neo-classical routines.

The two years 1958 and 1959 represent the high point of Polish composers' interest in twelve-note techniques, and it is at this stage that some members of the youngest generation come into the picture, notably Górecki and Penderecki. The roster of pieces which were written in these two years, regardless of their level of indebtedness to serial techniques, is both substantial and of a quality which began to match what was happening in the West. An analysis of the compositions selected in Table 7.1 demonstrates varying degrees and kinds of radicalism, from the oldest composer (Szabelski) to the youngest (Górecki).

Baird, for example, began to gain technical and expressive confidence in his *Four Essays*, especially in the outer movements (the second movement, on the other hand, looks backwards by using the 'Capriccio' of the Divertimento as a framework for elaboration). The first movement in particular shows how Baird had sidestepped the world of post-Webernian serialism, preferring sustained, cantabile lines and cogent harmonic movement to motivic fracturing and pointillist textures (Ex. 7.3). As early as the beginning of 1955, he had realised that his own lyrical gifts would find a better match with Berg, notably *Wozzeck* and the *Lyric Suite*: 'across the passage of time I began – entranced and at the same time frightened – to realise that that is how I hear music, how I myself wanted to compose'.[6] It would be erroneous, however, to look too closely for stylistic dependency on Berg (or, by extension, Mahler). Rather, Baird realised that Berg moulded technique to expression, and not vice versa; this was the chief liberating factor and was soon accorded a significant place in his oeuvre.[7]

Baird's pitch organisation remained true to twelve-note principles (he described the *Four Essays* as '99% dodecaphonic'[8]) and *Espressioni varianti* (*Ekspresje*) for violin and orchestra follows suit, although its technical range,

Table 7.1 *Polish Compositions 1957–9*

Composer	1957	1958	1959
Bacewicz	*Symphonic Variations*	*Music for Strings, Trumpets and Percussion*	*The Adventure of King Arthur* (radio opera)
Baird	String Quartet	*4 Essays*	*Espressioni varianti*
Dobrowolski			*Passacaglia na 40z5* for tape
Górecki	Sonata for Two Violins Concerto, op. 11	Epitaph	Symphony no. 1 '1959' 5 Pieces for two pianos
Kotoński		*Chamber Music*	*Musique en relief* Study on One Cymbal Stroke for tape
Lutosławski	*Five Songs*	*Funeral Music* Postlude no. 1	Postlude no. 3
Penderecki		*Psalms of David* *Emanations*	*Strophes* 3 Miniatures
Schaeffer	*Quattro movimenti* *Extremes*	*Tertium datur*	*Monosonata* *Equivalenze sonore*
Serocki	*Eyes of the Air*	*Musica concertante*	*Episodes*
Szabelski		*Sonnets*	*Improvisations*

in terms of row usage, rhythmic flexibility and timbral subtlety is hugely enhanced. Out goes the evidence of neo-classicism, in comes a heightened expressivity that at times seems to recall Szymanowski and even Bacewicz. It is one of the most impressive Polish works of the late 1950s. He was the first Polish composer to find his feet in this brave new world. With this piece, he achieved a balance of technique and expression which was to serve as the foundation stone for the rest of his short career (he died in 1981, aged fifty-three, just eight months after the death of Serocki, aged fifty-nine).

Serocki, in contrast, moved closer to the contemporary Western avant-garde and completed his move to post-Webernian serialism in *Musica concertante* (1958). There is now a concentration on a single series, a constructivist approach to macroform, refined pointillist textures comparable to recent works by Nono and an unusual complement of instruments (piccolo, soprano saxophone, bass clarinet, trumpet, two harps, large percussion section and fourteen strings) from which different ensembles are selected for each of the seven short movements. Its contemporary credentials are strong and Bogusław Schaeffer's view of it as 'a timid essay in serialism'[9] does it an injustice. At the time of its composition, it was at the cutting edge of Polish serialism, replete with a high degree of dynamic and registral

Example 7.3. Baird, *Four Essays* (1958), first movement, opening.

contrast, though its rhythmic character is somewhat anodyne (each movement maintains a constant, impartial metre and employs no tempo changes
of any kind). *Episodes* (1959) for strings and three percussion groups was
Serocki's turning point. On the one hand, it was his last piece to be substantially influenced by twelve-note processes, though Serocki was now more
interested in freely troping the twelve pitch classes than in adhering closely
to any one series. On the other hand, the piece gave indications of significant

new directions, partly inspired by the spatial dimensions of Stockhausen's *Gruppen*, which he had heard at Darmstadt the year before.[10] The notion of groups of sounds deployed spatially was particularly appealing (Górecki was also currently fascinated by this idea), though instead of emulating Stockhausen in terms of orchestral contrasts and technical procedures, Serocki chose to exploit string sonorities in a way only hinted at by his own Sinfonietta, Lutosławski's *Funeral Music*, or Penderecki's *Emanations*. Where Serocki led, others rapidly followed.

Schaeffer is an idiosyncratic figure. He first made his name as a critic, theorist and author of two milestones in Polish publishing: *New Music: Problems of Contemporary Compositional Technique* and *A Little Guide to Twentieth-Century Music*, both published in 1958. Schaeffer had assimilated an astonishing range of information, both technical and interpretative, and these and subsequent books, often liberally illustrated with musical examples, provided a primary source for most Polish musicians, even if, at times, they were overly polemical or factually unreliable. He did not emerge publicly as a composer until 1960, by which time he had, by his own count, written a large number of ground-breaking pieces. His *Music for Strings: Nocturne* (1953), which he has claimed as the first Polish (post-war) twelve-note piece, has had a shadowy public presence (it was not premiered until 1961) and no discernible impact. Its row is constructed as the simplest all-interval sequence, expanding stepwise either side of the initial pitch class. *Nocturne's* motivic and imitative antecedents are closer to Bartók than any Viennese example, but it remains a rather lumpen experiment. Schaeffer subsequently wrote a large number of piano pieces that have the air of technical exercises. Some of them – *Study in Diagram* (1956), *Free Composition* (1958), *Linear Construction* (1959) – show early evidence of Schaeffer's fascination with the role of notation as a mechanism for shaping or visually schematising compositional and performance practice; the twelve-note basis of these pieces is almost incidental to rapidly developing concepts of notational practice. *Permutations* for ten instruments (1956) is cast in pointillist mode, though the score of the last movement is conceived in a type of space-time notation. Although few composers moved without a backward glance from the old towards the new, there could not be a stronger nor more puzzling contrast than when the neo-classicism of *Quattro movimenti* (1957) is set against *Extremes* (1957, published in 1962), in which conventional signs and symbols (pitch classes, staves, metres) are totally replaced by new codes of conduct which seem to constrict rather than to liberate.

Schaeffer's didactic frame of mind was emphasised by *Tertium datur* (1958), the work with which he made his public debut at the 1960 'Warsaw Autumn'. Subtitled 'A Composer's Treatise for Harpsichord and

Instruments', it mixes conventional and graphic notation and conventional and experimental musical gestures. For the set of nine variations of the second movement, Schaeffer provides a diagrammatic plan; in each variation, there are eight 'phrases' (A–H), each made of rotations of one-, two-, three- and four-crotchet 'bars'. The instrumental ensemble is conventionally notated and functions as a cushion for the solo harpsichord. The notation of the solo part ranges from the totally specific to the speculative (Ex. 7.4). At this stage, Schaeffer had not yet mastered the difficult task of transferring sufficient input to the players to warrant his notational trials. There was, however, a considerable loosening of the pitch organisation into more flexible tropes and interval envelopes. Nevertheless, the schematic still controlled the intuitive.

One of the first composers to place his new serial work before the public was Kotoński. *Chamber Music* (1958) marked his return from the self-imposed 'internal' exile of the preceding years, when he had concentrated on ethnomusicological work in the Tatra mountains. This piece for twenty-one instruments is far from an academic affair and has more expressive warmth than have contemporaneous pieces by either Schaeffer or Serocki. Like the latter's *Musica concertante*, it is based on a single series, though *Chamber Music* has greater rhythmic flexibility and a broader motivic-timbral palette ranging from single notes to more contiguous thematic ideas (Ex. 7.5). Although Kotoński generally eschewed notational experimentation, he did produce a post-production graphic score for *Study on One Cymbal Stroke*, the first Polish piece of electronic music, created at Polish Radio's Experimental Studio. It was quickly followed by Dobrowolski's *Passacaglia na 40z5* (1959). Both works are brief in length and, if measured against what was happening in Cologne, Milan or Paris, rather basic. But that is not to diminish their symbolic importance in 1959. For each composer, this new creative resource was the start of a lifelong, though by no means exclusive interest in electronic music; together, they encouraged a long list of Polish composers who either dipped their toe in the waters (Penderecki's *Psalmus*, 1961, and Wiszniewski's *Db, Hz, Sec*, 1962) or made a more substantial contribution to the medium from the mid-1960s onwards (Schaeffer).

Penderecki's involvement with tape music was fleeting and his primary interests lay with instrumental possibilities. Like those of his contemporary, Górecki, his early student compositions drew on neo-classical models. In 1958, he was at his first crossroads. In *Psalms of David*, the third psalm is a patent derivative of Stravinsky's *Les noces* while the second ('Chorale') employs a twelve-note series in a conservatively melodic way. It is also noteworthy that this is the first Polish work since before socialist realism

Example 7.4. Schaeffer, *Tertium datur* (1958), second movement, harpsichord part, variations 4 (closing section) and 5.

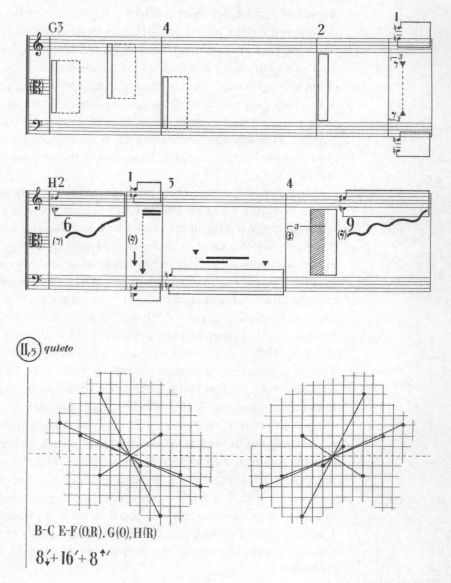

to have a transparently sacred dimension, a bold move for that time even though the execution of the task is carried out with a degree of objectivity away from any direct association with the established Roman Catholic church.[11] That same year, Penderecki began work on a quite different work, *Emanations* for two string orchestras, a successor and strong contrast to Serocki's neo-classical Sinfonietta, not least because the second

Example 7.5. Kotoński, *Chamber Music* (1958), second movement (♩ = 88), fig. 6.

Example 7.6. Penderecki, *Strophes* (1959) (♩ = 66, then touches 48 and settles on 55), bb. 69–71.

orchestra is tuned a semitone higher than normal. The traces of twelve-note invention here are overshadowed by a new concern for unconventional string sonorities, mainly rhythmic glissandi and pitch-bending by one third of a tone, for non-rhythmical tremolo and trills effected by heavy finger hammering on the string. Within two years, such explorations would dominate Penderecki's thinking (cf. the finger trills which open the First String Quartet, 1960), but in the meantime he wrote *Strophes*, the work which won him the top prize at the ZKP Young Composers' Competition mentioned earlier. It is effectively a mini-cantata (lasting about eight minutes), whose subtlety of instrumental and vocal inflection is one of the highlights of Polish music in the late 1950s (Ex. 7.6). It is perhaps the most ambitious of the three scores, although it does not make any advances in extending instrumental techniques. What it does do is appropriate pointillist gestures and combine them with an innovative selection of brief texts, by Menander, Sophocles, Isaiah, Jeremiah and Omar Khayyám, although by presenting them in their original languages the vocal contribution is colouristic rather than traditionally narrative. A solo soprano and speaker perform in tandem, interlacing conventional vocal production with a recitation that is notated as modified *Sprechstimme*. Through resourceful exploitation of the vocalists and a mixed chamber ensemble of flute, pitched and unpitched percussion and string trio, Penderecki creates a distinctively hyper-expressive sound world, a foretaste of the extroversion of his music of the 1960s onwards.[12]

Górecki's path was in some respects similar: an interest in vocal and instrumental pieces and a move through serialism towards new horizons. At times, these two contemporaries (Penderecki is two weeks older) seemed to be chasing each other's tail. Górecki's *Epitaph* was the work of a young composer who still had two years of compositional study to complete in Katowice, under the guidance of Szabelski. For a student composer who had inherited (and then savaged) the post-war neo-classical heritage in his *Sonata for Two Violins* (1957), and who had begun to show more avant-garde tendencies in his *Concerto for Five Instruments and String Quartet* (1957), the commissioning of a work for the 1958 'Warsaw Autumn' was an extraordinary break.[13] And the youngster demonstrated that, while matching Webern in terseness, he had his own approach to twelve-note organisation and was addressing the balance between serial and timbral concerns in a way whose individuality would become increasingly apparent in subsequent works.

Five Pieces for two pianos (1959) illustrates Górecki's unwillingness to maintain the centrality of the series. The fifth piece is an excellent example of a composer taking a series of twelve pitches and developing their potential

Example 7.7. Górecki, *Five Pieces* (1959), fifth movement, opening.

in contrary directions. The second of its two discrete halves, 'B', for Piano I only, turns quickly to complex twelve-note permutations while maintaining a regular pattern of subdividing each presentation of the series and sub-series into groups of three-, four- and five-note partitions. The permutational process rapidly becomes obscured, aided and abetted by high rates of change in dynamics, tempo, duration, register and attack, although there is little evidence of systematic serial applications to these parameters. And the final bar – an eleven-note chord followed by a solitary C sharp – suggests a denial of the serialist ideal, especially as it 'recapitulates' the essence of the first half of the piece, 'A'. 'A' is dominated not by the line but by the vertical (Ex. 7.7). It is a precise palindrome (Górecki has a penchant for mirror structures), with each bar dividing the twelve pitches between the two pianos in a simple procedure of alternating clusters (6:6; 7:5; 4:8; 9:3; 12:12; 3:9, etc.). The dynamic is almost entirely *ffff*, the rhythm a regular quaver pulse at a uniform tempo. The brutalising of neo-classicism in *Sonata for Two Violins* two years earlier is revisited here as Górecki constructs a new target: this brief but symptomatic confrontation with the linear, pointillistic world of early 1950s European serialism is a particularly vivid embodiment of a process that was taking place to some degree in the work of many Polish composers at this time.

The climax of Górecki's involvement in total serialism comes in the second movement 'Antiphon' of the First Symphony '1959' and in *Monologhi* (1960). This latter work is probably the closest any Polish composer came to the sound and technical world of pointillist total serialism. As in his next work, the orchestral *Scontri* (1960), Górecki deliberately sets out to explore the dynamic and durational properties of the numerical derivative of his twelve-note row (he also uses the number sequence to determine metrical change). Along the way, he is typically happy to modify his carefully mapped-out pre-compositional plan in order to admit intuitive use of material. *Monologhi* is constructed around the alternation and combination of its three instrumental groups, two of which consist each of metal percussion (suspended cymbals, gongs) and harp, while the third, which carries the kernel of the work, employs a solo soprano, pitched percussion (bells, vibraphone and marimba) and suspended cymbals. The text, Górecki's own, is subjected to extreme distortion and treated on a par with the instrumental parts. *Monologhi* displays an overwhelming sense of creative impatience and of a composer with a desire to break the serialist mould.

PART III

The search for individual identity

8 The pull of tradition

Bacewicz and Szabelski

Apart from the comic radio opera *The Adventure of King Arthur* (1959), Bacewicz was silent for two years before the premiere of her Sixth String Quartet at the 1960 'Warsaw Autumn'. In it, she made a belated attempt to come to terms with dodecaphony. She was far from convinced, however, that the move would prove fruitful, as she observed on at least two occasions that year:

> In writing [my] Sixth String Quartet, I want to sustain certain sections with serial technique, but at the same time I want to give it a different character than usual. Present-day pointillism does not interest me very much – it is perhaps a rather narrow path, a trend without a great future. On the other hand I am struck by electronic music: it invents new sound colours and new rhythms . . . I am less curious about experiments that combine creativity and its execution, such as aleatoricism, etc.[1]

> My Sixth Quartet was played at the Festival; it irritated some of the oldies (e.g., Sikorski) but surprised the youngsters. These latter thought that I am already incapable of moving forward, so they have begun to acknowledge me anew . . . The young are perhaps too surprised (that's their right!), but the middle [generation] endeavours to make music from this 'strangeness', not just experiments. In any case, there's no progress without freedom of experimentation.[2]

In fact, only the first movement shows real engagement with serial techniques, and they are applied only to pitch. Elsewhere, she is more at home with the sort of intuitive atonality which came to characterise her music partly based on tonal centres, partly reliant on the sequential passage work which peppers her music of the 1960s. What was not in doubt in the 1960s was her achievement in two particular spheres: firstly to have used her existing experience in devising non-repetitive developmental structures in which exposition and recapitulation play minor roles and, secondly, to have pursued her gifts for texture (pre-eminently in the slow movements of her music of the 1940s and 50s) and promoted them to the forefront of the best works of her last decade.

Each of the four movements of the Sixth Quartet is witness to her desire to move forwards on the first front, even if the traces of neo-classical rhythmic drive, especially in the 6/8 metre of the finale, sometimes do not mesh entirely with more reflective moments. But this admixture of the old and the new is quite deliberate and gives her music its character and edge. Bacewicz more successfully approaches the avant-garde on the second front in the opening movement (the initial combination of muted harmonics and glissandi is particularly alluring) and in the third, where she explores stasis and texture with great subtlety, detuning the first violin's E string down a semitone in order to exploit tritonal relationships with A natural. Such passages are among the first instances where it is possible to detect her interest in electronic music. Conversely, her unwillingness both here and elsewhere to use unconventional performance techniques or aleatory processes means that her rapprochement with new sound worlds remains somewhat restricted.

Pensieri notturni for chamber orchestra (1961) epitomises these trends and deservedly became one of her best-known pieces after its premiere at the Venice Biennale in April 1961. Despite obvious links with the Bartókian vein of 'night music', this work is more a consequence of the thematic and structural dissolution of the middle movement of *Music for Strings, Trumpets and Percussion*. It proceeds by means of loose associations between trills, elusive glissandi, daubs of individual colour, fleeting glimpses of motivic fragments, generally unconcerned about large-scale forward momentum. Bacewicz uses pedal points as periodic foci (G natural is prominent in the early stages) and with great delicacy allows the whim of the moment to dictate the piece's gentle, unforced trajectory (Ex. 8.1). Even the appearance of 6/8 gigue rhythms is tempered by the veiled discourse in which they form but one of many transient ideas. Only at the end, with its sequence of short phrases in the woodwind, does *Pensieri notturni* seem more grounded, touching an expressive and perhaps elegiac note. The closing bars disappear into the ether like the ending of Szymanowski's First Violin Concerto or Górecki's *Scontri*.

In the last eight years of her life, Bacewicz returned to something approaching her normal rate of output. This time, however, despite the success of *Pensieri notturni*, she harboured ever-increasing doubts as to the direction she might take when surrounded by so much that was new, some of which she found inimical. There were occasional backward glances, as in the nimble and spirited Divertimento for strings (1965), as well as new ideas, such as the exploration of Lutosławskian harmonic fields in the second and third movements of the Concerto for Orchestra (1962) and the 'Dialogo' in *Musica sinfonica* (1965). Among works which achieve an effective and persuasive balance of the several currents in Bacewicz's music are

Example 8.1. Bacewicz, *Pensieri notturni* (1961) (Largetto), fig. 4.

Contradizione (1966) and *In una parte* (1967). The former is cast in two movements, 'Grave' and 'Acuto', further emphasising her interest in developing new structural designs. It is a dynamic and highly expressive piece; the 'Acuto' movement is ample evidence, along with the one-movement *In una parte* (1967), that by this stage Bacewicz had found the means to create a symphonic allegro almost entirely from the aggressive juxtaposition of ever-changing lines and textures. Nevertheless, the methods of controlling rhythmic ebb and flow, or of creating momentum, are ultimately rooted in her neo-classical experience. The most curious experiment is the *Quartet for Four Cellos* (1964). This dark and pensive work makes few concessions. It too is cast in just two movements – 'Narrazione' and 'Riflessione' – both of which eschew formal stereotypes. Bacewicz chose this unusual ensemble because of its colouristic potential, and yet its high quotient of dissonance and the gritty determination with which the music shifts from introverted stasis to extrovert activity promote an unsettled, austere and almost pugilistic atmosphere which remains totally unresolved. For many observers, restless through-composition has been Bacewicz's strongest attribute, but for her it became a sign of unwanted creative tensions.

Baird was a great admirer of her music and detected that she had lost a degree of confidence: 'It seems that in the last years of her compositional life Grażyna Bacewicz was not spared from nervousness and anxiety, perhaps because it seemed to her that music was moving quickly forwards while she was lagging behind, losing touch.'[3] The fact that most works from the late 1960s borrow material from earlier works, sometimes wholesale, suggests a degree of uncertainty.[4] More pervasively, the 'Prelude' and 'Intermezzo' from the Partita (1955) furnished important thematic ideas for several of her last works, including *In una parte*, *Contradizione* and the ballet *Desire* (1968). The most intensive example of this patchworking of existing material is the central movement of the Viola Concerto (1968).

Bacewicz's output of the 1960s is but one example of the many works by Parisian-educated Polish composers trying to come to terms with an almost totally alien musical environment. More than most, she tackled the issues head on. For Bacewicz, engaging with the new could not be a token gesture; sometimes it worked, sometimes it did not, but she was not going to be a slave to any conventions, new or old. She rapidly developed a non-systematic free atonality, combined it with her extraordinary intuition with regard to rhythmic and formal structures, and produced music that was distinctive, impulsive and often more revealing of the turmoil of these years than that produced by more consciously avant-garde composers.

If at times her contemporaries thought Bacewicz had betrayed cherished neo-classical principles by essaying new compositional techniques and textures, they can but have been open-mouthed at the audacity of Szabelski, a member of the oldest generation who, like Szeligowski, had turned sixty in 1956. His output under socialist realism had been small: Symphony no. 3 (1951), *Heroic Poem* (*Poemat bohaterski*, 1952) and Concerto grosso (1954). These few pieces betrayed many of the signs of the times: monumentalism, baroque structures, a sombre tone that drew on both Hindemith and Shostakovich, though there was an unusual lack of folklore. His next pieces, the Concertino for piano and orchestra (1955), Second String Quartet (1956) and Fourth Symphony (1957), posited a tougher, more dissonant idiom. Szabelski appeared to be settling, like many of his contemporaries, including Bacewicz who was twelve years his junior, for a modest update of his existing style.

To what extent he was then influenced by the firebrand whom he had taken on as a student in 1955 is hard to determine, but a chronological comparison of the outputs of Szabelski and Górecki in the late 1950s suggests at the very least a strong mutual awareness. When *Improvisations* for choir and orchestra (1959) was premiered at the 1959 'Warsaw Autumn', in a programme which included Webern's Symphony and the premiere of Penderecki's *Strophes*, the shock was palpable. Szabelski strode into the avant-garde camp with the swagger of someone half his age. Contained within a simple ternary framework (Adagio–Presto–Adagio), this seven-minute piece runs the gamut of spare pointillist textures and occasional ensemble flurries created from basic twelve-note manipulations. Gone are any traces of motoric rhythms or neoclassical gestures. Most notable, however, is the fact that, for the first time in Polish music, the choral part had no coherent text but simply isolated syllables, treating the voices on a par with the orchestra. As one critic put it: 'By becoming openly involved in the avant-garde movement, Szabelski has, by virtue of his compositional authority, given his moral backing and active patronage to the youngest composers.'[5]

Szabelski's radical rethink was confirmed by *Sonnets* for orchestra (1958), *Verses* (*Wiersze*) for piano and orchestra (1961) and *Aphorisms '9'* for chamber ensemble (1962). He developed his new technique further by building structures from what he called 'mottos' (*hasła*), 'short, fairly distinctive motifs, a-thematic sound structures', which bore within themselves the seeds of new ideas that would provide new conflicts, tensions and contrasts (Ex. 8.2).[6] For Szabelski, this was the key to liberating himself from dodecaphonic expectations while at the same time remaining more faithful to twelve-note procedures than most other Polish composers, especially in the early 1960s. He uses the series as a basis for textural variations, often deploying it more or less complete for each motto, teasing the ear with unpredictable sequences of single pitches, flurries of notes and timbres, and chords of up

Example 8.2. Szabelski, *Verses* (*Wiersze*, 1961), first movement, opening.

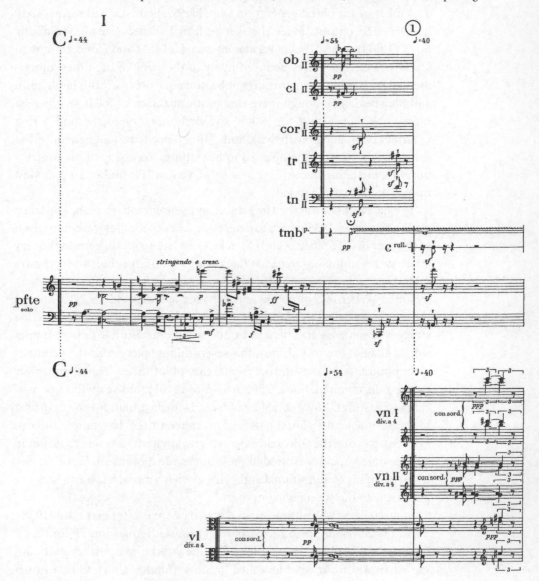

to twelve pitch classes. Incorporating his use of unpitched percussion, the results are often startling in their flamboyance (a surprise from so personally reticent a man as Szabelski).

Verses was premiered at the 1961 'Warsaw Autumn' in the same concert as Lutosławski's *Venetian Games* and Penderecki's *Threnody* and lost little in the comparison. The dynamism and energy of each of its four short movements are striking; regardless of tempo, the music is propulsive in a non-schematic way. As in Górecki's *Scontri*, finished a year earlier, ideas are bounced off each other, hocket-like, creating a rich variety of timbral-rhythmic textures and a compelling forward momentum. And the vibrancy of this score is aided by Szabelski's use of the piano as *primus inter pares*; in fact, *Verses* is one of the very few Polish concertante works from this period and it plays as significant a role in his output as does *Espressioni varianti* in Baird's.

Szabelski's next piece, *Aphorisms '9'*, is appropriately titled. Its small mixed ensemble of nine players led Szabelski to consolidate his textures less through verticalisation of the series than through linear means, highlighting both single sustained lines as well as contrapuntal groups rather than returning to the pointillism of *Improvisations*. The resultant five-minute score is genuinely aphoristic, a subtle balance of lyricism and vigour, proceeding by the same elastic process of tension–release. Szabelski further aligns himself with the younger generation by employing for the first time one of the new notational symbols (an upwards arrowhead indicating the highest note possible; its use, along with glissandi, also marks the climax).

The first of the three contiguous sections of *Preludes* for chamber orchestra (1963) is not only one of the clearest examples of the use of mottos but also reveals that their previously small-scale interaction has developed into longer-breathed instrumental choruses – four upper woodwind, five brass, unpitched percussion, piano and nine strings. Each of these five timbral blocks has distinctive material, a feature which is most memorably developed in the climaxes of the second and third preludes. In the second prelude, for example, hocketing brass are offset by group glissandi on the strings and repetitive figurations in the woodwind. In the hands of Lutosławski, textures like these would have been given some aleatory freedom to avoid any sense of motivic redundancy, but Szabelski, like Bacewicz, was unwilling to relinquish control in this way and perhaps relished the fixed, almost muscular heterophony that resulted. Szabelski's interest in block timbres is intensified in the one-movement Flute Concerto (1964), premiered by Gazzelloni at the Zagreb Biennale in 1965. The excision of all the orchestral woodwind not only offsets the soloist but simultaneously highlights the other family choruses, much as in *Preludes*. But his increasingly large-scale paragraphing is underlined by dividing the work into five sections dictated by the use of different sizes of flute: standard–alto–piccolo–bass–standard. The central section involving piccolo, brass and unpitched percussion (the whole framed by the string body moving in homophonic glissandi) is indicative of how Szabelski moved from the exuberant contrasts and tensions of *Verses* to a less hurried but equally symphonic discourse.

After a gap of four years, Szabelski produced a further surprise by composing a Fifth Symphony (1968), scored for chorus, organ and orchestra. Not only had the genre been ignored by most Polish composers since 1956 – Górecki's First and Lutosławski's Second (1967) being the most notable exceptions – but it marked a return to the monumentalism which had seemingly been discarded after his Fourth Symphony. And yet its gigantic chorusing (the brass here has strengths of 6.4.4.1), multi-layered heterophony (now mixing *a battuta* with *ad libitum*), pitch organisation, ostinati and repeated fragments all have their roots in the works of the mid-1960s. Its newly ecstatic and cosmic tone conjures up associations with Scriabin and Szymanowski (Third Symphony), as well as anticipating two works dedicated to the five-hundredth anniversary of the birth of the Polish astronomer, Copernicus, in 1473: his own *Mikołaj Kopernik* (1975) and Górecki's Second Symphony 'Copernican' (1972). The Fifth Symphony's two-part structure, the quotation in the closing moments of a sacred chant on the brass, and the central role assigned to the chorus have strong resonances in Górecki's music from *Old Polish Music* (*Muzyka staropolska*, 1967–9) through to *Beatus vir* (1979).

The most striking aspect of *Mikołaj Kopernik* and Szabelski's final work, the Piano Concerto (1978), is the sense that each is laconically made up of disparate fragments, with pared-down textures and structures. The Piano Concerto (which lasts less than seven minutes) is particularly idiosyncratic, its sequence of events open to interpretation as mere rambling or as an omen of postmodernism. It was an uncertain end to a career which had made the most radical shift in Polish music after 1956.

Baird

> I am not one of those people who wanted to wreck or ruin. I wanted, as far as
> I was able, to find myself in the stream of national tradition. Musical opinion
> calls me a romantic, which I acknowledge.[7]

It was evident from *Four Essays* that Baird was avoiding the more modish path to the new music of post-Webernian serialism. He had found Berg and admired the German's blend of an expressionist agenda with late nineteenth-century and early twentieth-century emotional candour. More trenchant was Baird's observation that Berg was able to flex the twelve-note technique to include, not exclude, possibilities for tonal reference. And whereas Berg was fond of pre-compositional formal designs, Baird preferred to trust his intuitions. Paradoxically, Baird remained more faithful to his twelve-note series than most, at least until the mid-1960s. At that point he relinquished that support while still composing works which in many respects sound as if they are dodecaphonic.

Although *Four Essays* marked his breakthrough, its stylistic juxtapositions (perhaps due to duplications with his incidental music for Shakespeare's *Henry IV* earlier in 1958, as well as to borrowings from *Divertimento*) militates against it as a defining statement. *Espressioni varianti*, on the other hand, the first of several concertante works he wrote over the next two decades (*Four Dialogues*, 1964, Oboe Concerto, 1973, *Concerto lugubre*, 1975 and *Scenes*, 1977), demonstrates several key mature features: a pervading lyricism (many thought it old-fashioned, or 'romantic', at a time when these were dirty words), an instinctive understanding of rhapsody as a structural vehicle and of the orchestra as a chamber ensemble, an avoidance of any newfangled technical device that he deemed inappropriate (and that meant all but a few notational ideas which enhanced his expressive range) and a parallel compositional ethos which emphasised the personal and the intimate rather than any suggestion of abstract formulation. These were evidence of his understanding of tradition; 'national' referred not to folklore (which, like Lutosławski, he never touched again after socialist realism) but to Szymanowski, Karłowicz and earlier composers.

The *Variations without a Theme* (1962) and *Epiphany Music* (1963) are especially persuasive examples of Baird's new direction. The title of the former is indicative of Baird's quest for an inner coherence reliant more on emotional expressiveness than on obvious technical procedures. Orchestration and, to a lesser extent, tempo are the main defining elements. He highlights solo instruments – saxophone, flute, violin, oboe and clarinet – as well as using the occasional tutti and string doubling (for example, the big but brief Bergian theme which emerges in the centre of the work). Other characteristics include quasi-tonal melodic inflections, occasional block textures whose inner variety is caused not by aleatory slippage between parts but by painstakingly composed-out variants for each instrument, and the use of intermittent pitch centres (e.g., the use of D sharp in the coda).

Epiphany Music epitomises Baird's artistic outlook in the 1960s and reveals that his abiding interest in literature was not confined to his vocal compositions:

> The work's title results from an attempt to transfer to music the
> constructional 'method' invented in literature by James Joyce, which he
> applies consistently from his youthful *Epiphanies* to *Finnegans Wake*.
> *Epiphany Music* is therefore a series of short impressionistic sketches of an

improvisatory character linked seamlessly together as an integral whole. It is a series of instantaneous, almost involuntary emotional manifestations; there is no pre-established schema in this piece and the sole formal determinant is the rapid and transient 'ebb and flow' of emotion.[8]

This process clearly has roots in preceding pieces, but *Epiphany Music* is far from being merely a sequence of unrelated ideas. On the macro-level, there is a deliberate move towards closure near the end, which recalls the opening palindromically in terms of instrumentation (for clarinet, percussion and, primarily, solo cello), motivic material and pitch organisation. Insofar as tempo indications in a seemingly improvisatory work have validity, the work progresses for the most part at an even Andante. But not for nothing is this qualified by indications such as 'agitato', 'improvisando', 'inquieto' or 'moderato', quite apart from numerous other markings which emphasise the Joycean concept of stream of consciousness. Discernible stages in the music's narrative are also distinguished, once again, by instrumentation for solos and duets, whose reflective utterances are punctuated by short flurries for larger ensembles. Pitch unisons (those on C, B flat and G being the most noticeable) act as temporary points of reference in an essentially dodecaphonic score.

The opening is a locus classicus of Baird's preferred way to start his compositions (Ex. 8.3) and bears an uncanny resemblance to the prophetic opening of Panufnik's *Nocturne*, composed fifteen years earlier. An open-string 'quasi niente' C on a solo cello (molto sul tasto) is accompanied by a gentle roll on the bass drum. The second entry accumulates new meaning: the cello C is now molto sul ponticello, the roll is on cassa piccola, there is an arabesque on bass clarinet, and the dynamic range of the crescendo–decrescendo envelope is slightly higher. At the third entry, the solo cello (*pp*, ordinario and pizzicato) responds briefly to this arabesque and a roll on a side drum is capped not only by a glissando ripple on the rim of a timpanum but also by a second arabesque, this time by clarinet and flute. By the time of the fourth entry (where the drum is now a tamburello basco), the only trace of the cello's rootedness on C is the initial grace-note, and the music moves off into a new area.

Baird's imaginative attention to detail and to the careful balancing of continuity and change is characteristic. As the piece progresses, other methods of realising ebb and flow and of subliminal association are brought into play (Ex. 8.4). These can be as traditional as eliding pitch classes – the transference of B flat from cello (the end of the first major section) to clarinet (bb. 24–5) – or using a pitch centre such as the surreptitious start of a pedal on G (b. 33), which in this case eventually explodes nine bars later

Example 8.3. Baird, *Epiphany Music* (1963), opening.

into the first brief Bergian melodic phrase (assai cantabile). The support given to the main melody instrument(s) at any one time is also signifi-cant (cf. the contrasts and continuities between the four main textures in bb. 25–7, 27–30, 30–4, which overlaps with the strings from b. 33). Baird uses instrumental shadowing at close quarters and at a distance: the tom-toms (bb. 30–4) pick up on the flute *frullato* (b. 30) before transferring their atten-tion to the clarinet, whose melodic and rhythmic profile is closely matched. Meanwhile, the 'quasi solo' claves in b. 32 elaborate the clarinet rhythm

Example 8.4. Baird, *Epiphany Music* (1963), bb. 24–34.

from three bars earlier. This associative process enables Baird to create a rich and allusive sequence in which the protagonists (the solo instruments) represent the 'I' of an intimate drama into which all of the participants are drawn.

Given Baird's literary interests, it was natural that he would be interested in music with text. He wrote three small song cycles for female voice and orchestra, all to poetry by female poets: *Love Poems* (*Erotyki*) to words by Małgorzata Hillar (1961), *Four Songs* to words by the Croatian poet Vesna Parun (1966) and *Five Songs* to words by Halina Poświatowska (1968). All three set epigrammatic, short-versed texts, perfectly suited to Baird's

Example 8.4. (*cont.*)

preference for allusory emotional utterances. *Love Poems* is graceful and
tender in tone, each of the six songs (apart from the all-embracing orchestration of the last) characterised by a particular instrumental complement.
Baird's chamber textures here have no brass and the only woodwind are
an alto flute and an alto saxophone which, along with a guitar, provide
the instrumental counterpoint to the solo soprano. The later two cycles,
for mezzo-soprano and chamber orchestra, are in contrast subdued and

desolate. The *Four Songs* are permeated by a deep-seated melancholy bordering on despair and alienation, while the *Five Songs* are preoccupied with abandonment, with matters of love and death, light and darkness. The latter's orchestration for just sixteen instruments is as delicate as in other works of the period, but the tone and tessitura is reminiscent of Szymanowski's early *Three Songs*, op. 5, in which poetic fragments by Jan Kasprowicz provoked some of the composer's darkest music.

The most sombre of Baird's pieces at this time, however, was his one-hour, one-act musical drama, *Tomorrow* (*Jutro*, 1964–6), based on a short story by that quintessentially troubled Polish writer, Joseph Conrad. As a genre, Polish opera had never really established itself in the twentieth century (Szymanowski's *King Roger* remained the only one in regular repertoire). After 1956, socialist-realist operas disappeared and few composers took up the challenge of a traditional genre in an artistic milieu dominated by concert music. Of those that did, Witold Rudziński was most active, composing the full-scale *The Commandant of Paris* (*Komendant Paryża*, 1958), *The Dismissal of the Greek Envoys* (*Odprawa posłów greckich*, 1962) and *The Shulamite* (*Sulamita*, 1964), the first of which is a late echo of socialist-realist subject matter. But of Baird's generation, none apart from the conductor-composer Henryk Czyz (1923–2002), who wrote two comic operas in the early 1960s, had composed anything notable for the operatic stage. Of those born in the 1930s, only Penderecki would contribute in a major way.

The impact of *Tomorrow* was considerable, not least because its subject matter was far from the exoticism of its Polish predecessors. It is set at night-time in a nameless place by the sea, at the edge of civilisation. The delusional Ozias (bass) waits for his renegade son Harry (spoken role) to return from abroad. His only neighbours are the blind carpenter Joshua (baritone), with whom he constantly argues, and Joshua's young daughter, Jessica (mezzo-soprano). Both Joshua and Jessica, for their different reasons, are eager for the outsider to return. When Harry does turn up, Ozias does not recognise him, and when Harry's advances on Jessica lead to attempted rape, Ozias kills him, all the while waiting for the Harry in his mind to come back, tomorrow: 'for the sake of fiction he destroys reality'.[9]

Tomorrow's librettist, Jerzy S. Sito, heightened the psychological and dramatic tension of the original, with the result that a sense of self-deception and delusion affects all of the characters. Joshua, a minor character once the opening scene passes, is preoccupied with the forces of nature – the sea, storms – and does not understand his daughter. Jessica, the only character who is not heartless, has built up an idealised picture of Harry and of their future together. Ozias's fantasy image of his son is so vivid that he cannot acknowledge the reality of the brutal ne'er-do-well who suddenly appears. Jessica is the only one who, at the end, has any understanding of what has happened and even she is left with her heart, and perhaps also her mind, broken by the experience. Certain parallels with Berg's *Wozzeck* and Britten's *Peter Grimes* (Polish premiere at the 1958 'Warsaw Autumn') are not hard to see. The most obvious debt is to Act III of *Wozzeck*: Baird's depiction of the rape scene and Harry's murder is contained in one twelve-note orchestral chord which builds up texturally and dynamically to a climax where the brass accentuate the chord three times as Ozias strikes his son dead. Krystyna Tarnawska-Kaczorowska has persuasively argued that Baird associates tonal events and instrumentation with certain characters.[10] Jessica, for example, is associated with the (alto) flute, alto saxophone and strings (cf. *Love Poems*).

Closely tied in with such timbral devices is Baird's use of gestural motivic types associated with specific emotional states, rather than with specific characters (in other words, the psychological temperature of the musical drama interested Baird much more than character delineation). Tarnawska-Kaczorowska identifies five of these, ranging from 'tenderness–affection–longing' (sustained strings, seconds and minor thirds) and 'love–lust–excitement' (alto saxophone) to 'anxiety–fear–foreboding' (string harmonics), 'distress–perturbation' (syncopation, especially on brass and percussion) and 'anger–irritation' (loud, fast, often violent chromatic flurries). These can serve only as spasmodic indications as the score is more broadly conceived than a list of motivic types might suggest, though the 'love–lust–excitement' and 'anger–irritation' motivic types are the most ear-catching. It would be tempting to reference such emotional embodiments to other works (the use of the alto saxophone is an obvious possibility), but it is more prudent to see their wider implications in an associative rather than a concrete way, in keeping with Baird's compositional ethos.

And yet Baird invited such a comparison in his next major orchestral piece, *Sinfonia breve* (1968), where the build-up to the main climax of its first movement, 'Epos', (Ex. 8.5) is an evident chordal variant of the crescendo from *Tomorrow*'s rape scene and the climactic three iterations which marked the murder of Harry. In *Sinfonia breve*, however, a resolution of the critical moment is achieved by inserting a new chordal climax at this point and the escape is led by a solo oboe; *Tomorrow* has no such closure. *Sinfonia breve* is also a signpost to the future. The contrasts between solo timbres, of which the oboe is paramount (it is the sole representative of its family amongst the otherwise triple woodwind), and the more muscular tuttis of

Example 8.5. Baird, *Sinfonia breve* (1968), first movement, bb. 70–3.

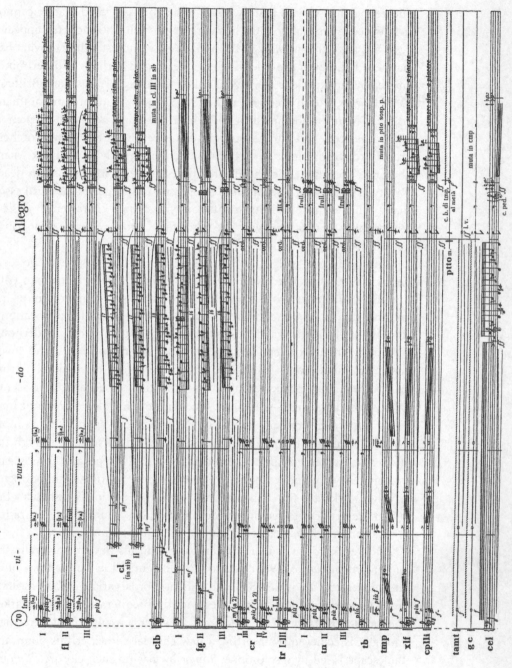

Example 8.5. (*cont.*)

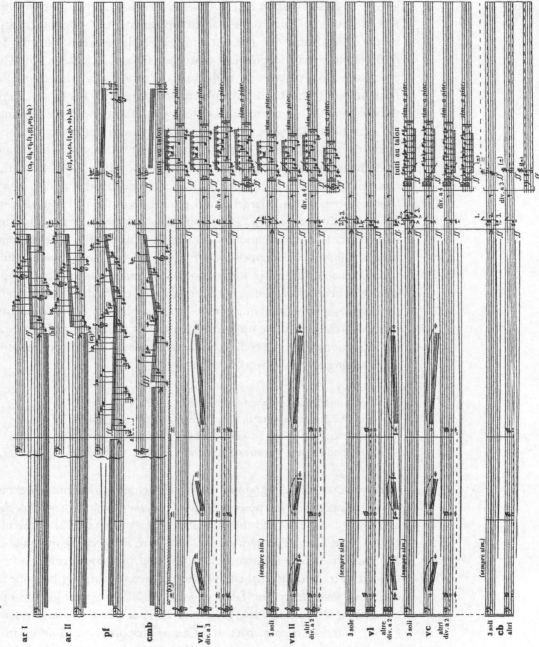

a larger orchestra than in *Epiphany Music* creates greater tensions in which Baird seems to back off from sustained confrontation. The decade is capped by the Third Symphony (1969), composed eighteen years after the Second Symphony with its prescient sobriquet, 'Quasi una fantasia'. The Third Symphony's four movements, with a total duration of some sixteen minutes, relate in outline to classical symphonic structure, with the finale carrying the weight of the argument (a procedure which Lutosławski was refining at the same time). There are familiar protagonists (clarinet in the first movement, the oboe elsewhere), though the solo–tutti dialectic is tilting away from the former towards groups of instruments. Where the 'ebb and flow' was perceptible in the intimacy of chamber dialogue, it is now at least as likely to occur between larger family groups, as in the first tutti sequence in the opening movement. The symphony even breaks with Baird's own indifference to the convention of a rousing ending – something he seemed to have diligently sidestepped for over a decade – by concluding the finale with a climactic tutti and a fortissimo trill for wind, brass and pitched percussion. There is little sense, however, of a modernist slant on symphonic development, rather that of a composer reassessing the dramatic potential of a full orchestra to face up to certain issues of technique and expression the attractions of which could no longer be denied. As he commented in 1973, talking about this work:

> Up to now I have rebuked reality rather mildly and calmly. Now I am becoming angry, sceptical, bitter. This could not have continued without influencing my work. I do not want to write untruths. I want to distance myself and that is why my current music is more vehement.[11]

Baird's quasi-autobiographical search for genuine, transmittable expression continued with the powerful cantata *Goethe-Briefe* for baritone, choir and orchestra (1970) and the orchestral *Psychodrama* (1972) – 'the most brutal piece I have ever written'.[12] These were followed by the emotionally indicative *Elegy* for orchestra (1973) and *Concerto lugubre* for viola and orchestra and his final composition, a second work for baritone and orchestra, *Voices from Afar* (*Głosy z oddali*, 1981). There were less obviously charged pieces, such as *Play* (1971) and *Variations in the Form of a Rondo* (1978), both for string quartet, and *Canzona* for orchestra (1980), with its irresistible use of instrumental chorusing. Nevertheless, the overwhelming tone of Baird's music after *Tomorrow* was sombre.

Baird's impassioned setting of love letters between Goethe and Charlotte von Stein draws not only on Wagner's *Tristan und Isolde* (an early motivic allusion), late Mahler and Berg but also on Schoenberg (*A Survivor from Warsaw*) and Webern's two cantatas. Nearer home, there are parallels with the vocal writing in Penderecki's *St Luke Passion* (1966) and *Dies Irae* (1967), though Penderecki's pieces are more public displays of wracked emotion than the essentially private vehemence of Baird's score. The contrast between orchestral and choral eruptions and the intense restraint of the solo baritone reinforces Baird's sensitivity to textual nuance, as may also be observed in the valedictory *Voices from Afar*. It is perhaps appropriate that the latter work's three poetic fragments by Iwaszkiewicz, who had written texts for several works by Szymanowski, should inspire Baird at times to emulate the latter's sense of heightened awareness. The opening movement, 'I Stand by the Eternal Lake', with its sustained octave G naturals and quiet contemplative mood, recalls in pared-down terms the world of Szymanowski's Third Symphony. But where Szymanowski celebrates life, love and God, Baird chooses poetry about life recollected from beyond or on the brink of death. In the final song, 'In the Church', the protagonist, standing in front of a statue of the martyred St Agatha, rails against God and his inaction in the face of the world's natural and man-made disasters ('Silence is Your system. What is there on Your side?'). The bitterness of this text is complemented by concentrated musical images, powered by variants of the 'Dies Irae' motif, and a pained, inconclusive resolution in which Baird returns to the plangent tones of arguably his favourite instrument, the oboe.

The elegiac anguish of these scores also permeates the purely instrumental works of Baird's last decade. Yet Baird's view of the world, as expressed through his music, is by no means limited to that of fateful resignation, especially in the chamber and concertante works such as *Play* and the Oboe Concerto. *Scenes* for cello, harp and orchestra, with its subtitle 'Conversation, Dispute and Reconciliation', gives a deliberately anthropomorphic slant to the genre of the double concerto. Autobiographical stimuli are never far from the surface (*Concerto lugubre* was dedicated to his recently deceased mother). To what extent *Psychodrama* had a personal dimension is impossible to determine, but it remains one of the most compelling post-war Polish orchestral scores and perhaps his greatest achievement. Within its span of under nine minutes (it is one of his shortest compositions), it accumulates a counterpoint of tensions that is breathtaking in its emotional rawness. It underlines the fact that Baird's strength lay in the invocation of semi-abstract musical drama characterised by an intuitive subtlety of detail, penetrating psychological insight, and a powerful sense of unease. Moments of rest are deceptive and unnerving, confrontation is impulsive and brutal. His outlook and spirit were romantic, laced with a very personal twentieth-century angst.

Lutosławski

Lutosławski's relationship with the past was altogether more considered. After the careful explorations of the *Five Songs* and *Funeral Music*, it became evident to Lutosławski that he had come to a crisis point in the Three Postludes. Their composition was spread over two years: no. 1 was completed in September 1958, no. 2 in August 1960, and no. 3 in April 1959; a fourth postlude was abandoned. The last to be completed, no. 2, is also the most retrospective and is a lame cousin of the so-called 'blurred toccata' style of the Concerto for Orchestra's second movement. The first Postlude, the only one which Lutosławski was later prepared to conduct, is notable for the harmonic–timbral stratification of the twelve notes in its outer sections (the central section sounds tired and ineffective in comparison). Against a carefully judged continuum of string harmonies and utilising a ten-bar rhythmic pattern, four groups of instruments flicker in almost pointillistic fashion, their fleeting motifs based on a sequence of crab-like chromatics (oboes, high piano), thirds (trumpets and harps), tritones and minor ninths (flutes, xylophone and celesta) and perfect intervals (clarinets, low piano). This potent exploration of the harmonic spectrum was to resonate in later works. The third postlude is at once the most daring and the least successful. Its attempt to engineer a macro-rhythmic accelerando and intensity of momentum by repeating a sequence of ten discrete timbral–thematic ideas, on the second, third and fourth occasion reducing their duration, is too patent and arch. The final iteration, where each idea is given only one bar, is cut short after only seven bars and the ensuing climax of repeated quaver chords, whose orchestration harks back to *Little Suite*, fails to gel with what precedes it. Nevertheless, the schematic significance of the experiment cannot be underestimated, as it not only provided the basis for the finale of *Venetian Games* (1960–1), but also found real fruition in works such as the Second Symphony (1967) and, most spectacularly, *Livre pour orchestre* (1968).

The story of Lutosławski's escape from this impasse is well known. He heard Cage's *Concert for Piano and Orchestra* in a radio broadcast in 1960 and had a flash of inspiration: a degree of controlled aleatoricism would liberate him from the micro-rhythmic cul-de-sac of the Three Postludes. *Venetian Games* was the first product of this new outlook and marks the second pivotal point in Lutosławski's career. Later in the 1960s, Lutosławski sent the manuscript score to John Cage and wrote in his covering letter: 'You became a spark in the powder-keg – I am inexpressibly grateful to you.'[13] The conventional wisdom, and one led and fostered by the composer, has been primarily that the freeing of the composer and performers from the need to coordinate musical lines rhythmically enabled Lutosławski to develop a new expressivity and genuine flexibility in the design and implementation of his fledgling twelve-note harmonic language. This gave Lutosławski's compositions from 1961 onwards both a variety and a stylistic identity that made his music stand out not only from that of his compatriots but also from that of composers in other countries. In fact, his solution to the 'tumult' was quite unlike any other and made him the least typical of all Polish composers after 1956. It was a truly imaginative leap, lending his music a resonance and character which had enormous compositional potential. From this moment, Lutosławski had secured his creative future, and he knew it: 'A composer's individual technique is like alcohol in an addict's veins. Three small glasses are enough to get him drunk. A little invention is enough to compose a musical work.'[14]

There were, however, other facets to this shift. Firstly, there was his willingness between 1961 and 1964 to embrace a raw, edgy tone rather than the considered, almost suave persona he cultivated elsewhere. Prime examples are the blunt contrasts in the outer movements of *Venetian Games*, the dramatic confrontations of 'Le grand combat' in *Trois poèmes d'Henri Michaux* for forty-part choir, woodwind, brass and percussion (1963), and the energetic jousting of the String Quartet (1964). Other composers, as different as Bacewicz and Górecki, were also going through their own creative turmoil at this time, and Lutosławski's more extrovert avant-gardisms should also be regarded as part of the general Zeitgeist. Secondly, the desire to concentrate on harmony, and to keep the twelve pitch classes more or less in play at any one time, curtailed his opportunities for highlighting individual lines, although there are a few exceptions, such as the flute obbligato in the third movement of *Venetian Games* or, in a different way, the chamber interplay of the String Quartet. In this regard, he presented a strong contrast to Baird's concurrent focus on the solo melodic line. Thirdly, and as a direct though not inevitable result of his basic reliance on twelve-note harmonies, articulated by what he called variously 'limited aleatoricism' or 'aleatory counterpoint', Lutosławski had to rethink radically the small-scale musculature of his music. To borrow syntactical terminology, he could determine medium-scale form – chapters, paragraphs, sentences – by flexing the duration, dynamics, density, register and timbre of the 'ad libitum' sections, but how was he to characterise these at the level of clause, word or even syllable? The question was not simply one of liberating rhythm, but whether the motif, the staple element of his earlier music, had a meaningful place in an overwhelmingly harmonic idiom. It is in this domain that some of the most interesting developments took place in his music of this decade.

Venetian Games occupies a Janus-like position. The second movement's 'blurred toccata' is conventionally metred, but Lutosławski's handling of the material masks this framework. In the macro-accelerando of the finale, the individual ideas are now freed of metric constraints and instead of appearing purely sequentially are piled upon one another until the resultant 'chaos' is decisively exploded and demolished. Its formal logic, however crudely realised, has an organic inevitability which the third Postlude had not achieved. When Lutosławski's approach to melody is considered, the flute solo in the third movement is notable for its construction from a series of distinct motivic fragments, some of which seem to have sprung from an earlier style period, although together they form an early example of his mature 'cantilenas'. These motivic fragments are lifted from the first movement and it is here that Lutosławski's tussles in characterising his textural–harmonic blocks first appeared. The first movement has two developing and contrasted interlocking blocks. Each textural block is as differentiated from the other as Lutosławski could manage; and each is marked by a sharp percussive punctuation, an almost filmic intercutting device he first tried out in the macro-rhythmic accelerando of the third Postlude and one to which he returned on many occasions (in *Slides* (*Przezrocza*), 1988, it becomes the work's raison d'être). The first movement of *Venetian Games* works because neither block is quite the same on each of its four statements, the first being altered by adding timbral–motivic material on successive appearances, the second by shifting harmonic content and varying a basic set of motivic ideas. A stark abstract design is achieved by moderating an underlying constancy with elements of addition and variation.

The first block is characterised by an unchanging twelve-note chord in the woodwind (other pitch classes above, between and below the notes of this chord are added subsequently by other instruments). There seems to be a plethora of motivic material here, although there are only nine motivic types, with each of the seven woodwind having different versions. There are short motifs whose durational values can be extended or which can be repeated to create longer variants; and there are accelerando–decelerando patterns built on the same principles. But what is striking here, as elsewhere in the score, is the profligacy of the motivic invention. The first movement in the published score is, in fact, a second version; Lutosławski revised and completed the score after its partial premiere at the Venice Biennale in April 1961. The woodwind material of the earlier 'Venice' version of the first movement, still anchored by the same twelve-note chord, is even more disparate. There are virtually no variant motifs shared between the seven players and some of the long-breathed ideas seem to have come from a very traditional background. At this first stage in the design, melody is predominant. Lutosławski evidently thought this was too disparate and unwieldy, and his natural leaning towards order led him to devise the series of nine motivic types in the final score. A comparison with the content of his next work, *Trois poèmes*, reveals that he has ironed out almost all traces of motivic individuality. Dotted rhythms have disappeared and homogenised groups of two to six semiquavers become the norm. This has a philosophical irony. In trying to developing his concept of 'collective ad libitum' and of releasing players from 'the often absurd demands which some composers have made of performers in the last few years'[15] Lutosławski actually reduced their individuality for the greater good of the whole. Restoring character to the motivic components of his harmonic blocks after *Trois poèmes* would be a major preoccupation.

At this stage, Lutosławski was primarily interested in the myriad ways in which such blocks could be constructed harmonically, and it was this exploration which proved to be a more than adequate replacement for traditional motivic and contrapuntal devices. Throughout his career, Lutosławski carried out extensive sketches before committing himself to a composition. In his exploration of twelve-note harmony, he quickly recognised that constructions which had limited interval content had more sharply differentiated character, and therefore greater dramatic potential, than those that mixed interval classes. For instance, close semitonal clusters (interval class 1) have very limited expressive properties, and he used them sparingly, either as a starting point or destination of wedge-shaped harmonic movement. Lutosławski also divided them up into smaller clusters (e.g., spanning a perfect fourth) within which the individual lines articulate melodic fragments where intervals larger than 1 give the cluster air to breathe (e.g., the choral writing in *Trois poèmes*). On the other hand, the two whole-tone scales (interval class 2), have greater resonance and character (the opening of *Trois poèmes*). As Stucky, Homma and Charles Bodman Rae have demonstrated, certain configurations became more central to Lutosławski's thinking than others.[16] Many of them are symmetrical above and below a central axis, such as the woodwind chord in the first movement of *Venetian Games*, which is based on interval classes 2 and 3. Other recurrent two-interval configurations include 2 and 5, 3 and 4, 4 and 5, and 5 and 6. Of course, the number 12 is rich in subdivisions, as composers from Webern to Reich have discovered to their benefit, and so Lutosławski was able to devise a huge range of harmonic patterns based on one, two, three or more interval classes. As his experience grew, he transferred this principle to linear pitch organisation. Lutosławski's genius lay not so much at this preparatory, local stage of composition but in creating sequences of harmonies which articulated his traditionally based structures in a modernist way. The role of the motif and the line as generators of form was re-imagined and transformed.

Example 8.6. Lutosławski, *Trois poèmes d'Henri Michaux* (1963), orchestral full score with choral short score, figs. 127–135.

It still took Lutosławski a few attempts to sort out his preferred notational strategies. In *Trois poèmes*, several methods of notating the aleatory articulation of the harmonic blocks were put under trial (Ex. 8.6): in the first movement, 'Pensées', there are passages that superimpose different metres within a one-second downbeat (1/2, 3/4, 5/8, 7/8 and 9/16). There are also passages using space-time notation where two types of accelerando–decelerando patterns, using stemless note-heads, appear from their spacing to have been originally mapped on graph paper. At the start of the final 'Repos dans le malheur', the space-time notation is much looser. But it is the notation of collective ad libitum passages which dominates and which proved to be the most durable.

The music of *Trois poèmes* has an extraordinary freshness and elasticity which comes from an astute command of how materials can be linked or contrasted in terms of interlocking harmonic designs, timbral articulation and use of register. It is also unusual in its use of two conductors, one each for choir and orchestra, a feature which gives an extra aleatory dimension to the performance as well as a pugnacious angle to the central 'Le grand combat'. This movement demonstrates Lutosławski's habitually succinct handling of resources. Its tone is rougher because only here does the unpitched percussion take part, paralleled by pitchless screaming and shouting by the chorus (in the outer movements their music is pitched). Lutosławski was undoubtedly encouraged in this adventurous composition by Michaux's vivid poetry. Whether Lutosławski knew at the time of the Belgian's visual art (his drawings often show a swirling mass movement of figures across the page), or his use of mescalin for artistic purposes, is hard to tell.[17] But they provide an uncanny parallel with Lutosławski's music.

It is significant that Lutosławski should have chosen at this juncture to turn to chamber music, a medium for which he composed relatively few pieces. And the String Quartet has maintained its pre-eminence among them. On a technical level, it was a challenge to his ability to adapt twelve-note harmonies to four players. The medium's timbral limitations equally compelled him to reinvestigate motivic character and to pay greater attention to linear aspects. And although he had originally not intended to provide a full score – not least because he had composed harmonic–textural blocks which were often considerably longer than hitherto and because he therefore wanted to give the players more responsibility for coordination – he acceded to their request.

The Quartet is structured in two movements, 'Introductory' and 'Main', a pattern elaborated by the Second Symphony three years later. In its motivic material, the Quartet is related to Three Postludes and *Venetian Games*, though in an emaciated form. The first movement proceeds by means of a brutal intercutting between a conversational series of unrelated motivic 'mobiles' (Lutosławski's own term, derived from his interest in the sculptures of Alexander Calder)[18] and jagged octave C naturals. The cumulative sense of nervousness is answered by the second movement, which has greater sense of purpose, proceeding in broad spans characterised by texture (tremolando, pizzicato, glissando etc.), but without recourse to the

Example 8.7. Lutosławski, String Quartet (1964), coda section, fig. 48.

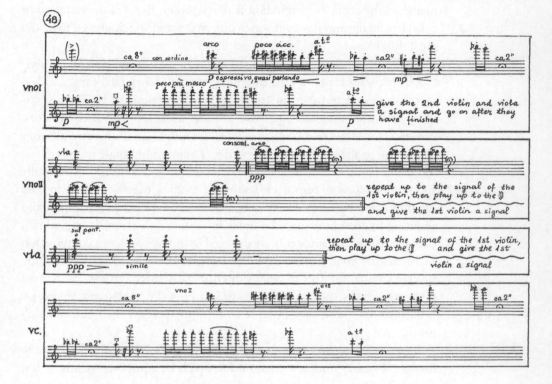

extended instrumental techniques filling any number of contemporaneous Polish scores. The three final subsections of the movement – the climactic 'Appassionato', a chorale-like texture with repeated 'morendo' markings, and 'Funebre', which eventually evaporates in a brief coda – provide a refined and extended version of *Funeral Music*'s concluding 'Apogeum' and 'Epilogue', i.e., a climax and a resolution. These subtitles have invited many commentators to see the presence of death in this conclusion.

Maja Trochimczyk characterises the 'Funebre' section as 'an extended *pathopoeia* . . . a musical figure of mourning', suggesting further that the work is 'an allegory of human life ending in death and, possibly, resurrection'. And she further cites the phrase 'in paradiso' applied by Tadeusz A. Zieliński to the many concluding moments in Lutosławski's scores where the music disappears upwards into nothing (Ex. 8.7).[19] John Casken is captured by the transcendental quality of this section and, more particularly, of the coda which 'does have something of the resurrection about it, where *individual* instruments present flashbacks of earlier material, newly optimistic, and *ascending* . . . towards the final moments of onomatopoeic bird song reminiscent of Messiaen's "angels" . . . the *Funèbre* has cleared the way for a new vision, the realization of something other, emanating from the very core of the *Funèbre* itself.'[20] The String Quartet was an important breakthrough. It tested out the efficacy of a structure where the first part was exploratory but unresolved, followed by a second which directed the musical argument forward to a point of climax and calm resolution. As Casken puts it, in speculating on Lutosławski's initial response to Cage's 'spark in the powder-keg':

> Is it possible that at this moment he conceived the idea that he could engage his listener in a new musical poetry, an elusive and haunting fantasy of detail in which his twelve-note pitch groups could intertwine and migrate towards a climactic point, beyond which a new level of experience would be inevitable?[21]

Lutosławski's next large-scale piece was to be his most problematic, the Second Symphony, his first substantial work for full orchestra since the Concerto for Orchestra thirteen years earlier. Its end-weighted structure is a development of the two-movement design of the String Quartet. Here the two movements are titled 'Hésitant' and 'Direct'. Like its counterpart in the Quartet, 'Hésitant' is a loose agglomeration of motivic–textural ideas. Unfortunately, there is little in the way of dialectic. What in a chamber composition may be an intriguing discourse can sound stretched and aimless in an orchestral context, especially if the motivic material is amorphous and there is not a taut rein on the sequence and interaction of different textures. This does eventually occur (from fig. 27), but by that stage the impression of hesitancy and purposelessness is so strong that when the movement growls to a close on low bassoons and trombones it is as if the entire process has deflated. The movement overplays its titular card, leaving 'Direct' to start again from scratch, with little symphonic or expressive relationship with the first movement. This it does with considerable energy, introducing the strings playing arco (they play only a few pizzicato chords in 'Hésitant') and motoring forwards by textural superimposition as well as juxtaposition. Among features worth noting are the passing use of quarter-tonal inflections in the strings (cf. parts of the String Quartet) and Lutosławski's reworking of the textural foreshortening of the early stages of a macro-rhythmic accelerando. It is less mathematically schematic than its predecessors and its ramshackle progress is enhanced by an increased brutality. What is intriguing is the return of Lutosławski's faith in metred music, which he introduces at fig. 133 in order to propel the music forward to its final stage where, as Stucky puts it, 'macrorhythmic accelerando merges with microrhythm'.[22] Unfortunately, Lutosławski rather miscalculates the

Example 8.8. Lutosławski, *Livre pour orchestre* (1968), first chapter, opening.

climactic 'collective ad libitum', which refuses to die, and the escape is considerably enfeebled. Instead of a sense of another world, the symphony ends with a straggle of lower strings echoing the end of 'Hésitant'. It was, perhaps, a necessary experiment (Lutosławski himself harboured doubts about it), because the two orchestral works that followed learned all the lessons and took Lutosławski's music onto an altogether higher plane.

Both *Livre pour orchestre* and the Cello Concerto (1970) have maintained a prominent place in the international concert repertoire. Each work benefits from a memorable beginning that also holds the key to the whole composition. In *Livre*, it is an A minor triad draped in a diaphanous sheen of string glissandi and quarter-tones (Ex. 8.8). It has many predecessors (such as the writing for female voices in *Trois poèmes*) but none approaches it for sheer sensuous allure. Few concertos begin so strikingly yet with such deliberately unremarkable material as in Lutosławski's Cello Concerto: the soloist playing up to twenty statements of an open D, *p* and *indifferente*. The success of both pieces is essentially down to two factors: strongly characterised development of material and innovative (and successful) structural designs that spring from their opening ideas. *Livre* fulfils the structural ambitions of *Venetian Games*: it is a four-movement end-weighted form, with the first three discrete initial 'chapitres' linked by brief, deliberately under-characterised 'intermèdes'. Lutosławski's subtle sleight here (although there are intimations of subliminal structural linkage between the third and fourth movements of *Venetian Games* and in the Second Symphony) is to prolong the third 'intermède' to merge with a string cantilena (initiated by two solo cellos) so that the listener is initially unaware that the final 'chapitre' has actually begun. What then follows is an irresistible macro-rhythmic accelerando – the most sophisticated of them all – leading seductively yet relentlessly to its explosive destruction, the aftermath of which transcends the turmoil with high strings and a pair of flutes. Of all Lutosławski's quiet conclusions – and those of the String Quartet and *Mi-parti* (1976) run it close – this is arguably the most fulfilling.

The sound world of *Livre* is full of marvels. The opening string idea grows organically to create a movement full of self-motivation (some of its material is related to the third song in Lutosławski's *Paroles tissées*, 1965, noted for the exquisite delicacy and poetic restraint of its orchestration), a mini end-weighted structure in itself. The first three 'chapitres' re-emphasise Lutosławski's appreciation that metred music is necessary for tempi above a median level (the initial stages of the work's later macrorhythmic accelerando are written more freely, only to be gathered in as the rate of change accelerates). But metre itself, as seen in parts of *Trois poèmes*, does not prohibit a blurring of pulse, as the second 'chapitre' amply demonstrates. The third 'chapitre', another blurred toccata, develops the quarter-tonal inflections of the first and provides an early example of the 'weeping semitone' which was to come into its own in subsequent works. After these three scherzi, the low string cantilena of the fourth 'chapitre' provides a momentary resting point, full of lyrical intensity and at a register and pace which speaks more eloquently than its prototype in the Second Symphony's 'Direct'. It sings, and it is perhaps no accident that Lutosławski employs here the long-breathed notation he devised for the choir in *Trois poèmes*.

If *Livre* emphasises the seductive colouristic aspects of Lutosławski's music of the late 1960s and 1970s, the Cello Concerto undoubtedly demonstrates his uncommon sense of drama in music. The fact that it refers to recognisable concerto features – three movements, the cadenza, and a vigorous interplay between soloist and orchestra – cannot hide the fact that Lutosławski meticulously re-examined their potential to create a quite different and arresting scenario. Most blatantly, he recast the cadenza as an introduction for solo cello; over four minutes pass (nearly a fifth of the entire concerto) before there is any orchestral response.[23] Lutosławski has thus set up a stark dialectic between a solitary, isolated soloist, alternately indifferent and mildly energised (successive motivic musings in this Beckettian monologue are marked 'un poco buffo ma con eleganza', 'marciale', 'grazioso', etc.), and the external forces, firstly antagonistic trumpets. The introduction functions as an expressive metaphor of the entire concerto, and the ensuing three movements explore different ways in which the solo cello interacts with these other forces. In the first movement, there are four carefully orchestrated episodes, each initiated by a solo cello pizzicato ('a symbolic invitation to a dialogue'[24]), which progressively animate a co-operative relationship with woodwind, strings and percussion; as each episode begins to assert itself, 'the brass intervenes, destroying this initiative'.[25] After a brief recollection of the initial D naturals, the cello tries a new tack, embedding itself in one of Lutosławski's most extensive lyrical cantilenas. It is backed in this endeavour by both divisi strings and woodwind. The intensity of the cello line, 'molto espressivo, dolente', is contained not least in the figure of weeping seconds accented by appoggiaturas. Towards the end of this central movement, the cellist and strings unite in an impassioned unison, a final statement of the 'dolente' figuration which propels itself towards a bold confrontation with the full brass at the start of the finale. At last, soloist and tutti lock horns. The progress of the conflict is full of twists and turns: the cello emerges battered, but not defeated, and flees the scene in a short coda. As Arnold Whittall has elegantly summarised: 'One factor connecting the work with most other successful concertos is that the soloist is not simply characterized as a perpetual, quixotic outsider, but is also engaged, Orpheus-like, in confrontation with, and ultimate conquering of, the hostility of the (orchestral) Furies.'[26]

Such an interpretation, with its literary, mythological and musical references, was about as far as Lutosławski himself might have gone, but he was never totally comfortable about extra-musical associations. And yet he lived in a country and at a time of Communist control when every utterance, be it political or artistic, was examined for its symbolic meaning. Of his works without text, the Cello Concerto has invited the most speculation about its extra-musical symbolism. Lutosławski laid the foundations in his early commentaries, but soon admitted: 'I'm horrified to see how one can be carried away by my careless mention of the dramatic conflict between the solo part and the orchestra.'[27] That has not stopped others, beginning with Mstislav Rostropovich, who commissioned and premiered it, from seeing the drama as representing the individual acting both in concert with society and struggling against its more inimical aspects. Given the date and place of its conception and preparation (1968–70, when Poland and the Soviet Union were experiencing civil unrest and individual opposition against Communist authority), it is hardly surprising that real-life parallels were drawn.[28] However tangential such parallels, the musical means used to create this undeniably dramatic concerto reinforce the idea that the initially indifferent individual, who then initiates dialogues, blossoms lyrically in the central movement and confronts the orchestra, at the end achieves a *tutta forza* triumph. These stage-posts are marked by clear pitch-class emphases – D, E, E, D and A – suggesting a deliberate progression. And it becomes transparent that the utter transformation of the character of the cello writing is Lutosławski's central concern, with its various stages regarded as rites of passage.

A couple of Lutosławski's own comments on the Cello Concerto question any simplified dramatic interpretation. So it is that, rather than understanding the introduction as full of portent, he sees it as having a 'frivolous atmosphere . . . the occasional state of inertia produced by the repetition of these notes [D naturals] doesn't seem seriously to contradict that at all'.[29] He thereby throws the emphasis away from the D naturals, both symbolically and structurally. But was he simply trying to put those who sniffed around too closely off the scent? Instead of drawing a connection with the Concerto's opening with the high cello A naturals in the coda, he links the opening D naturals with the emphatic climax earlier in the finale, which he more closely identifies as 'the climax of the composition. Just before the coda, where the orchestra is playing tutti, one chord is repeated at intervals of one second and this is immediately followed by a continuous chord *fortissimo* which goes on for fifteen seconds. The similarity is obvious.'[30] Indeed, he sees the coda as having 'no obvious direct connection with the dramatic event . . . Just as a work of literature has its epilogue, its postscript, so the coda has a particular role to play here.'[31] Lutosławski is at variance with most commentators here, not least because the proportions and dynamism of the structure demand a stronger moment than a mere epilogue. The coda does provide this resolution, akin in function though not in tone to the transcendentalism of other Lutosławski examples, which are themselves much more than postscripts. Rae comes closest to reconciling this difference: 'Symbolically, the soloist reaches a separate climax, at the very end.'[32] Not only symbolically, but musically too, the cello has the last word.

In the early 1970s, Lutosławski showed a renewed interest in serial procedures. In *Preludes and Fugue* for thirteen strings (1972), for example, each of the seven preludes begins with one hexachordal pitch-class trope and ends with its interlocking partner. This complementarity allows him to realise a mobile form for the one and only time in his career. Where all seven preludes are programmed, they must be played in the given order, but when fewer are performed their order is discretionary; hence the desirability for the hexachordal complementarity. Furthermore, the Fugue may be edited down when a selection of Preludes is performed. In one sense, this rare use of mobiles (Calder again) mirrors Lutosławski's compositional procedures, which consisted of making numerous individual sketches which would eventually be sorted and woven together. Here, though, he left some of this process to the performers, showing that he had not altogether abandoned an interest in what some of his more radical colleagues were doing (though it is noticeable that many, including Baird, Górecki and Penderecki, were far more conservative in this regard). His purpose was evidently to explore a new approach to end-weighted form (his reconfiguring here of a familiar eighteenth-century structural pairing was a successor to his formal rethinking in the Cello Concerto). The significant aspect is, however, less the play with structure and more the artful way in which this contemporary fugue is realised. The six fugue 'subjects' are differentiated in both material and character. As he was wont to do in his sketches (and in the introduction of the Cello Concerto), ideas are given character 'tags': *cantabile, grazioso, lamentoso, misterioso, estatico* and *furioso*. He also uses his fondness for motivic ad libitum textures (the finale of *Venetian Games* and the String Quartet are perhaps the best parallels) by having not single-line subjects and answers but bundles of two or three thematically related lines (Ex. 8.9). Even though the sketch-based origin of *Preludes and Fugue* is particularly transparent, it is a virtuoso display of craft within a textural sound world which emphasises the increasingly lyrical and intimate nature of Lutosławski's music.

The dreamscapes of Robert Desnos's poem 'Les espaces du sommeil' proved irresistible to Lutosławski, who would return to Desnos's surrealist poetry in his last work with voice, *Chantefleurs et Chantefables* (1990). When composing *Les espaces du sommeil* (1975), however, Lutosławski was drawn not only to Desnos's text but also to the structural match with his own creative processes: 'its musically tempting imagery, its conveniently pliable structure, and its recurring textual elements'.[33] Indeed, Lutosławski annotated his copy of the poem,[34] highlighting (sometimes with dynamic markings) the text's divisions. These enabled him to create a series of episodes beginning 'Il y a toi', the longest of which forms the main end-weighted section, whose animated texture is quietened by a coda consisting of several short segments each initiated by the words 'Dans la nuit'. The restrained lyricism which had been the abiding feature of *Paroles tissées* is enriched and darkened by using a full symphony orchestra as well as a baritone voice instead of tenor. *Les espaces* also demonstrates Lutosławski's ongoing recourse to the linear deployment of the twelve notes in order to create a constantly shifting harmonic background. This was especially significant where a sense of line was inherent to the concept of a composition (e.g., the Cello Concerto or *Preludes and Fugue*). It was one way to break down any sense of monolithic twelve-note harmony, and he used it with special eloquence in the central slow section formed by the two 'Il y a toi' segments (figs. 24–82) which precede the climactic section of *Les espaces* (Ex. 8.10). Lutosławski's technique of deriving a non-dodecaphonic melodic line with varying interval content from background harmony created by sequences of twelve notes based on limited interval classes (in this instance, 2 and 5), is a particular feature of his pitch organisation. A freer variant of this procedure was employed in the first section of *Mi-parti* to mesmerising effect.

Mi-parti is often regarded as marking the return of Lutosławski's concern for melody, although this aspect of his compositional aesthetic had been

Example 8.9. Lutosławski, *Preludes and Fugue* (1972), fugue, figs. 38a–41.

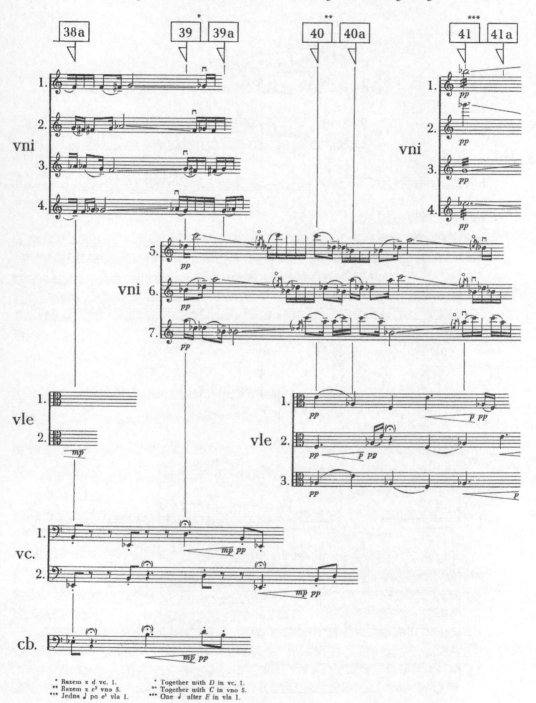

* Razem z d vc. 1.   ' Together with *D* in vc. 1.
** Razem z c³ vno 5.   " Together with *C* in vno 5.
*** Jedna ♩ po e¹ vla 1.   *** One ♩ after *E* in vla 1.

Example 8.10. Lutosławski, *Les espaces du sommeil* (1975), figs. 63–70.

evident to some degree for many years. His increasing lyricism in the early 1970s was something different and the opening of *Mi-parti* was the culmination of his harmonically derived melodic ideas. In this instance, the basis is a series of eight twelve-note string chords which, by seemingly intuitive transposition of individual pitches (involving changes of between two and six notes between successive chords), transposes itself up a semitone each cycle. The process is faster and more sophisticated than in *Les espaces* (there are links too with the opening of *Livre*) and is considerably enhanced by the emergence not of just one melodic line but of a growing polyphony of wind instruments. Each line maintains a clear rhythmic and articulatory character and is simultaneously enhanced by drawing ever-changing pitch classes from the shifting chord sequence in the strings. For Lutosławski, however, this opening was problematic: he was dissatisfied with the masking of the melodic threads by the rather 'muddy' harmonic texture in the strings. As his preceding music had increasingly demonstrated, he was searching for new ways in which to animate his undeniably rich harmonic language. And with a tiny work for oboe and piano – *Epitaph* (1979) – his melodic invention found release from overt harmonic constraints and he entered the final phase of his compositional career.

Serocki

The works with which Serocki began to establish a truly distinctive voice were *Episodes* for strings and three groups of unpitched percussion and *Segmenti* (1961), scored for single wind, four percussionists, electric mandolin and electric guitar, harpsichord and celesta, piano and harp (other strings are omitted completely). Their instrumentation alone indicates a composer fascinated by timbre: guitar and mandolin had been used five years earlier in *Heart of the Night* and would resurface in *Impromptu fantasque* (1973) for three to six mandolins, three to six guitars and six recorders. Such explorations (and there are several other strands in his music) mark Serocki out from his contemporaries because he preferred vibrant hues to uniformity of texture. In that sense, works like *Symphonic Frescoes* (1964) and *Forte e piano* (1967) find kindred spirits in Górecki's *Scontri* and Lutosławski's *Venetian Games* rather than in Penderecki's *Threnody* for fifty-two strings. Serocki was reluctant to abandon the avant-garde aesthetic and he concentrated his efforts on an energetic search for new ways in which instrumental colour and performance techniques might be put to intricate rather than generalised expressive ends.

The significance of *Episodes* lies in its (then) novel stage disposition and exploitation of the instrumental forces: twenty-four desks of violins form a semicircle around the conductor, with ten desks of violas across the front of the stage and eight desks of double basses across the back. Two lines of four desks of cellos radiate from the conductor to trisect the violin semicircle, with the three percussion groups placed at its ends and apex. The layout functions as a series of routes along which Serocki moves the sound, creating powerful currents and counterflows. The four episodes – 'proiezioni', 'movimenti', 'migrazioni' and 'incontri' – have a symphonic cogency which arises from Serocki's energetic exploitation of the properties of the ensemble and its layout. The strings are the main conduit and, for the first time in Polish music, Serocki uses them as a source for mass movement of clusters and scalic figures. As yet there are no special notations, no unprecedented playing techniques. The 'proiezioni' episode functions as an exposition, gradually revealing the range of combinations, from unisons to large chordings, from a single desk to the entire ensemble. The sequence of transitions and confrontations is handled with enormous flair and drama. The two central episodes are shorter, with 'movimenti' assigned to the percussion, whose gradual crescendo acts as an enormous upbeat to 'migrazioni'. This virtuoso scherzo – a descendant of long-forgotten toccatas – has a galvanising effect as tiny semiquaver motifs dart in a myriad of directions. Few Polish composers could or wanted to match the sheer panache and speed demonstrated here, not least because many of them were losing interest in metred music with a definable pulse. But perhaps the most impressive section is the last, where Serocki gathers together various characteristic patterns from the preceding episodes (Ex. 8.11). The 'incontri' episode is not just a series of 'meetings' but a sequence of vigorous, even frenetic debates, demonstrating Serocki's instincts for musical argument, even when most of the material is athematic.

Serocki seems to have taken breath at this point, because his next piece, *Segmenti*, written after a pause of over a year, abandons the movement of mass sounds of one or two instrumental families. He turned instead to the aperiodic and ametric exploration of a chamber ensemble of highly variegated instruments, some of which, especially the piano, are played in unconventional ways. There are still spatial features in the score, though Serocki makes subtler and less systematic use of the layout's potential. *Segmenti* is more interested in local colours and tensions created by contrasts in timbre, density, register and figuration and less in development or long-term continuities. He achieves this by mixing points of sounds, sustained lines (the opening flute solo) and moments of ensemble (a passage for six maracas, a fragmented sequence of wind chords, and the brief central climax for all but the unpitched percussion, which then provides the escape).

It was a small but landmark step from the segmentation of musical structure within a controlled sequence of events to the creation of a work in

Example 8.11. Serocki, *Episodes* (1959), bb. 299–308.

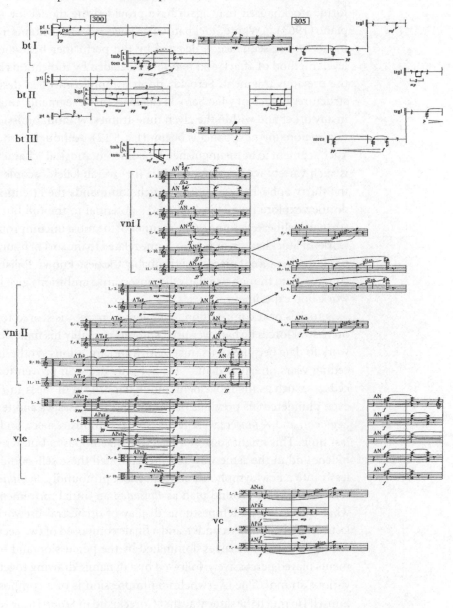

open form. And while there had already been a few Polish essays in open form, Stockhausen may again have provided the model for *A piacere* for piano (1963).[35] Where Stockhausen's *Klavierstück* XI contains nineteen fragments whose sequence is decided by the performer but whose dynamic level, method of attack and tempo are decided by indications at the end of the previous fragment, Serocki adopts a more controlled design. The ten structures in each of what Serocki called its three 'segments' must be played, in any order and within the given time-frames, without omission or repetition, before the next panel is begun (Ex. 8.12). Although Serocki intended 'each segment to be distinguished by a different musical "character"',[36] there is such variety within each that it is the overall kaleidoscopic sequence of the thirty aphoristic structures which commands the attention. Not only do they explore the piano keyboard's potential to the full but each is also strongly delineated, some in the manner of the most uncompromising piano works of Stockhausen or Boulez, some related to the sort of figuration he had used in other recent pieces. It is probably the best-known Polish open-form composition, though its relatively conservative ambitions give it the air of a workshop experiment.

Serocki's next composition, *Symphonic Frescoes*, is scored for the largest orchestral forces he had ever used and was arguably his most accomplished work to date because of its imaginative and ambitious synthesis of the preceding years of experiment.[37] He not only drew on proven technical procedures, such as the movement and juxtaposition of ideas in *Episodes*, but even plundered his previous pieces for specific passages and textures: both *Segmenti* and *A piacere* were fertile sources in this respect, and not for the last time. This might suggest a Bacewicz-like impasse, but Serocki was not hidebound in the same way and incorporated these self-quotations seamlessly into a new, symphonic context. More profoundly, *Symphonic Frescoes* follows the same ground plan as *Episodes*: an initial movement hinting at what is to follow, a tempestuous display of orchestral fireworks (this one lasting barely ninety seconds), and a finale composed of two sections, a slow sequence of sound masses dominated by the percussion and other instruments played percussively, followed by a dynamic drawing together of these various strands. The overwhelming impression is of a composer enjoying himself (in much the same way that Górecki did in *Scontri* four years earlier). His timbral palette is vivid and he is extraordinarily adroit in his use of what Szabelski called 'mottos' as a means of generating symphonic momentum. And even though he makes more use than before of new notational devices and introduces new sound sources (in the third fresco, he requires the brass to strike the mouthpieces of their instruments with the palm of the hand), he still maintains an almost Lutosławskian control over those parameters

Example 8.12. Serocki, *A piacere* (1963), one of three 'panels'.

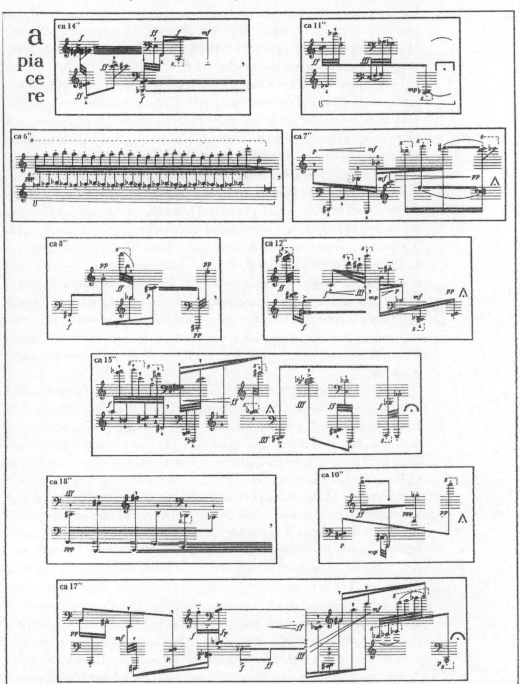

which he regards as his sacrosanct domain. There are ad libitum passages, but there is no real aleatoricism. Pitch organisation is also controlled, not beholden to any one system or procedure, although the burgeoning influence of Lutosławski's ad libitum twelve-note chords gives added resonance to the design of Serocki's harmonic blocks.

In *Continuum* for six percussionists (1966), Serocki returned to his interest in the timbral and dramatic potential of percussion allied to the polyphonic movement of sound in space. Here, he placed his performers not on the stage but around the auditorium, anticipating Xenakis's *Persephassa* (1969), also written for Les Percussions de Strasbourg. For his palette of colours, Serocki assembled over 120 instruments, mainly unpitched, dividing them among the players to create two types of sets. The set-up for three of the players includes a vibraphone and marimba or xylomarimba, temple blocks and tam-tams; that for the other three includes bells or glockenspiel, maracas, suspended bottles, bass drum and bongos. All players have cymbals, and a range of other instruments is dispersed among the six. Co-ordination is maintained by giving signals notated in the score. Rhythmic precision as such was of diminished importance, with Serocki highlighting broader contrasts of timbre between the players and between the work's thirty-six segments to provide a somewhat gentler sense of momentum than hitherto. The end result almost approximates (in fixed form) the principles governing *A piacere*.

In pursuing new performance techniques in the cause of a greater sound spectrum, Serocki was of course aligning himself with a range of composers from abroad as well as from Poland, foremost among them Penderecki and Szalonek. But neither Pole had quite Serocki's bravura and esprit, which erupted in *Forte e piano* (1967), premiered by Alfons and Aloys Kontarsky in Cologne the following year. Once again, familiar traits – swirling arabesques, sharp textural and dynamic contrasts – are put at the service of an almost pugnacious scenario, with the two pianos at the centre of the action. Serocki maintains the dissonant harmonic idiom of *A piacere* in the piano parts, which are governed by chords rather than semitonal clusters, thereby assuring greater depth and variety. Each of the customary four sections is carefully delineated. The first, for example, consists of attempts, each more robust than its predecessor, to rise from the depths of low timpani and piano thuds towards a more active higher tessitura. Serocki invigorates this process by masterly use of the orchestra and by cross-cutting these attempts at liberation by layering them asynchronically with accelerandi and ritardandi. The customary scherzo is brief and draws the soloists into its web of swirling chromatic motifs; on its dissolution, the soloists embark on what Zieliński calls a 'lyric fantasy',[38] accompanied in turn by sustained strings, trombone and cello glissandi, before succumbing to one of Serocki's typical short climaxes built from an accumulation of ad libitum fragments (in this instance, without strings). The concluding developmental synthesis, high-lighting percussive playing techniques (including harps and low strings), is more discursive than usual. In the final climax, the soloists abandon all pretensions of being concerned with precise pitch classes and join in with white- and black-note forearm clusters.

The culmination of Serocki's large-scale orchestral pieces of this period is *Dramatic Story* (1970), whose original designation as a ballet score has left no trace of extra-musical narrative; nor has the piece departed in any great sense from Serocki's habitual 'symphonic' template. *Dramatic Story* is remarkable, however, for its change of tone. It would appear that Serocki had been considerably influenced in the development of a more relaxed and enriched harmonic language, and the introduction of fledgling cantilena passages, by the finely honed example of Lutosławski's works of the 1960s. There are numerous instances of twelve-note chords, many of which have a quasi-tonal aura because of the internal disposition of intervals. Some chords are harmonically static (e.g., composed of the three diminished sevenths or divided modally into 'white' and 'black' notes), others use registral shifts, such as the narrowing from a tutti of three different twelve-note chords (shades of the climax of the second of Lutosławski's *Trois poèmes*) to land on a unison B natural at the end of the first of the three main sections. A few moments later there even appears to be a homage to the delicate skein of string glissandi which begin Lutosławski's *Livre*. This is one of many exam-ples of chords of fewer than twelve notes and of the use of glissandi, some of which are detailed to mark quarter-tone inflections between adjacent semitones.

As *Dramatic Story* indicates, Lutosławski was not the only Polish composer to devise end-weighted structures. The Lutosławski connection is also per-ceptible in the major role played by string cantilenas in this work, which for the most part are not in unison but are series of (usually) twelve-note chords moving homophonically. They are differentiated from most of the other chordal patterns only by differences in speed and articulation: their slow-moving homophony gives their upper and lower melodic profile greater presence. Serocki places these cantilenas at strategic points within each of the three sections, and purely from a structural point of view they remain *Dramatic Story*'s single most memorable idea. In each instance, they impart a feeling of sensual repose, unique in Serocki's output; conversely, in Lutosławski's music they are normally endowed with a degree of forward propulsion.

The first cantilenas follow closely on the opening arabesques, hinting at their potential significance. Contrary motion between the upper and lower half of each chord sequence is typical, and there is no clearer example of this than a passage which begins with a twelve-note semitone cluster and expands symmetrically outwards in concertina fashion, in seven stages, to a span of over two and a half octaves with a chord made up of what Lutosławski analysts would recognise as dominated by interval classes 1, 3 and 4 (Ex. 8.13). There are three cantilena groups in the final section, the third of these bringing the work to its close. Their presence in this final, developmental section reinforces the impression that they, and not the work's extrovert ideas, are where the 'real' story lies. There is one moment, however, that suggests that such an interpretation is perhaps too easy. As the final section builds up to what is certainly one of Serocki's most brutal climaxes, he introduces a trio of clarinets blowing high-pitched 'raspberries', produced by playing on the mouthpiece only (they later produce glissandi and play while biting the reed). Anticipating Lutosławski's use of brief brass fanfares to puncture the otherwise calm atmosphere in the coda of *Mi-parti*, Serocki seems to be suggesting that a certain tongue-in-cheek quality would not go amiss at this critical point in *Dramatic Story*. Serocki's sense of humour was notorious, and this spilled over, along with the clarinet sounds, into a real piece of musical fun, *Swinging Music* for clarinet, trombone, cello and piano (1970) (Ex. 8.14).

It is in the nature of synthesis to be retrospective and it is clear that for much of the 1960s Serocki was reworking one particular macro-structure alongside a number of other musical ideas. There was little sign, however, that he was prepared to compromise on his own modernist agenda, and this gave his music a distinctive profile when most of his compatriots, especially in the 1970s, seemed to be moderating their aesthetic and stylistic position. A significant element was his continuing search for new sound sources, which was essentially a result of his intense curiosity about instrumental virtuosity and its compositional uses. Several pieces explore the potential of the recorder, including *Impromptu fantasque* and *Concerto alla cadenza* for recorder and orchestra (1974), in which the soloist plays the full range of six recorders (and detached mouthpieces) from sopranino to gran basso. Both works use extended instrumental techniques and new textures with considerable bravura, as is characteristic of Serocki's music in the 1970s. While *Fantasmagoria* for piano and percussion (1971) attempts to harmonise the percussive potential of the piano with actual percussion in a free-flowing discourse, his writing for recorder exuberantly invades the timbral territory of electronic music through multiphonics (cf. Szalonek's woodwind experiments), glissandi or quasi-stochastic sound fields. The element of fantasy, of intuitive consequentiality, continued to fascinate Serocki (as in *Fantasia elegiaca* for organ and orchestra, 1972), and he achieved it by giving sufficient leeway to the performer, usually through detailed graphic notation. With

Example 8.13. Serocki, *Dramatic Story* (1970), bb. 72–81.

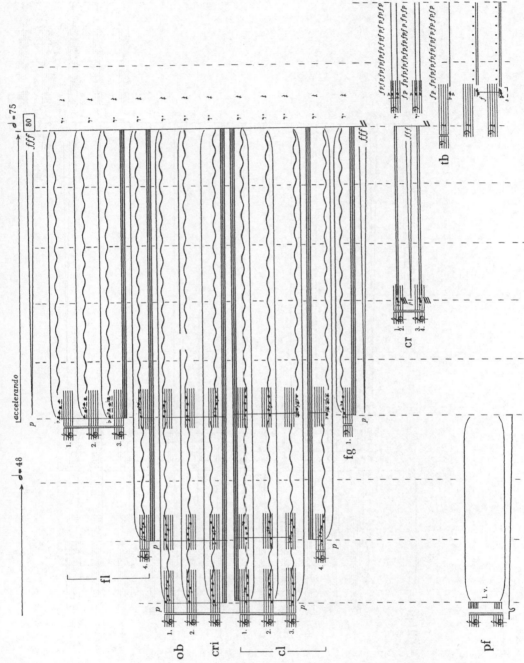

Example 8.13. (*cont.*)

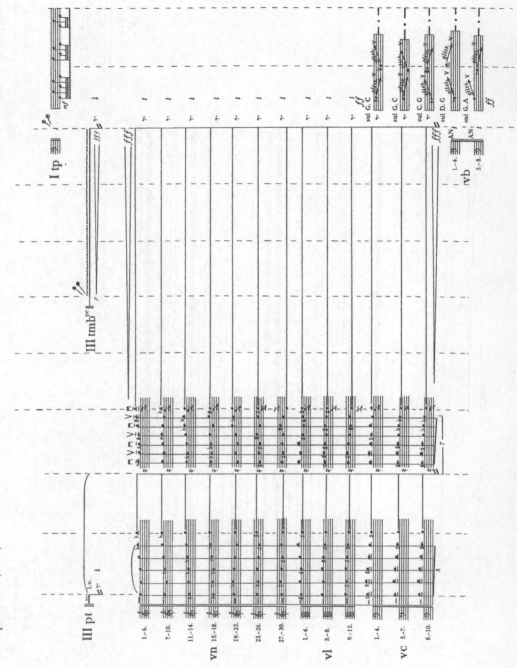

Example 8.14. Serocki, *Swinging Music* (1970), leading up to letter M.

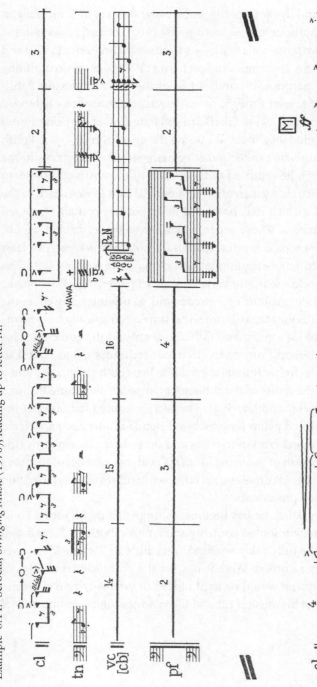

a mix of delicacy and dynamism, his music evokes a state of sonic delight, often tinged with humour and eschewing easy programmatic associations.

Serocki's final two large-scale works – *Ad libitum* for orchestra (1977) and *Pianophonie* for piano, electronics and orchestra (1978) – show no dimming of his exploratory nature and stand as two of the most impressive Polish works of the decade, even though, to some ears, their aesthetic belonged more to the experimental 1960s. Like Baird and Lutosławski, Serocki evinced no interest in the modal or tonal idioms or the evocation of a past Polish culture that were surfacing in the music of many of his compatriots in the 1970s. In *Ad libitum*, he returned to the notion of the abstract mobile, to the idea of kaleidoscopic segmentation first essayed in *A piacere*: each of the work's five 'pieces' (which may be played in any order) contains between five and eight segments, whose order is likewise to be performed 'ad lib'. Few Polish composers paid much attention to mobile structures, not least because they held to a more traditional view of narrative content. If *Ad libitum* highlights Serocki's relish for variable abstract patterning, *Pianophonie* revisits the spatial dimensions of *Episodes* and *Continuum* as well as the genre of the concerto for the sixth time, this time electronically transforming much of the soloist's music and diffusing it around the audience. This was the only time Serocki turned to electronic techniques, and he did so only because the electronic interface would be live (both the pianist and a sound engineer in the centre of the audience manipulate the sound through ring modulation, delay and layering). The work's assured handling of the resonantly transformed piano timbres, two extended cadenzas, an isolated brass 'chorale', sectional cross-references and propulsive jazz rhythms (the last an orchestral cousin of *Swinging Music*) is evidence enough of Serocki's ability to shape a coherent dramatic narrative which dares to avoid tried and tested compositional procedures.

Even more than Baird, he has become an unjustifiably forgotten composer, and his contribution to contemporary music both in Poland and abroad has yet to be fully acknowledged. Very little of his music has ever been commercially recorded. Were it not for the chronicle recordings of the 'Warsaw Autumn', it would be hard indeed to form any proper assessment of the acuity of his musical ear and the vividness of his compositional imagination.

9 Sonorism and experimentalism

The 'Polish School', sonorism, and electronic music

Among the terms and labels attached to Polish music after 1956, those of
the 'Polish School' and 'sonorism' are the most frequent and among the
most elusive. The term 'Polish School' was not a new one: Mycielski had
evoked a Polish musical school at the Łagów conference in 1949, though its
meaning then was quite different,[1] and the term was subsequently used in
the preface to the programme book of the first 'Warsaw Autumn' festival
in 1956, essentially in reference to Polish music since Łagów.[2] But the term
was reborn in the foreign press a few years later as visiting journalists tried
to come to grips with Poland's avant-garde developments of the late 1950s
and early 1960s, though it remained 'somewhat enigmatic to Polish musical
circles'.[3] As Danuta Mirka has commented:

> The unifying features of this music were sought chiefly on the aesthetic plane,
> in its strong, ardent expression and the dynamism of its formal processes.
> Both of these qualities were equally strange to the experimental 'asceticism'
> of Western music in the 1950s and hence were all the more noticeable in the
> music coming from Poland . . . Characteristically enough, when foreign
> observers concentrated on the aesthetic unity of Polish music as an integral
> phenomenon in musical life, Polish critics reacted by turning their own
> attention to the variety and wealth of its stylistic resources.[4]

In defining further this variety and wealth, most commentators on
Lutosławski have been at pains to indicate that he stood somewhat outside the phenomenon of the 'Polish School': 'he witnessed the appearance
on the musical scene of younger colleagues, such as Penderecki and Górecki,
who, together with Baird and Serocki, laid the foundations of the "Polish
School" of the 1960s'.[5] Such a viewpoint is based on generational as well
as stylistic criteria, and by implication includes other composers such as
Bacewicz, though not, as has been seen, the idiosyncratic Szabelski.

Perhaps 'Polish School' was an inevitable construct; its danger lay in
the misrepresentation its imprecision engendered. Certainly, there was a
common purpose in the years after 1956, partly retrospective (the attempt
to ignore, erase the evidence of or move beyond socialist realism), partly

speculative, as most Polish composers shared a burning desire to make up for lost time. The spirit of these years gave an impression of unity, even though there was ample evidence, not only from live performances, of clear stylistic and aesthetic differences between composers. And it was not as if those who reported back to the West on Polish developments were lacking in materials. PWM turned manuscripts into published scores at an impressive rate (many of the major new pieces from 1958 onwards were published within months of their premiere) and, from the outset of the 'Warsaw Autumn', the state record company, Polskie Nagrania, issued 'chronicle' live festival recordings, often within hours of the performance. But dissemination of these scores and recordings was very limited outside Poland. Today, even more so than forty years ago, the lack of readily available materials from these years, apart from the works of a handful of composers who have Western publishers, serves only to perpetuate the myth abroad of the 'Polish School'.[6] The label remains an entry point for discussion but has little more than a rather confined geographical–historical relevance.

The term 'sonorism', however, despite being sometimes lazily overlapped with 'Polish School', is one which it is possible to define with greater confidence. Its origins may be traced back to a proposal in 1956, made by Chomiński, that the study of sound as such would bring new insights, particularly to twentieth-century music. In 1956, of course, Polish music was only just emerging from the doldrums, so 'sonoristics' (*sonorystyka*, from the French *sonore*) had no relevance to recent Polish composition. Chomiński's intention was to discuss music on the basis not of traditional parametric approaches but of its qualities as sound; he wanted to open up a debate on music from Debussy and Stravinsky to the *Klangfarben* of the Second Viennese School and beyond without having to be hamstrung by the quantifiable technical aspects of the composer's craft.[7] Twelve years later he published the first in-depth survey of new Polish music, in which he applied his theory to a range of contemporary composers, from Baird and Lutosławski to Górecki, Penderecki and Schaeffer.[8] Under the heading of 'sonoristic language', he used terms such as 'sonoristic technique', 'musical sonoristics', 'sonoristic devices' and 'sonoristic structures', rather than the more generalised term 'sonorism' which emerged later. In his broadly conceived account, Chomiński identified five areas of enquiry: sound technology, temporal regulation, horizontal and vertical structures, the transformation of sound, and form. The composer's coordination of these areas, according to Chomiński, amounted to 'sonoristic regulation'.

A more succinct summary of the phenomenon had been made in 1966 by Zieliński, who listed what he saw as the main elements, unencumbered by the term 'sonoristics' and closer in spirit to compositional practice:

(1) sound colour (often enriched by new means of articulation); (2) dynamics; (3) sound shape in time and space (its length, width, and thickness, organization of lines and bands, points, inflections and arabesques on various patterns); (4) motion and stasis (various means of motion, motion in three-dimensional space); (5) combination of simultaneous layers of sound; (6) integration and variability of sound image in the temporal course.[9]

Because these elements were often employed to create 'broad-brush' sound shapes, the results came to be labelled abroad as *Klangflächenmusik* or 'sound-mass music'.

Neither Chomiński nor Zieliński attempted a detailed theoretical synthesis, and thereafter the currency of 'sonoristics' seemed to diminish – some Polish historical surveys ignored it altogether.[10] Gradually from the mid-1970s, however, a few Polish musicologists revisited the issue, now known as 'sonorism', as they attempted to define more closely the music of the 'Polish School'. Most attention was paid to Penderecki:

> Penderecki's instrumental music . . . may be labelled today as classic
> sonorism. In it were realised all the typical features of this trend. There
> ensued a fundamental change to the hierarchy of musical values: in place of
> melody, harmony, metre and rhythm, sound became the form-creating,
> tectonic agent. Pitch as such ceased to have a vital role – colour was now
> dominant. The sound shape became the essential architectonic unit instead of
> the motif.[11]

More recently, Mirka has not only attempted the overarching analytical synthesis which has eluded others but has also written the most insightful account of the issues surrounding sonorism.[12] Based on a study of seven works by Penderecki written between 1959 and 1962, her exhaustive analysis draws on structural linguistics and mathematical set theory. She detects numerous interlocking systems at work which involve considerations of timbre, articulation and pairs of binary opposites in the areas of pitch, dynamics and time (continuous–discontinuous, mobile–immobile, high–low, etc.). It is an important development in the analytical–theoretical discourse begun by Zieliński and Chomiński, although Penderecki remains dubious of the sonoristic label, as no doubt do other composers.

Among the works composed between 1959 and 1964 which are generally cited as significant examples of sonorism are Baird's *Study* (1961), Górecki's three-part cycle *Genesis* (1962–3), Kilar's *Herbsttag* (1960), *Riff 62*, *Générique* (1963) and *Diphthongos* (1964), Schaeffer's *Equivalenze sonore* (1959) and *Little Symphony: Scultura* (1960) and Penderecki's complete output from

Anaklasis (1959–60) to *Canon* (1962). These works, as well as a number of electronic pieces by Kotoński, Dobrowolski and Penderecki, represent sound explorations of varying intensity as well as giving some inkling of the stylistic variation held even within this ostensibly hard core, though the works by Baird and Kilar are arguably less appropriately included than the others. A slightly later contribution was made by Szalonek, whose *Les sons* (1965) initiated his fertile examination of the sonoristic potential of a range of instruments, primarily the woodwind. There are, of course, many pieces by other composers which share some of the textural and timbral concerns of these ground-breaking compositions, but which in essence could not be called sonoristic. These include Bacewicz's *Pensieri notturni* and Quartet for Four Cellos, Lutosławski's *Trois poèmes* and Serocki's *Episodes*. The rationale of such pieces is still based on the play of 'melody, harmony, metre and rhythm'; new sounds are subservient to the argument conditioned by the other elements. The key factor in the differentiation between these and fully sonoristic pieces is the use to which new sounds are put. In Górecki's *Genesis* and Penderecki's *Polymorphia* (1961), for example, the rationale is based on the 'sound shape' or the 'sound mass'. Sonoristic principles are therefore integral, form-building, rather than incidental or decorative.

There were close technical and expressive parallels between the high point of sonorism and developments in electronic music in Poland. Dobrowolski and Kotoński were the leading pioneers, but even their output was patchy in the years after the Experimental Studio was established at Polish Radio. Dobrowolski's first essay, *Passacaglia na 40z5*, is effectively a short sketch, mixing four layers of sine tones and white noise in a mildly contrapuntal discourse. *Music for Magnetic Tape no. 1* (*Muzyka na taśmę magnetofonową nr 1*, 1963) is a far more accomplished work, both technically and musically, and its indebtedness to Stockhausen's *Studie II* is understandable. Its sound sources are both electronic and *concrète* (human voice and piano), treated to a range of filtering, ring modulation, and echo devices typical of the period. It is also clearly the work of a composer with an ear for traditional development, because its narrative progresses from mainly the purely electronic towards the *concrète* (the original sound sources become more evident, aided by a significant increase in sustained 'melodic' material). The score, with full technical information and 45 rpm recording, was published by PWM a year later.[13]

In the Polish context, Dobrowolski was also one of the first to pioneer the combination of pre-recorded tape and live performers.[14] *Music for Tape and Solo Oboe* (1964) neatly interlocks its live and stereo recorded elements in a chamber environment (Ex. 9.1); it had three successors: for tape and piano (1972), double bass (1977), and bass clarinet (1980). Dobrowolski

Example 9.1. Dobrowolski, *Music for Tape and Solo Oboe* (1964), 4'00"–4'10".

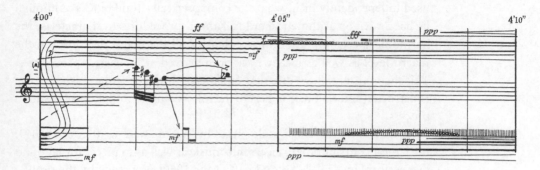

subsequently transferred the idea into the orchestral sphere, alongside his interest in spatial music, first explored in *Music for Strings and Four Groups of Wind Instruments* (1964). In *Music for Strings, Two Groups of Wind Instruments and Two Loudspeakers* (1967), the five constituent sound sources are placed around the concert hall and their spatial interaction brought to a climax in the rapid hocketing of the closing moments. The work is significant because it underscores the close relationship between the electronic studio and the move by certain composers towards a sonoristic approach to musical material. Dobrowolski's position is not as extreme as Penderecki's. Although he maintains a high degree of continuity and blocked textural homogeneity (the two wind groups are identical and are treated as mutual echoes of each other), he develops the music in an evidently symphonic manner. This discourse also allows for an almost Bairdian motivic lyricism in his writing for the woodwind, partly stemming from his experience in composing *Music for Tape and Solo Oboe.*

In the early 1960s, Kotoński concentrated on his concert music, although he maintained a strong interest in music for tape. After the earlier *Study on One Cymbal Stroke*, there was a break until *Microstructures* (1963), the first Polish stereophonic tape piece. Kotoński's source material was percussive (wood, glass, a mechanical saw), as befitted the author of *Percussion Instruments in the Modern Orchestra* (1963).[15] The level of micro-structural transformation, what Kotoński described as 'granularity', is quite sophisticated for its time and the discontinuous temporal and textural fluidity within a wide dynamic range produces a vivid sonoristic soundscape.[16]

After a further break, Kotoński then became the first Polish composer to gain extensive experience in foreign studios. *Klangspiel* (1967), realised at the Studio for Electronic Music in Cologne, follows stylistically in the path of *Microstructures*. On the other hand, *AELA* (1970), made in the Polish Radio studio, has closer parallels with the mass sonorism of

Penderecki's music of the early 1960s. It is based entirely on sine waves, used independently or in what the composer calls 'tone blocks'. Although he has drawn on arithmetical or logarithmic procedures to characterise the harmonic spectrum, duration and density, all the major decisions on the macro-level as well as locally have been arrived at by chance procedures. This theoretically allows different versions of the piece's nine episodes to be constructed and Kotoński is alert to the role a computer might play in such a process.[17]

Apart from a few small-scale pieces by Wiszniewski written in 1960–3, the largest contribution to electronic music as well as to pieces for tape and live performance in the second half of the 1960s was made by the prolific Bogusław Schaeffer. In 1966 alone he produced at least two tape pieces – *Assemblage* and Symphony – plus the Trio for flute, harp, viola and tape. *Assemblage* is an easy-going, almost jazzy collage of moderately treated violin and piano sounds – a far cry from the intense seriousness of Dobrowolski and Kotoński. The four-movement Symphony, however, was the longest piece of Polish tape music to date, at seventeen and a half minutes. Like Kotoński's *AELA*, the published materials include the basic graphic score, a 45 rpm mono recording (a mainly electronic version made by Schaeffer and his studio engineer, Bohdan Mazurek), as well as technical data and descriptive information necessary for different realisations. The graphic score is the crucial element, because it is this rather than the data that is the starting point for the piece. As such, it ties in with Schaeffer's numerous other works whose scores are intended to be inspirational for the interpreter rather than definitive. The results may be 'sonoristic' in their interlocking sound masses, but their graphic origins are a long way from the more tightly controlled sonorism of Penderecki. Indeed, apart from their interest in new sound sources and their deployment, one could hardly find two composers more diametrically opposed in their compositional aesthetics.

Penderecki

Penderecki once summarised his transition from student composer to international figure in the late 1950s as follows:

> Hindemith, Honegger – they were the twentieth-century composers, apart from the already popular Bartók and Stravinsky, who interested me. Later came the new wave of interest in the Viennese School and the discovery of what had been happening in electronic music. The new world of electronics influenced the shape of my output in the 1960s.[18]

Although he worked in Polish Radio's Experimental Studio on many occasions in the early 1960s, mainly composing incidental music for the theatre and radio, Penderecki produced only two concert pieces involving tape. The second of these, *Canon*, uses the technology to provide playbacks of earlier sections of the live performance, their function being simply to increase the canonic layers and therefore the textural density. Its formulaic nature compares unfavourably with his more intuitive pieces. The other work, *Psalmus*, is for tape alone. It belongs to the strand of Polish *musique concrète*, utilising the voice of one of the most accomplished Polish performers of contemporary music, Halina Łukomska, in a manner reminiscent of Stockhausen's *Gesang der Jünglinge*. Although its tone is reflective and restrained, it nevertheless parallels in electronic format many of the more extrovert features of Penderecki's concert works of 1960–2.

In these three years he produced seven works of what Teresa Malecka called 'classic sonorism': *Anaklasis* (1959–60), *Threnody to the Victims of Hiroshima* (1960), the First String Quartet (1960), *Dimensions of Time and Silence* (1960, rev. 1961), *Fonogrammi* (1961), *Polymorphia* (1961) and *Fluorescences* (1961–2). They are evidence of Penderecki's exhilarating sense of freedom, not just from the stifling neo-classicism of his youth but also from what he saw replacing it in Polish music, the insidious avant-garde hegemony of serialism. More than that, he felt free from the constriction of traditional musical parameters: rhythm and metre, harmony and melody, and many aspects of form. In this respect, electronic music appears to have been a major catalyst, and he quickly transferred its focus on timbre, register, dynamics and unconventional shaping of materials (splicing, filtering, tone modulation) into the sphere of traditional performance outlets, the one area of past practice which he continued to endorse wholeheartedly. The consequences included finding new ways of playing instruments, most famously the orchestral strings, and new notations to replace those he had abandoned (though these two aspects are not mutually dependent). This he did with such fervour, energy and originality that, within months of the world premiere of *Anaklasis*, at the Donaueschingen Festival in West Germany in October 1960, he was being touted as the brave new face of Polish music, a symbol of cultural rebirth and the figurehead of the 'Polish School'. His definition of the new sounds became the touchstone for 'sonorism'.

Too often, Penderecki's innovative outlook has been taken as indicative of a creative shallowness or sensationalism. He certainly intended to shock, but his purpose was serious. The titles were objective rather than descriptive, with the exception of *Threnody*, which was first performed in 1961 under the non-committal title, *8'37"*. Several of them were drawn from the

Greek (*anaklasis* – refraction of light, or an iambic rhythmic figure; *poly-morphia* – many-formedness; *fonogrammi* – sound-writings) or had quasi-scientific overtones. At this stage in his career, there is little to support the assumption that his explorations were primarily for emotionally expressive reasons, rather that he was fascinated by experiments in sound in which structure was determined by sharp contrasts and interlocking progressions of shape, contour, texture and colour. On severing his links with conventional musical modes of conduct,[19] he turned to the visual arts for support and inspiration:

> I am looking for deeper interconnections between painting and music . . .
> For me the most important issue is the problem of solving colours, colour
> concentration, as well as operating the texture and time. There are, for
> instance, paintings in which – through multifariousness – we achieve an
> impression of space and time. The task of music is to transplant all these
> elements of time and space, colour, and texture onto music.[20]

He went further in his programme note for the premiere of *Dimensions of Time and Silence* at the 1960 'Warsaw Autumn':

> The composition is an attempt to transplant some technical premises of Paul
> Klee and Yves Klein into the language of sound. These analogies are apparent
> in the segmental operation of various colours and structures, linked on the
> basis of 'penetration' (Klee) and in the insertion of static segments operating
> through vibrating 'sound space' or just their own resonance (Klein).[21]

Penderecki was thus one of a number of Polish composers in the early 1960s (like Baird and Zygmunt Krauze, b. 1938) who found significant exemplars outside music. While it would be foolish to conclude that all of Penderecki's pieces at this time were equally indebted to the visual arts, the bold visuality of his sketches – what might be termed 'graphic imaging' – supports analysis based on architectural sweep and proportion as well as provoking questions about macro-structures, subsections and local detailing, especially insofar as they avoid connections with musical antecedents.

The matter of what Chomiński called 'temporal regulation' is especially important. In outline, some of Penderecki's pieces follow the proven effi-cacy of ternary design (*Anaklasis*, *Threnody*, *Polymorphia*), but such is the ubiquity of ABA structures that little extra can be read into his usage of it. Its cushioning effect against the startling content of these pieces is an undeniable aspect, but little more so than a frame or outer proportions of a painting. Perceptions are certainly more challenged where the frame is open-ended, as in both versions of *Dimensions of Time and Silence* and the String Quartet. While a work's subsections may be viewed as part of a progressive continuum, the search for conventional form-building often misses the point; all these pieces are more through-composed than recapitulatory. Their impact lies in local (atemporal) and cumulative (temporal) juxtapositions, in superimpositions and interpenetrations of the painterly abstraction of sound shapes. These processes determine the perception of form, whether abstract or narrative, while the content of the sound shapes provides the local detail, the colour and texture. The greatest attention has been paid to the local detail, essentially the new sonorities and their sources in new instrumental techniques (needless to say, the notation of these details is an important corollary factor). Penderecki's approach to the larger concerns of form, on the other hand, is conventional, with no suggestion of mobile structures.

Although there were initial indications of new sonorities in 1958–9, especially in *Emanations* and *Three Miniatures*, it was in 1960 that Penderecki decisively jettisoned the past. Among the new sounds and techniques that he introduced for string players were, in *Anaklasis*, (*a*) quarter-tone clusters, clusters which (*b*) were static or (*c*) moved in a uniform glissando, (*d*) the concept of 'highest pitch possible', (*e*) striking the strings with the palm of the hand (strings as percussion) and (*f*) playing between the bridge and tailpiece. In the String Quartet, (*g*) playing on the tailpiece and (*h*) striking the (upper) body of the violin with the fingertips or the nut of the bow also joined the catalogue. This last feature was extended to all instruments in the revised version of *Dimensions of Time and Silence*, which shares with *Threnody* a particular new sound-texture, (*i*) where the low strings are played on the tailpiece and on the bridge. The most difficult technical task was presented at the start of the String Quartet, (*j*) where the score requires the players, senza arco, to 'set the string in vibration by pressing it strongly with the finger, with simultaneous trilling'. In *Polymorphia* and *Fluorescences*, players are additionally required to tap (*k*) their music stand with the bow or (*l*) their chair with the nut.

Anaklasis also involves percussion as a timbral foil, to which *Dimensions of Time and Silence* adds a forty-part mixed choir and *Fonogrammi* a solo flautist playing piccolo, flute and alto flute. The work with the most varied palette, *Fluorescences*, is scored for large orchestra, including quadruple woodwind, a brass section of 6.4.3.2, and six percussionists. Although described by Penderecki at the time of its premiere at Donaueschingen in October 1962 as 'a terminal balance-sheet',[22] *Fluorescences* is less a summation of the preceding two years of mainly string and percussion experiments than a one-off riotous adventure of 'a sorcerer's apprentice'[23] into the sound

potential of the other orchestral families. At times, it does resemble a catalogue of effects, insofar as it introduces instruments that are not being played
in new ways but are recognised rather for their innate sound world (type-
writer, musical saw, siren, flexatone, etc.).

Penderecki shapes his sounds in versatile ways. These range from a single
pitch class played solo or unison in conventional manner – the simplest
form of homogeneous sound – to complexes of heterogeneous material
using extended instrumental techniques. While it is beyond the scope of
this study to examine the full range of sound shapes which are witness to the
range of binary opposites (static–mobile, high–low, active–passive, loud–
soft, long–short, etc.), the following topic areas are indicative: (i) exploration of a single pitch class, (ii) clusters, (iii) heterogeneous sound shapes,
(iv) homogenous or canonic inventions and (v) percussion.

Firstly, the exploration of a single pitch class. As exemplified by *Dimensions of Time and Silence*, this can be a short, clear-cut episode (A flat, fig. 3),
a note which emerges from and/or disappears into other ideas (A natural,
fig. 17) (Ex. 9.2), or has a structural denotation on more conventional lines
(D natural, fig. 103). There are other instances where a single pitch class
functions as a major segment in its own right: in *Polymorphia* (A natural, figs. 46–53, lasting almost one minute) and *Fluorescences* (C natural,
figs. 68–85, lasting over two minutes), the common pitch is subjected
to a range of timbral variation and, in the latter case, also of rhythmic
articulation.

Secondly, and most fundamental to the concept of 'sonorism', is the broad
topic of the cluster. Clusters may begin and/or end as a single pitch class and
fan out stepwise – e.g. the start of *Anaklasis* on A (Ex. 9.3), or the series of
overlapping wedge clusters at fig. 18 in *Threnody* – or by glissando, such as
the start of *Polymorphia* on E or the sequence of different pitch classes which
initiate a series of expanding–contracting clusters in *Threnody* (Ex. 9.4). The
most varied example is the energetic respiratory layering which follows the
musing on A natural in *Polymorphia*. The intervallic ambit of clusters may
be fully formed at inception, totally static or animated as it were from inside
by very fast or very slow vibrato or irregular tremolo, with or without mutes,
sul ponticello or sul tasto (e.g., the closing minute of *Threnody*).

Most graphically, clusters can migrate. Such moments underline the fact
that what is melody is also harmony, at once a novel synthesis and a double negative. The first memorable example is the conclusion of *Anaklasis*
(Ex. 9.5), where five string clusters on harmonics disappear upwards, one
after the other, offset by interjections from percussion, harp and the inside
of the piano (cf. the strings-only sequel in *Threnody*, figs. 16–17).

Clusters such as these are habitually created from semitones or quarter
tones, though their intervallic constituents are of generally lesser importance

Example 9.2. Penderecki, *Dimensions of Time and Silence* (*Wymiary czasu i cisze*, 1960–61), figs. 14–21.

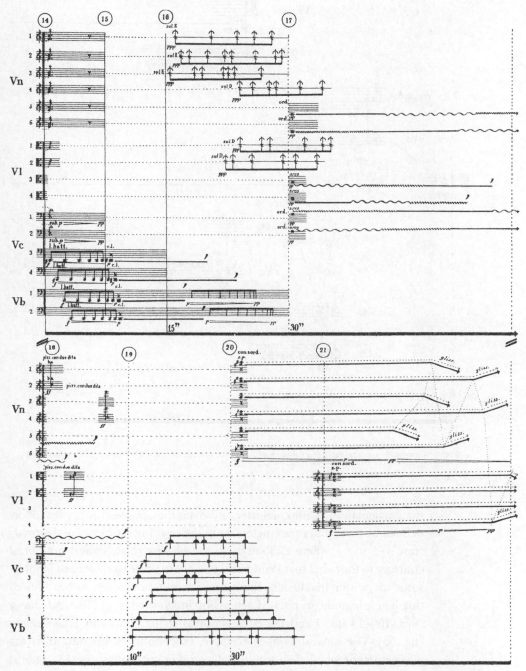

Example 9.3. Penderecki, *Anaklasis* (1959–60), opening.

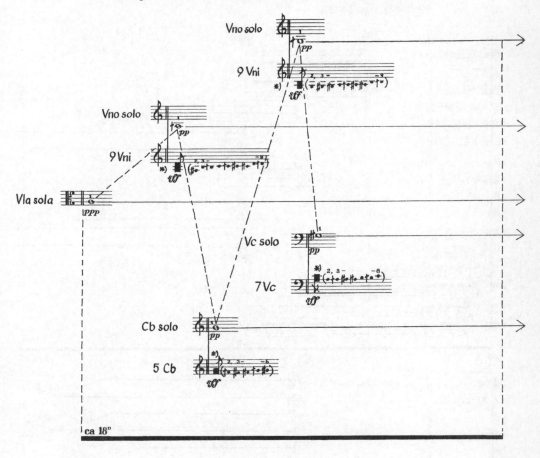

*) Każdy instrumentalista gra wyznaczony jego instrumentowi ton, tak aby równocześnie zabrzmiała cała skala ćwierćtonowa między podanym dolnym i górnym dźwiękiem.

than articulation, timbre, register and dynamics. Some clusters are totally defined by these latter parameters, as in the opening moments of *Threnody* (figs. 1–5 incl.), where all the strings are playing their highest note. And contrary to the belief that Penderecki was not in the least interested in intervallic 'air' within his clusters, there are a few instances where he has allowed this. These include the pitched percussion in *Dimensions of Time and Silence* (figs. 100–14 incl.) and the triple-stopped string chords in *Fluorescences* (fig. 55). The most organised example, exceptional in his output, is the pizzicato chordal accelerando in *Polymorphia* initiated at fig. 33. Against 'highest-note' violin pizzicati, the other strings hocket between two different twelve-note harmonic constructions – a ladder of perfect fourths and a

Example 9.4. Penderecki, *Threnody* (1960), fig. 10.

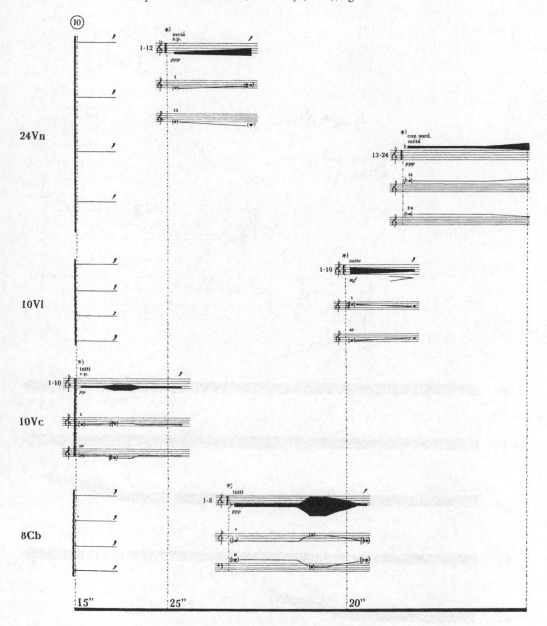

*) Dokładna realizacja w głosach. / Genaue Ausführung ist in den Stimmen angegeben.
Exact notation is given in the parts. / L'exécution précise est indiquée dans les parties.

Example 9.5. Penderecki, *Anaklasis* (1959–60), fig. 113.

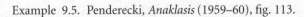

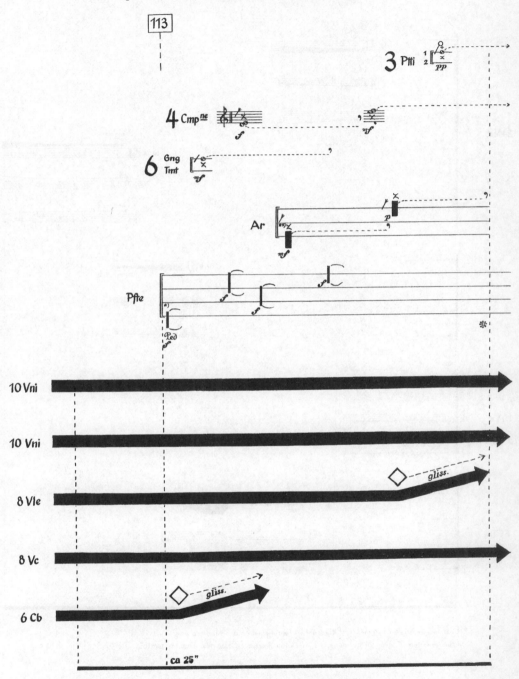

*) Kawałek drewienka (ołówek) rzucić na struny i pozostawić do wybrzmienia-do znaku ↑.
**) Struny uderzać miotełką jazzową (tremolo).

combination of the two whole-tone scales separated by a minor third. Despite these exceptions, clusters remain essentially close-packed and homogeneous. When they are dispersed into smaller fragments, even silence increases the level of heterogeneity. And when Penderecki prefers gradual shifts to blunt confrontations, he uses dispersal to mask the joins. Whether fully or partially formed, such sound shapes employ one of two basic organisational methods: heterogeneous sound shapes and homogenous, often canonic inventions.

The first of these (the third topic in this survey) is created aleatorically, with differing degrees of heterogeneity. There are several instances in the opening section of *Dimensions of Time and Silence*. At fig. 10, each of the six pitched percussion instruments plays its own twelve-note sequence within the 4" block. At fig. 16 (see Ex. 9.2), violins and violas introduce a six-voice scattering of rapid non-rhythmical tremolos between the bridge and tailpiece (high, *ppp*); at fig. 19, the lower strings provide its counterpole, playing on the bridge and tailpiece (low, *f*). A varied version of this latter texture is to be found in *Threnody* at fig. 62 (Ex. 9.6), where the two sound sources are organised in layered patterns of accelerando and decelerando (cf. Lutosławski's use of tempo in creating orchestral sound blocks in *Trois poèmes*, figs. 35–84). Examples of variegated sound blocks are equally numerous, e.g. figs. 6–9 in *Threnody*. Gradually taking over from the work's opening texture, the strings are divided into four successive blocks, each of which enters in sequence playing the same four rotations of seven textural motifs, none of which is conventional.[24] Elsewhere, Penderecki applies rotational or permutational principles to pitch (*Dimensions of Time and Silence*) and rhythmic patterns.

At this point, the survey comes to a crucial junction, because it is evident in these works of the early 1960s that Penderecki was not so enamoured of what a painter might call free brush strokes or total intuition that he felt he could dispense with more traditional means of organising the interior of his sound shapes. Examples of rotation in a rhythmically aleatory environment are at one end of this spectrum. At the other end lies the fourth topic area, that of unmetred or metred canonic inventions. The most striking of these notationally are the apparently encephalographic lines (the second version of *Dimensions of Time and Silence*, fig. 149, and *Polymorphia*, fig. 11) where the curves and points of a putative melodic line are used as canon fodder (Ex. 9.7).[25] This feature may also be observed in a programmatic context in *Dies Irae*. This texture is also but one of a number of instances in this period when Penderecki regulates the flow of time by means of one-second 'bar lines' (cf. the String Quartet, the revised conclusion of *Dimensions of Time and Silence*, and the permutational wind canon at fig. 20 in

Example 9.6. Penderecki, *Threnody* (1960), figs. 62–3.

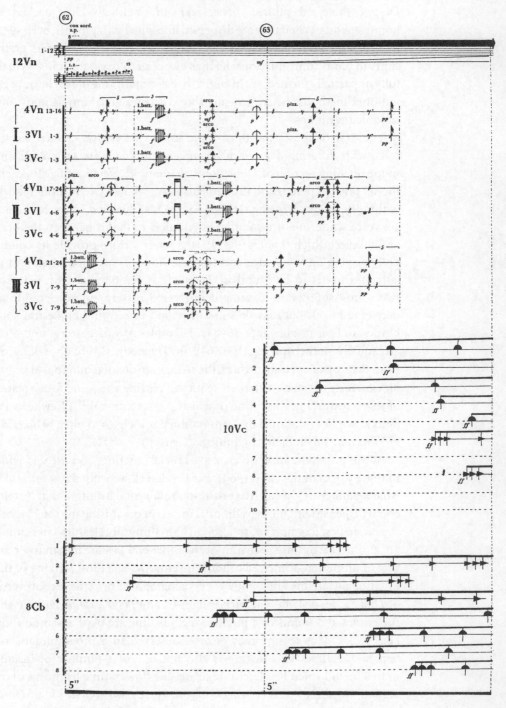

Example 9.7. Penderecki, *Dimensions of Time and Silence* (1960–1), figs. 144–53.

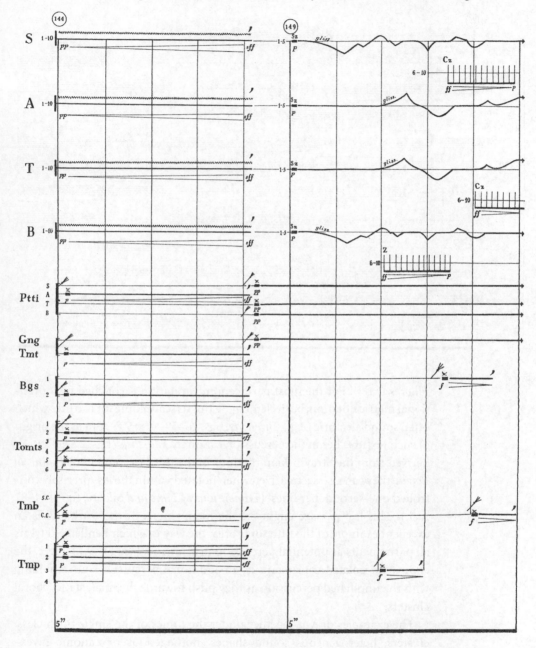

Example 9.8. Penderecki, *Threnody* (1960), fig. 26.

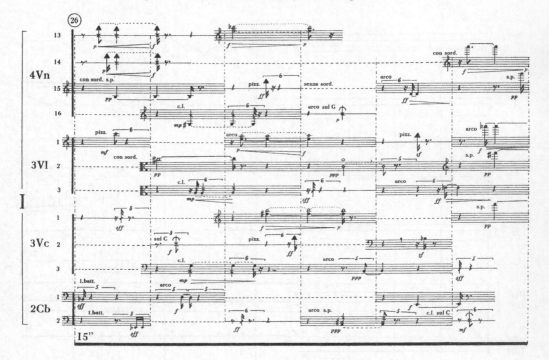

Fluorescences). For the most part, canonic imitation is couched in conventional metric notation, both elements acting as scaffolding for textures which often sound aleatoric (e.g., *Threnody*, figs. 26–59) (Ex. 9.8). But as the origin of such textures lies in the percussion canon in *Anaklasis* (figs. 22–37), itself derived from the Stravinskian rhythms in the third movement of *Psalms of David*, they can also seem driven when notated within the less precisely controlled one-second 'bar lines' (*Dimensions of Time and Silence*, figs. 144–87 incl.). This last passage engineers the main climax of the work and is an excellent example of the fifth topic area, the way in which Penderecki treats all participants as potential percussion instruments (see Ex. 9.7). Here, the choir uses isolated consonants as an additional percussive source, joining with the unpitched percussion as they push towards the final, static, choral clusters.

The examples drawn together under the topics of the single pitch class, clusters, heterogeneous sound shapes, homogenous or canonic inventions, and percussion, have indicated properties which properly belong to considerations of their larger structural context. If, however, these features are regarded as moment-by-moment foci, much as the content of a non-narrative abstract painting, then despite music's temporal dimension the overall structure of a work might be regarded as relatively insignificant. Some works operate within a loose ternary design, others are less recapitulatory, and the differences between the two doubtless shape perception. But it would be mistaken to value one over the other. It is of interest how the sound shapes are gathered together in what, to borrow another artistic term, might be called 'panels'.

In the two best-known ternary designs – *Anaklasis* and *Threnody* – the outer panels are dominated by unmetred textures and various types of cluster. Their central panels are metred, more airy, pointillistic and rhythmic, with strong imitative or canonic underpinning. In *Anaklasis*, the central panel is also concerned with what Penderecki called 'interpenetration', or overlap: a highly rhythmic section for unpitched percussion 'bleeds' into the pitched percussion, which in turn gradually overlaps with a pointillistic string section. The content of the final panel, although it recalls the cluster element of the first, is largely independent. It has a sense of textural focus that suggests it is moving forwards rather than confirming the past. In *Threnody*, a complex serially controlled three-part canon utilises some of the textural motifs from earlier in the piece (see Ex. 9.8), underlying the sense of dispersal, before bringing them to the fore in a brief, climactic hocket (figs. 56–63). The return to a fully clustered texture is engineered by a series of overlaps, the joins masked by the grating *fortissimo* of the sole appearance in *Threnody* of the tailpiece–bridge combination (i) mentioned earlier. The final panel therefore slips in quietly, acting as a vague reminiscence rather than a confirming recapitulation. In both works, the ternary design is therefore defined more by contrast between the inner and outer panels rather than by any firm intention to create closure.

The String Quartet and both versions of *Dimensions of Time and Silence* are fascinating examples of open-ended structures. The String Quartet, notionally the briefest of these pieces at six minutes, is a binary structure in which the first 'panel' (up to 3'10") furnishes material for the second. The inner timing of the entire work is regulated by one-second 'bar lines' grouped in fives; each double-page spread of the score is a minute long. The first panel consists of a lengthy series of slow-burning heterogeneous interpenetrations (0'20"–2'50") framed by smaller, clear-cut textural groups. The central section of interpenetrations is constructed on the basis of arithmetical operations rather than the closer serial workings of the central panel of *Threnody*. As Krzysztof Bilica has shown, various number series are in operation, the figures referring to the number of 'events' beamed together in any one part.[26] On the level of macro-structure, the relationship of the

Quartet's second panel to the first is comparable to that of a pointillistic dispersal of a cluster. The second panel is a procession of fragmented ideas based on figures or events in the first panel. And although there are local areas of coherence or momentum, its discourse is marked by a strong sense of dispersal. Not even an eighteen-second recollection of the first panel's hectic heterogeneity (4'58"–5'16") is sufficient to quash the sense of fleeting formal coherence. The 'textural–motivic' structural dissolution has perhaps its closest Polish parallel in the central movement of Bacewicz's *Music for Strings, Trumpets and Percussion*, composed two years earlier.

It is no accident that the discussion returns frequently to *Dimensions of Time and Silence*. It is the clearest example of Penderecki's understanding of the value of the mathematical procedures and structural connections between different components that he observed in the abstract visual arts, especially Klee's paintings: 'My piece *Dimensions of Time and Silence* also consists of a dozen or so closed cells, which form in themselves separate wholes and are juxtaposed on the principle of imposition.'[27] These 'dozen or so closed cells', each clearly defined from its neighbours in its parametric profile, are presented in sequence in what appears to be the first of the piece's 'panels', sometimes abutting, sometimes overlapping in relay. Penderecki groups them into larger sets, firstly percussion, then strings (from fig. 12) (see Ex. 9.2), then percussion (fig. 22), including a metred rhythmic passage from fig. 28, and finally vocal (fig. 46), with a brief percussion cell at the end (fig. 50). At this point, in what seems to be a second 'panel', Penderecki does something quite unexpected: he retrogrades the cells from fig. 28 back to the very beginning (figs. 54–82 incl.), adding on the retrograde of the metred passage (figs. 28–45 incl.) for good measure (figs. 83–102). He has thus created an essentially palindromic form, framing it apparently as a separate entity, with the unretrograded choral–percussive idea at the core of what is now understood not as a double panel but as a ternary structure.

It is shortly after this juncture that the first and second versions of *Dimensions of Time and Silence* diverge. The first minute remains the same in both: the choir takes charge, as if to suggest that everything up to fig. 103 has been merely introductory. From initial alto D naturals, the choir reaches a *fortissimo* semitonal cluster spanning over three octaves. From this moment (end of fig. 107), in the first version, the choir has a brief passage and is followed (as in the published score) by reiterated notes on pitched percussion. Then the choir launches the rest of the piece *a cappella*. Its text in this first version consists of a magic square favoured by Webern: SATOR AREPO TENET OPERA ROTAS. This concluding panel, predominantly a Webernian choral texture, is a startlingly effective contrast to what precedes it. It both complements and contradicts it, but it has little connection materially or stylistically. After the premiere, Penderecki ejected the final choral section completely, and its replacement not only ties in with aspects of the first section, notably the choir's percussive rotational patterns on the consonants B D G K P T, but it is stylistically more of a piece. In one sense, this creates a more unified and balanced score (the piece now lasts well over twelve minutes compared to the original eight to nine). But there is perhaps a lingering question: did Penderecki demonstrate a more conservative trait by wanting to tie in the final section more securely, thereby shying away from the more colourful, stark panelling of the first version?

The suggestion of traditional closure is most apparent in *Polymorphia*, where lapidary evolution is more central than confrontation, resulting in an organicism which is almost symphonic. It is the most tautly controlled of all these pieces in its expressive temperature and in the compatibility of its various cross-referenced materials. From the dark depths of the opening E natural, Penderecki builds up a quasi-electronic texture, almost like a gloss on the opening of Wagner's *Das Rheingold*. Its use of open clusters (made up of whole tones, thirds and fourths, as well as the customary quarter tones and semitones) also brings a degree of luminosity to the cluster formations. And the extended episode on A natural further enforces the sense that the purportedly aharmonic, atonal nature of sonorism is on the verge of dissolution.

The greatest surprise is yet to come. There has been no rational explanation why *Polymorphia* should end with a chord of C major. The composer has said that not only was this final chord the starting point for the piece but also that it is the resolution of the preceding cluster. This is theoretically arguable, and indeed the preceding emphases on certain pitch classes and the open clusters may retrospectively be seen to augur such a conclusion. (In fact, this final gesture has the same cadential function as its counterpart in *Threnody*: would a diatonic triad instead of the two-octave quarter-tonal cluster at fig. 70 in *Threnody* have had any less impact than here?) The value of the C major triad lies not in any putative harmonic consequentiality that confirms a traditional process but in its radical challenge to what Penderecki had established as his norms.[28] If it was more than a temporary and puzzling shock tactic, his subsequent pieces would no doubt absorb its implications.

Throughout the 1960s and into the early 1970s, Penderecki's orchestral works maintained a strong though not exclusive connection to sonorism. Foremost among them are the two works whose title underscores Penderecki's continuing interest in sound manipulation, *De natura sonoris* I (1966) and II (1970–1). Among the other notable features are Penderecki's development of works which, by their concertante nature, represent a significant compromise with the abstraction of 'high' sonorism: Sonata for cello and orchestra (1964), Capriccio for oboe and eleven strings (1965), Capriccio for violin and orchestra (1967), Partita for harpsichord, electric and bass guitars, double bass and chamber orchestra (1971) and the First Cello Concerto (1972), which shares material with the Concerto per violino grande (1967). The culmination of this period was the First Symphony (1973), which can truly be regarded as 'a terminal balance sheet' of the instrumental music up to this point.

Whether Penderecki was ever a fundamentally radical composer is a matter for debate. His later career indicates that he is more conservatively grounded than the two non-Polish composers with whom he was often linked in the 1960s: Xenakis and Ligeti. There are some superficial similarities between them, but the working methods are quite different. There is no equivalent in Penderecki to Xenakis's stochastic theories or Ligeti's micropolyphony. Penderecki's strength lies not in the preparatory or inner detail but in the immediate drama of extreme contrasts, in an almost visceral expressivity. This became quickly apparent in his renewed interest in traditional choral music, as distinct from the asemantic percussiveness of the vocal writing in *Dimensions of Time and Silence*.

Unusually for Polish music in the 1960s, Penderecki's music from 1962 is dominated by choral composition. Penderecki began his departure from sonorism with Stabat Mater (1962) for three unaccompanied choirs. The vocal writing picks up where the second movement of *Psalms of David* had left off four years earlier. Its indiosyncratic amalgam of plainchant tradition, *Sprechstimme*, spoken passages 'quasi una litania', chromatic counterpoint and clusters was a potent and prescient mix. Although it follows *Polymorphia* in ending with a diatonic triad (D major), the effect is rather different in that it is a conceivable resolution to the pitched material which precedes it. The other major factor is that this is a work with a sacred text, written and premiered at a time when such a composition was a major symbolic statement. But it paled into insignificance when it was absorbed into the mould-breaking *Passio et mors Domini nostri Jesu Christi secundum Lucam* (commissioned 1962), which was premiered in Münster in West Germany on 30 March 1966 and given its Polish premiere three weeks later in Kraków. The *St Luke Passion* was the first large-scale oratorio-like work by a Polish composer since the nineteenth century and its scale and ambition were startling. There then followed a series of major choral compositions which, if not directly sacred, pursued themes involving compassion and concern for humanity: *Dies Irae*, dedicated to the victims of Auschwitz, *Cosmogony* (1970), composed for the twenty-fifth anniversary of the United Nations, and the two-part *Utrenia* (*Jutrznia*) – 'The Entombment of Christ' ('Złożenie Chrystus do grobu', 1970) and 'The Lord's Resurrection' ('Zmartwychwstanie Pańskie', 1971). *Canticum canticorum Salomonis* (1970–3) and *Magnificat* (1974) complete this group, although it is worth mentioning in this context Penderecki's first opera, *The Devils of Loudun* (*Diabły z Loudun*, 1969), which also has connections with religion, albeit with an emphasis on human corruption and venality.

In the eyes of some commentators, Penderecki's works of high sonorism were now to be regarded as a staging post to the grander, more 'meaningful' oratorio-related genre established by the *St Luke Passion*. If this is true, then the innate qualities of the early works are demeaned and the transparent 'messaging' of the texted compositions is raised to new heights of symbolism. Those who viewed the sonoristic pieces as representing the best of the Polish avant-garde were more likely to view Penderecki's new direction as a compromise too far. A cynic might suggest that Penderecki realised, having seen in the case of *Threnody* the effect an emotive title could have on a work's perception and success, that his particular talents could be especially eloquent when topics of religion, persecution and the plight of humanity were invoked. And there were many resonances in Polish society and history which could be struck, hence his electronic score for the radio play, *Brigade of Death* (*Brygada śmierci*, 1963), based on diary entries made in 1943 by a Polish inmate of a Nazi extermination camp in Lwów, and hence the dedication of *Dies Irae* 'Oratorium ob memoriam in perniciei castris in Oświęcim necatorum inexstinguibilem reddendam'. Even the two movements of the Concerto per violino grande were titled 'Quasi purgatorio' and 'Suoni celeste'. What is undoubted, however, is that Penderecki's *St Luke Passion* broke out from the confines of specialist contemporary music and into the repertoire of broad concert programmes, reaching a spread of audiences at home and abroad that was unrivalled in the Polish context until the worldwide success of Górecki's Third Symphony (1976) twenty-seven years later.

The *St Luke Passion* followed hot on the heels of Britten's *War Requiem* (1962) to become the 'sacred' music phenomenon of the late 1960s. Its success was rarely unqualified and opinions have frequently been divided.[29] At the New York premiere in 1969, 'all the Right People were there – Copland, Carter, Cage, Sessions, Babbitt, Feldman . . . The reception at the end was powerful and prolonged, the cheers finally winning out over the boos.'[30] Harold Schonberg wrote one of the most perceptive reviews, including in his comments:

Can this be one of those pieces of modern music for people who hate modern music? . . . Whether or not *Saint Luke* lives as a viable piece of music, it does illustrate a movement that tries to take music out of abstractionism into something that has a direct contact with life and reality . . . The audience at the Carnegie Hall concert may have been in on the birth of neo-romanticism in the 1970s.[31]

The heart of the controversy lies in the Passion's retrospective nature, in the revivification of an eighteenth-century genre associated primarily with Bach and certain of its associated stylistic, rhetorical and linguistic traits. In the process, Penderecki reclaimed many of the musical parameters he had so brusquely abandoned in 1959, thereby seeming to undermine his commitment to sonorism as an integral compositional approach, preferring to utilise its colouristic features as but one of several disparate resources. The main critical concern seemed to be whether this new heterogeneity was too dependent for its coherence on its programmatic context. Was it a genuinely musical synthesis or subservient to extra-musical forces? Having explored a largely abstract sound world, Penderecki was ready to give greater attention to programmatic genres, such as the oratorio and opera, and his subsequent career has shown that both vocal and instrumental streams have been pursued more or less in tandem. He is on record as saying, for example, that a number of smaller instrumental pieces are offshoots of larger vocal pieces and were composed simultaneously: *De natura sonoris* I is 'paired' with the *St Luke Passion*, *The Awakening of Jacob* (*Przebudzenie Jakuba*, 1974) with *Magnificat*.[32] This suggests that he saw no substantial stylistic difference between pieces with and without text. This is correlated by the unusual case of *Cosmogony*, where 'the collage of texts does not influence the musical form; the musical form is autonomous. Text and music meet only at one point (the chord on the Copernican word "sol" [sun]).'[33]

The *St Luke Passion*, on the other hand, is driven by the text, which characteristically draws on other sources: St John's gospel, excerpts from five Old Testament psalms and the Lamentations of Jeremiah, plus several non-biblical and liturgical texts. Self-standing musical structures, such as the Passacaglia in Part II (fig. 16), are rare; the burden of narrative and reflection is borne by clearly defined conventional arias (with and without chorus), recitatives (spoken) and choruses (accompanied and *a cappella*), some of which become major set pieces. The more obviously dramatic sections ('The Taking of Jesus', 'The Mocking before the High Priest' or 'The Mocking of Christ on the Cross') furnish Penderecki with opportunities for violent expressive textures, which he seizes with a faultless sense of timing (less is more in this regard). But the main expressive weight lies on the reflective sections, notably the several unaccompanied psalms, such as the 'Miserere' towards the end of Part I. Indeed, the Passion is exceptionally, even indulgently riven with a lacerating penitence. Here, as elsewhere, the music is saturated with the intervallic components of the BACH motif. This cell and a not dissimilar four-note motif which opens one of Poland's most famous hymns, 'Holy God' ('Święty Boże'), are integral foreground components of the underlying twelve-note pitch organisation. Recurrent foci on individual pitch classes (e.g. G and D naturals in Part I) and the periodic brief two-chord refrain on the word 'Domine' are two of the other agents with which Penderecki seeks to bind the Passion. He revisits the major-chord endings of *Polymorphia* and the Stabat Mater by ending on an E major triad to the words 'Deus veritatis'. Whether this conclusion is an attempt to bring a sense of release to the Passion as a whole, or just to the unresolved cadentiality of the 'Domine' motif, is hard to tell. Its thunder is certainly stolen by the D major chord retained at the end of the Stabat Mater a few minutes earlier. More tellingly, this triadic exclamation mark has an even more jarring effect here than in either of its predecessors. It satisfies no long-term musical nor textual need (the work ends, after all, with 'The Death of Christ' and a final psalm) and is too brief and simplistic a response to a substantial programmatic work of such dark power, grit and plangency.

No such accusation can be levelled against *Dies Irae*. Penderecki gives full rein to his rapidly developing sense of the apocalyptic; in so doing, he anticipates themes and their treatments in *The Devils of Loudun*, the *sacra rappresentazione*, *Paradise Lost* (*Raj utracony*, 1976–8) and his third opera, *Black Mask* (*Czarna maska*, 1984–6). The final 'Apotheosis' has a seriousness to counterbalance the preceding two sections, 'Lamentatio' and 'Apokalypsis', and any suggestions of easy resolution are denied. A *fortissimo* choral unison at the word 'victor[ia]' is firmly quashed and the work ends with a reiteration of the affecting mezzo-voce 'Corpora parvulorum' [The bodies of children] from the opening 'Lamentation'. *Dies Irae* was the first Polish work to address the Holocaust explicitly and on the world stage, though Maciejewski's *Missa pro defunctis* (1946–59), Wiechowicz's *Letter to Marc Chagall* and *Kinoth* (1963) by Zbigniew Bujarski (b. 1933) are important forerunners.[34] Penderecki realised his project not as a transcendence of the horrors of Auschwitz (cf. the intention and tone of Górecki's Third Symphony, 'Symphony of Sorrowful Songs', composed nine years later) but as a fire and brimstone sermon on the Day of Reckoning. His selection of texts is characteristically imaginative: the classic *Dies Irae* is jettisoned in favour of the Book of Psalms, Corinthians and Revelations, as well as excerpts from Aeschylus' *The Eumenides*. And rather like Britten (*War Requiem*) and Tippett (*A Child of Our Time*), he also draws on contemporary texts: most of the opening

'Lamentatio' turns to harrowing Holocaust poetry by Broniewski, Aragon and Różewicz. The central 'Apokalypsis' is among the most overwhelming music he has written, with many of the sonoristic effects from the early 1960s now put to use in an illustrative, almost cinematic way (Ex. 9.9).

The two other smaller-scale vocal and orchestral works of this period – *Cosmogony* and *Canticum canticorum Salomonis* – are less narrative, using their texts and the voices for generalised effect. Despite the fact that the former has an intriguing selection of texts set in their original lanuguages – Ovid and Lucretius, da Vinci and Copernicus, and words by Yuri Gagarin and John Glenn during their first space flights – such is the way they are used that the choral input is but one more sound source, its detail as subservient to the enveloping sound shapes as the orchestral material. *Cosmogony* is therefore closer to the traditional symphonic poem than to oratorio-related genres. It may also be regarded as a secular 'act of worship', with the luminescence of a major triad (E flat) on the word 'sol' placed not at the end but at the mid-point, allowing it both time and space to reverberate through the rest of the piece. The role of the voices (a sixteen-part choir) in *Canticum canticorum Salomonis* is much more central, even though its Latin text is also treated in a liberally asemantic way. Befitting its erotic subject matter (the Old Testament Song of Solomon), the language is seductive, the physicality of its sound world sensuous where *Dies Irae* was brutal (cf. the individual quarter-tone inflections in the voice parts and the use of conches (or ocarinas) at the beginning, and the carefully pitched instrumental and vocal 'glissandi' from fig. 21). It straddles the divide between the sacred and profane tendencies in Penderecki's music, a theme explored in different ways by the two stage works which flank it, *The Devils of Loudun* and *Paradise Lost*.

Penderecki's appetite for large-scale sacred choral works had been whetted by the *St Luke Passion* and continues to this day (*Seven Gates of Jerusalem*, 1996, and *Credo*, 1998). In one sense, the two-part *Utrenia* forms the sequel to the *St Luke Passion*. And yet its atmosphere and musical language are markedly different. Most obviously, this is a work whose inspiration lies not in old Catholic traditions but in Orthodox rites which Penderecki witnessed in north-eastern Poland, the USSR and Bulgaria. Colouristically, this is evidenced by its massed choralism, the use of animated and harmonised chant, the emphasis on extreme vocal registers (very low bass, falsetto tenor) and, in Part II ('The Lord's Resurrection'), the inclusion of authentic wooden and brass bells and pulsating dance rhythms.[35] No less importantly, its heightened vocal and instrumental ecstasy and its submersion of textual meaning in rapturous and mystical paraphrase, which it shares with *Cosmogony* and *Canticum canticorum Salomonis*, comes from an intensified rapprochement

Example 9.9. Penderecki, *Dies Irae* (1967), 'Apokalypsis'.

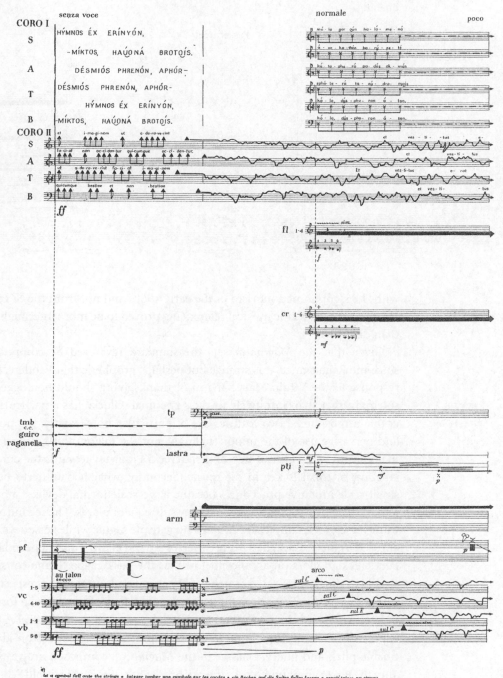

Example 9.10. Penderecki, *Magnificat* (1974), fifth movement 'Passacaglia', opening.

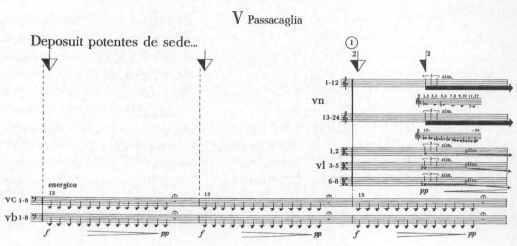

with the symphonic sonorism of the early 1960s and not from the *St Luke Passion*, whose specific musical referencing proved to be more intermediate than definitive.

Given that the *Magnificat* sets the standard text used by composers since the Renaissance, it is strange but perhaps prophetic that Penderecki's response to the Virgin Mary's hymn of thanksgiving should be doggedly solemn rather than intuitively joyous. The final 'Gloria' has a particularly gothic atmosphere. Two features are of particular note. Firstly, the novel and pervasive use of the minor (tellingly, not the major) third, especially melodically, was a crucial step on Penderecki's journey towards the emancipation of tonal forces in his music. Secondly, what had hitherto been small-scale imitative procedures became large-scale formal devices, a portent of structural underpinning in many subsequent pieces. The second and third verses, for example, are cast as a huge triple fugue, while verse seven is encased in the passacaglia setting of verses six and eight. This is a peculiarly Pendereckian gloss on an ancient form, as the passacaglia theme consists simply of thirteen repeated crotchets, D natural and A flat in the respective verses (Ex. 9.10). This tritonal relationship, the first of many to be found in later works, is brought to the fore when the concluding orchestral A flat is preceded by a unison choral D on the word 'Israel'. The focus on identifiable pitch and interval classes in the *Magnificat*, composed only a year after the First Symphony, marks the real break with sonorism: Harold Schonberg's perception of Penderecki's incipient neo-romanticism was about to be confirmed.

Górecki

The sensation of the 1960 'Warsaw Autumn' was the premiere of Górecki's *Scontri*. Quite apart from atomising the conventional orchestral layout, it was the first instance of a Polish composer apparently disregarding any formal or musical coherence in favour of a reckless pursuit of extremes. In terms of its orchestral and structural scale, it towered over its rivals; even comparable compositional cauldrons such as Serocki's *Episodes*, Penderecki's *Anaklasis* or Lutosławski's *Venetian Games* seemed to have milder ambitions. Just as Górecki had dealt with neo-classicism in the *Sonata for Two Violins* three years earlier, so now he wanted to explode the myth of serialism. He had already begun to undermine it in the first movement of Symphony '1959', where his twelve-note matrix is presented crudely as a dense homophonic recitative on the strings, denying it the conventional linear or contrapuntal subtleties and interlocking it with percussion in a series of block contrasts unprecedented in Polish music. In *Scontri*, the string texture had been transformed into a squirming, three-octave semitonal cluster (fig. 6).

What distinguishes Górecki's clusters from Penderecki's simultaneous exploitation of them is that in *Scontri* they form but one component in a teeming multitude of ideas. Where *Anaklasis* and *Threnody* are characterised by a restricted timbral palette, however unconventional, and are dominated by stasis rather than galvanised movement, *Scontri* explodes with a startling and panoramic array of melodic, harmonic, rhythmic, timbral and dynamic fireworks. Nor is Górecki timid in his time-scale: in the longest single-span Polish orchestral piece of its time at some seventeen minutes, his invention never flags. A great part of its energy comes from its restless and metred rhythmic character. When this is combined with an unpredictable pace of change in other parameters, particularly timbre and texture, the music lives on a combination of volatility and apprehension. On a technical level, far from being incoherent, the work is planned meticulously and realised intuitively. Its pitch organisation – one principal twelve-note series and three minor ones – also furnishes number series used to create dynamic and durational sequences. And these are integrated with a structural template consisting of six sections, subdivided into twenty-eight 'sheets' more or less corresponding to the double-page spread of the printed score. In turn, each sheet was originally intended to unfold a rotationally variant order of the four orchestral families. In sum, Górecki designed a kaleidoscopic patchwork to operate at different levels; in reality, as the work progresses, he frees himself from his original plan and proceeds by instinct. Like Penderecki, his reliance on earlier procedures was being overtaken by an increased confidence in his independence of them.

In retrospect, *Scontri* was a last Polish hurrah for the orchestral block-buster; it was Górecki's *Rite of Spring*. His next major project was conceived on a more modest scale, though its expressivity was commensurately intensified. It is in the three parts of the *Genesis* cycle (1962–3) that he comes closest to the type of high sonorism espoused by Penderecki. Nevertheless, there is never any doubt, in terms of style and the way materials are used, that Górecki's aesthetic is quite distinct. He has a great command of musical narrative (little patience here with the abstraction of sonorism), a confidence in the pacing of through-composed structures and an unabashed relish in bold timbres, ritual and ostinato (especially in the unusually scored second and third parts, *Canti strumentali* and *Monodramma*). As Patkowski commented on *Canti strumentali* in a radio review of the 1962 'Warsaw Autumn': 'The rich range of colour . . . has a strong, immediate, as it were physiological effect. This sonic hedonism of Górecki, characteristic of the nascent Polish school, confers on *Canti strumentali* a special rank.'[36]

The first of the cycle, *Elementi* for three string instruments (violin, viola and cello), is one of the least ingratiating and yet most powerfully sensuous of post-war Polish compositions. The combination of 'genesis' and 'elements' is indicative of Górecki's desire to probe the essence of sound. The musical material may be similar to Penderecki's arsenal of string effects, but there is a vehement dissonance and breathtaking momentum to its deployment which other composers rarely attempted and which can make some brands of sonorism seem diluted or sluggish in comparison. This is through-composition with a vengeance and the fact that he is still initiating a piece with a detailed pre-compositional and serially derived ground-plan is even more astonishing than in the case of *Scontri*.

As expected, the finished product almost completely masks its organisational origins. There are clues. The last of the work's twenty-two 'fragment groups' (Górecki's term) outlines the twelve-note series which sourced Górecki's pre-compositional decisions (Ex. 9.11). It is disguised by overlaying three partitions of the series (violin: notes 5–4–3–2–1; viola: 6–7; cello: 8–9–10–11–12), each note doubled at the fifth below; the final dislocation is caused by the fact that the instruments were detuned a few minutes earlier, making this apparently clear sequence purely nominal (identifiable pitch classes play a greatly reduced role in any case in *Elementi*). The row's sequence of eleven intervals is used to create a palindromic pattern of 'fragment groups' based on their numerical equivalents, first in prime, then in retrograde: 11–5–11–2–9–6–11–3–13–5–11/11–5–13– etc. These figures then successively determine the number of events within each 'fragment group', although Górecki replaces any serial derivations for dynamics and timbre with simpler and shorter number sequences. As a

Example 9.11. Górecki, *Genesis* I: *Elementi* (1962), fig. 25.

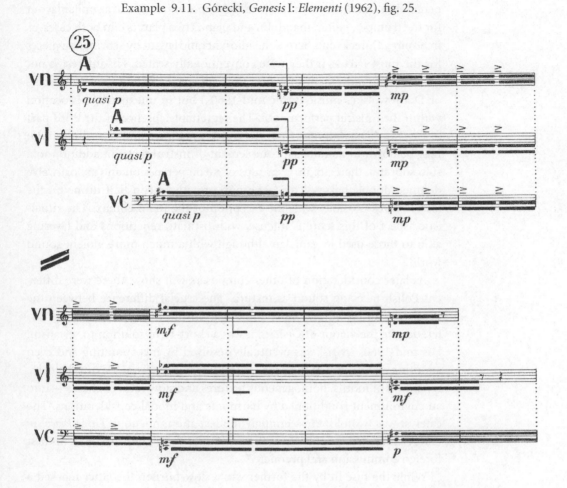

further example of Górecki's deliberate denial of the row's significance, and rather like a painter scraping down one surface before building further layers above it, he varies wildly the criteria for implementing these events. They can be sequential, concurrent, they can be a sustained texture or a short, sharp chord. In this way, the ground-plan is superseded by the expressive demands of the moment. Nevertheless, Górecki is careful not to present the work as a free-for-all and shapes his textures into paragraphs, marking out the mid-point (fig. 15) by a striking change in pace, timbre and dynamic.

Górecki's interest in spatial layouts was at its height in the late 1950s and early 1960s. *Genesis* is no exception. The three players in *Elementi* are placed at the back and at either side of the front of the stage, separated by between six and twelve metres. In *Canti strumentali* for fifteen players, the violins, violas, percussion and flutes form two lozenge shapes either side of a similar layout for the trumpet, guitar, mandolin and piano (two players). In both cases, as in *Scontri*, Górecki cuts across the idiosyncratic layout by scoring the pieces for the most part as if they were conventionally seated. His interest is not in schematic movement of sound through space (as in Serocki's *Episodes* or Dobrowolski's music in the mid-1960s) but in unexpected dislocation within the musical performance. The regrettable absence of the third part of *Genesis*, *Monodramma*, from the concert platform and recording studio may be down to its unusual complement of instruments: in addition to a solo soprano, there are three groups of metal percussion and six or twelve detuned double basses. This last group provides a constant drone on the lowest notes possible, with the exception of the main climax. The ritualistic aspect of this score is intense, with ostinati, repetitions and layering akin to those used in gamelan although with a much more violent sound world.

As later consideration of other composers will show, there were different Polish takes on sound as texture. The crucial difference between the Pendereckian brand and Górecki's angle on the issue is that for the latter, despite the vigour of *Genesis*, it was a short-term solution to serialism. His mid-1960s 'crisis' was eventually resolved by incorporating and even adopting anew some of the broader features of sonorism – textural blocks, repetition of motifs, homogeneous textures and slow rates of change – into an environment conditioned by harmonic and modal considerations. The catalyst was twofold: the seemingly modest and innocuous *Three Pieces in Old Style* for strings (1963) and *Refrain* (*Refren* for orchestra, 1965), his first foreign commission and premiere.

While the fuse lit by the former was a slow-burner, the latter marked a more obvious turning point in his career. Unlike Penderecki, Górecki had not established himself as a major presence abroad, although his First Symphony was given its first complete performance at Darmstadt in 1963. This situation was partly due to his natural diffidence in the public sphere, but also because his output was neither huge nor easily programmed (although *Monologhi* won the ZKP's Young Composers' Competition in 1960, it was not until 1968, in West Berlin, that it received its first performance). After *Scontri*, Górecki had to all intents and purposes retreated from public view, just at the moment when Penderecki and, to a lesser extent, Lutosławski were being increasingly celebrated abroad. They had already set out on stylistic and technical paths that were to prove durable. Górecki, on the other hand, while not in any way disowning *Scontri* or *Genesis*, went back to the drawing board, taking his time before embarking on the road that was to lead to the Third Symphony and beyond.

Even in a system of state subsidies for creative artists, it was always necessary for them to take on work other than major official commissions. Lutosławski wrote some three dozen popular songs (foxtrots, tangos, waltzes) under the pseudonym 'Derwid' throughout 1957–64; Baird and Serocki continued to write significant film scores into the 1960s; Penderecki wrote a considerable amount of incidental music for marionette theatres (1957–67) and many composers were connected with mainstream theatre. Górecki was no exception to this trend, although he took on rather less of this type of work than many others. One piece of what might so easily have been hack work, *Three Pieces in Old Style*, was to prove immensely significant for his musical development. At the time, it passed more or less without notice and seemed marginal to his main output, especially when Górecki failed to give the work a customary opus number. The piece had been commissioned by the head of PWM, Tadeusz Ochlewski, for an 'Evening of Early Polish Music and Poetry' in Warsaw. Górecki's response was to compose a set of three modal pieces, the last of which was an unusual rendition of a sixteenth-century, four-part Polish royal wedding song. Five features here were prescient: the use of church modes, the incorporation of pre-existing music, the use of an harmonic 'aura' (the first five notes of the Dorian mode form a backdrop for the four-part harmonised song in the same mode), the isolation of the song's tenor line for special attention, and the homophonic stacking of the tenor to create parallel harmonisation (in this instance, on all eight notes of the mode). This last feature, which can be traced back as far as the 'Russian Dance' in Stravinsky's *Petrushka*, was to become an essential component in Górecki's modal music in the 1970s. Innocuous though it is, *Three Pieces in Old Style* marked the first decisive break with the sonorism of *Genesis*.

The second break was *Refrain*. Its ternary design and atmosphere, informed by palindromic patterns at all levels, seems to hark back to Messiaen's *Les offrandes oubliées*. Confrontational hockets in the central section between brass, timpani and woodwind–string chords are framed by material which, as in Messiaen's piece, has a calm, transcendental aura. In fact, *Refrain* is quite unlike any other Polish or European piece of its time and the outer sections mark a radical shift in Górecki's aesthetic. Unlike those contemporary works which were re-engaging with mainstream traditions of musical narrative (as varied as Bacewicz's Divertimento and Penderecki's *St Luke Passion*) and those who were still working through the issues of sonorism (Szalonek's *Les sons*), Górecki was staking out a distinctive territory of expressive restraint. The music of the outer sections is metred, quiet, non-confrontational, conventionally notated and played, and exceptionally slow-moving. The opening section unfolds as a series of palindromic melodic refrains on the strings, starting and finishing on C natural, each refrain developing the intervallic detail of its predecessor from within, like a sequence of organic inhalations and exhalations. And while the chant-like melodic ambit concentrates on semitones (its first statement being confined to an outline C–D flat–C, later expanding to a maximum range of a minor third), its harmonic design is whole-tone and its implementation relates back to the third of the *Three Pieces*. The melody is stacked in open octaves, five parallel lines moving in a four-octave range bounded by C–E flat and c'''–e flat'''. Each subsequent refrain adds the pitch class a whole tone higher in each of the five octaves, so that by the sixth refrain (Ex. 9.12) Górecki has a full whole-tone cluster moving in parallel with the melody, a harmonically clarified descendant of the string cluster at fig. 6 in *Scontri*. The friction between melodic and harmonic intervals is finely judged to keep the music pulsing, despite its marking of ♩ = 26–8. In the concluding section, Górecki progressively reduces the texture back to the original octave C naturals, though by a different route.

Perhaps the most striking aspect of *Refrain* is its control of time. Gone is the sensory hustling of *Scontri* and *Elementi*. Instead, the ritualistic repetitions of the other parts of *Genesis* are brought to bear on a recognisable melodic, harmonic and rhythmic language in a totally original way. This amalgam leads to a perception of time in which the metabolic rate has been drastically reduced (how many other composers have used such a slow tempo marking?); even in the 'fast' central section, movement is more apparent than real because of the tight harmonic and rhythmic control. The transparency of material and compositional process is extraordinarily eloquent. In its stripping away of serial and sonoristic inessentials, in its abstract agenda, *Refrain* arguably presented the most individual resolution to date of the post-1956 tumult.

Just as had happened after *Scontri*, Górecki again turned after *Refrain* to a group of ensemble pieces with an overarching theme. Where, in Górecki's eyes, *Genesis* had been primarily about compositional technique, the four pieces called *Little Music* (*Muzyczka*) were concerned with character: 'all the *Musiquettes* are composed on the same principle: the utmost economy of musical material'.[37] The first three were composed in 1967, the fourth in 1970. Standing quietly behind Górecki's new compositional targets were his developing confidence in repetition at the level of motif and refrain and the concomitant dispensing with obvious forward momentum. Where Lutosławski's motivic and harmonic materials were designed to create movement towards an identifiable goal, Górecki in the late 1960s frequently put his faith in ideas which give the strong impression of operating outside time, not least because of their slow and almost imperceptible rate of change.

Example 9.12. Górecki, *Refrain* (1965), sixth refrain (first half).

In the vocal music of the 1970s, such features emphasised thoroughgoing modality and gentle contours, creating a strongly meditative atmosphere.

The bristling energy of the *Little Music* series brings the material–time continuum into sharp focus, especially in *Little Music* IV for clarinet, trombone, cello and piano. This idiosyncratic line-up will be considered later in the discussion of Krauze, but the work itself is notable for its structural template and, despite its relatively short duration (nominally nine minutes though performances can last at least five minutes longer), its characteristically abstract approach to materials and time. Its binary design is defined by the brutal contrasts between the aggressive motivic reiterations in the first movement (*ffff*) and the largely quiescent chant of the second (*mp–ffff–mp*). Material is reduced to a bare minimum and emphasises extremes not only of dynamics but also of register and pitch organisation. These features are particularly apparent in the first movement, where the piano confines itself almost exclusively to the low bass register while the other three instruments are concentrated at the top of their ranges. Intervallically, there is a reiterative focus on the tritone (principally C–F sharp) and the semitone. Górecki also brings proceedings to a halt on five occasions by inserting huge general pauses. Such bleakly confrontational obsessions are far in excess of those made by either Górecki's or Penderecki's works of the early 1960s, let alone other Polish music, because *Little Music* IV makes so few compromises with conventional musical procedures. Again, closer parallels are to be found in the visual arts, as if each sound block is one panel in a sequence, to be viewed as an atemporal totality. Although its restricted pitch material is bluntly repetitive, and its performance techniques unexceptional apart from the extreme demands made on the performers' stamina and lip, its redefinition of what abstract sonorism can embrace is just as potent as the phenomenon's acknowledged high point at the start of the 1960s.

In between *Little Music* III for three violas and *Little Music* IV came two significant orchestral works, *Old Polish Music* (*Muzyka staropolska*) and *Canticum graduum* (1969). Despite a residue of obscuration in some of the pieces in the late 1960s (e.g., Górecki's use of scordatura throughout *Little Music* III), the most striking aspect of this period is the central position of modal idioms and references, both direct and oblique, to old Polish music. Unlike Penderecki's appropriation of Bachian devices for traditional narrative and expressive ends, Górecki's utilisation of even older artefacts was much more abstract, as his refrain-based structures demonstrate, and more geared to re-establishing a sense of Polish identity than striving for a universality based on foreign idioms, techniques or ambitions. He was implementing, consciously or not, Szymanowski's dictum of 1920:

Our music must recover its age-old rights: absolute freedom, and complete liberation from the yoke of 'yesterday's' norms and precepts of creativity. Let us be nationalistic in the cultivation of our ethnic peculiarities, but let this nationalism aspire without fear to that state in which its elevated values become all-embracing.[38]

This developing aspect of Górecki's ethos is most keenly felt in *Old Polish Music*. The principle of the contrapuntal accrual of motivic roulades in *Choros* I for strings (1964) and *Little Music* II for trumpets, trombones, two pianos and percussion is released from its chromatic constraints into a modal environment. The stark antiquity of this Aeolian fanfare, centred around an absent G natural, is totally at variance with other Polish music of the time (the opening of Lutosławski's *Livre* provides an interesting comparison). So also is the schematic design of developing and interlocked refrains, with their exceptionally slow rate of textural and harmonic change. Each of the three main refrains is distinctive: (a) a series of *ff* fanfares expanding from the initial duet to four pairs of brass instruments, maintaining constant modal pitch classes, (b) a less characterised, ametric idea for horns, focussed on the 'missing' G natural from (a), and (c) a complex series of quiet, sul ponticello string chorales which evolve from the string 'after-images' which came at the end of the early (a) sections. This last idea takes as its material the tenor line from a well-known Renaissance hymn, Wacław z Szamotuł's *Already Dusk Is Falling* (*Już się zmierzcha*), a line which had already featured in a little unpublished piece for string quartet, *Chorale in the Form of a Canon* (1961), and would be used again at the start of the First String Quartet (1988). Górecki deliberately mistreats the tenor by subjecting it to dodeca-phonic manipulations, thus denying it its 'natural' ambience (it was already bereft of its original context). By the time this refrain has expanded from its initial two-part homophony to a full twelve-part texture on its fourth appearance, it has acquired a modernistic rationale of some considerable presence, a ghost of the twelve-note matrix at the start of the First Symphony '1959'. It is as if Górecki is still playing out the creative and technical tensions between old and new, in music unmoved by conventional expressive concerns.

The final word is given, as if in atonement, to the old (Ex. 9.13). Górecki cites a two-part medieval organum 'Benedicamus Domino', whose pitches had furnished the material for the opening fanfare. This iconographic quotation, whose function is partly recapitulatory, partly metaphysical, is played sotto voce by two trumpets 'with no shading at all', against a sustained texture in which a corona of all the 'white' notes between octave G naturals is gradually added (shades of *Refrain* and a foretaste of the conclusion of the

Example 9.13. Górecki, *Old Polish Music* (*Muzyka staropolska*, 1969), start of coda.

Second Symphony, 'Copernican', 1972). This was neither the first nor last time that Górecki used a transcendental coda. Within the year, *Little Music IV* would also rely on the calming effect of a chant-like conclusion: 'the static modality of its coda clearly represents a transcendence of the previous events and a critique of the violence that informs them'.[39] The codas of *Canticum graduum* and *Ad matrem* (1971) follow suit in a more harmonious fashion, while the Second Symphony emulates *Old Polish Music* by incorporating a Renaissance musical fragment. Górecki was not alone, of course, in seeking resolution to preceding musical argument; different though their agendas were, Lutosławski also used his codas for similar reasons, though few other Polish composers placed such structural emphasis on them.

That Górecki was testing out a number of different, but related paths forward is attested by *Canticum graduum*. This unduly neglected work, commissioned by West German Radio and premiered in Dusseldorf under Gielen, reveals a gentler, warmer disposition, drawing on the harmonic language of *Refrain*. There is no let-up in concentration, however, as its characteristically forthright performance instructions demonstrate: the opening 'sempre legatissimo, ben tenuto, molto cantabile, con massima espressione e grande tensione' is succeeded in the coda by 'cantabilissimo e tranquillissimo'. Such strongly worded instructions underline the fact that, for Górecki, straightforward materials have enormous latent power. And the prolonged and intense scrutiny of stringently restricted material is in part due to the composer's practice of testing his ideas repetitively at the piano. The work's profile is governed by an inexorable expansion from D by two octaves in each direction, the inner harmonies created from the alternation of the two whole-tone scales. This harmonic plan is articulated by an animated version of the palindromic rhythmic patterns in *Refrain*, and at the moment of greatest expansion and density these simple procedures produce a wall of sound with uncommon resonance. Typically, this power is not now released by hyperactivity, as in *Refrain*, but by a coda which refines the example of the last of the *Three Pieces in Old Style* by intimating the presence of a Dorian chant against a harmonic cushion drawn from the notes of the same mode. Like its immediate successor, the astringent *Little Music IV*, it proposes much which Górecki's voice-based music of the 1970s fulfils.

Szalonek

Although the high point of sonorism was during the first half of the 1960s, and the abstract potency of its effects had been tempered by a range of composers with their developing individual stylistic and linguistic agendas, one composer pursued his explorations with unusual fervour in the second

Example 9.14. Szalonek, *Aarhus Music* (1970), part of section E. Copyright 1971 by Seesaw Music Corp. – New York. Reprinted by permission.

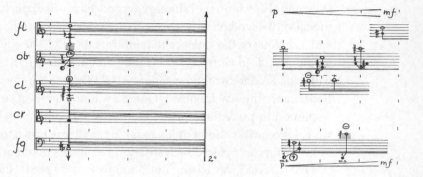

half of the decade and into the 1970s. Szalonek became the new standard-bearer for sonorism: where Penderecki had focussed on new string sonorities, Szalonek was fascinated with woodwind instruments. Although he was a comparative late starter in finding a distinctive voice, he gave early indications of a new direction in the Concertino for flute and orchestra (1960–2). Its essentially dodecaphonic technique is deployed in an exceptionally fluid texture, although it is most intriguing for its experimental treatment of the solo flute (*frullato* and pitch bending) and in one passage where the orchestral woodwind and brass are required to play on the mouthpieces of their instruments, a feature later used by Serocki. The Concertino's dedicatee was the Italian virtuoso, Gazzelloni, who gave the premiere at the 1963 'Warsaw Autumn'. Szalonek's discussions with Gazzelloni led him to investigate further the idea of extended instrumental techniques for woodwind and, in a series of works stemming from *Les sons* for orchestra – Szalonek's 'compositional manifesto'[40] – he brought his systematic explorations to bear on a range of chamber and orchestral works. Most of these draw attention to non-woodwind instruments, e.g. *Mutanza* for piano (1968), *1+1+1+1* for one to four string players (1969), and *Piernikiana* for solo tuba with passively resonating piano or tam-tam (1977). In fact, in a sequence of over a dozen works, only two are exclusively for wind instruments: *Quattro monologhi* for solo oboe (1966) and *Aarhus Music* for wind quintet (1970) (Ex. 9.14).

Szalonek's investigations were carried out with quasi-scientific precision and in the context of a philosophical consideration of the history and nature of sound and of the nature of musical perception.[41] He was primarily intrigued by what he called 'combined sounds', spurred on by Bruno Bartolozzi's work on woodwind multiphonics, not least because the latter's account of these sounds seemed to Szalonek to be too imprecise in its attempt to fix the relationship between technical means and verifiable aural results.[42]

To this end, Szalonek developed an explicit performing methodology involving new fingering, the identification of overtone combinations, unorthodox embouchures as well as techniques involving playing on mouthpieces alone. He pinpointed three levels within his combined sounds – foreground, background and 'colour' – giving precise cause-and-effect examples from his own scores. Needless to say, these developments gave rise to many new notational issues and, with characteristic concern for the end result, Szalonek prefaced his published scores with the most meticulously detailed explanatory notes in contemporary Polish music.

Szalonek's purpose was not purely abstract. He was intent on re-establishing 'contact with the natural expressive potency and richness of sound as structured by the physical interaction of man with his surroundings, whether as active performer or active perceiver'.[43] Not for nothing is *O Pleasant Land . . . (Ziemio miła . . .*, 1969) a powerful symbol of this mission. Szalonek described this cantata, whose text pleads for the innocence and beauty of the natural order against 'fear and horror, streams of blood and the gleam of falling iron', as having 'the character of a protest song'.[44] The narrator – a role that can be taken by a singer of any tessitura – uses not only natural speech and *Sprechstimme* but also sings the outer sections by following a precise interval-class notation whose mean pitch level is immaterial in a context dominated by unpitched ideas. The narrator, thus dislocated, becomes both performer and perceiver, a latter-day Wanderer searching for a new order in a tarnished landscape.

The compositional results of Szalonek's studies were anything but dry: 'they still shock us with their dramatic exposure of a dark world of primordial expression through sound: a world of heightened yet naturally sensuous immediacy, possessing an animal-like intensity of utterance'.[45] This is particularly true of those pieces which make few concessions to audience sensibilities, and interestingly these tend to be works for chamber ensemble, such as *1+1+1+1, Aarhus Music* and *Improvisations sonoristiques* for clarinet, trombone, cello and piano (1968), which are as formidably uncompromising in their timbral–harmonic explorations as Górecki's *Elementi*. A more familiar mode of gentle impressionistic sound-painting, leading to substantive developmental musical textures, was introduced by *Les sons*, whose opening is among his most magical. It is not too far-fetched to hear the influence of Ravel's woodwind scoring at such moments. Four flutes play scattered staccato harmonics in a spacious soundscape, followed by flute *frullato* and other performers blowing across the necks of bottles. Succeeding textures, grouped in paragraphs, explore a wide range of instrumental sonorities which, as in music by both Penderecki and Lutosławski, are juxtaposed, overlapped and interpenetrated. In a strategy which also reappears in later pieces (e.g., the second and third movements of *Mutazioni* for chamber orchestra, 1966), Szalonek subsequently groups like instruments into chordal choruses. These work in rhythmic consort, both homophonically and heterophonically, to energise the main climax, whose hockets and rapid flurries seem to be participating in a massive jam session.

The link with Lutosławski's principles of structural design is sometimes very strong and places many of Szalonek's pieces as much in the sphere of pre-war modernism as in the experimental avant-garde. In *Proporzioni* for flute, viola and harp (1967, rescored for flute, cello and piano in 1970), for example, Szalonek parallels Lutosławski's preference for end-weighted schemes. *Proporzioni* begins with three discrete sections that are succeeded by a symphonic drive towards an explosive climax and a concluding coda. The opening section is one of Szalonek's most memorable and underlines his highly refined ear for captivating sonorities: sporadic 'highest-note' pizzicati on the viola are counterpointed first on the harp by tuning-key glissandi articulated by plectrum and later by flute *frullato*, a three-part invention in all but name. This slow, unassuming texture is succeeded by two other texturally delineated but inconclusive sections – a largely chordal duet between the harp and the two melody instruments in which pitch patterns are rotated mosaically, and a cadenza for the flute alone. Both of these sections are almost entirely conventional in their methods of sound production. The sense of structural incompleteness is resolved in the final two sections, which provide the main thrust of the piece in a manner comparable to Lutosławski's earlier *Venetian Games* and forthcoming *Livre*. Where Lutosławski rarely glances backwards after the main climax, Szalonek recapitulates isolated fragments of the second section in forming the coda of *Proporzioni*.

Szalonek's structural mastery is due not only to his understanding of large-scale contrasts and progression (his music is never about sound for sound's sake), but also to his mastery in combining instruments, whether or not they utilise the 'combined sounds' of woodwind multiphonics. He brings a concluding stability to the first movement of *Mutazioni*, for example, by a triple layer of high cantabile solo double bass, tiny con sordino glissandi in the upper strings, and gently punctuating chordal chimes on the celeste. In the third movement, he uses distinctive timbres (quasi-Morse-code patterns on clarinets, followed by repeated marimba figurations with string pizzicati) as resonators for the commentaries and interventions from other instruments which eventually lead to the main thrust of the movement and of the work as a whole. In his pieces for solo instrument, he is equally adept at shaping the context of his sound material. There is a natural flow and dialogue between novel and conventional sounds in *Quattro monologhi*, a relaxed counterpart to Berio's *Sequenza* VII for oboe composed three years

Example 9.15. Szalonek, *Mutanza* (1968), section B.

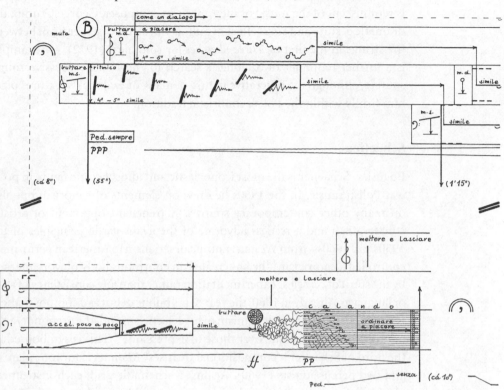

later. The fourth monologue is a rare example in Szalonek's music of mobile form: like Lutosławski, he prefers to maintain full control over what he regards as the major parameters, usually allowing the performer only a modest extension of traditional interpretative freedom (more rarely, as at the climax of *O Pleasant Land . . .* , he does occasionally give the instrumentalists a compendium of textures to play 'a piacere', paralleling the point in Lutosławski's end-weighted structures where the greatest simultaneous diversity is to be found).

Mutanza for piano is deliberately less propulsive. This is in large part due to the fact that most of the action takes place inside the instrument with a variety of accessories applied not before but during the performance: these comprise four cylindrical steel rods for rubbing or bouncing vertically or horizontally on the strings, approximately thirty steel ball bearings which are poured onto the strings, a nylon cork for rubbing on the sounding board, a nylon brush and twenty sticks of plasticine (Ex. 9.15). Vivid and bizarre though some of these sound producers are, what is noticeable is the ruminative time-scale which allows the performer to improvise at leisure on the various sound complexes.[46] At times, Szalonek's enquiring spirit is reminiscent of the music of the American composer, George Crumb; the dramatic gesture and aural effect of pulling out strips of paper from between the strings in the first of *Three Sketches* for solo harp (1972), for example, is a further reminder of Szalonek's search for new and expressive sound sources, although the reiterative nature of many of Szalonek's textures place him firmly within the Polish sonoristic tradition.

Schaeffer

Bogusław Schaeffer is the most iconoclastic and idiosyncratic figure in post-war Polish music. In the 1960s he drew on elements of sonorism but also on many other contemporary sources. A trenchant opponent of artistic conservatism and a restless advocate of the avant-garde principles of the 1950s and 1960s – from Western European serialism to American performer-controlled aleatoricism – he has created an enormous body of work marked by the spirit of ceaseless experimentation rather than any consistency of style or language. Already in 1960, the year of his public debut as a composer, there is ample evidence of the dynamism of his eclecticism and 'the preponderance of problems of technique over those of expression'.[47] This is symbolised by the third of Schaeffer's 'compositional treatises', *Montaggio* for four pianists and two percussionists (1960). Against a schematic grid, each instrument plays a defined sequence of thirty four-second blocks of material. To this Schaeffer adds layers of stylistic counterpoint: 'a virtuoso piano, a strict piano, an aleatory piano and a percussion piano . . . This results in . . . various structures and various styles of interpretation . . . . the composition is an attempt at a new formal system within strictly set limits.'[48]

A more complex version of this principle lies behind *Topofonica* (1960), in which forty solo instruments perform sequences of small motivic fragments in a mosaic which is both highly structured (a 'passacaglia of instrumental timbres')[49] and open to certain interpretative variables (e.g., four pages use three different ink colours to mark out alternative instrumental combinations). Its heterogeneous sound world is still controlled by intellectual rather than timbral pursuits. In complete contrast, the multiple polyphonies and unconventional performance techniques in the five short movements of the orchestral *Little Symphony: Scultura* reveal a composer fully capable of using mass sound shapes to create a coherent expressive argument which stands comparison with contemporaneous pieces by Ligeti, Xenakis and Penderecki. Were Schaeffer concerned with a personal musical identity, such shifts would seem illogical or inappropriate. Instead, he wanted to examine composition as an activity to be pursued for its own ends. Furthermore, he did not regard himself always as the prime figure in the process, though the difference between Schaeffer as puppet-master and as disinterested man of ideas is not always self-evident.

In fact, Schaeffer was the first Polish composer to devolve substantial compositional responsibility to the performer, and he was able to do this not least because of his voracious appetite for new notational procedures. The best-known example is the one-page graphic mobile, *Nonstop* (1960), whose realisation may last anything from six minutes to eight hours. Structurally and notationally, it foreshadows a number of pieces, including the stage composition *TIS MW 2* (1963), *Two Pieces* for violin and piano (1964) and *Quartet 2+2* (1965), whose duration may be anything between four minutes and four hours. With a typically wry twist, *Nonstop*'s notation includes syllables from his own name (Ex. 9.16). Among the performance instructions are several which encapsulate the musical and theatrical extremity of Schaeffer's intentions:

1. Sounds should be constantly varied; repetition of sounds should be avoided.
2. For each repetition of an element with the same symbol there should be a different rhythmic, dynamic and articulatory response.
3. The performer must try – as far as possible – to link small elements together into larger groupings (e.g., left-hand glissando + right-hand chord + whistling + foot-stamping = 'a motif').

    The performer of the piece must be male with a baritone voice; when the piece's duration is prolonged, between 3 and 8 pianists may take it in turns.[50]

The premiere by Krauze and John Tilbury, designed by the composer and with the participation, among others, of the avant-garde visual artist and founder of the experimental Cricot Theatre in Kraków, Tadeusz Kantor, did not take place until 27 October 1964. It lasted for seven hours thirty-eight minutes and is often cited as the first Polish musical happening.[51] The link with Kantor was a significant symbol of Schaeffer's developing aesthetic. Kantor's search for what in 1956 he had called 'autonomous theatre' and his belief that 'what is important about theatre is the process rather than the product'[52] found enormous resonance in Schaeffer's output.

After 1960, Schaeffer continued to provoke the musical establishment. He published polemical articles and books on contemporary music issues, including *Classics of Dodecaphony* (1964) and culminating in his mammoth *Introduction to Composition* (1976). His most notorious spat was in 1971 with the neo-classical composer and acerbic critic Kisielewski, but others too have seen Schaeffer as a charlatan, too prone to conceptual theorising and too

Example 9.16. Schaeffer, *Nonstop* (1960).

nonstop

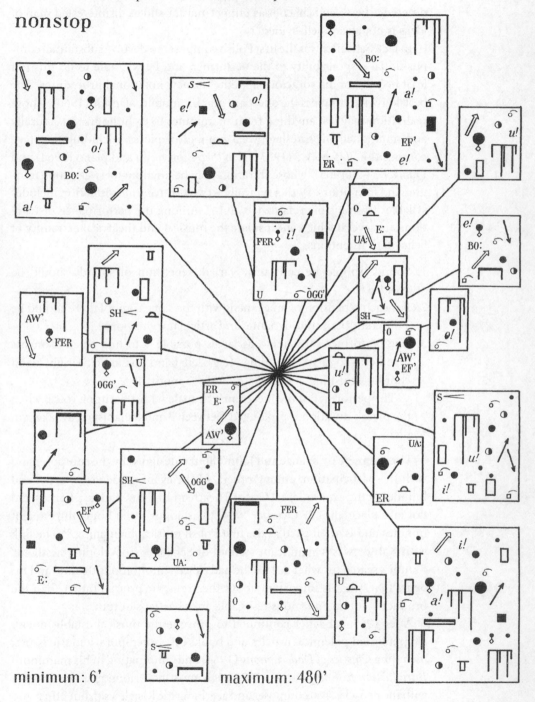

minimum: 6'   maximum: 480'

unconcerned for the musical result.[53] That is to misunderstand Schaeffer's goals, which are always to challenge expectations and perceptions. And while he may overstate his case, there are many works which genuinely advance the boundaries of contemporary music. He was, for example, the only Polish composer to explore the interface with jazz extensively (there are, of course, other isolated examples, such as Kotoński's *Selection* I for electric guitar, clarinet and alto and jazz saxophone, 1962, or Serocki's *Swinging Music*). In *Course 'j'* (1962), scored for woodwind, strings and percussion with a jazz sextet based on the line-up of the Modern Jazz Quartet, Schaeffer charts a path from his own environment (aleatoric, post-serial improvisation) via graphic notation towards a more conventional jazz idiom. *Music for MI* [the vibraphone player Jerzy Milian] (1963) is effectively a concerto whose central movement is for jazz sextet. But, rather than repeat the experiment of *Course 'j'*, Schaeffer incorporates a solo soprano and six reciters who, at one stage in the explosive first movement, muse simultaneously on the nature of 'melody' and 'word'. Elsewhere in the movement there is the performing instruction 'continue until such time as the audience shows irritation' and the pianist plays excerpts from Schaeffer's earlier solo piano piece, *Articulations* (1959). Such digressions and distractions are integral parts of his theatricality, and in the second movement of *S'alto* for alto saxophone and chamber orchestra (1963) members of the orchestra read out excerpts from Dostoyevsky's *The Possessed*. While there are more conventional examples, such as *Jazz Concerto for Orchestra* (1969) or *Blues I* for two pianos and tape (1972), the jazz works of 1963 point irrevocably in the direction of theatre, and not just music theatre in the line of Kagel.

Crucial to Schaeffer's development at this juncture was the formation in his home city, Kraków, of the new music ensemble, MW2 (Młodzi Wykonawcy Muzyki Współczesnej – Young Performers of Contemporary Music). The core line-up of MW2 – two pianists, flute, cello, a dancer and three actors – was led by the pianist Adam Kaczyński, one of the foremost Polish exponents of new music. MW2 gave numerous Polish premieres of music by composers such as Cage, Busotti, Castiglioni, Andriessen, La Monte Young and Pousseur. And while it performed music by a number of Polish composers, especially those like Bujarski, Łuciuk, Krzysztof Meyer (b. 1943) and Marek Stachowski (b. 1936) who also lived in Kraków, its primary focus was on Schaeffer's music, or, as he termed it, instrumental theatre. The first of a long line of 'stage compositions' was *TIS MW 2* for actor, mime, dancer, soprano, flute/violin, cello/alto saxophone, and two pianos, premiered in Kraków in April 1964.[54]

As one of its main axioms, *TIS MW 2* ranks the musical performance of musicians and non-musicians equally. It also attempts 'absolute decomposition . . . the ends of the composer are, above all, the non-schematism of the formal structure and the indefiniteness of this composition as a whole even for its performers'.[55] Schaeffer provides a basic framework: the piece, lasting some thirty minutes, is performed in two parts, the first in almost complete darkness (just sufficient to make out the mime and dancer), the second in full light. The actor recites excerpts from a novel, *Pałuba* (The Hag, 1891–1903), by the Polish writer, Karol Irzykowski (whose life as critic as well as author, and whose use of this novel to confront the pretensions and masks of established society, may be regarded as a precursor of Schaeffer's own position and credo). The other seven performers are allowed to pick up on the text's generalised opposites, such as the discrepancy between representation and reality, but may use only one phrase – '. . . for several years she had led a life full of phantom dreams' – to guide their individual response to their sequence of sonic fragments.

A series of stage compositions followed in quick succession, including *Scenario for a Non-Existent but Possible Instrumental Actor* (1963), *Audiences I–V* (1964), *Quartet for Four Actors* (1966), *Fragment* (1968) and *Hommage à Irzykowski* (1973). Added to these must be *Howl* for reciter, two actors and instrumental ensemble (1966), a setting of excerpts from Allen Ginsberg's poem. Although there is a through-composed score, there is no notation of pitch and other parameters are indicated only in general terms. More significant are the eight 'idioms' governing the actions of all the performers apart from the reciter: 'chaos', 'anything', 'jazz', 'bruitisme-noises', 'action music', 'melodies', 'dull strokes', 'concentrating attention on oneself'. Given the nature of Ginsberg's inflammatory poem – with its hallucinatory ode to New York drop-outs and excoriation of Moloch, a Canaanite idol to whom children were sacrificed – and Schaeffer's colourful response, it is hardly surprising that this was one of the works to which Kisielewski took exception at its premiere (by an expanded MW2) in Warsaw in March 1971. Not only does he reveal, despite his post-war championing of creative freedom, his own inability to cope with the concept of happenings but he also demonstrates that the avant-garde progress of Polish music was subject to the checks and balances of public opinion.

> Quite a number of composers during our century have committed artistic suicide, for example Stockhausen, Boulez, Cardew . . . so why shouldn't Schaeffer be added to the list. After his recent manifestation at the Warsaw Philharmonic I set about conferring titles on him, e.g.: Schaeffer – the Dandy, Schaeffer – Conqueror of Americanism, Schaeffer – Spirit of the Age,

Schaeffer – Pagan God of Narcotic Youth . . . and, saddest of all: SCHAEFFER – PRINCE OF SUPERFICIALITY.

. . . The author of *Monosonata* told me recently that, if music has an inevitable tendency towards disintegration, it is necessary simply to accelerate that collapse. Congratulations, well done, if somebody is bent on being a grave-digger . . .

. . . Schaeffer wants to seduce these youngsters in a somewhat strange way, snobbishly, modishly, and in the 'foreign fashion' . . . *Howl*, by the 'rabid' American Allan Ginsberg, – a rebellion against civilisation yelled-out from the stage by psychedelics and drug addicts – is the latest Western fashion (Schaeffer en vogue – quelle misère!) . . . *Howl* was not very clever (or rather was mightily stupid) in its literal naturalism and vociferous expression: old jokes, rather unpleasant. Besides dragging on interminably, the naturalistic convention did not entirely seem to win over youngsters brought up on television, so the success proved to be somewhat sickly (perhaps Schaeffer is already too old, too in earnest for homegrown candidates for psychedelia?!) . . . And so Schaeffer, destroying our sensitivity, achieves his commendable purpose of the inevitable hastening of the end of music. But what is the rush – he will perish with the music. Suicide![56]

Schaeffer responded robustly, as was to be expected, but he soon faced a creative impasse of sizeable proportions. He 'disappeared' compositionally in 1973 and emerged two years later. Musically, the result of this internal exile was the rather tame sonoristic idiom he adopted in the two orchestral 'Harmonies and Counterpoints': *Warsaw Overture* (1975) and, in a bizarre shift of creative emphasis, *Romuald Traugutt* (1976), a hommage to the leader of the short-lived 1863 uprising against the Russian occupying forces. He gradually reasserted his old experimental will, as in another hommage, this time to the master of conceptual arts, Joseph Beuys (*Voice, Noise, Beuys, Choice*, 1984). And while Schaeffer has continued to create musical works, he has achieved greater fame and popularity both at home and abroad as the author of satirical and comic plays for the straight theatre. The very aspects of his work in the 1960s which had so outraged audiences and critics by their perceived disrespect to musical traditions have led, since the early 1980s and especially in the 1990s, to a relaxed, humorous and broad-based appeal which lacks nothing in sophistication nor critical edge. The musical outsider found a home in the theatre.

10 A significant hinterland

**Seven composers: Kotoński ◆ Kilar ◆ Bujarski ◆ Block ◆
Moszumańska-Nazar ◆ Meyer ◆ Stachowski**

It would, of course, be all too easy to ignore the music of other composers in the 1960s, not least because so little of it is still performed. Nevertheless, the extensive publications by PWM, and the less accessible recordings, do reveal how a broad swathe of composers participated in sonorism and its aftermath. It quickly becomes apparent that Penderecki's sonoristic techniques were appropriated selectively by others and that his usage of them cannot be taken as representative of Polish avant-garde music in the 1960s. The music of composers who developed their own extended instrumental techniques and notation (Szalonek), or borrowed selectively from what rapidly became a common pool of effects, is often markedly different. Some composers placed these effects in a more rhythmicised or metred context, others were more open to a transparent pitch organisation, some highlighted individual instruments in a chamber or orchestral setting. Some exploited the tensions and sense of apprehension that the new sonorities could evoke (Penderecki, Górecki, occasionally Baird) while others encouraged less anxious responses (Bujarski, Kotoński, Kilar, Serocki). For Schaeffer it was experiment itself which had pride of place. The majority of composers explored sonorism more or less simultaneously with Penderecki and Górecki, i.e. in the early 1960s, though a few came to it later in the decade (Szalonek). Some, like Penderecki, retained elements of 'high' sonorism into the 1970s, others transformed its underlying principles into quite different music in which pitch was paramount (Górecki, Kilar). And even those who were not in the least interested in Penderecki's brand of sonorism, such as Baird, Lutosławski and Serocki, were able to draw their own conclusions from his explorations and respond accordingly.

Kotoński's concert music of the early 1960s is an understated amalgam of pointillism and sonorism, in which percussion plays a major role. In the Trio for flute, guitar and percussion (1960) and *Canto* for mixed ensemble (1961) he demonstrates a keen ear for variegated rather than uniform sonorities, which unfurl in a relaxed and quasi-improvised manner. Even in works with larger forces – *Musica per fiati e timpani* (1963) and *Concerto per quattro* (1965), though with the exception of a late surge of group sonorism in *Music for Sixteen Cymbals and Strings* (1969) – the music is orientated towards small instrumental combinations in which the individual sound is more significant than the larger mass, and clusters are of marginal importance. This aligns him more closely with Baird than Penderecki or Górecki, not least because his lyrical impulse is uppermost. This is especially clear in the three chamber pieces completed in 1964 – *Pezzo* for flute and piano, *Monochromia* for solo oboe, and the Wind Quintet – and their many successors. Even in *A battere* for violin, viola, guitar, harpsichord and three percussionists (1966), where all the instruments are treated percussively, the tone is refreshingly undogmatic and Kotoński's interest in jazz (cf. Kilar and Schaeffer) surfaces in the rhythmic patterns and sonorities.

Although Kilar's concert career did not blossom fully until after the 1960s, his participation in Polish music dates back to the early 1950s when he was still a teenager. His rapprochement with serialism was confined to *Herbsttag* for soprano and string quartet. In *Riff 62* for orchestra, he brought a rough, jazzy quality to sonorism by emphasising the roles of the two clarinets, three saxophones, quadruple trumpets and trombones and percussion; in contradistinction to Penderecki, the strings (thirty-six violins and twelve double basses) have a very minor role. In fact, Kilar does not appear to have engaged deeply or consistently in the sonoristic experiment: *Générique* and *Springfield Sonnet* (1965) lack the compositional rigour of their contemporaries and the four-minute *Diphthongos* for choir, percussion, two pianos and strings has only a fleeting novelty value for its setting of words and shouts from Trobriand Island songs. Traces of diatonic harmony begin to emerge in *Springfield Sonnet*, which ends on a secondary seventh, and a strong metrical drive surfaces from time to time. These features begin to coalesce in *Solenne* (1967), which bears a close resemblance to the style and content of Górecki's *Refrain* and *Little Music* II of the same year, as well as anticipating *Old Polish Music*.

From this point on and through the 1970s, Górecki and Kilar, both of them from Katowice in southern Poland and both enamoured of the culture of the Tatra Mountains, seem to have vied with one another as they explored modal and tonal harmony and high degrees of repetition in a highly distinctive way. Initially, Kilar also favoured slow tempi, as in *Training 68* for clarinet, trombone, cello and piano and *Upstairs–Downstairs* for two children's choirs and orchestra (1971), where the passivity of his musical material is in strong contrast to the pent-up energy of Górecki's contemporaneous scores. There are occasional flashes of electricity, as in the jazz-like break towards the end of *Training 68*, or the growling whole-tone clusters and diminished triads which ambush the insouciant minor third A–C which is sustained throughout *Upstairs–Downstairs*. The early evolution of this dyad into an A minor chord is finessed at the very end by the substitution of the upper major third for a lower one, forming a conclusive F major triad. That the whole piece is reliant on such a progression is symptomatic of Kilar's distance from robust musical dialectic. He seemed at this point to be settling for a gentle surface sweetness, confirmed by the *Prelude and Christmas Carol* (*Przygrywka i kolęda*, 1972), in which even the canonic elaboration of an ancient Polish carol seems decorative rather than of conceptual significance.

Zbigniew Bujarski, the forgotten member of a famous generation, was the first Polish composer to investigate scientifically, rather than impressionistically, the harmonic and melodic potential of microtonal clusters, which he called 'synthetic monophony'. He was still a student, and in 1958 he found little support for his ideas. His subsequent compositions – the orchestral *Zones* (*Strefy*, 1961), *Kinoth*, *Chamber Piece* for voice, flute, harp, piano and percussion (1963) and especially *Contraria* for orchestra (1965) – share superficial similarities with Penderecki's sonorism. And yet Bujarski's creative sensitivities were more finely detailed, suggestive rather than bludgeoning. These were brought to bear on pieces that quickly established his credentials as a humanitarian. *Kinoth* is an early Polish commemoration of past atrocities, provoked by three excerpts from the Lamentations of Jeremiah 'in memory of the Jewish generation of the annihilated'. The innocuous title of *Chamber Piece* hides the fact that, with a few deft brushstrokes of instrumental colour, it sets three poignant Japanese texts on the US bombing of 1945, ending with the words 'on the ruins of the school, the rays of the setting sun extinguish . . . Hiroshima, Atomic City' (Ex. 10.1). In the privacy of its emotional tone and the piercing clarity of its musical ideas, it is memorably lacking in any kind of sensationalism (and provides a telling contrast to Penderecki's post-titled *Threnody*). *Contraria*, on the other hand, is a swirling multi-layered tapestry, highly variegated, playful and seductive rather than aggressive. In the tantalising richness of its colouristic and harmonic detail it is closer to Serocki than Penderecki.

Augustyn Bloch (b. 1929) is another essentially lyrical composer, and much of his energy has been channelled into music for voice, both in concert repertoire and in opera. He also demonstrated an early aptitude for ballet scores such as *Voci* (1962), *Awaiting* (*Oczekiwanie*, 1963) and *Gilgamesh* (1969). His first major success, *Espressioni* (1959), to a text by Iwaszkiewicz and written for his wife, the soprano Halina Łukomska, is, despite its twelve-note pitch organisation, more remarkable for its heightened lyricism in the lineage of Szymanowski. *Meditations* (1961), with its setting of Old Testament texts, heralded a lifelong interest in biblical and

Example 10.1. Bujarski, *Chamber Piece* (1963), conclusion.

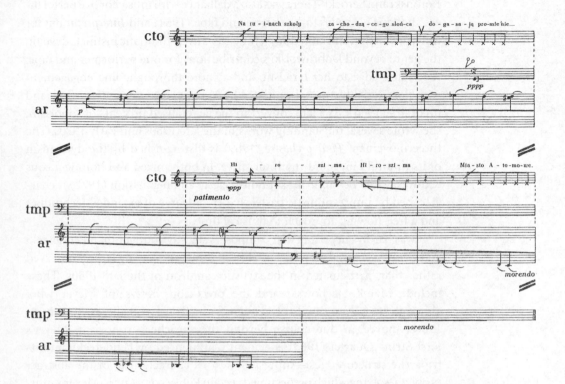

religious themes (paralleling, rather than imitating Penderecki's focus) and is delivered in a style which borrows contemporary idioms as appropriate. In many works he shares with Kotoński a relaxed manner and preference for light textures, though he has a keener sense of drama. Like Kilar and Górecki, he was loath to abandon metre for timed general blocks of sound, as in the dynamic *Dialoghi* for violin and orchestra (1964). His moderation of Pendereckian sonorism and eschewal of most extended instrumental techniques is best observed in one of his finest orchestral pieces, *Enfiando* (1970), where the mass movement of sound and propulsive rhythms are carefully detailed. Bloch has a powerful neo-romantic streak and an attitude that refuses to take the more portentous aspects of contemporary music too seriously, without in any way diminishing the contemporaneity of his musical language.

As a near contemporary of Baird, Kotoński and Serocki, Krystyna Moszumańska-Nazar took an oblique view of sonorism, although the closing moments of *Music for Strings* (1962) make clear reference to certain sonoristic traits, albeit within an overridingly neo-classical context. In that sense, she is arguably closer to Bacewicz, although her evident fascination with percussion throughout the 1960s and 1970s aligns her with Kotoński and Serocki. There was also a dalliance with music for live performers and tape – *Exodus* for orchestra and tape (1964) and *Interpretations* for flute, percussion and tape (1967); the latter's lively dramatic instincts develop the genre beyond Dobrowolski's contributions for one performer and tape. A tougher edge to her lyricism, and a more thoroughgoing engagement with post-serial textures, is initiated by *Variazioni concertanti* for flute and orchestra (1966). As a late convert to the generalised precepts of sonorism, she wrote several outstanding works in the late 1960s and early 1970s. The three-movement *Pour orchestre* (1969) is distinguished by the dynamism of its timbral range and rhythmic drive, in both mixed and homogeneous textures, while *Bel canto* for soprano, celesta and percussion (1972) is characterised by impressionistic pastel shades, a degree of extended techniques and a free-flowing approach to musical time.

It was hardly surprising that composers slightly younger than Penderecki and Górecki showed an initial interest in sonorism, having largely observed rather than participated in the stylistic cauldron of the late 1950s. These include Marek Stachowski and the precocious Krzysztof Meyer who, although they were pupils of Penderecki in Kraków in the early to mid-1960s, moved in due course beyond their teacher's sonorism. Meyer's First String Quartet (1963) is evidently influenced by Penderecki, and its tripartite structure 'Tesi–Antitesi–Sintesi' is characteristic of the abstract problem-solving which preoccupied certain Polish composers. Meyer's intuitions rapidly led him in a more conservative direction. He chose to align himself with a range of older composers, such as Bartók, Stravinsky and Shostakovich, as well as compatriots such as Lutosławski and Bacewicz. He is a prolific composer and one for whom traditional genres such as the concerto, sonata, string quartet and symphony became paramount. The significant works of the 1960s include the Violin Concerto (1965), the Fourth Piano Sonata (1968), the Second String Quartet (1969) and his first three symphonies (1964, 1967 and 1968), the last two of which have a choral component. His emphatic rejection of sonorism and of most avant-garde tendencies was striking in one so young, and the idioms and genres he selected inevitably draw comparisons with music of the inter-war and post-war periods. There are contemporary textures and timbres, but these are usually incidental to a language in which tonal pulls and familiar nineteenth-century signposts govern the overall flow and structure, as in the Violin Concerto. Meyer's energetic and finely wrought music is not at heart concerned with a radical re-evaluation of past traditions like that of Górecki, Lutosławski or Penderecki, nor can it be said to anticipate the postmodernisms of the 1980s, although his subsequent referencing of pre-existing music is perhaps anticipated by the Stravinskian allusions in the Second Symphony.

Stachowski's First String Quartet (1965) and *Neusis* II for two vocal ensembles, percussion, cellos and double basses (1968) remain close to Penderecki. Within two years, however, Stachowski had branched out in two different directions. *Audition* II for flute, cello and piano (1970) is notable for its loose interplay between the three performers; there is no full score and the extended passages when the pianist plays inside or on the body of the instrument, or places objects on the strings, are notated in the sort of graphic notation evolved by Schaeffer, Łuciuk and Szalonek. Its strong aleatory procedures intimated that Stachowski was moving into the field of experimental music promoted by the piece's first performers, MW2. And yet its periodic focus on a single pitch (D natural) suggests a desire for conventional underpinning, as it also does in the three-movement orchestral *Irisation* (1970). The iridescence implied in the latter work's title symbolises the colouristic as opposed to sonoristic essence of Stachowski's music at this time, and its resonant harmonic language, volatile sound shapes and symphonic instincts lean more in the direction of Lutosławski than Penderecki.

Krauze and Sikorski

If sonorism of the Pendereckian mould emanated from Kraków, Warsaw maintained a polite distance, preferring, in the music of Lutosławski, Baird, Serocki and others, to develop a closer architectonic relationship with detailed rhythmic and pitch organisation. Of the younger Warsaw generation who graduated in the early 1960s, two composers quickly became preeminent: Zygmunt Krauze and Tomasz Sikorski (1939–88), son of the composer Kazimierz Sikorski. They were both his students, the latest in a line that had already included Bacewicz, Baird, Kisielewski, Krenz, Palester, Panufnik and Serocki. From the beginning, they each showed a determined individuality which defined a different stream in contemporary Polish music.

Already in his student works – *Malay Pantuns* (*Pantuny malajskie* for contralto and three flutes, 1961), *Five Unistic Pieces* (*Pięć kompozycji unistycznych* for piano, 1963) and *Triptych* for piano (1964) – Krauze had established his musical aesthetic. This was based on the concept of 'unism', a term drawn from the paintings and theories of one of Poland's most distinguished inter-war artists, Władysław Strzemiński (1893–1952). While Penderecki's references to Klee and Klein in 1959–60 were soon superseded by other concerns, Krauze's allegiance to Strzemiński has been durable. For the first time in Polish music, a composer drew deep sustenance from Polish visual arts. Szymanowski, for example, had preferred figurative folksiness to the modernist abstract art of his time and appears to have expressed no interest in Strzemiński and the Polish Constructivists, who flourished in the central Polish city of Łódź in the 1920s and 1930s. A major influence on Strzemiński and others had been the reductive abstractionism of the Russian Suprematist artist, Kazimir Malevich, who exhibited his paintings in Warsaw in 1927. Strzemiński had already formulated a theory of unism and a few years later realised its principles in 'compositions of minute, logically arranged parts merging with the monochromatic surface of the canvas'.[1] In the early 1930s, Strzemiński completed a long series of paintings entitled *Unistic Compositions* and in 1934 defined their underlying concept:

> The type of composition for which Unism is striving is . . . optical unity, visual unity of the shapes and their link with the plane on which they are placed, as well as with its borders . . . Organic and real unity is possible only by means of the Unistic system of equally significant interrelated elements constituting a rhythm which is infinitely continuous; this process of building up on the principles of equal significance is substituted for the process of contrasts.[2]

Aspects of these ideas might be applied to a number of Polish compositions in the early 1960s, on the local level of individual sound blocks, but the structural basis of these pieces, be they by Lutosławski, Penderecki or Serocki, lies precisely in 'the process of contrast' which is anathema to the unistic ideal. And therein lies the striking difference in Krauze's outlook, which adheres closely to Strzemiński's formulations.

Despite its intense simplicity, *Malay Pantuns* (cf. Ravel's approach to the *pantun* or Kilar's modernist treatment of Trobriand Island texts in *Diphthongos* three years later) is not yet fully unistic – its minimal material, delicate rhythmic repetitions and restrained tone mask a fairly dissonant harmonic language which has roots in serialism. *Five Unistic Pieces* has a more abstract agenda: five short 'panels' related only by a common thread of rhythmic patterns based on primary numbers. Each panel explores a different, circumscribed idea, with a steady degree or gradual trajectory of dynamic and/or registral contrast. The fourth, for example, 'sempre mezzo forte, ma molto intenso', has a sequence of thirteen nominal eight-note chords, which, without using the sustaining pedal, are merged note-by-note into the next (cf. Lutosławski's *Mi-parti*) while moving more or less stepwise up in register (Ex. 10.2). This veiled and suggestive musical process has no pretensions to 'the big statement', something that Krauze also learned from Strzemiński.

Example 10.2. Krauze, *Five Unistic Pieces* (1963), start of no. 4.

Several of Krauze's later pieces are more extrovert, including *Triptych* and *Esquisse* for piano (1965, rev. 1967) and String Quartets nos. 1 and 2 (1965, 1970). Borrowing its layout from winged altar paintings, *Triptych* gives the performer optional routes through four panel combinations in which, based on his experience in *Five Unistic Pieces*, gradations of dynamics, rhythmic activity and registral placement are explored. The music is shorn of thematic–motivic identity, with the rates of parametric change in the unfolding of the pitch content providing the work's *raison d'être*. *Esquisse* was composed when Krauze was making a name as an interpreter of graphic and improvised scores outside Poland (although he was accustomed to extended instrumental techniques as a performer, his own piano compositions in the 1960s use the instrument conventionally). He had already premiered Schaeffer's *Nonstop* and in 1966 won the International Gaudeamus Competition for Performers of Contemporary Music in Utrecht. *Esquisse*'s febrile fragmentation, replete with long pauses, is very much of its time, and suggests that he was happy to entertain a greater degree of contrast than in the earlier piano pieces. The two string quartets are likewise more expressionistic than might have been expected. In the angular First Quartet, the transitions between parametric extremes are shortened to the point where they constitute a more recognisable dialectical process. The Second Quartet refines this process (it is played legato throughout) and reasserts the unistic aspect: its elasticated shifts in textural intensity are articulated by heterophonic shoals of pitches in contrasting degrees of chromatic proximity. Once again, local parallels may be found elsewhere (the first movement of Lutosławski's *Trois poèmes*), but here the exaggerated ebb and flow constitutes the main musical substance, a reiterative process that has as many connections with the experience of studying a Strzemiński painting as it has with musical perception.

One of the underlying precepts of unism is an equation between unity and minimal variety of material. Krauze seemed to approach Strzemiński most closely in three other works of this time: *Piece for Orchestra* no. 1 (1969), *Piece for Orchestra* no. 2 (1970) and *Voices* for fifteen instruments to be selected from a prescribed list (1968, rev. 1972). In these works Krauze opted for a much slower and more uniform metabolic rate, a constant articulation ('legatissimo sempre'), and, in each of the last two works, a clear division of the panels by lengthy pauses (cf. Górecki's use of extensive silence in his contemporaneous *Little Music* IV). All of them, like their predecessors, revolve around the movement of pitch classes; there are, therefore, no unpitched instruments. In the two *Pieces for Orchestra*, the instruments are grouped into homophonic but heterogeneous ensembles (five and seven respectively), although some heterophonic leeway is permitted within and between groups as they interpret the proportionalised space–time notation (Ex. 10.3). The overall effect is of lapidary suspended animation, a trance-like state in which individual timbres and consonances emerge in an unusually beguiling way. Krauze also expected each listener to make his own piece from the sound he heard:

> I would prefer the listener to be able to immerse himself in listening to different musical details and fragments rather than being assaulted by a band of attractions, alterations and surprises. This music is discreet. It does not attack the listener. Instead, he has been assigned an active role: he hears only those musical fragments and details that suit him. He chooses them himself, because it is easy to know this music. He therefore knows what may await him. He also knows, if a given fragment has disappeared for a while, that it is sure to return.[3]

This type of musical narcotic, underlined by its subdued dynamic level, seemed more palatable to Polish audiences than Schaeffer's *Howl*. Krauze's

Example 10.3. Krauze, *Piece for Orchestra no. 1* (1969), beginning.

intimate and undemonstrative focus on pitch roulades is quite unlike anything else in Western music at that time. A work like *Piece for Orchestra* no. 2 is diametrically opposite to Penderecki's energetic breast-beating, although there are some similarities to Górecki's music of the time. As in the other two pieces, strange diatonic harmonies emerge from the mist, though here the music achieves a post-romantic lyricism, as if hearing a distant orchestral resonance through a distorting filter with fluctuating inner dynamics. *Voices* signals the direction which Krauze would develop in the 1970s. For instance, the fifteen instruments should not be exactly in tune. And the list of instrumental options omits the standard orchestral representatives: it includes piccolo and recorders, but not the flute, the brass may be chosen from the cornetto, tuba or sousaphone, while the pitched percussion is expanded to include balalaika, lute, banjo, etc. And foreshadowing later ensembles is the possibility of incorporating rarely used instruments – traditional, folk, old, electronic, toy or self-made sound sources. This democratisation of instruments and the implication that amateur musicians can participate in contemporary music does have certain parallels in Schaeffer's aesthetic, but it does not herald any kind of free-for-all: 'The dynamic level of the instruments must be absolutely equal . . . Mutes may be used to achieve the proper balance. The softest instruments should be amplified.'[4] This democratisation came to fruition especially in subsequent works which incorporated folk music and unusual instruments.

As part of his career as a performer, Krauze was the pianist and leader of one of Poland's few ensembles dedicated solely to contemporary music, Music Workshop ('Warsztat Muzyczny'). Poland had no dedicated mid-size chamber ensembles for new music, although both Music Workshop (based in Warsaw) and MW2 (Kraków) did expand their forces from time to time. Despite, or arguably because of its unusual line-up – clarinet, trombone, cello and piano – Music Workshop attracted composers from at home and abroad; in its heyday in the late 1960s and 1970s, it performed widely. Among the Polish works composed for Music Workshop were Kilar's *Training 68*, Kotoński's *Pour quatre* (1968), Krauze's *Polichromia* (1968), Szalonek's *Improvisations sonoristiques*, Dobrowolski's *Krabogapa* (1969), Górecki's *Little Music* IV, Serocki's *Swinging Music* and Tomasz Sikorski's *Untitled* (*Bez tytułu*, 1972). Later on, younger composers like Eugeniusz Knapik (b. 1951) wrote for Music Workshop, whose legacy and commissioning brief were taken up in the 1990s by a younger ensemble, Nonstrom. There is thus a sizeable body of unusually scored Polish chamber music, a repertoire with considerable variety. At one end of the spectrum is Krauze's *Polichromia*, which displays the same characteristics, but at shorter length, as the *Pieces for Orchestra*. At the other end are the extrovert works, already discussed, by Szalonek and Górecki, whose *Little Music* IV symbolises his many underlying contiguities with Krauze's music. And while neither work by Dobrowolski or Kotoński could be said to be as distinctive, they do pinpoint the technical and expressive range of Music Workshop as an ensemble. The best-known work of all is Serocki's *Swinging Music*, not least because it is prepared to cock a snook at many of the new sonoristic conventions of extended instrumental techniques (see Ex. 8.14). With his keen ear for sonorities and an unbounded sense of humour, Serocki treats the four instruments as a jazz combo, creating a rhythm section out of palm hits on the trombone mouthpiece and open neck of the clarinet, or articulating the salient 'tu, ta-ta, tu, ta-ta' rhythm on each instrument: a plastic brush sharply drawn across the piano tuning pins, blowing across the barrel of the clarinet, striking the sides and belly of the cello with alternate hands, or playing a 'silent' note on the trombone.

Tomasz Sikorski's contribution to Music Workshop reinforces the essentially minimal ethos not only of much of the music promoted by the ensemble but also Sikorski's own distinctive voice. This he established in a series of works in the mid-1960s – *Antiphons* and *Echoes* II (1963), *Prologi* (1964), *Concerto breve* (1965) and *Sequenza* I (1966) – in which the music proceeds by means of chains of small ad libitum fragments grouped in larger sequences. The quasi-improvisational chordal fragments are deployed antiphonally or as live or tape playback echoes in a reiterative heterophony that is obsessive and, like some of Krauze's pieces, achieves a disembodied, altered state, particularly in the cumulative resonances and polymorphic character of *Antiphons* and *Echoes* II (Ex. 10.4). *Prologi* is characterised by its mix of triadic ideas, diatonic scales and more dissonant material; his use of four-note cells, constructed from pairs of perfect fourths, is a feature of this and other compositions, where tritonal harmonies or pedals become a regular feature.

Sikorski's pervasive nervous energy and unremitting focus on reductive processes occasionally approached the sonoristic values apparent elsewhere in Polish music (*Concerto breve, Sequenza* I), mainly by developing flickering, amorphous and quasi-stochastic textures. But in the works of the late 1960s, he returned to an introspective, often fractured idiom which focussed on one or two key notions. In one of his rare comments on his compositional intentions, he described *Sonant* for piano (1967) in the following terms:

> This work is based on the contrast between the attack and decay of sound. The work's construction, above all its temporal organisation (augmentation of rhythmic values, approximate values, whose duration depends each time on the timbral characteristics of the piano), as well as its 'form' (static aspect, repetitions of structures, etc.) are the consequences of the distribution of *Sonant*'s sound material in two strata: those of attack and decay.[5]

Example 10.4. Sikorski, *Echoes* II (1963), Sequenza III, in which the material is
pre-recorded twice and one of the two voices is eliminated, leaving only its
resonances.

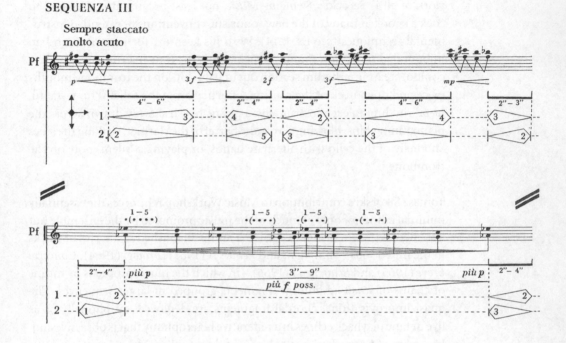

By the time of *Homophony* (1970), Sikorski had intensified the concentration of his material: 'It is a proposal for static, one-dimensional music. In
this work, both the sound material and its structuring are reduced to a
minimum.'[6]

Homophony's instrumental forces reiterated Sikorski's lifelong interest
in specific timbres (it is scored for twelve brass, piano and gong) and he
reinforced his fascination with the interface of diatonicism and dissonance
in utilising a six-note bitonal chording, a combination of first-inversion G
major and second-inversion B flat minor triads (Ex. 10.5). His fundamentally diatonic language is particularly evident – even exposed – in the pared-
down minimal reiterations of his Music Workshop commission, *Untitled*.
He had, by this stage, defined his musical persona as uncompromisingly
austere in terms both of material and its deployment and of the timbral–
expressive world which he explored (cf. Górecki in the late 1960s). He largely
eschewed the temptations of orchestral sonorism (although in *Holzwege*
for small orchestra, 1972, he achieved an almost Messiaen-like luxuriance
both texturally and harmonically), usually preferring an ascetic palette in
which his intense and often bleak reiterative meditations could be given full

Example 10.5. Sikorski, *Homophony* (1970), fig. 23.

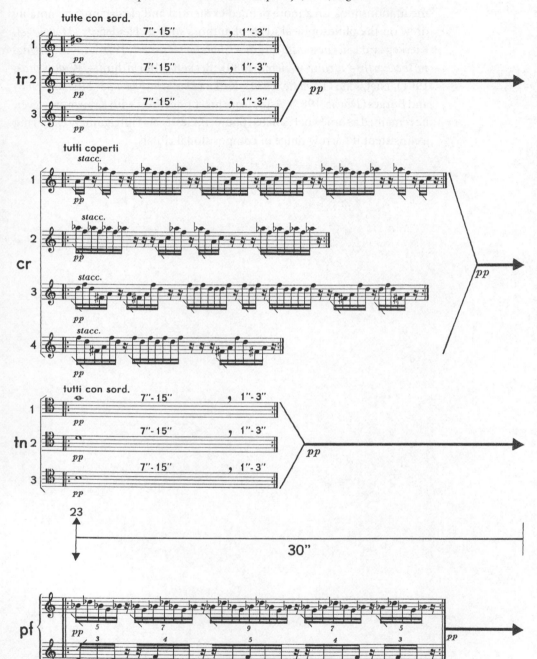

rein outside traditional modes of discourse. In the 1970s and 1980s, these meditations took on a more defined existential and elegiac hue: he notably drew on the philosophical ideas of authors such as Heidegger (*Holzwege*), Kierkegaard (*Sickness unto Death – Choroba na śmierć*, 1976), Joyce (*Strings in the Earth – Struny w ziemi*, 1980), Beckett (*Afar a Bird – W dali ptak*, 1981), Nietzsche (*La notte*, 1984), Kafka (*Das Schweigen der Sirenen*, 1986) and Borges (*Diario*, 1987). Aside from his connections with Krauze, however, he remained a somewhat isolated figure, tirelessly and intriguingly exploring a consistent if narrow range of compositional rituals.

PART IV

Modernisms and national iconographies

11 Pursuing the abstract

During the second half of the 1960s and well into the 1970s, most Polish composers went through further stages of reassessment and reorientation after having achieved their initial modus vivendi with avant-garde music from Western Europe and America. In some cases, such adjustments can be marked by specific compositions and dates – Górecki's *Refrain* (1965) and *Ad matrem* (1971), Penderecki's *St Luke Passion* (1966) and First Violin Concerto (1976), or Lutosławski's *Livre* (1968) and *Epitaph* (1979). For other composers, the process was more gradual although sometimes equally radical. And for some, change was minimal: Baird and Serocki, for example, were but two of the Polish modernists who maintained their dedication to the ideals which they had espoused in the early 1960s.

A substantial number of other composers, mainly those born in the inter-war years, maintained active contact with aspects of Polish modernism while at the same time making stylistic modifications or softening their tone. Dobrowolski and Kotoński are representative of this trend. Dobrowolski's continuing interest in new instrumental techniques (*Music for Tuba Solo*, 1973) and electronic media (culminating in his only exclusively digital composition, *Passacaglia for TX*, 1988) was matched by his preference for non-descriptive titles, such as the six pieces titled *Music for Orchestra* (1970–82). Of these, the last three admit more traditional elements, such as the use of a focal pitch class in no. 4, 'A-la' (1974), in which, in almost Lutosławskian fashion, 'A constitutes the centre of symmetric vertical structures'.[1] The 'Passacaglia' subtitle of no. 5 (1978) is but one of many Polish post-war pieces which use this compositional principle; it also flags up an intriguing disintegration of the passacaglia principle in which dodecaphonic techniques are combined with a process in which instruments peel off from the reiterated theme with their own ad libitum version. The resultant sound-mass is more subtle and layered than in his more densely continuous scores and itself may have been a response to the more strictly defined procedure which Górecki had used in the first movement of his Third Symphony in 1976.

While Dobrowolski's titles and mode of discourse denoted abstract musical thought, Kotoński has been more inclined towards programmatic ideas, even though his language and preferred genres have still been largely rooted in his music of the 1960s. One of his pervading themes has been the element of 'air': *Aeolian Harp* for soprano and ensemble (1973) and the orchestral works *Wind Rose* (1976), *Bora* (1979) and *Sirocco* (1980). He has also combined electronic means and chamber groupings to compose four works devoted to the four seasons, beginning with *Spring Music* (*Muzyka wiosenna*, 1978). His affinity with nature is shared by other composers, including Zbigniew Bargielski (b. 1937), whose first two string quartets are entitled 'Alpine' (1976) and 'Primaverile' (1980).

On a technical level, Bargielski is a good example of a composer who shares with Lutosławski a fundamental concern with pitch organisation and its role in the musical evolution of a composition. In works since the early 1970s, he has developed what he terms 'Zentrumsstrukturen', a procedure which isolates 'the dominant sounds that function as centres of the individual formal segments'.[2] His links with Lutosławski are further emphasised by the structural rationale of the two-movement Third String Quartet 'Still Life with Scream' (1985): 'Preparation' is followed by 'Action', a clear reference to Lutosławski's notion of 'Hésitant' and 'Direct' in his Second Symphony. This link does not, however, indicate a comparable musical language, as Bargielski's quartet draws on several features of Penderecki's arsenal of string techniques from the 1960s. Furthermore, Bargielski's use of instrumental timbres is as important to 'Zentrumsstrukturen' as pitch organisation, and the combination of three of his favourite instruments – guitar, accordion and percussion – with orchestra in *Trigonalia* (a neologism combining 'trigon' with 'bacchanalia') (1994) is indicative of his constructivist outlook. The ways in which composers use titles is as varied in Poland as elsewhere. Serocki's customarily signify a procedural idea, while Baird's often indicate either a genre or a state of mind or emotion. Dobrowolski's are matter-of-fact, Bargielski's poetically surreal (especially in his music for accordion). Tomasz Sikorski, whose repetitive, cellular structures are arguably the most unremittingly abstract in post-war Polish music (and yet imply a high degree of fragility), deliberately counterpointed his music with evocative titles, many drawn from literature.

Traditional titles and genres, such as the symphony, concerto and string quartet, played an increasingly significant role in the music of many composers who during the 1970s and 1980s openly acknowledged their identification with the gestural and formal clarity of eighteenth-century practices. Once again, attention is drawn to those composers born, like Bargielski, between the mid-1920s and the mid-1940s, such as Moszumańska-Nazar, Bujarski, Stachowski and Meyer. Perhaps not insignificantly, these four were all educated and based in Kraków and so shared a common musical environment that was by no means the same as that of nearby Katowice (the home of Górecki and Kilar) or of Warsaw. (Regional compositional differences had been a feature during the 1950s and 1960s, and they remain strong today.)

As the oldest of this Kraków group, Moszumańska-Nazar clings most closely to timbral concerns, although there is a notable toughening of her musical language not only in the linear tensions of her two string quartets (1974, 1979) but also in the epic and hard-edged confrontations of the orchestral *Rhapsody* II (1980) and *Two Dialogues* (1994). At times, the determined muscularity of her thematic ideas and robust orchestration recall the uncompromising amalgam of contradictory forces in Bacewicz's music of the 1960s, although by the 1980s, while heterogeneity was more commonplace in Polish music, hard-edged atonal argument seemed decidedly outmoded.

Bujarski, Stachowski and Meyer all demonstrate in differing ways that Polish composers in the 1970s began to renew contact with past eras. All three revisited neo-classicism in a determined attempt to break out of what they evidently saw as the faded glories of sonorism and its generalised concepts of pitch, rhythm and structural momentum. Bujarski has always favoured a seductive sound world, lyrical, suggestive and reflective, and this continued to moderate any neo-classical leanings. It is apparent in a range of pieces, from the neo-romantic inflections of the oratorio *El hombre* (1973), with its dark-hued settings of poetry by Eliot, Eluard, Whitman and Ionesco, to the Szymanowskian sensuality of his response to Polish poetry in *Gardens* (*Ogrody*, for soprano and orchestra, 1987). Bujarski's better-known works are his four string quartets (1980–2001), three works for strings – *Musica domestica* (1977), Concertos for Strings I and II (1979, 1992) – and the orchestral *Similis Greco* I (1979). *Musica domestica*'s ancestry in the heterophonic 'bundling' of Lutosławski is subtly combined with a rich harmonic language and quasi-eighteenth-century figurations that together anticipate the postmodernist trends of younger Poles in the 1980s. The first Concerto for Strings, for solo violin and seventeen string players, though less virtuosic than its successor, illustrates Bujarski's move towards a neo-tonal idiom. The heightened expressiveness of both the soloist and ensemble even suggests parallels with the music of John Tavener, although it does not preclude a strong sense of harmonic and motivic momentum. It is, within the Polish context, an exceptionally impassioned and eloquent work, as is *Similis Greco* I, which Bujarski, who is also a painter of considerable originality, designed as a tribute to the 'irrational light effects of the ecstatic, visionary and mystical paintings by El Greco' (Ex. 11.1).[3] This latter work, harmonically luminous and unerringly handled in its colours and pacing, adds a certain air of antiquity to Bujarski's language. Yet its patent seriousness and intense contemplative quality differentiates it from more febrile postmodernism.

Stachowski, by nature mild-mannered and modest, is another casualty of the critical tendency to focus on the major figures at the expense of those who

Example 11.1. Bujarski, *Similis Greco* I (1979), letter B.

work in their shadow. In defining his voice after a brief period of experimentation around 1970, he moved gradually towards an unusual combination of neo-classical and impressionist impulses. En route he evinced a fascination with ritual and the exotic in the Lutosławskian *Chants of Thakur* (*Śpiewy thakuryjskie*, to words by Rabindranath Tagore, 1974), simultaneously consolidating his use of focal pitch centres, including second-inversion major triads, as in the conclusions of both the orchestral *Poème sonore* (1975) and the song cycle *Birds* (*Ptaki*, 1976) or in the frequent unisons of *Quartetto da ingresso* (1980). Stachowski's seven named or numbered quartets (1963–2001) form a representative group in terms of their textural clarity and intimate expression. *Quartetto da ingresso*'s unabashed saturation with G naturals and their 'resolution' onto C at the end, as well as the frequently tonal implications of melodic figurations, is counterpointed starkly by sections of greater dissonance and fragmentation. This confrontational but curiously undramatic dialogue is characteristic of many of Stachowski's works and stands in some contrast to the more animated pitch organisation and structural practices of Lutosławski, whom Stachowski holds in high regard and with whom he shares many local technical procedures.

Stachowski's use of titles such as 'Canzona', 'Serenata' or 'Intermezzo' (*Birds*) or 'Sinfonia' and 'Pezzo gioioso' (Divertimento, 1978) are reliable indicators of the neo-classical trend in his compositional ethos. Although his music still utilises a wide range of more typically modernist devices, his music is characterised by a degree of asceticism, such as in his spare settings of d'Annunzio in *Madrigale dell'estate* for voice and string trio (1984) (Ex. 11.2). Occasionally, he indulges in greater harmonic and timbral luxuriance (*Sapphic Odes* for mezzo-soprano and orchestra, 1985). More recently, Sonata for Strings (1991) holds true to tonal and metric stability, alongside reiterative and scalic figurations; sometimes the music borders on the stylistic simplicities characteristic of Kilar, especially in its reduced interest in confrontational argument.

The youngest composer of this group is the most prolific and the most obvious heir to Bacewicz. Meyer has to his credit eleven string quartets and much other chamber music, six symphonies and numerous concertos. He is unusual for his generation in having concentrated on traditional genres rather than on the programmatic or picturesque, and in this he follows closely in Bacewicz's footsteps as well as linking himself with one of his idols, Shostakovich. He shares with both composers a high level of nervous energy and, although his sense of musical humour may lack Shostakovich's particular irony, it is used with precision and flair. The connection with Shostakovich (and Bacewicz) is underlined by Meyer's string quartets. Their focus progresses from the lucidity and emotional refinement

Example 11.2. Stachowski, *Madrigale dell'estate* (1984), conclusion of no. 1.

of no. 4 (1974) to the intimate lyricism of no. 8 (1985) and the energetic post-Bacewicz, quasi-Beethovenian intensity of no. 10 (1994). He shows a natural affinity with the medium, and in several cases has set out, albeit conservatively, to rethink its potential scenarios: no. 5 (1977) gives the cello a primary concertante role and foregoes unconventional playing techniques, no. 6 (1981) opens by deconstructing eighteenth-century gestures around a C natural pedal, while in the short no. 7 (1985) the instruments are muted throughout and for much of its length are explored in varied pairings (Ex. 11.3). Meyer's quartets, like Bacewicz's before him, are less easily defined as neo-classical as they tend to draw more on early nineteenth-century

Example 11.3. Meyer, Seventh String Quartet (1985), opening.

gestural modes than on early twentieth-century refractions. The same is not true of his lighter instrumental and orchestral works, many of which use classical stylisation and citation for genuinely witty and deconstructive purposes. The capricious mocking of cadential formulae in the Piano Concerto (1979, rev. 1989) is followed by three quirkily affectionate orchestral tributes: *Hommage à Johannes Brahms* (1982), the cello concerto *Canti Amadei* (1984) and *Caro Luigi* (Cherubini, not Nono!) for four cellos and orchestra (1989).

Meyer's musical personality is often eclectic and his approach to pitch organisation includes not only tonal referencing but also linear twelve-note procedures (for example, the serial use of an all-interval row in the Third Symphony). His indebtedness to Lutosławski is apparent in the Fourth

Symphony (1973), where he shows his metrical sure-footedness not only in the animation of complex harmonic blocks but also in his masterful control of the conventional symphonic allegro. Lutosławskian echoes are also heard in the Fifth Symphony (1979), which, despite its chamber scoring, is a substantial work with a clear end-accented architecture. Meyer's motivation for the Shostakovich-inspired Sixth 'Polish' Symphony (1982) – in which he refers to three well-known Polish patriotic songs – was a symbolic act of defiance and commemoration which was bound up with the national turmoil of the early 1980s, a feature of Polish music discussed in greater detail in the next chapter.

Lutosławski

Lutosławski refused to be drawn into such extra-musical arguments, although there is circumstantial evidence that certain works may have been associated with external events (*Funeral Music* with the Hungarian Revolution or the Third Symphony, 1983, with the Polish situation in the early 1980s). Even if this is true, there is never any sense that Lutosławski's music is dependent on non-artistic perspectives. Furthermore, while he was deeply engaged in a refined reconciliation between modernist and pre-modern ideals, like some of the composers discussed above, his primary focus on pitch and its integral role in devising rhythmic and gestural patterns meant that he avoided weak or derivative language in which not all parametric implications had been radically considered. For him there could be no idle gesture, no indulgent pause, no flaccid rhythm. The preparations for his last period had been long and compositionally arduous, but when he was ready there was no hesitation in his manner nor in the music.

The final phase of Lutosławski's career began with *Epitaph*. This modest piece for oboe and piano, anticipating several other solo and duo pieces which for the first time since *Dance Preludes* gave non-orchestral players the opportunity to include his music in their repertoires, is significant for a number of reasons. Firstly, it realises Lutosławski's goal of a coherent melodic language, still based on carefully controlled intervallic schemata, without the necessity for explicit harmonic underpinning. Secondly, his characteristic intent to create drama from opposites (here they are a *lamentoso* cantilena and a Papageno-like bird song) achieves a suitably Mozartian dialogue (Ex. 11.4) which reaches a confrontational climax before the more consonant epilogue. Its composition gave Lutosławski enormous confidence in this more exposed melodic language, also shown in later chamber works, such as *Partita* (1984) and *Subito* (1992), both for violin and piano. *Partita*'s title is functionally descriptive, whereas *Epitaph* and

Example 11.4. Lutosławski, *Epitaph* (1979), opening.

Grave (1981) had been memorial tributes. *Partita* is his most extended duet, with three movements linked by ad libitum interludes (a developed echo of *Livre*). His preface to the score acknowledges its indebtedness to Baroque rhythmic–gestural language and yet at the same time suggests that this is illusory. This is typical of his determination to view his music as essentially independent of associations, whether with idioms of other composers and periods or, for that matter, with extra-musical contexts. And yet *Subito*'s volatile shifts of mood, the close interaction of the two players and the violin's near-ecstatic lyricism (Ex. 11.5) seem to allude to that quintessential work of Szymanowski's middle period, 'La fontaine d'Arethuse' from *Myths*. One might also question whether the Ravelian lightness of touch in *Chantefleurs et chantefables* and the late-romantic traits in the Piano Concerto (1988) are substantive or transitory features. Underlying these and other backward glances is Lutosławski's perhaps unconscious desire not only to strengthen contact with the mainstream of European music to which he felt he always belonged but also, as Stucky has eloquently argued, to revisit the synthesis of old and new which two of his own works of the 1950s – Concerto

Example 11.5. Lutosławski, *Subito* (1992), fig. 6.

for Orchestra and *Funeral Music* – had so successfully achieved.[4] Nowhere is this desire clearer than in the Third Symphony and nowhere is its realisation more complicated by divergent demands on the listener's attention.

At one level, this is the most brilliant and dynamic score in his oeuvre. It revels in orchestral sonorities (it was written for the Chicago Symphony and its conductor Sir Georg Solti) in ways that outshine even the Concerto for Orchestra. At another level, its structural intentions are overlaid or even subverted by the expressive power of the musical ideas. Lutosławski described its continuous outline structure as consisting of 'two movements, preceded by a short introduction and followed by an epilogue and a coda'.[5] One key feature unmentioned here is the motif of the repeated octave E naturals which opens and closes the symphony and occurs at crucial stages in the design of this thirty-minute work. Such is the arresting impact of this motif that its appearance at either end is more than just a pair of quotation marks; it calls into question the function of return in an output normally preoccupied by progression. Furthermore, the motif's appearances in the body of the work – sometimes on E, sometimes extended or varied – are designed to mark out the ever-lengthening stages not only in the introduction and first movement (three episodes) but also in the early parts of the second (cf. the use of 'Il y a toi' in *Les espaces*). Its syntactical purpose seems clear.

A second aspect – the use of 'set piece' canonic toccatas (figs. 32 and 49) – also has structural implications as well as recalling comparable passages in Concerto for Orchestra and *Funeral Music*. The set pieces have a specific gravitas which counterpoints the repeated-note motif and suggests a change of both pace and focus. The second toccata is of particular significance, because it is here, and not earlier, that the second movement begins to gather strength for what is expected, on Lutosławski's previous form, to be the climax of the movement and the work's dénouement. Although there is a climax of sorts (fig. 77), it is so lacking in affective resonance that it can only be regarded as a minor event in the larger scheme of things. Consequently, Lutosławski's own vision of a second movement followed by an epilogue and coda may reasonably be interrogated. An alternative, even parallel reading is to understand the epilogue and coda as extensions of the developing argument of the second movement and not as commentaries upon it. This is supported by the way in which (from fig. 81 onwards) both the toccatas and interlaced cantilenas eventually merge to create an intense and powerful recitativo texture (saturated with minor thirds) that becomes the symphony's new and most significant centre of gravity (Ex. 11.6). This recitative creates such an expressive momentum in what is normally described as the Epilogue and Coda that it provides strong evidence that the *real* climax has been reserved for the very end. At fig. 99, the apogee of this process doubles as the final brief drive (a sparkling piece of canonic writing for pitched percussion and piano in one of Lutosławski's contracting and ascending harmonic 'wedges') to a final fortissimo chord, itself a version of the typical Lutosławskian climax. Here, however, instead of the gradual resolution of tension that characterises many of his previous works, such as *Livre* or *Mi-parti*, the 'escape' consists simply, and cadentially, of four repeated E naturals. An abiding impression of the Third Symphony, when placed alongside its immediate predecessors in Lutosławski's

Example 11.6. Lutosławski, Third Symphony (1983), figs. 81–2.

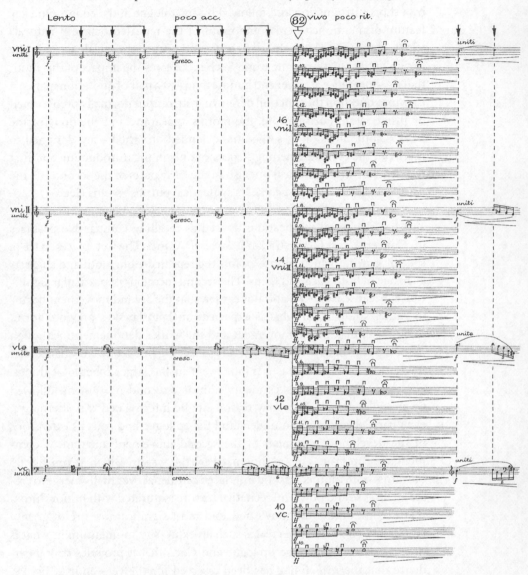

orchestral output, is that it is motivated by line (cantilena, recitative, canon) rather than by harmonic movement (block chordal contrasts or sculpturally shaped harmonic movement). The success of *Epitaph* had been translated into symphonic terms in a multivalent fashion that demonstrated yet again the technical and expressive richness of Lutosławski's compositional vision. Its immediate international success in concert halls, broadcasts and commercial recordings was remarkable in the context of contemporary music in the mid-1980s.

There followed a series of three pieces under the title *Chain* (1983, 1985 and 1986). The technique of presenting a musical argument as an overlapping relay of ideas had been a notable feature of Lutosławski's compositions for many years, going as far back as the Concerto for Orchestra. In these three works, he elevated this 'chain' technique to become the structural backbone. It is not, however, a passive process, and he keeps alive his essentially developmental approach by shaping and contrasting the different links in the chain to achieve a satisfying dramatic whole. Each of the three pieces has a distinct persona, although all three advance Lutosławski's new-found melodic confidence. With just fourteen players, the ten-minute *Chain* 1 bridges the divide between chamber and orchestral music, allowing for both intimacy of detail and richness of timbre (the opening ad libitum section of the orchestral *Chain* 3 also demonstrates the significance of instrumental colour in clarifying the chain technique). The four-movement *Chain* 2, for violin and orchestra, gave Lutosławski particular satisfaction, not only because he was, once again, working with an inspirational soloist (Anne-Sophie Mutter) but also because he had found an expressive balance of fine proportions between 'the shaping of pitch (i.e., melody, harmony and polyphony)' and what he by this stage in his career deemed a lesser concern, 'the organisation of time'.[6] The suppleness of transitions between *ad libitum* and *a battuta* passages (from both an aural and notated perspective – they are not always readily identical) is a mark of his acumen in exploiting pulse, rhythm and phrasing. It symbolises, alongside the melodic aspect, the relaxed ease with which he synthesised new and old gestural conventions. *Chain* 2 is a clear example of the refocussed function of twelve-note chords: they appear only a handful of times, at critical structural points in the two fast movements where their impact is all the greater for their rarity. There are also moments, both stylistically and procedurally, where, as in the expressivity of the solo writing and seemingly intuitive chaining of sections in the later *Subito*, Lutosławski again recalls Szymanowski's practices in works such as his First Violin Concerto and *Myths*.

Reconciling the present with the past is, for some, the most problematic aspect of Lutosławski's Piano Concerto. He set out deliberately to marry his own idiom with 'traditions of nineteenth-century pianism. With the traditions of Chopin, Liszt and Brahms'.[7] This might seem an uncharacteristically confessional change of tack, but Lutosławski had frequently cited early twentieth-century composers, including Debussy and Stravinsky, as his role models. They too had utilised preceding traditions to enrich and advance their own work; Lutosławski's Piano Concerto is simply another variant of his own modernist–classicist synthesis. Its gestural language, quite apart from its stylistic affinities with a range of other composers including Ravel,

Bartók and (*pace* Lutosławski's own comments) Rachmaninov, is evidently a continuation of what, to borrow Whittall's term 'classicizing strategies',[8] had already been mapped out by many preceding works, including the five-movement orchestral *Novelette* (1979). In the Piano Concerto, such strategies are observable on local and structural levels, in the melodic, harmonic and textural idioms as well as in the sequence of larger events.

The most discussed aspect, to use Lutosławski's somewhat guarded acknowledgement, is the finale's 'allusion' to the Baroque chaconne (viz. his similar caution in describing *Partita*). As always, he was anxious that his reliance on the past should be seen as referential rather than reverential, thus preserving his compositional autonomy. Lutosławski's chaconne – a conjoining of two ideas, the first intermittent, the second sustained in a mini-sequence – is a series of seventeen orchestral statements which, with one or two alterations and additions, completes a traditional circle of fifths to conclude the main part of the movement. The piano, meanwhile, is engaged in its own complementary process whose divisions are designed not to coincide with those of the orchestral chaconne. This part-mechanistic, part-developmental combination is rich in ambiguities; Lutosławski has created a distinctive take on the chaconne form and, simultaneously, given a masterclass in the chain technique. Even so, what seems new and fresh has clear antecedents not only in his own oeuvre but also in the wider modernist fascination with the kind of lapidary formations characteristic of Stravinsky and Messiaen. Nevertheless, the coda and final 'cadence' of this finale bespeak a much more traditional practice. While some of Lutosławski's works end by a process of reduction and withdrawal, others, from *Preludes and Fugue* to the Fourth Symphony, suggested to Lutosławski the need for a short rousing conclusion. In his discussion of the Piano Concerto, Whittall perceives 'less a resolution in the traditional, grandly romantic sense than an abrupt concession to closure'.[9] Perhaps the problem is even broader: the chaconne is a self-contained unit and does not possess sufficient weight and unified momentum to bring the Concerto as a whole to a convincing close. The coda is therefore a necessarily separate device which, brilliant though it is, does not wholly integrate with or fully resolve what precedes it.[10]

The Fourth Symphony, Lutosławski's most compact, is a taut and focussed exploration of the power of melody to shape a work into something that is infinitely more expressive than the original ground plan might suggest. As in the Third Symphony, the Fourth in many ways defies its outline description (a two-movement form with epilogue and coda). Its thematic integration, the impact of moments of rhythmic rest and the structural significance of carefully placed pitch unisons all conspire to reshape the work. At its heart

Example 11.7. Lutosławski, Fourth Symphony (1992), opening.

is post-romantic thematicism, and in its various forms this creates the over-arching dynamic of the symphony. Its deeply memorable opening (tolling E naturals initiating a four-note harmony over which unfurls a clarinet melody of exceptional poignancy) may be directly related to the texture (also based on E) which begins the Third Symphony's 'epilogue' (Ex. 11.7). On its two further appearances, this cantilena texture is developed by processes of upward transposition, extension and amplification, until it is decisively countermanded prior to the commencement of the 'second' movement at fig. 22, barely one third of the way through. Such is the strength of the 'first' movement's cantilenas that when such textures and intense lyricism occur again in the 'second', each time launched from a unison pitch in the middle register – A natural (figs. 43–6), B flat (64–73), C natural (73–82) and A flat (82–5) – the 'second' movement's opening scherzando section appears to be diversionary rather than substantive (even though its main theme, at fig. 23, does become entwined in the symphony's developmental processes). Lutosławski adds a further diversion at fig. 73 (a gradual accumulation of pinpricks of sound), a set-piece texture which he reintegrates into the developmental fabric partway through by recalling the disruptive trumpet motif which had appeared after the first cantilena at fig. 4. Thereafter, the motivating force of the symphony is sustained lyricism – balancing the three cantilenas at the beginning of the work – as it drives towards the climax, escape and coda.

When considering the relationship of content and form, it seems self-evident that those works in which structural concerns are paramount (especially those in the 1960s and 70s) present few conflicts with their musical material which, by and large, is rooted in twelve-note harmonic patternings. It is a reasonable conjecture to suggest that, from 1979 onwards, after jettisoning the twelve-note chord as the main compositional component in favour of melody, Lutosławski was encouraged to look beyond the immediate structural confines of two-movement or end-accented form towards a more intuitive, developmental 'fantasia' which would, as the Third and Fourth Symphonies imply, be driven by his instinct for multivalent dramatic and thematic tensions of the kind that were pursued so memorably by Szymanowski in his middle period.

Penderecki

Penderecki's music has shown a more deliberate search for synthesis. Thinking back to the mid-1960s, he has opined that: 'The contemporary artist, despite his longing for universality, is fragmented and alienated. For me, the conscious use of tradition became an opportunity for overcoming this dissonance between the artist and the audience.'[11] Initially, this change was most apparent in his vocal and choral music, but in the mid-1970s he signalled a conscious shift of emphasis by turning to orchestral music with exclusively generic titles (he had already used the First Symphony to provide a summation of and official farewell to his sonoristic idiom). The First Violin Concerto, written for Isaac Stern, marked an irrevocable turning point, initiating six more concertos[12] and four further symphonies (several more have been planned). If that was not enough to mark him out from his compatriots even more than in the 1960s, this move was integral to his conscious attempt to reclaim what he saw as the most significant aspects of music of the past. He looked beyond the lightness of conventional neo-classical utterance to a darker idiom based on late-romantic gestures. The comparisons made most frequently, including those by Penderecki himself, have been to Bruckner and Wagner, although there are strong cases for looking also at Liszt (in terms of motivic density) and the Polish neo-Straussian composer, Karłowicz (in terms of post-romantic aesthetic).

There had already been intimations in the *Magnificat* of what some commentators saw as a degenerative softening of his radical sonorism, and this surfaced even more clearly in the compact orchestral miniature, *The Awakening of Jacob*. With panache and urgent structural momentum, it creates in music the sense of terror and wonderment evoked by Genesis 28 – portentous brass chords, unearthly ocarinas (a follow-up to their use

Example 11.8. Penderecki, First Violin Concerto (1976), harmonic kernel, bb. 6–7.

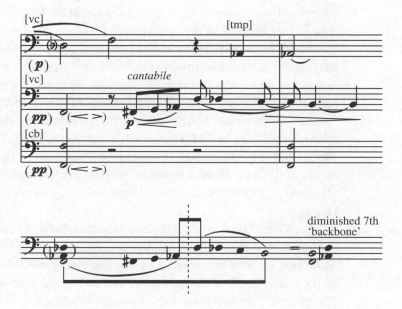

in his recent Old Testament piece, *Canticum canticorum Salomonis*), and a pattern of rising and falling semitones separated by tritones which have been at the core of Penderecki's pitch material ever since. It is tempting to see in the shifting directions of this stepwise and gapped motif the movement of the angels up and down the ladder of Jacob's dream, although whether their saturated presence in subsequent pieces carries anything like the same conviction is arguable.

One of the clearest examples of this motivic obsession comes in the exposition of the First Violin Concerto. The opening is characteristic of this new period: a slowly repeated note (F) is subsumed into a first-inversion D flat major triad (the rising sixth, minor and major, will become a prime melodic feature in later works) and then counterpointed by the pitch class a tritone distant (B).[13] In this instance (Ex. 11.8), the tritone is elaborated by chromatic movement F–A flat (ascending) followed by D to B (descending), a figure whose two interlocking tritones (F–B framing A flat–D) articulate a diminished-seventh chord. It is little surprise, therefore, that Penderecki's music shows an intense degree of tonal instability. Even when the music achieves a momentary sense of rest, it is often caused by focus on a triad or single pitch class which in turn is countermanded by another at a distance of a tritone (e.g., the A major triad followed by one on E flat minor at b. 70 or the D–A flat sequence before the 'development' begins at b. 84). The juxtaposition of minor triads a tritone apart was to become a trademark, especially when orchestrated on low woodwind and brass (the opening of the Second Symphony, 1980, or the conclusion of the Flute Concerto, 1992). As a further example of the importance of such pitch relationships, one of the intermittent ideas in the Violin Concerto (it had already occurred in *Magnificat*) is a chordal combination of a major-minor triad with a root note a tritone lower, sometimes dubbed the 'Penderecki' chord.[14] The full realisation of this construct comes, however, at the very end, when the solo violinist adds a further note (high C sharp) a tritone above the fifth of the C major-minor triad and its tritonal bass F sharp (Ex. 11.9). This formation may usefully be seen as a pair of two diminished triads (with their inherent tritone and minor thirds) a semitone apart; its pre-eminent interval classes (1, 3 and 6) symbolise the essence of Penderecki's new harmonic and melodic language.

If the Violin Concerto crystallises important aspects of Penderecki's pitch organisation, it also signifies his new conservatism. Aleatory rhythms and ad libitum sections are replaced by thoroughgoing metred notation, with all the implications of compositional and directorial control that implies. The gestural language harks back to earlier models, too, as does the relationship between orchestra and soloist. That said, there is an intention on the composer's part to avoid obvious structural divisions, even though there are signs of an underlying sonata structure. The work's discursive character is due to the multiple digressions that inevitably affect a work of some forty minutes' duration.[15] These digressions consist essentially of pauses or interruptions to the flow of the musical argument – short quasi ad libitum solo phrases, sudden shifts in tempo and rhythm (cf. the two 'tempo di marcia' segments which are interposed just before the 'recapitulation' and in the middle of the second cadenza – Wolfram Schwinger finds these interludes 'inexplicable'[16]), or the placing of the intermittent chords described above. Writing recently about the Concerto Grosso for three cellos and orchestra (2000), Andrzej Chłopecki neatly encapsulates Penderecki's process in large-scale single-movement works: 'the carousel of main motives, melodic illustrations, harmonic progressions, rhythmic figures and textural shapes keeps turning in successive variants . . . in a bravura exchange of arguments and ripostes, statements and negations'.[17] As this suggests, Penderecki's approach to rhapsodic discourse differs from that explored by Szymanowski or Lutosławski in that the contours of the argument are less sharply defined and welded together. A major cause is that his pervasive melodic–harmonic language is so intervallically restrictive and plainly repetitive that no amount of rhythmic, articulatory or even contrapuntal variation, nor occasional textural or thematic cross-references,

Example 11.9. Penderecki, First Violin Concerto (1976), conclusion.

can shape the large span of a musical argument in a conventionally dramatic manner. Instead, this essentially lyrical music is reliant on its localised affectivity.

Penderecki took a different tack in the Second Cello Concerto (1982), which he structured as three expanding alternations of slow and fast sections concluded by a slow coda. There are traces of recapitulatory elements in the later sections, but the unheralded interpolation of seven vivacious variations during the final fast section is a striking example of his

Example 11.10. Penderecki, Second Cello Concerto (1982), Variation III leading into Variation IV.

diversionary tactics (Ex. 11.10). The sketches reveal that Penderecki at one stage subtitled the Concerto 'Rondo capriccioso' and its sectional alternations still mimic the form's traditional use of episode and refrain.[18] Despite the capricious insertion of brief cadenzas and fugatos, Penderecki this time also constructs large-scale paragraphs (the second fast section is a particularly successful, goal-directed perpetuum mobile), and the overall structure provides a coherent vehicle for the intimate, developmental dialogue of solo cello and orchestra. Its obsessive motivic ideas, stark contrasts and nervous

Example 11.11. Penderecki, Second Cello Concerto (1982), opening.

energy make for one of Penderecki's most compelling concertos. This is partly because it reinterprets elements from his sonoristic past. The slow sections, for example, are introduced by a distant, simplified relative of Penderecki's block textures of the early 1960s. Here, it consists of quietly reiterated quavers and shallow glissandi in the upper strings (Ex. 11.11). Their initial high B natural is, again, counterpointed by its polar opposite (a low F), the resulting tritone establishing an air of uncertainty, even of imminent cataclysm which the Concerto proceeds to exploit.

Penderecki's pervading evocation of doom and gloom – an exaggerated if less inherently dynamic version of eighteenth-century *Sturm und Drang* – is intensified here and elsewhere by his basic orchestral palette, which is not that of a water-colourist or seductive impressionist. Multiple doublings, extremes of high and low register, sombre chording and the contrasting use of solo instruments, usually as agents of melancholic lyricism (cor anglais, clarinet, bassoon, trumpet and orchestral violas are among Penderecki's favourites), lead to brutal contrasts which as often as not are the main force for structural momentum, given the basic monothematicism of his motivic invention. The results can be crude, blustering and aggressive, or contrarily lyrical, elegiac and melancholic. The expressive intent, therefore, linguistic and stylistic changes notwithstanding, is essentially unchanged since *Threnody*, *Polymorphia* or the *St Luke Passion*.

Example 11.12. Penderecki, String Trio (1991), opening of first movement.

In subsequent concertos, Penderecki developed his procedure of local and large-scale contrasts. Although the Viola Concerto (1983) recalls its two immediate predecessors in many respects, it is cast on a more modest scale and is notable for (i) its introduction of a type of vigorous string theme which pivots above and/or below an open string (an echo of one of Bacewicz's characteristic ideas), in addition to giving the impression that it is about to initiate a fugato, (ii) a certain stiffening of the rhythmic joints in fast tempi which contrasts strongly with greater flexibility in slower tempi and (iii) a lightening of texture and subsequent easing of expressive tensions. These features are developed in his more recent chamber music, including the String Trio (1991) (Exs.11.12 and 11.13) and Clarinet Quartet (1993).

The Second Violin Concerto (1995), however, returns to the ambitious dimensions of earlier concertos. Like Lutosławski, Penderecki has had the

Example 11.13. Penderecki, String Trio (1991), opening of second movement.

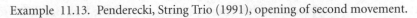

good fortune to have been able to write for extraordinary performers, some of whom, like Rostropovich and Mutter, they had in common. Penderecki's Second Violin Concerto was composed for Mutter and its unusually complex interlacing of elegiac and dynamic modes not only seems geared to her interpretative talents but is also the most impressive embodiment of Penderecki's free-wheeling reconsideration of concerto structure (its subtitle, 'Metamorphoses', summarises Penderecki's essentially developmental approach to his chosen material). On the one hand, he reinforces classic sonata-allegro signposts: in contrast to some of his earlier concertos (where there can be two cadenzas), there is only one large, highly virtuosic cadenza, placed conventionally towards the conclusion and both announced and quitted orchestrally by robustly tonal cadential figures. On the other hand, the Concerto's agenda places the spotlight less on concertante elements than on the free-rein lyricism of the solo writing. Not untypically, the orchestral background pulses funereally (occasional joined by fanfaring trumpets and bells) alongside other tutti expressions of anxiety against which the soloist becomes the representative of private and more subtly detailed emotion. The Concerto's most memorable section is its extended elegiac conclusion. This further underlines his embrace of tonality and, according to Mutter, may be interpreted programmatically: 'It opens with a scene of burial, in which the soul triumphs over the body and soars aloft to heaven.'[19] Such an observation is a timely reminder that much of Penderecki's symphonic musical thought originates in his music with text, both sacred and secular.

There is a tendency to discuss Penderecki's instrumental works in the context of the operas and large-scale oratorio-like works, especially in Poland. Thus the Second Cello Concerto and the Second Symphony (1980) are associated, for example, with *Paradise Lost*, the Third Symphony (1988–95) with *Black Mask*, and the String Trio and Clarinet Quartet with his most recent opera, *Ubu Rex* (1991). There are many linguistic and technical comparisons to be made and it is probably true that what in a nominally abstract context, such as a concerto or symphony, sounds uncomfortably visceral is perfectly at home in works where sin, purgatory, plague and scatology – and redemptive resolution – form the crux of the drama. Indeed, his music has often been characterised as filmic (with regard to his music since 1975, Nino Rota is sometimes cited, usually pejoratively) or as akin to Grand Guignol. Penderecki, however, is untroubled by transference from textual and visual media to the concert hall. His 'abstract' music continues to invite programmatic interpretation, as is revealed by Tomaszewski's comments on the use of a well-known carol in the Second Symphony:

> Almost in passing among the multitude of contrasting themes, the beginning of the Christmas song 'Silent Night' can be heard, *pianissimo* and *quasi da lontano*, like music from a distant memory, from a childhood world. The song opens up a realm of experience that encompasses equally the rebellion and triumph, the catastrophe and resignation of the funeral march. In Penderecki's homeland, Poland, the Second Symphony was immediately

understood as national music, an immediately and subjectively 'romantically' affective tone, which gave expression to the painful memory of the struggle, suffering, and hope of the Polish people.[20]

Outside Poland, this may seem to border on hyperbole, and Schwinger for one has been dismissive of the quotations of 'Silent Night', calling them 'foreign bodies'.[21] Polish reception of Penderecki is a fascinating topic in itself and, primarily up to the early 1990s, the phenomenon was closely entwined with his ability to tap into national sentiment, as the following chapter will show. Taken in isolation, the Second Symphony is problematic more for its unrelenting earnestness and its faux late-romantic Germanic monumentality. A more bullish tone characterises his next completed symphony, no. 4 (1989), also cast as a substantial single span. Its title 'Adagio' is somewhat of a misnomer, as it also pays considerable attention to scherzando material. Furthermore, its progress is marked by the same kind of alarums and excursions that have already been observed in the concertos: and such is the attention paid to a succession of individual instruments that together they almost fulfil the role of concertante soloist. The Symphony was given the noted Grawemeyer Award in the United States in 1992, seven years after Lutosławski won it for his Third Symphony.

In his collection of lectures, *Labyrinth of Time*, Penderecki writes of the symphony as the salvation of musical civilisation, casting himself as a latter-day Noah, utilising the genre as a means of processing 'the experience of our century', arguing that it represents a 'musical ark which would make it possible to convey to coming generations what is best in our twentieth-century tradition'.[22] He has a particularised view of the history of the genre:

> I would like to continue the music that was cast at the beginning of the [twentieth] century: the tradition of writing symphonies. Sibelius, Bruckner, Shostakovich and Prokofiev were the last composers of my era writing the big forms. Then the tradition disappeared; no one was interested in picking up and continuing these big forms.[23]

These comments beg a range of responses, and one may seriously question, for example, the assumption that the symphony is the most appropriate vehicle for today's composer of orchestral music, or the names on his list of admired predecessors (Mahler, unusually, is omitted while Sibelius is perhaps a surprise inclusion), or his unqualified view of the symphony as a 'big' form.

Example 11.14. Penderecki, Fifth Symphony (1992), Tempo di marcia before
fig. 37.

The most clearly structured single-movement symphony is the Fifth (1992), although even this reinforces the impression that Penderecki's grasp of symphonic drama is built on fractured narratives. The concept of the 'Tempo di marcia' returns, acting initially as a hesitant 'trio' to the main Scherzo. The allusions to Mahler (horn and trumpet motifs, military percussion, grotesque clarinet, off-stage brass) seem referential rather than ironic (Ex. 11.14). And while the influence of Shostakovich is apparent in the orchestration and thin contrapuntal textures, they lack the bite and edge which marks the Russian's psychological acuity. Most strangely (although explicable because the commission came from South Korea), Penderecki resorts to the passacaglia once more in order to incorporate a simple Korean folksong as its theme after the brief opening Vivace. Its most notable feature is the fact that the song rotates just three pitch classes – F, B flat and C – which emphasise precisely those intervals which have least interest for Penderecki, the major second and perfect interval. He makes little attempt at intervallic integration, and the song seems as incidental as the Mahlerian references which follow.

The most drawn-out composition chronologically, the Third Symphony (1988–95), is the only one which has separate movements, five in all. This bestows additional structural clarity and the opportunity to relish his command of both individual structures and the expressive temperature of the whole: the hiatuses and tortuous cross-referencing in previous works are greatly reduced. The monotonal, discontinuous Passacaglia theme of the fourth movement relates back to that in the *Magnificat* and provides the foundation for a terrifying textural accrual and climax and the subsequent Tristanesque use of cor anglais. The 'danse macabre' of the finale evokes both Shostakovich and Berlioz and, like the highlighting of the percussion in the second movement's 'Allegro con brio', is a reminder of the music's ancestry in the opera *Black Mask*. The heart of the symphony lies in the central Adagio, in which the ghosts of Wagner, Bruckner and Mahler are summoned to create one of Penderecki's most affecting slow movements. At such moments, he achieves a rare harmonic luminosity.

Given that Penderecki's focus is habitually on line, timbre, tempo and dynamics, his concert music of the past quarter century relies on plain-speaking rhetoric, on readily absorbed intervallic and rhythmic repetitions, and on the reinterpretation of models drawn from major symphonic composers of the past. In today's world, he remains stylistically very much a loner and attempts to remain impervious to the contemporary world outside by immersing himself in his work at home outside Kraków: 'I escape here into intimacy, a world close to silence.'[24] As a result, he claims to be nearing the perfect, cathartic synthesis for which his symphonies, concertos and, more recently, chamber music, are staging posts:

> I practise various musical forms looking in them for the answer to pervading questions and doubts. Search for order and harmony is associated with the feeling of collapse and apocalypses . . . the world of music is an ideal world. Therefore I am very glad to turn to a pure musical form not contaminated by externality. I wander and roam entering my symbolic labyrinth. Only a roundabout way may lead you to fulfilment . . . And it seems to me that I am getting close to the essence of music.[25]

12   Music and symbolism I: sacred and patriotic sentiment

Church and State

Meyer's incorporation of familiar patriotic and religious melodies in his 'Polish' Sixth Symphony (see Chapter 11) was occasioned by the imposition of martial law on 13 December 1981.[1] The gesture was not uncommon in the early 1980s and formed part of a continuum stretching back many decades (Ex. 12.1). In the post-war years, the patriotic song 'Song of Warsaw' ('Warszawianka', 1831) had been a source for Woytowicz's Second Symphony and Panufnik's *Heroic Overture*, works which commemorated Polish heroism during the Second World War. Even further back, Paderewski had radically adapted the opening phrases of the folk melody to the *Dąbrowski Mazurka* (1797) – later to become Poland's official national anthem – and secreted it in the finale of his Symphony 'Polonia' (1909) as part of his contribution towards the fight for Polish independence. It might well have seemed, to the outside observer, that such struggles in the sphere of cultural affairs had been resolved once the thaw had begun in the mid-1950s. This was far from the case, because the societal problems under the PZPR had not been resolved and would not be until an acceptably democratic system was established in 1989. During the intervening decades, there were several major crises in Poland that involved both the independence of cultural activity, religious expression and the common well-being of ordinary citizens (Appendix 4 charts a selection of events for the twenty-five years between 1966 and 1990). Central to these phenomena was the election of Cardinal Karol Wojtyła of Kraków to the papacy on 16 October 1978. This galvanised the Polish population in an unprecedented manner and was a crucial inspiration in the establishment of the Solidarity (*Solidarność*) trade union, led by Lech Wałęsa, in 1980. It also occasioned a number of compositions dedicated to Pope John Paul II, including Górecki's *Beatus vir* (1979) and Penderecki's *Te Deum* (1980).

The relationship between Church and State, already severely tested at the time of socialist realism, was to prove crucial on all fronts. The Church became a focus of opposition to the Party as well as a sanctuary within which open discussion and artistic events could take place without hindrance (they sometimes had to be conducted in great secrecy, especially after December 1981). Many composers gravitated towards the Church,

Example 12.1. Opening phrases of five Polish patriotic hymns and songs: (a) 'Mother of God' ('Bogurodzica'), (b) *Dąbrowski Mazurka* (the Polish national anthem), (c) 'God, who has protected Poland' ('Boże coś Polskę'), (d) 'Song of Warsaw' ('Warszawianka') and (e) 'Hymn of 1910' ('Rota').

although some, like Baird, Lutosławski and Serocki, stayed determinedly secular and wedded to essentially abstract ideals.[2] Yet the shift to religious composition was irreversible once Penderecki had demonstrated with the *St Luke Passion* that it was possible to embrace sacred themes more or less with impunity. The symbolic significance of the fact that this large-scale oratorio was premiered in 1966 – the Millennium of Christianity in Poland – cannot be overestimated, even though it had been commissioned to mark the seven-hundredth anniversary of Münster Cathedral in West Germany. After the performance there on 30 March, the first Polish performances were in secular contexts – in the Kraków Philharmonic Hall on 22 April[3] and in the courtyard of Kraków's Wawel Castle in June, when some fifteen thousand people attended.[4] Its impact in bringing the Church into the public arena of contemporary music was staggering, and Penderecki pursued sacred themes in many subsequent works.

He was not alone, however, and the roster of sacred Polish works by other composers is substantial. Among those who have contributed to the repertoire have been Bujarski (*The Birth – Narodzenie*, 1983) and Meyer (*Te*

Deum, 1995; Mass, 1996), as well as lesser-known figures such as Andrzej Koszewski (b. 1922), Józef Świder (b. 1930) and Romuald Twardowski (b. 1930). Even the former socialist propagandiser Witold Rudziński has written a number of works with religious connections, such as *Gaude Mater Polonia* (1966) and *Ostrobramska Litany* (1994). The particular strand of compositions dedicated to the victims of war (usually associated with the recent Polish experience) has already been cited in the music of Maciejewski, Penderecki and Bujarski, and is reinforced by other works, including *Musica humana* (1963) by Zbigniew Penherski (b. 1935), *Requiem for the Victims of War* (1971) by Zbigniew Rudziński (b. 1935) and *Holocaust Memorial Cantata* (1992) by Marta Ptaszyńska (b. 1943).

Two composers stand out for their consistent application. Juliusz Łuciuk represents a large group of composers, some of them still at the start of their careers, who dedicate themselves to approachable and functional music for the Church. Their idioms are typically tonal or modal and relate stylistically to ancient chants and popular hymnody. Although in the 1960s Łuciuk was a gentle-voiced participant in Polish sonoristic explorations, since the composition of his oratorio *Francis of Assisi* (1976) he has concentrated on sacred music. This includes settings of texts by the Pope, such as the short anthem *O Polish Land* (*O ziemio polska*, 1987), and devotional oratorios, including a tribute to the patron saint of Poland, *Sanctus Adalbertus Flos Purpureus* (1997), and *Litany to Our Lady of Supraśl* (1998).

The music of Augustyn Bloch, which shared many of its characteristics in the 1960s with that of his contemporaries, has in recent years shown a marked leaning towards antique and ecumenical religious materials, while keeping his distance from any hint of ecclestiastical functionality. Bloch's works on religious themes range from the mystery opera *Ayelet, Daughter of Jephtha* (*Ajelet, córka Jeftego*, 1967), written to commemorate past and present martyrs to inhumanity, to the orchestral *Abide with Us Lord* (1986), in which a brief phrase from Luke 24 and part of a Protestant prayer are uttered. Even in his choral works, he has shown a reluctance to compromise his essentially modernistic, though sometimes quizzical language. Where he has introduced changes has been in his referencing of the patterns of ancient chant, be it Byzantine, Jewish or Gregorian, or the Lutheran chorale, as in the *a cappella* setting of texts from the Book of Isaiah in *Anenaiki* (1979), dedicated to John Paul II, *For Thy Light Is Come* (1986), and settings from the Book of Psalms, *Thou Shalt Not Kill!* (1990), which is an extended series of meditations for baritone, cello and orchestra dedicated to Pastor Dietrich Bonhoeffer and Father Jerzy Popiełuszko, the Polish priest murdered by the security forces in 1984.

Given Poland's history, since the late eighteenth century, of having to establish its national identity against a background of partition, Nazi occupation and Soviet political and cultural pressure, it is hardly surprising that composers sometimes sought to express their national solidarity through works, and materials, which both commemorated and signified their Polishness and the centrality of the Roman Catholic church during periods of vicissitude. Three composers, born within a year of each other in the 1930s, have for reasons of their profile – caused in large part by their music with sacred connections – dominated this characteristic area of recent Polish music.

Penderecki

Penderecki has carved out a very particular niche. Since the *St Luke Passion*, he has pursued a high-profile musical relationship with the Polish Roman Catholic church and its hierarchy, he has generally chosen monumental themes and forms, and he has utilised the best-known patriotic and sacred hymns as emotive icons. He had already become accustomed to making dedications to victims of atrocities (*Threnody*, *Dies Irae*) and the coincidence of events and anniversaries in Poland in the early 1980s led him to a series of individual compositions that eventually grew into the *Polish Requiem*. Its five dedications are tied into a national psyche that is especially alert to the concept and realities of martyrdom. The 'Lacrimosa' (1980) was commissioned by Wałęsa to mark the tenth anniversary of the fatal Gdańsk riots of 1970, the *a cappella* 'Agnus Dei' (1981) was composed on the night of the death of the Polish Primate, Cardinal Wyszyński, and performed at his funeral two days later, and the 'Recordare' (1983) celebrates the beatification in 1982 of Father Maksymilian Kolbe, the Franciscan monk who volunteered to die in place of another inmate at Auschwitz (Oświęcim) in 1941. Furthermore, the first part of the 'Dies Irae' (1984) commemorates the fortieth anniversary of the deaths of tens of thousands of the capital's citizens during the Warsaw Uprising, while the 'Libera me' (1984) is dedicated to the thousands of Poles murdered by the Soviet Army at Katyń in 1940.[5]

These associations are bolstered by Penderecki's use of well-known Polish tunes, a practice he had first employed in the *St Luke Passion*. In its 'Crux fidelis', he had utilised as pitch material a four-note motif drawn from the ancient Polish supplication 'Holy God', thereby drawing attention not only to his compositional craft but also to his underlying aesthetic. In the *Te Deum*, he had given a central role to the early nineteenth-century 'God, Who Has Protected Poland' ('Boże, coś Polskę'): 'For us, that quote has not just a sentimental but a political significance.'[6] It is a powerful and highly expressive passage, although the counterpointing of its conventional hymnic choralism 'quasi da lontano' (cf. the marking for 'Silent Night' in the Second Symphony) with an anguished soprano solo ('Salvum fac populum tuum Domine') recalls any number of nineteenth-century operatic scenes – with an on-stage heroine and off-stage chorus – which are then cruelly shattered by a dramatic denouement. It should also be noted that Penderecki has also quoted music from other traditions. His opera-oratorio hybrid *Paradise Lost*, with its subject matter of the Last Judgement, was composed just before the Second Symphony and *Te Deum* and incorporates not only the Bach chorale *O große Lieb* but also, in the concluding set-piece Passacaglia, the more predictable *incipit* of the *Dies Irae* chant. There are further external references to both Polish and foreign music and texts in *Credo*, though he eschewed them in *Seven Gates of Jerusalem* because he felt they would be a distraction: 'I tried to write a work free of any residue – without any inspiration which would simply be superficial here.'[7]

When Penderecki returned to 'Holy God' in the 'Recordare' of the *Polish Requiem*, he used it in a fuller version and with the first verse of the original Polish text in order to make a direct emotional and spiritual contact with a wider audience (Ex. 12.2). It is an excellent example of his ability to deploy pluralistic means for expressive ends, and the stylistic integration with its more modernist chromatic context is considerably assisted by the intervallic content of the Polish hymn (two semitones embracing a minor third). The hymn is initially offset by violas and then (in a manner developed from the *Te Deum*) by a solo soprano singing the Latin text. It subsequently plays the role of an intermittent *cantus firmus* supporting increasingly elaborate layers in Penderecki's habitual chromatic vein. Of the other discrete sections, the 'Lacrimosa' emphasises Penderecki's tonal leanings, his fondness for the Tristanesque motif of the rising minor sixth and descending semitone, and the Verdian tone of the more sustained sections of the Requiem (Ex. 12.3). Curiously, Penderecki reserves his most terrifying music in the 'Dies Irae' for the 'Confutatis maledictis' section towards the end rather than for the start, which instead has the air of a skeletal 'danse macabre'. As if to underscore the interchange of dramatic and symphonic modes in his work, Penderecki gives the *Polish Requiem* an extra section, a finale in which texts from elsewhere in the Offertorium and from the Psalms provide a rationale for a thematic resumé of earlier parts of the work.

The mixture of different musical traditions in the *Polish Requiem* places it stylistically between the Second Symphony and *Black Mask*, with the Second Cello Concerto being its closest instrumental counterpart. Penderecki's other two large-scale oratorio-like works are closest to the Third Symphony and betray a considerable easing of tone and an increasing willingness to

Example 12.2. Penderecki, *Polish Requiem*, 'Recordare' (1983), opening, incorporating reference to Polish hymn 'Holy God' ('Święty Boże').

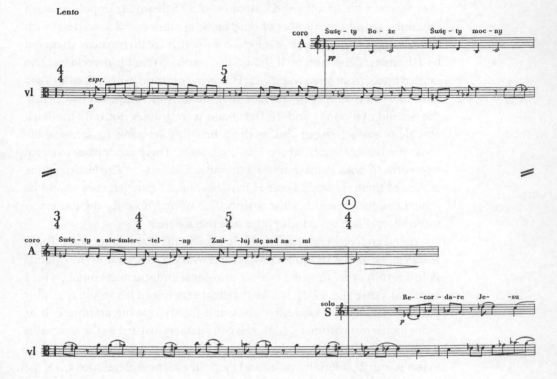

adopt thoroughgoing tonality. Both *Seven Gates of Jerusalem* and *Credo* make use of tonal hymnic choruses to frame and intersect what are markedly extended pieces; the latter work is particularly characterised by a high level of sweet consonance, often caused by choral movement in thirds. What passes as harmonic movement in these works is often merely cadential part-writing over and around a root-position triad, and the overall language can veer from Fauré to Orff or Prokofiev. *Seven Gates*, written to celebrate the three-thousandth anniversary of the founding of Jerusalem, remains an occasional piece with some moments of unusual instrumental colour, but it lacks the dramatic or narrative momentum of its predecessors. Arguably its most telling feature is the use of a narrator in the sixth movement to tell the story of the prophet Ezekiel's account of God bringing bones to life in the desert and creating a huge army for the Israelites. The genre of accompanied recitation in concert as well as religious works has interested a number of Polish composers, but this is one of its most prominent examples. Furthermore, the sixth movement symbolises, along with the chorale-like citation

Example 12.3. Penderecki, *Polish Requiem*, 'Lacrimoso' (1980), soprano entry.

of two Polish liturgical hymns in the 'Crucifixus' in *Credo*, the increased closeness of Penderecki's output to the 'house style' of everyday ecclesiastical worship, even to the point that its placing in the structure and manner of delivery suggests a cross between a heightened biblical reading and a sermon.

The original intention behind *Credo* was that it would be part of a Mass. In the early 1990s, Penderecki had tried out settings of other movements, including two *a cappella* miniatures – *Benedicamus Domino* and *Benedictus* (1992) – and a powerful *Agnus Dei* which was performed and recorded in 1995 as part of a joint-authored *Requiem of Reconciliation*.[8] He soon realised that the *Credo* would make a substantial piece on its own. This is such a recurring pattern in his *modus operandi* (for instance, the gestation of the First Violin Concerto and the Second and Fourth Symphonies) that it suggests an inherent monumentality in both his compositional language and aesthetic. His monumentalism exists both in single-span structures and in multi-movement works, although a recent renewed interest in chamber music suggests a possible shift towards a more conversational tone. The monumentality is also emphasised by his presumably deliberate economy of means across musical parameters. While, for example, there are some extraordinarily subtle and unexpected moments of orchestration, the abiding impression is of a heavy etching of colours and shapes, of a deliberately restrictive timbral palette and an increasingly predictable textural range. The same may be said of his harmonic, thematic and gestural language. He is not alone in this, as will be seen. Even so, his desire for a tough-minded synthesis in the *Polish Requiem* has led, via the expressionistic and *buffo* extremities of his last two operas (especially *Ubu Rex*) as well as through the more modulated romanticism of his symphonic works, to a seriously soft-focussed work like *Credo*. With no trace of irony, *Credo* rejects modernism as if it is outmoded or unintelligible (cf. Łuciuk's or Kilar's sacred output) and instead embraces a range of anachronistic elements that provide succour and comfort rather than a challenging dialectic. For many listeners, it remains a puzzle why Penderecki has so unequivocally abandoned the radicalism of his music of the 1960s. An alternative view is that Penderecki is essentially the same composer, simply one who has retreated from the front line. The language may have changed, but the basic building blocks of his structures, the concentration on line rather than harmony, the forceful tone contrasted with an intently personal contemplation of sound, the determinedly confident manner underlaid by a sense of expressive anxiety, the fascination with both the profane and the sacred – these strikingly characteristic features have remained constant.

'In Penderecki's approach, man seeks, beseeches, but also struggles with God for his rights, introducing his personal feelings into liturgical prayer.'[9] Regina Chłopicka's observation on the sacred music has broader implications: it underlines his essentially emotional compositional impulse as well as his search for a communicable language based upon his own experience. Penderecki has not been afraid to go out on a limb at several crucial stages in his career. Undeterred as ever by external criticism, he prefers, as he has put it himself, to seek the safety of his private labyrinth in which he can continue his quest for universality.

Górecki

Although at the start of the 1960s it may have seemed that Górecki and Penderecki shared certain technical features, their compositional agendas and underlying aesthetics were always quite distinct. The fact that, since 1970, they have both contributed to repertoire that includes symphonies, chamber and sacred music (Górecki has no interest, however, in opera) is simply indicative of trends shared by a number of their colleagues. And whereas Penderecki has quite clearly preferred to create a body of work, even his own tradition, within specific genres, Górecki seems to have shown no particular desire to establish such dynasties.

Górecki is particularly devoted to *a cappella* choral works of modest scale, not all of which have a direct liturgical connection. *Euntes ibant et flebant* (1972), a setting from the Psalms, is less concerned with the narrative of the text and much more with the harmonic implications of the first three notes of the Dorian mode, creating resonant hazes by duplicating the effect of acoustic echo. At crucial points in the structure, new pitch classes are introduced, always with minimum fuss and maximum expressive effect. *Amen* (1975) develops this concept, on the one hand emphasising the text by conversely reducing it to the one word 'Amen' and on the other by using contrary-motion patterns within the mode, building on an idea explored six years earlier in the instrumental *Old Polish Music.* Górecki seems intent on achieving an ecclestiastical tone but one clearly filtered through his own creative sensibilities. Later works which straddle the concert–church divide include one of Górecki's best known choral pieces, *Totus Tuus* (1987), premiered in Warsaw's Victory Square at an open-air mass conducted by the Pope on his third visit to Poland. Its quietly meditative repetitions, interlocked strains, and mainly tonal progressions derive from the many idiomatic arrangements he had already made of Polish hymns, such as the five *Marian Songs* (1985).[10] Unlike Penderecki, Górecki has not been tempted to place such humble hymns in a larger context, and many of them remain unperformed.

His largest unaccompanied choral work, *Miserere* (1981), amplifies the procedures explored in earlier pieces. It is, almost coincidentally, his one obvious tribute to the social and political turbulence of the Solidarity years and, more specifically, was inspired by the brutal beating-up of Solidarity activists in the northern town of Bydgoszcz in 1981. It was not performed, however, until 1987. In keeping with his aesthetic practices established in the 1970s, especially in the Third Symphony, Górecki was interested in the transcending of evil, not its depiction. The protracted textural accrual from low bass to treble which constitutes the first twenty minutes of *Miserere* is an exceptionally bold reliance on one basic mode (A Aeolian), on persistent homophony and just three words: 'Domine Deus noster'. This is truly reductive and testing for listeners and performers alike. Once again, he evidently wishes to induce a state of concentrated meditation which, at significant moments, will be elevated to a different plane by a shift in bass note or in textural density, though not, as elsewhere, by introducing any note foreign to the prevailing mode. Instead, to create a sense of resolution in the coda – a custom which he developed during the 1960s – he relies purely on the introduction of newly resonant chording, of a bass-line descent to low D natural, and of two new words, 'Miserere nobis'. Its monumentality is prayerful rather than imposing, and yet it has enormous physical and spiritual impact precisely because of its total focus on the ultimate goal of what Ivan Moody calls 'a post-penitential meditative calm'.[11]

Herein lies the clue to most of Górecki's structures, not least those concert pieces with sacred or patriotic associations in which he combines voice(s) with orchestra. The first of these, *Ad matrem* (1971), prefaced the sequence of three large-scale pieces of the 1970s for which Górecki is best known. Regrettably, this little masterpiece has almost completely escaped attention.[12] A bare summary of its component parts cannot convey the way in which they are placed with consummate precision and without a wasted note in the trajectory towards the brief, contemplative coda. The sequence of events – an elongated crescendo on pulsating unpitched percussion (which attracts violent woodwind and brass reiterations of a B flat–E natural tritone), the first of two choral interjections with the words 'Mater mea', a luminous orchestral passage based on a dominant thirteenth, a lugubrious dirge related to material from *Little Music* III, and the one and only appearance of the solo soprano ('Mater mea, lacrimosa dolorosa') singing a modal motto – sounds almost implausible, so varied are its materials in style and content and so frugal their deployment. That, of course, is the work's strength. It is a remarkable synthesis of the abstract and the programmatic, and it convincingly marks, alongside the Second Symphony, Górecki's passage into a new period.

Although Górecki shares almost nothing with Penderecki and has little in common with Lutosławski, he does share with the latter an acute understanding of the value and significance of dramatically effective harmonic organisation. This becomes increasingly apparent during the 1970s. It also becomes clear that he is thinking again on a monumental scale, really for the first time since *Scontri*. His focus is partly on the wonder of the universe (Second Symphony) and partly on the celebration of his faith (*Beatus vir*). In between these two works is the Third Symphony, in which he explores the ascendancy of good over evil.

The Second Symphony 'Copernican' was written to mark the five-hundredth anniversary of the birth in 1473 of the great Polish Renaissance astronomer.[13] In attempting to encompass his compatriot's shattering discovery that the earth moved around the sun, Górecki composed two movements, in the first of which the 'monstrous and violent "mechanism of the world" turns and parades itself in a manner that is both awesome and apocalyptic'.[14] Utilising huge orchestral forces, Górecki revisits the harmonic idiom of *Canticum graduum* in a manner that is both exultant and fatalistic. He is not simply in awe, however, as the central quiet episode of the movement might suggest; this grinding, repetitive music may also be understood as a metaphor for the harshness of spiritual and creative life in early 1970s Poland. The resolution comes in the second movement, itself a greatly expanded version of the reconciliatory codas of preceding works. As if to reinforce the image of man's struggles in life, the solo baritone hauls himself slowly from the depths and is shortly joined by a female figure (solo soprano). Together, they ecstatically proclaim the magnificence of the Lord's creation: 'The sun to rule by day . . . The moon and stars to rule by night.'[15] Their translation from the physical to the spiritual dimension is then confirmed by the entry of the choir, singing Copernicus's own words – 'What indeed is more beautiful than heaven, which of course contains all things of beauty?' – to a four-part fragment of Polish Renaissance homophony. Characteristically, this citation is at pitch (Dorian mode), and its pentatonic 'black-note' orchestral backdrop completes the chromatic spectrum as if to symbolise the integrity of the image. The biblical symbolism of the two human figures, the carefully harnessing of white- and black-note formations (day and night?) and the coherent harmonic designs (the final inexorable crescendo–decrescendo on black-note pentatony is not only a boldly simple gesture but an extraordinarily liberating moment) form a transcendental 'positive' to the intimidating 'negative' of the first movement. As in *Ad matrem*, Górecki has created a dramatic tableau with an unerring sense of the dynamic potential of slow-motion and suspended animation.

The gestation and premiere of *Beatus vir* provide an insight into creative, religious and political conditions in Poland in the late 1970s. Cardinal Wojtyła commissioned Górecki in 1977 to write a work to commemorate the nine-hundredth anniversary of the death of his illustrious predecessor, Bishop Stanislaus, put to death by King Boleslaus II in 1079. The commission caused Górecki great problems with the Party in Katowice (he eventually resigned the Rectorship at the Higher School of Music) and, when Wojtyła was elevated to the papacy in 1978, the political significance of the commission and its approaching performance was greatly magnified.[16] Górecki realised that there was great interpretative leeway in this ancient story of Church–State relations, one which would not escape the attention of any living Pole. He therefore dismissed any idea of a narrative account, determining instead to emphasise the spiritual doubts and moral aspects, again in an attempt to transcend tragedy with meditation. The score is certainly austere, shorn of any decorative element until the bell-like conclusion. Its motivic-harmonic material is built on a four-note trope (B–C–D–E flat) which connects to Polish folk and hymnal patterns, as in 'Holy God'; its tonal plan is geared to classic, but simply effective contrasts of C minor and E flat major. Typically, Górecki is largely uninterested in the principles of *Durchführung* that are characteristic of conventional oratorio methods, constructing *Beatus vir* from amplified gestures based on everyday church music. His manipulation of these materials is never routine, even when he appears to be indulging in simple repetitions or cradled alternating chord patterns. There is no easy comfort here, but an almost monastic severity.

Eclipsing even Penderecki's *Threnody* in its notoriety and international impact, Górecki's Third Symphony became in the early 1990s an international topic of conversation and debate. In equal critical measure it was hailed and slated, although the public devoured the first CD recording, with sales reaching over a million, not to mention the dozen or so coat-tailing recordings which followed. No other recording of a piece of contemporary music has had such success across so many cultural and social strata; its adoption as source material by the media (a mixed blessing indeed) continues to keep it in broad circulation. A large part of its appeal was its non-institutional expression of sacred and patriotic sentiment – death, familial loyalty, sacrifice and transcendence – which by nature of Górecki's treatment of the genre emphasised these sentiments over and above a specifically Christian message. Nevertheless, the symphony was unceremoniously lumped together with the work of composers as varied as Arvo Pärt, Tavener and Giya Kancheli as the product of 'holy minimalism'and other epithets.[17] This soubriquet is even more senseless than the generalised assumptions of the 'Polish School' or 'sonorism' and arises, one suspects, from two main and sometimes deliberate misunderstandings. Firstly, the secular and sacred musical traditions of Central and Eastern Europe are not only different from those in the West but also of comparable validity. They give rise to alternative interfaces with concert traditions that do not necessarily comply, for example, with long-standing practices of Austro-German *Durchführung*. Rather, they are more likely to find kindred traditions in France or Russia, and one is strongly reminded of Szymanowski's strictures in the 1920s on the hegemony of the Austro-German tradition and the need for Polish composers to break away from its stranglehold. Secondly, the term 'minimalism' is too recent to be meaningfully definitive, as any discussion of American or Dutch examples reveals. Only rarely do Polish examples approximate the high-energy pulsing characteristic of Reich or Glass; this rapprochement, however, is normally the result of native folk-based models rather than of emulation, as in Kilar's *Sparking Dance* (*Krzesany*, 1974) or Górecki's Harpsichord Concerto (1980). Some members of the younger generation, however, have established clear links with the music of Louis Andriessen (see Chapter 15).

The decade and a half that separated the symphony's composition and its international success is often ignored, leading to the downplaying of its striking originality in the context of mid-1970s European music (viz. the similar position of *Refrain* in the mid-1960s). At a time when both Lutosławski and Penderecki were themselves reconsidering their compositional priorities, Górecki was already refining his existing modal and structural concerns to produce a work exceptional even within his own output. It is a 'Symphony of Sorrowful Songs', comprising three slow movements for solo soprano and orchestra, lasting almost an hour. There is no dissonance that does not relate to modal or tonal inflections, there are no signs of extended instrumental or vocal techniques (these he had abjured some years earlier), no disjunction, no decorative distractions. Most importantly, there is no second-hand stylistic referencing, although if predecessors were to be sought they might be found, distantly removed, in the music of composers as varied as Bach, Schubert, Tchaikovsky and even Debussy.[18]

At the heart of the Third Symphony lie its texts, each dealing with a different aspect of a woman's response to death, each with a Polish context: (i) a fifteenth-century lament of the Virgin Mary for Christ on the Cross, (ii) a prayer to the Immaculate Queen of Heaven inscribed on the wall of a Gestapo jail in 1944 by an eighteen-year-old highland woman, and (iii) a folksong, whose text may date from the Silesian Uprisings (1919–21), in which a mother mourns for her missing son.[19] Each of these texts is treated

differently. The first is framed by an extraordinarily evocative canonic texture in which the theme is an amalgam of two Polish religious songs – a
beggar's Lenten hymn and a song of praise to the Lord – whose combination symbolises the bittersweet message of the Crucifixion. On a purely
musical level, the movement illustrates a fine synthesis between the melodic
and harmonic properties of modes, enabling a resonant balance between
continuity and change. The second movement is the only one which does
not have what Penderecki called 'residue'. Instead, Górecki creates one of
his many cradling progressions where two harmonies rock to and fro. Its
simple charismatic pattern provides the impetus, and eventual climax, of the
young woman's prayer. Górecki uses a similar cradling sequence in the final
movement, though this he borrowed from Chopin's Mazurka op. 17/4. He
also makes an almost imperceptible reference to the climactic chord in the
development of the first movement of Beethoven's Third Symphony. These
two references (Ex. 12.4), again made at pitch, are less quotations than private symbols for the composer; they deepen the listener's appreciation, but
they do not determine his or her response. Both here and in the first movement, Górecki has moved beyond basic sacred and patriotic sentiment to
another plane of understanding. He has transcended not only the vileness of
death and war, which he refuses to depict, and instead has sought resolution
through contemplation. His goal has not been to make obvious connections
with the Polish Church nor with localised history and folk traditions but
to use their repertoires and more subliminally those from 'art' music to
attain the sort of universalism advocated by Szymanowski. And it can be
no coincidence that, at the conclusion of the theme of the first movement's
canon, Górecki should employ one of his dearest motifs, a three-note turn
that he shares with Szymanowski and the latter's Stabat Mater, the most
significant Polish sacred choral work from the first half of the twentieth
century.

Kilar

Kilar has pursued a distinguished career as a film composer long after
his colleagues had their youthful dalliances with the medium. Since the
1950s he has written over a hundred film scores for leading Polish directors, including Kazimierz Kutz (*Salt of the Black Earth*, 1969), Krzysztof
Zanussi (*Balance Sheet*, 1973; *Full Gallop*, 1996) and Andrzej Wajda (*The
Shadow Line*, 1976; *Pan Tadeusz*, 1999). Kilar has had particular success
in the last decade working with directors based outside Poland, including Francis Ford Coppola (*Bram Stoker's Dracula*, 1992), Roman Polanski
(*Death and the Maiden*, 1994) and Jane Campion (*The Portrait of a Lady*,

Example 12.4. Górecki, Third Symphony (1976), third movement, soprano entry.

1996). His forte is amiable pastiche, often couched in memorable melodic phrases that bear the marginally varied repetitions required by much late twentieth-century mainstream cinema. These features are amply illustrated by his neo-klezmer theme for Polanski's *The Pianist* (2002), the true story of the extraordinary wartime survival of the Jewish pianist and composer Szpilman, a contemporary of Bacewicz, Lutosławski and Panufnik.

The cross-influence from film to concert music in Kilar's output is perhaps symbolised by his willingness to crop his score for Zanussi's film about the Polish martyr Father Maksymilian Kolbe (*A Life for a Life*, 1990) to create the orchestral *Requiem for Father Kolbe* (1996), in which the all-pervasive theme from the film (redolent of the intervallic twist of the hymn 'Holy God') is marginally repackaged. Although Kilar has produced little over a dozen concert scores since 1970, they have caused considerable controversy in Polish musical circles. This arises from their increasingly minimal content and, in the works with religious associations, their aesthetic credibility. In contradistinction to both Górecki and Penderecki, Kilar often seems intent on relocating sacred subjects rather than intensifying their spiritual relevance in a secular world. Kilar's *Mother of God* (*Bogurodzica*, 1975), for example, discards the medieval tune (except as a motto at the very end) and resets the text in a manner which emphasises its original role as a military prayer before battle. In *Exodus* (1981), the cinematic dimension becomes central. Taking as inspiration a passage from Exodus 15 (where Miriam, tambourine in hand, leads a dance in praise of the Lord's defeat of the Egyptians, whom he had just engulfed in the Red Sea), Kilar's score resembles music from a Hollywood biblical epic. As a sample of the symbolism perceived by some in Polish music of the 1970s and 1980s, the response of Chłopecki to *Exodus* is instructive:

> Kilar first thought of writing the piece as early as 1979, during John Paul II's first pilgrimage to Poland. However, at a press conference, he said that his intention was to write a Solidarity anthem. This seems to explain everything. What we have is a musical, political poster – vivid and propagandist. *Exodus* means the crossing of the Red Sea by the Poles, the political picture of 1981. An expression of a street demonstration in which the 'Domine Deus' is made to sound like political slogans, like the chanting of demands and the tossing of banners in the wind. The piece is populist rather than popular . . . It appeals to instinct and reflects the expression of the masses who rose in rebellion. Also, it is hypnotic. It is the art of revolution and refusal, but also of a live TV broadcast and pop culture; the art of intense and indirect expression meant to appeal to the imagination of the masses.[20]

Example 12.5. Kilar, *Exodus* (1981), bb. 64–77.

And yet it is hard, if Chłopecki is to be believed, to suppress the feeling that Kilar's tongue is at least partly in his cheek. The score's 'oompah-oompah' reiteration of E major and its catchy melodic hook (Ex. 12.5), the neo-Ravelian build up of texture which eventually erupts into a brief statement of *Boléro*'s rhythmic ostinato, have considerable panache even if they and the quasi-militaristic tone pall into kitsch by the end of its thirty-minute span. The militaristic aspect resurfaces in *Victoria* (1983), an inexplicably trite fanfare for John Paul II on his second visit to Poland, in which Kilar set a four-hundred-year-old message sent by the Polish King Jan III Sobieski to Pope Innocent XI ('Venimus, Vidimus, Deus Vicit') after his famous victory over the Turks at Vienna in 1683. In other works, Kilar attempts to recreate the realities of congregational prayer (the chanting of the 'Ave Maria' in *Angelus*, 1984) and, in the central 'Corale – Largo religiosamente' of the Piano Concerto (1997), entrusts the soloist with a double-handed chording of a 'Benedictus' chant.

There is little sense in these works that Kilar – who is an unassuming man – is engaged in anything other than a coincidentally postmodern attempt to locate his Roman Catholicism in the public arena. Like both Penderecki and Górecki, Kilar has tested the boundaries between secular and sacred, especially in terms of the performing environment. Nowhere is this more tangible than in his recent *Missa pro pace* (2000), commissioned by the (secular) Warsaw Philharmonic to celebrate its centenary and premiered by them in January 2001. The work is marked by an asceticism that is enervated and pious to a fault. Its problematic nature is characterised by its lack of musical dialectic or of any innovative departures from the standard text (the 'pro pace' aspect is completely unaddressed). Kilar seems uninterested in responding to the vividness of the liturgy: the inert setting of the Credo, from the 'Crucifixus' to the 'Amen', is a particular instance. *Missa pro pace*'s blanched perspectives offer a stark contrast to recent sacred music by Penderecki, Łuciuk and others. If nothing more, it provides an alternative view of the relationship between music and Roman Catholicism in Polish society.

13 Music and symbolism II: vernacular and classical icons

The relationship between Polish composers and the Roman Catholic faith has had religious, political and social significance, not least in the way in which composers, bolstered by their creative and religious freedom since 1956, gradually took opportunities from the mid-1960s onwards to put music at the centre of the State–Church divide and to explore spiritual issues more openly. In combatting the anti-religious tenets of communism, it might have been expected that composers would also have severed all associations with the secular musical materials appropriated by post-war socialist realism. As has already been observed, however, in the music of Bacewicz, Lutosławski and others, the stylistic bedrock of most immediate post-war music – a kind of Slavonic neo-classicism – had resonances in later decades. As far as folk music was concerned, it seemed to have been consigned to history by contemporary Polish composers, so tainted had it become by association with Stalinism[1] and so out of kilter with avant-garde ambitions. In the late 1960s, however, there were signs in concert music of a renewed interest: Bacewicz's Viola Concerto has folk traces and both Górecki and Kilar were edging in that direction through their moves towards modality and the citation of old Polish music. What ensued was a process of reclamation of the vernacular, a major attempt to cleanse the memory and to reconfigure the significance of folk culture for composers tiring of mainstream modernism. In some cases, there was a parallel identification with classical art music, as has already been seen in Górecki's Third Symphony.

Kilar

Kilar, for one, had given early signs of impatience with sonorism (*Upstairs–Downstairs* and *Prelude and Christmas Carol*). Four orchestral works came to symbolise his populist approach to Polish folk music and particularly to the music and scenery of the highland (*góralski*) region and its environs such as Podhale and Orawa: *Sparking Dance* (*Krzesany*), *Kościelec 1909* (1976), *Grey Mist* (*Siwa mgła*) for baritone and orchestra (1979) and *Orawa* for strings (1986), a lively and succinct reimagining of a traditional highland string band (*kapela*). *Grey Mist* frames the three verbatim verses of a simple highland lovesong (a shepherd sings to his sweetheart, asking the mist to part so that the moon can light his way to her), whose intervallic content – four fifths of a pentatonic scale – is less pointed than the many highland tunes with sharpened fourths and flattened sevenths. The picturesque evocation of a Tatra mountain enveloped in mist is created by the simple orchestral overlapping of whole-tone and modal configurations within stable, almost sonoristic block textures. The characteristic 'kick' (or rhythmic snap) of the original tune informs much of the orchestral material, as do simple canons and the occasional tritones. There is no pretence other than to venerate, almost iconically, the sanctity of the highland tradition.

Kilar's target in *Kościelec 1909* is more ambitious, although it is paced in the same leisurely way. The title refers to the year and location in the Tatra mountains of the death of Karłowicz. With its three labelled themes – of the Mountain, of the Call of the Abyss, of Destiny – Kilar evokes not only Karłowicz's music (such as the three *Eternal Songs*, 1906) but the symphonic poems of Liszt and Tchaikovsky. Stylistically, of course, it has little in common with any of these composers, although its pattern of alternating and developing sections bears the same distant resemblance to symphonic dialectic that had also been explored by Górecki (*Old Polish Music*). Kilar, however, saw this more as a series of freeze-frames (Karłowicz was, incidentally, a frequent photographer of the Tatra mountains as well as an experienced mountaineer), conceiving it as the 'stopping and extending in time of these few tragic seconds'.[2] As has already been observed in the *Missa pro pace* and other works, Kilar's music is often reductive, and this attenuated concept of time accorded with his natural instincts, regardless of any picturesque programme.

Between them, Kilar (*Exodus*) and Górecki (*Scontri, Ad matrem*) have provided many of the sensations of the 'Warsaw Autumn' festivals. *Sparking Dance* was one of the most infamous (it was premiered at the 1974 festival), because Kilar bluntly contradicted the abstract trends of his colleagues in favour of an illustrative, rhythmically dynamic portrait of 'mountain dwellers' spontaneity and . . . a rustic fresco'.[3] It was as if Kilar was trying to recreate in music the sharply etched woodcuts and colourful paintings of highland life made, in a memorable blend of folk and neo-classical traditions, by the Polish artist Władysław Skoczylas (1883–1934). The shock of Kilar's new primitivism was palpable. It opened up new and not always welcome vistas on what contemporary Polish music might represent (the effect was akin to the scandals caused by Les Six in France at the end of the First World War). Nevertheless, while rejecting the generally atonal, unrhythmicised aspects of sonorism, Kilar still drew on some of its techniques to conjure a rough-hewn score, celebrating vigorous highlander dancing and wild festivities in vivid blocked colours. Even the colouristic, quasi-onomatopoeic glissandi for full orchestra – precipitous descents or dizzying ascents between highest and lowest notes of each instrument (Ex. 13.1) – are eclipsed by the riotous anarchy of the ending. After the main climax, a 'molto rustico' simulation of a folk string band seems too cute by far and is soon obliterated by a plethora of ad libitum orchestral whoops and yells, accompanied by 'as many sonagli, sheep-bells, triangoli, crotali, cencerros, campanelli da messa etc. as possible'. Kilar is cocking a proto-postmodern snook at avant-garde conventions while creating a whole new set of his own. The regular rhythms, pulsating percussion, textural build-ups, dynamic contrasts, steady tempos, simplified gestural and harmonic language and easily assimilable motivic content not only informed the three succeeding folk-related works but also the later pieces in which the focus switched from secular to sacred icons.

Krauze

Kilar was not, however, the first to break the sonorist mould with folklore. Krauze had already shown in the 1960s his clear independence of general trends and did so again in 1972 in a work that challenges even more strongly the expectations of an orchestral piece in the concert hall. By 1970, 'Warsaw Autumn' audiences were perfectly attuned to music with unusual instrumentation, spatial placements, or electronic input. *Sparking Dance* challenged in terms of its aesthetic and its material, but in other aspects it was conformist. Krauze's *Folk Music* (1972) has a more radical agenda, one that reinvents his long-standing devotion to unistic composition. Whereas in earlier examples, such as *Piece for Orchestra* no. 1, there was a low level of textural variation, *Folk Music* has forty players, marshalled unconventionally and spatially on stage (echoes of Górecki's *Scontri*) and divided into twenty-one groups of between one and six players. Each group plays independently its own sequence of folk material (several dozen items in total from a range of East and Central European countries, although with a strong Polish presence), in its own time and key, all playing *pianissimo possibile* unless highlighted momentarily by the conductor. The flow pattern of the work is circular (as was implied by some previous pieces), with no macro-structural shaping apart from a continuous pedal E flat and a final tutti crescendo. The expressive intent is therefore minimal and disinterested, except, as the composer is careful to advise, that 'the most important interpretative element in the composition is for each of the instrumentalists to imitate a rustic and folk-like style of playing'.[4]

For Krauze, this 'rusticity' is neither picturesque nor patriotic, simply his way of toying with different material which might be thought of as

Example 13.1. Kilar, *Sparking Dance* (*Krzesany*, 1974), p. 16.

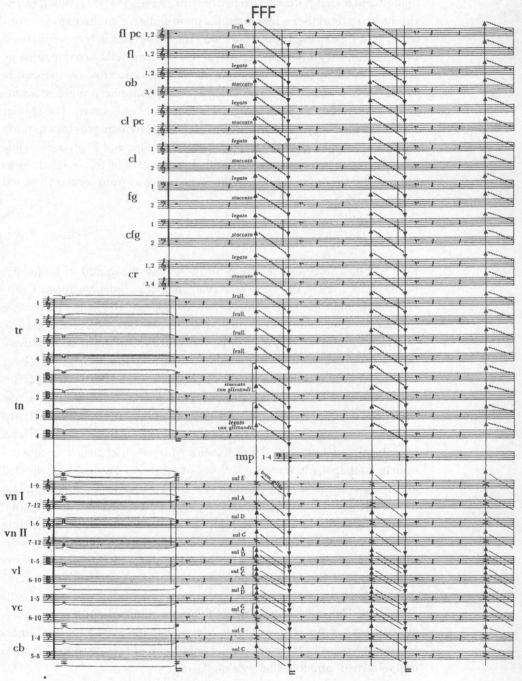

maksymalna ilość dowolnych dźwięków / as many sounds ad lib. as possible

Example 13.2. Krauze, *Aus aller Welt stammende* (1973), opening.

having either or both of those attributes. He is, rather, maintaining his fascination with abstract, quasi-repetitive patterning, now with borrowed material, as the subsequent *Aus aller Welt stammende* for ten string players (1973) shows. Having meticulously transcribed four separate 'worldly' melodies (*światówki*) from the south-east of Poland, Krauze treats each one heterophonically and extensively in its own 'panel' (Ex. 13.2). The material is further blurred by requiring each player to stand (or sit) as far apart from the others as possible, to find his or her own tempo, expression and articulation while remaining faithful to the folk style of the original melodies. Krauze thus extends the heterophony from the three or four written parts to up to ten (what Lutosławski called 'bundling' in his *Preludes and Fugue* composed the previous year). The initial effect of a mimicked folk string ensemble rapidly gives way to an aurally teasing, quasi-canonic texture of evolving roulades. The original material is distanced as well as subsumed, and the technical success of *Aus aller Welt stammende* would prove to be a signal influence on Krauze's subsequent oeuvre.

Creative play with found objects permeates much of Krauze's music and was most flamboyant in those works incorporating non-classical instruments. *Idyll* (1974) develops from *Folk Music* into a bucolic landscape wherein a quartet of players (originally the four members of Music Workshop, including Krauze) improvises blithely on a range of folk instruments (hurdy-gurdies, bagpipes, folk fiddles, shepherds' fifes, sheep bells), accompanied by a tape of country and farmyard noises. This is folklorism of a different hue. Krauze has been one of Poland's foremost improvisers – a rare compositional activity in Poland (cf. Bogusław Schaeffer's contribution to music theatre in the 1960s) – and his works for solo piano are delicate and imaginative contributions to extended techniques on the piano (*Stone Music*, 1972; *Gloves Music*, 1973) as well as a droll but serious commentary on the relationship between new music and that of the past (*The Last Recital*, 1974).

The group improvisation sponsored by Music Workshop led to larger ensemble pieces and the incorporation of mechanical instruments, as in *Automatophone* for guitars, mandolins and music boxes (1974). The overlay of live and pre-ordained material emphasises the composer's interest in the relationship between happenstance and process, with the balance here tilted firmly in favour of the latter. The first version of *Automatophone* formed part of Krauze's exploration of installation art which he had investigated in *Spatial-Music Compositions* nos. 1 and 2 (1968–70) created in co-operation with an interior designer and a sculptor. In 1974, he presented *Fête galante et pastorale* for six live ensembles, including folk instruments, and thirteen tapes (1974) during the Musikprotokoll festival in Graz in twenty-six rooms in Eggenburg Castle. Thirteen years later, the still strongly unistic *La rivière souterraine* (1987) was performed at Metz in a specially constructed walk-through maze of seven 'space cells'.

It became apparent during the 1970s that Krauze was using folk sources for quite different ends to those of Kilar, or even Górecki, and that his focus was on other compositional avenues. There are occasional sacred or political references, such as the inclusion of 'God, Who Has Protected Poland' and other found material in both *Soundscape* (1975) and *Tableau vivant* (1982) – 'a piece about silence, fear, anger and obsessiveness'[5] which also refers obliquely to the opening notes of the Polish national anthem as part of its immediate response to 13 December 1981. In another work connected to the martial law period, *Piece for Orchestra* no. 3 (1982), Tarnawska-Kaczorowska has detected motivic ancestry in *We, the First Brigade* (*My, Pierwsza Brygada*), a famous soldiers' song from the First World War.[6] In contradistinction to patriotic citations by other composers, these references are so reworked and absorbed as to be incidental to Krauze's overriding obsessions: finding new ways of exploring unistic expression, investigating the relationship between lyricism and brittleness, and refracting his material through a semi-ironic, semi-abstract lens. At times, the results may be desultory, but at others challengingly prescient of the postmodern trends developed by the next generation of Polish composers. Among his most representative recent works are *Arabesque* for piano interior and chamber orchestra (1983), *Quatuor pour la naissance* for clarinet, violin, cello and piano (1984) and *Symphonie parisienne* (1986), whose ruthless motivic persistence is reminiscent of Górecki's music of the late 1960s. The Piano Quintet (1996) – with its concluding quote from the Adagietto of Mahler's Fifth Symphony – and the Second Piano Concerto (1996) accommodate rhapsodic lyricism, gamelan-like timbres and an occasionally minimalist rhythmic thrust within their ornamented textures; *Adieu* for out-of-tune upright piano and orchestra (2003) reinforces the underlying whimsy in much of Krauze's music.

Górecki

With regard to their folk associations, Górecki's compositions are comparatively modest and he generally leaves the original folk material unadorned. He has been content, for example, to arrange several sets of folk songs for mixed *a cappella* choir in an idiomatic and unassuming manner, beginning with *Broad Waters* (*Szeroka woda*, 1979) and including, most recently, *Five Kurpian Songs* (1999). His reverence for these simple melodies is the same as in his settings of church songs; indeed, he sees them as coming from the same sacred–vernacular stock. On the few occasions when he has evoked folk traditions in his concert music, he has done so in unexpected circumstances. His Harpsichord Concerto was another 'Warsaw Autumn' surprise, in 1981, not only because it was sparkling, short and snappy, with a total duration of only nine minutes, but also because it brought together in its two complementary movements the twin 'poles' of Górecki's compositional aesthetic, forming a sacred chorale prelude and a secular round dance. The first is *minore*, linear and largely in compound time (a developing D Aeolian chant-like string theme decorated by keyboard figuration) while the second is conceived, as it were, at right angles to the first: *majore*, vertical and in duple metre (chordal folk-style material juxtaposed by alternations of solo and strings). The material appears to be Górecki's own, although Malecka believes that the interlude in the first movement is related to the same church song, 'People, My People' ('Ludu, mój ludu'), that Penderecki was to use in *Credo*.[7]

There are further stylistic references to Polish folk idioms in the body of chamber and orchestral music which Górecki composed after a hiatus in the early 1980s caused by ill health and by what the Poles call 'internal exile' (i.e., silence caused by a withdrawal from public life, usually for political reasons). In the trio *Recitatives and Ariosos: 'Lerchenmusik'* (1984–6), for example, these include snap rhythms and emphatic tritones, often placed as sharpened fourths above solid diatonic chording. The second movement develops an arioso style which bears all the hallmarks of highlander melodic improvisation. In all these instances, however, the allusions are couched in contemporary terms – such as doublings at the minor ninth – which might just as easily come from modernist traditions as from any perception of the acidulous tone of certain folk idioms (cf. the Arioso of the Second String Quartet, 'Quasi una fantasia', 1991). And while the insistent, grinding repetitions so characteristic of his music may have roots in folk practice, they are as determinedly abstract in their rituals as Kilar's remain programmatic (Krauze is a closer parallel).

The First String Quartet, like the Second, has a Bartókian, even Stravinskian flavour in its vigorous reshaping of folk dance. The instruments are paired off to provide strident melody-and-accompaniment textures in which Górecki's alert variation of metre and motivic phrasing (itself based in folk practice), with much repetition of short phrases, results in a level of high energy unusual among his compatriots. In the closing stages of the First Quartet, he presents simply the dance accompaniment, as if the melody is too distant a memory (this passage is even recollected *tranquillo* in two movements of the Second Quartet). The process of distillation is nowhere clearer than the motif of semitonally clashing pairs of perfect fifths; it performs a critical structural function in the First Quartet interlocked with a canonic idea that had already appeared in two earlier works, notably *Old Polish Music* (Ex. 13.3). Not only do these two ideas develop in tandem to form the first section but they return to form a recapitulatory coda, the fifths dovetailing with the memory of the central 'dance' (Ex. 13.4) before the canon appears in full for the first and last time. As this and other works show, Górecki is entranced not only by his Polish, vernacular heritage but also by art music, and sees compositional potential in their juxtaposition. In the chamber music in particular, he explores both the treatment and structural function of these two strands, sometimes of the alternation of enhanced statements, sometimes more subliminally, as in the several allusions to Beethoven that follow on from the subliminal citation in the finale of the Third Symphony. Central to these explorations is Górecki's renewed attention to the developmental and recapitulatory aspects of form.

The shaping of *Recitatives and Ariosos* (a title which implies processes of alternation as well as neo-Baroque concerns) is achieved by means of instrumental focus (the three movements successively highlight the cello, clarinet and piano) and a stepped decrescendo (in which the finale has a familiar role as a quiet resolution), although tempo contrasts are limited: the work retains the Third Symphony's concept of three slow movements.

Example 13.3. Górecki, First String Quartet 'Already it is Dusk' ('Już się zmierzcha', 1988), opening.

*) The viola is always 'en dehors' (but not too much). It is the *cantus firmus* from the song
  "Already it is Dusk" by the 16th century Polish composer Wacław z Szamotuł.

Example 13.4. Górecki, First String Quartet 'Already it is Dusk' ('Już się zmierzcha', 1988), bb. 307–18.

The musical contents of the first two movements are recalled cyclically in the finale (a new development for Górecki), but not before he has sprung a subtle surprise. In keeping with the stepwise melodic character of the central movement and its tonal pungencies, he initiates the finale with a melodic–harmonic phrase that amalgamates a vespers melody with what sounds like an echo of the opening of Beethoven's Fourth Piano Concerto. The reference becomes more explicit as the movement proceeds, but unlike instances in many earlier pieces it is never quoted verbatim or at the original pitch. It has become less an icon than an integral part of the developmental procedure, which at times is aggressively antithetic to the peaceable nature of the original sources. On the other hand, the derivation of some of the material in the 'Arioso' of the Second String Quartet from a Chopin Polonaise is hard to believe, so removed has it become from its source, and underlines the greatly reduced role in Górecki's thinking of the cleansing iconographic citation.

The Beethovenian connections and cyclic procedures such as intervallic, tonal and thematic cross-references are even more elaborate in the Second String Quartet. Its subtitle 'Quasi una fantasia' evokes immediate parallels with Beethoven's use of the term (Piano Sonata op. 27/1), and the repositioning of materials (usually at the same pitch) in different movements cuts across the formal division of the work into four movements. More significant than these reappearances is a sequence of three 'Beethovenian chords' (Górecki's own term) – B flat, E flat and A – which act collectively as carefully placed moments of repose and, separately (mainly the chord of B flat), as tonal reference points, especially in the two fast movements. It is, of course, but a small step from such procedures to the type of iconography featured in earlier works, but here it also symbolises the classicising of Górecki's structural processes at all levels, wherein he leans upon composers such as Beethoven and Schubert with whom he feels a special affinity. Thanks to their example, he felt able to essay more elaborate medium- and long-term structures while retaining tried and tested features such as the exposed plangency of slowly unfolding melodic lines (first movement) or the concluding citation (a not entirely convincing quote from the opening of 'Silent Night').

The Beethovenian strength of purpose in the two string quartets is tempered by the sense that Górecki enjoys playing off one unlikely idea against another, sometimes, as in the reference to 'Silent Night', with little explanation. Krauze might empathise; Penderecki, whose *buffo* mode is terribly solemn, would probably not. In the context, the passing reference to the opening of Szymanowski's highlander ballet *Mountain Robbers* in the 'Arioso' of *Concerto-Cantata* for flute/alto flute solo and orchestra (1992) seems incidental. The almost postmodern accommodation of brash circus-style music in *Concerto-Cantata* and in the quixotically named *Little Requiem* for piano and thirteen instruments (1993) is a different matter, although there are hints of such material in the Second String Quartet. These two works amply illustrate the playful aspect of Górecki's personality (the sacred implications of their titles are misleading, and the Baroque-style movement headings in the *Concerto-Cantata* simply reinforce preferences ingrained since before the First Symphony '1959').

Concerto-Cantata forms a continuum with both the intense pastorale of the First Quartet and the frolics of the Harpsichord Concerto, furthermore framing its mix of languid wistfulness and stomping extroversion (shades of Shostakovich) within an abridged palindromic structure (again, a reminder of past procedures). In a sense, *Little Requiem* follows suit, although there is a palpable air of melancholy that derives from its more dynamic contrasts between folk-related musings and the jolly (?) circus romp of the third movement. Despite the often captivating ideas and its fluid, associative structure (like that of the Second String Quartet, the division into four movements masks other cross-currents), it raises many more questions of stylistic and expressive coherence than any of its immediate predecessors. On the one hand, it is a throwback to his student works like the Piano Sonata (1956); on the other hand, it assumes an attitude of unconcern about conventional closure which diverges strongly from the contemporary efforts of Lutosławski or Penderecki.

14 Emigré composers

The possibility for Polish composers to travel abroad – the immediate period of martial law aside – has been an important feature of Polish musical culture since 1956. Many of those born after the Second World War have studied in Europe or the United States, sometimes on scholarships funded by Lutosławski's Grawemeyer award. One or two have spent extended periods outside Poland, but it is noticeable that the vast majority of this generation still live and work in their native country. The same is not true of those born between the wars. Bujarski, Kotoński and Stachowski are firmly rooted and receive most of their performances at home, while a few – like Górecki and Kilar – combine an international presence with a wish to live and compose in Poland. Penderecki is a special case – his output is predominantly commissioned, premiered and performed outside Poland and he remains the most peripatetic of Polish composers. Lutosławski had a similar international trajectory, although he had a settled home in Warsaw. There is, however, a large group of composers, mainly born between the mid-1920s and mid-1940s, who have moved abroad (some for political reasons), usually to take up teaching positions. These include Dobrowolski (Graz, 1976), Meyer (Cologne, 1987), Ptaszyńska (USA, 1972), Schaeffer (Salzburg, 1986) and Szalonek (Berlin, 1973), all of whom have disseminated many important aspects of contemporary Polish music not embodied by composers with higher international profiles. And all have maintained active contact with Polish musical circles, sometimes sharing in the aesthetic, cultural and socio-political concerns of their colleagues living in Poland.

Szalonek was a case in point. Having resigned his position at the Katowice Higher School of Music in 1972 in protest at political interference, he succeeded Boris Blacher as Professor of Composition at the Hochschule der Kunste in West Berlin. Without compromising his innately investigative compositional credo (he developed, for example, a compositional technique called 'selective dodecaphony', which bears resemblance to Lutosławski's patterned twelve-note manipulations), Szalonek began to work with more conventional instrumental techniques, as in what he called his 'classical' *Little B–A–C–H Symphony* for piano and orchestra (1981). In part an extended chorale prelude on *Christ ist erstanden,* its references to neo-classical idioms become increasingly blatant before being shattered at the end of the first movement ('Beats'). The consequent to this is 'Noises', a short reflective coda which has echoes of Górecki's custom and practice. After finishing the work, Szalonek dedicated it to John Paul II, not in celebration but in thanksgiving for the Pope's survival of the assassination attempt on his life in St Peter's Square on 13 May 1981. Carl Humphries detects signs of alienation in the music that followed, suggesting that it

> bears traces of the emotional scars and uncertainties of exile – a certain nightmarish anguish becomes mixed with the child-like mischievousness that often lightened the tone of earlier works. The compositions produced in the 1980s, such as *D. P.'s Five Ghoulish Dreams* (1985) . . . seem to go further in this direction, allowing the sonoristic aspect to give rise to extreme juxtapositions of strident density and minimalistic emptiness that produce a surreal feeling of estrangement from the safety and familiarity of ordinary social existence.[1]

In the 1990s, however, Szalonek's music seemed more reconciled, especially in those works that, in concentrating on the transformational powers of art and music, maintain a strong link with his experimentations of the 1960s. He was still fascinated by variable versions of his music, as in *Medusa's Head* for 1–3 flutes or recorders (1992), the first of a three-part cycle devoted to the rehabilitation of the legendary Greek Gorgon. And multiphonics play a large role in the solo of the two-movement concerto *L'hautbois mon amour* (1999), an immensely powerful interplay of neo-classical and experimental idioms with a Lutosławskian dialectical drama underlying the confrontational first movement and the bittersweet keening of the second.

Szalonek also tapped into patriotic and sacred sentiments, but without banners or badges, as in the complex polyphonies and luminous harmonic idiom of the unaccompanied twelve-voice *Miserere* (1997). There are, for example, integral Polish elements in *Prayer* and *Silver Prelude* (1993), two earlier *a cappella* settings of Polish poems invoking both God and nature within the landscape of the Beskid Mountains south of Szalonek's birthplace, although the undaunted modernism of the music makes no attempt to locate itself in Polish folk culture. Instead, the music keeps faith with the experimental tradition by giving each of the sixteen voices considerable temporal independence; as the composer indicated, each one sings 'to oneself and God'.[2] His most stunning work of the last decade is his only string quartet, *Symphony of Rituals* (1991–6). Premiered at the 2002 'Warsaw Autumn', it dares all by starting with that most clichéd of openings, instrumental tuning, and proceeds with equal daring to explore musical arguments of symphonic proportions, occasionally touching on Polish folk traditions but more importantly challenging the listener's perception of time, material and idiom. Like his near-contemporaries Baird and Serocki, Szalonek deserves wider international recognition for the depth and individuality of his musical thought. Not unexpectedly, his domicile outside Poland seems to have been of little help in disseminating his own music abroad, and his career followed a pattern already laid down by emigré Polish composers of older generations. Of those who left Poland in the post-war decade, three are of particular interest.

Roman Haubenstock-Ramati, having studied under two composers with strongly contrasting aesthetics (Malawski and Koffler), held positions at Polish Radio and *Ruch Muzyczny* in Kraków and at the Polish branch of the ISCM before emigrating to Israel in 1950. He then returned to Europe where he worked at Universal Edition in Vienna (1957–68) and was Professor of Composition at the city's Musikhochschule (1973–89). With this pedigree (he also taught at Darmstadt), it is no surprise that his music displays a thoroughgoing modernism, often involving mobile forms and graphic notation. And although ten of Haubenstock-Ramati's works have been performed at the 'Warsaw Autumn' since 1961 (neither he nor his music was banned like Panufnik's, partly because he had a profile as a writer, not as a composer, when he left and there were therefore no cultural or political repercussions), his music shows no signs of being Polish in spirit or execution and belongs wholeheartedly to the Austrian tradition which he found so amenable.

Roman Palester, although only twelve years Haubenstock-Ramati's senior, had had a prominent role in Polish music both before and after the Second World War. Unusually, he was able to move between France and Poland with relative ease in the post-war years, deciding in 1951 to take advantage of the option of exile and staying in Paris. Almost immediately he became head of the Polish section of the American-run Radio Free Europe in Munich (1952–72), which did not endear him to the Polish authorities; like Panufnik, his name was proscribed in Poland until 1977, although the performances of his Variations for Orchestra (1955) in Katowice in 1958 and of the Fourth Symphony (1948–52) at the 1958 'Warsaw Autumn' were a political aberration comparable to the performance of Panufnik's *Tragic Overture* in Warsaw in November that same year. Never a prolific composer, Palester's output after 1951 numbers some twenty new works premiered in his lifetime, including Missa brevis (1951), String Trio (1959), a one-act 'action en musique' *La mort de Don Juan* (1961), *Metamorphoses* for orchestra (1968), Viola Concerto (1978) and the Fifth Symphony (1977–84). With the hyperactive Fourth Symphony, Palester began to absorb twelve-note techniques, anticipating in his flexible treatment the approach adopted later by many composers in Poland. And while there were a few later experiments in open form and a freer rhythmic language, he preferred to engage in conventionally notated thematic development, based on twelve-note rows, aligned with a post-romantic expressiveness. In the Fifth Symphony, the emotional intensity embraced valedictory citations from lieder by Schubert and Brahms ('O Tod, o Tod, wie bitter bist du'). Unlike Haubenstock-Ramati, he created several works which in their differing ways renewed his contact with Polish culture, including *Concertino for Harpsichord and Ten Instruments on Old Polish Dances* (1955), *Three Poems by Czesław Miłosz* (1977) and *Hymnus pro gratiarum actione* (Te Deum) (1979), which he dedicated to the Pope.

The composer who made the most of what he could out of exile was Panufnik. Having leaped, as he memorably put it, 'from my Polish position of No. One to No One at All in England' in 1954, Panufnik still managed to secure a publishing contract with Boosey and Hawkes and eventually landed the Music Directorship of the City of Birmingham Symphony Orchestra (1957–9). He then decided to relinquish regular employment and to return to composition full-time. Of these three emigré composers, Panufnik produced the most distinctive and internationally acclaimed body of work and he worked with many eminent conductors and soloists, including Stokowski, Solti, Ozawa, Menuhin and Rostropovich. His 'English' period produced eight new symphonies, a range of orchestral works and concertos, the cantata *Universal Prayer* and chamber music, including three string quartets. The titles of his two books – *Impulse and Design in my Music* (1974) and *Composing Myself* (1987) – give a clue to the main creative tension in his composition and to his orderly approach to life and work. Before he left Poland, he had given ample evidence of the role of pattern and clarity in his music, and these features became even more marked after 1960, as did the sometimes contradictory pulls of intuition and intellect. Habitually, he created a visual maquette of the overall design of a piece – often symmetrical and/or geometrical in character – which he then realised in every parameter in jewel-like detail. Sometimes the result could be dry and overly schematic (*Metasinfonia*, 1978), but usually he achieved an intriguing balance (a notably complex example is *Sinfonia di sfere*, 1975).

From the very beginning of his time in England, Panufnik expressed in music his ineradicable Polishness. This was given a particular sheen in *Sinfonia sacra* (1963), the work which began a revival in his creative fortunes. Composed ahead and in commemoration of the thousandth anniversary of the establishment of Christianity in Poland (cf. Penderecki's *St Luke Passion*), the Symphony draws systematically on the opening intervals of 'Mother of God' (*Sinfonia votiva*, 1981, also draws on this hymn). *Sinfonia sacra*'s 'intervallic integrity, cool archaisms, detached formal rituals and directly emotional devices – brass fanfares, militaristic percussion, expansive string cantilenas'[3] not only relate back to his 'Polish' period but also anticipate the defining characteristics of later works. At the heart of his developing pitch organisation, which crystallised in a new way in *Reflections* for piano (1968), was the notion of an all-pervasive intervallic cell, most commonly a three-note combination F–B–E. Along with their permutations and sequential transpositions, such cells ensured a tonal/atonal fluctuation, which in conjunction with the patterning of other parameters gave the impression of a musical language that was both restlessly mobile and inherently static. Nevertheless, he was not so wedded to any one system that he could not leaven such ascetic procedures with other figures, such as his fingerprint major-minor chording.

Even though his music often gives the impression of being hermetically sealed, it becomes especially powerful when it breaks away from large-scale symmetries and the dangers of predictability and when it pursues several simultaneous layers of activity. This is especially true of the later symphonic works, such as the last two symphonies: *Sinfonia della speranza* (1986), with its passionate cantilenas and prismatic reflections of the F–B–E motif, and the Tenth Symphony (1988). Many works have descriptive titles suggesting an extra-musical dimension: the subtitle of the Third String Quartet – 'Papercuts' ('Wycinanki') – refers to the work's origins in the same symmetrically designed folk artefacts that inspired *Sinfonia rustica* in the late 1940s. Some works are linked to specific events in Poland, observed from afar by the exiled composer. *Katyń Epitaph* (1967) reflects on the atrocity of 1940,[4] *Sinfonia votiva* is linked with the image of the Black Madonna in Częstochowa and the striking shipyard workers in Gdańsk, and the Bassoon Concerto (1985) is dedicated to the memory of Popiełuszko, murdered the previous year.

While Palester visited Poland after he was de-listed in 1977, Panufnik refused to return until there was a democratic government. That must have seemed a forlorn hope, but in 1990, a year before he died, he journeyed to Poland for the performance of eleven of his works at that year's 'Warsaw Autumn'. To Polish audiences, he was still much of a mystery even though the festival had programmed his works on a regular basis since giving *Universal Prayer* its Polish premiere in 1977. There was considerable curiosity in his return as one of Poland's most notorious exiles from the socialist-realist years, but, as with other emigrés, he and his music were still viewed as being largely outside the Polish experience. Strong efforts have since been made by publishers, performers and musicologists to reintegrate Panufnik into the collective history of post-war Polish music, and certainly he has the highest profile there of any emigrés of his generation. He will be considered by many, however, still to have two nationalities and two bodies of work which remain situated primarily in their geographical and cultural place of origin, whatever the composer's attempts to bridge the gap.

15 Young Poland

It would be all too easy to gain the impression that contemporary music in Poland has always revolved around the 'Warsaw Autumn'. This festival does, after all, have an extraordinary record for international exchange and for the promotion of Polish composers. It takes place in the capital, supported by other Warsaw-based institutions in the press, broadcasting and recording industry. The broader picture, however, reveals a significant dispersal of activity across the country, largely the result of the post-war establishment of regional centres of output: the state-owned music publisher PWM is in Kraków, the principal Polish Radio orchestra is located in Katowice, and the Music Academies (previously known as PWSM – State Higher Schools of Music) are to be found in major cities across Poland. In music publishing, further diversity came in 1974 with the establishment of the Authors' Agency in Warsaw (in conjunction with ZKP). And as a sign of new pluralism in the dying moments of communism in Poland, and at the moment when PWM was going through a difficult period, an independent imprint was established in Poznań. The driving force behind the co-operative venture Brevis (set up in 1990) was two composers of the post-war generation: Lidia Zielińska (b. 1953) from Poznań and Rafał Augustyn (b. 1951) from Wrocław. Their motivation was simple: to raise the profile of their own generation at a liberating moment in Polish history.

The role of music festivals other than the 'Warsaw Autumn' has also been particularly significant. Both Augustyn and Zielińska, for example, have been closely involved in contemporary music festivals in their respective cities as well as having served terms, like many of their colleagues, as members of the repertoire committee of the 'Warsaw Autumn'. In Warsaw, during the politically and economically difficult mid-1980s, the 'International Young Composers' Forum' (subsequently 'International New Music Forum') provided temporary rivalry for the 'Warsaw Autumn', while at the end of the decade there were biennial 'Encounters of Young Composers' in Gdańsk. And in 1989, the Kraków section of ZKP set up the annual 'International Music Days of Kraków Composers'.

Even in the mid-1970s there was a sense that the dynamics of Polish music were beginning to shift away from those who had been born before the Second World War. By the beginning of the 1980s, very few of the best-known Polish composers were actively involved in teaching composition; some, sadly, had died prematurely, some had emigrated, others were figureheads with active international careers. In the mid-1970s, a musical vacuum began to develop at precisely the time that social and political unrest, aided by the gross mismanagement of the Polish economy, paved the way for the establishment of Solidarity in 1980. Those born in the 1950s were then in their early twenties and were increasingly unafraid of becoming involved in the struggle for a new Poland, on both the political and cultural front. And the symbol of change for them, as the 'Warsaw Autumn' had been for older generations in 1956, was a festival of new music.

The MMMM – 'Młodzy Muzycy Młodemu Miastu' (Young Musicians for a Young City) – was held annually in 1975–80 in Stalowa Wola, an industrial new town in the otherwise delightful countryside of south-east Poland. Despite its laboriously alliterative title (with its echoes of socialist slogans and recall of the name of MW2), this festival provided a major launching pad for several young composers.[1] MMMM – whose symbolic patron was Charles Ives – was organised by a young musicologist from Kraków, Krzysztof Droba, and was particularly associated with the early careers of a trio of composers from Katowice: Eugeniusz Knapik (b. 1951), Andrzej Krzanowski (1951–90) and Aleksander Lasoń (b. 1951).

The terms 'new tonality' and 'new romanticism' were much bandied about at the time. Although not exclusive to Poland, of course, these epithets and associated trends arose as a delayed reaction against the complexities of total serialism imported from Darmstadt and, more immediately, as a riposte to sonorism. Added to the notions of new tonality and new romanticism was what Lutosławski called 'a new type of melody'.[2] A comparison of the changing focus in the music of both Lutosławski and Penderecki, not to mention other composers, shows that there were many divergences in the realisation of these 'new' goals. In this context, it is notable that three of the composers named so far in this chapter – Augustyn, Knapik and Krzanowski – studied composition with Górecki in the early 1970s, just at the moment when he was turning to modal and melodic writing.

Completing the roster of this group are a number of significant Warsaw-based composers, including Stanisław Krupowicz (b. 1952), Paweł Szymański (b. 1954) and Tadeusz Wielecki (b. 1954). As will be seen, many of this generation have continued to pursue mainstream genres and repertoire when opportunities have arisen, not least because this is where Polish performers had developed considerable expertise. Most of them, however, have avoided monumentalism and abstract symphonism. A few have been drawn to extra-musical patriotic sentiment (though less overtly than their elders), some have contributed to sacred genres (some with postmodern remove), and a few have tackled opera. There has been no appetite, however, for 'new complexity'. Where this generation of Polish composers has developed an extra dimension has been in the more experimental outlets already mapped out by Schaeffer and Krauze, such as electronic music, multi-media or music theatre.

The 'Stalowa Wola' generation

For much of the 1970s and 80s, Knapik pursued a double career, as composer and pianist. He was following a noble Polish tradition of composer-performers, after Bacewicz, Krauze and Tomasz Sikorski, and in tandem with several of his contemporaries who advocated much more than their own music, such as Krzanowski (accordion) and Wielecki (double bass). Knapik's repertoire included Messiaen,[3] a composer who, along with Górecki and Ives ('Listen to Ives, how much freedom there is!'[4]), has been a signal influence on Knapik's compositional development (Partita for violin and piano, 1980). The steady, sustained chording supporting an ecstatic solo voice in Knapik's *La flûte de jade* for soprano and orchestra (1973) has a symbiotic relationship with Górecki's Second and Third Symphonies while simultaneously indicating a rapprochement with twentieth-century French music. *Le chant* (1976), a setting of part of Valéry's 'Le cimetière marin', adopts a more expressionist approach to shifting chromatic spectra as well as containing dark-hued remnants of block sonoristic textures. The placing of the solo soprano at the end clearly recalls Górecki's consolatory codas and also confirms parallels with Lutosławski's endings. In a second 'sea' piece – *Comme au bord de la mer . . .* for ensemble (1977), another setting of Valéry, this time recited on interpolated tape excerpts – Knapik moved more decisively towards his own version of lyrical 'new tonality' (or, perhaps more accurately, 'new modality'). This feature characterises several chamber works written at this time, notably the String Quartet (1980).

In the two-movement quartet, Knapik set out to reinterpret what he understood as the 'specific gravity' of the Beethoven quartets.[5] In advance of Górecki's string quartets, although in quite different ways, he examines the gravitational pull of consonance within a dissonant context. The first movement veers masterfully between fixed points of euphony by means of cadential sidesteps, multi-directional glissandi and scalic runs. Triadic integration, not just the reconciliation of opposites, lies at the heart of the formal design, which, like Bujarski's first two quartets, is rooted in the sonata principle. Among recurrent figures are an arpeggiated E flat minor chord, a chordal refrain B–D–A (anticipating Górecki's 'Beethovenian chords' in his Second String Quartet), and the chord of E major. Apart from the diversionary E flat minor triad, these chords are theoretically linked by the cadential circle

Example 15.1. Knapik, String Quartet (1980), start of second movement.

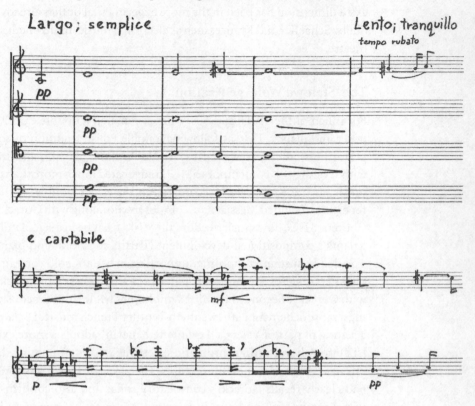

of fifths, whose selective properties Knapik exploits both brazenly and with subtlety. An equally tangible connection between them is the motivic extraction of minor thirds, a feature which is carried over into the second movement (Ex. 15.1). The intervallic concentration in this movement is strongly reminiscent of Lutosławski's pitch organisation, although the recurrence of ideas at pitch aligns Knapik more with Górecki, as does the concluding semi-dissonant chorale. But the almost Wagnerian plagal cadence at the start of the movement and the modified plagal cadence onto the concluding 'tonic' E major chord bespeak, like the features of the first movement, a confidently individual approach to the intercutting of and bridging between triadic and non-triadic material.

There had been several hints that Knapik was interested in late-romantic idioms, such as the Mahlerian inflections in Partita and in his imaginatively reflective *Islands* (*Wyspy*) for strings (1983), his third piece on the theme of water. Little, however, could have prepared either the composer or his audiences for what followed. In 1987, Górecki had turned down the offer of an operatic collaboration with the Belgian director and artist, Jan Fabre.

Fabre turned to Knapik, and with only one or two exceptions Knapik has since devoted himself to stage and concert music for voices and orchestra. Some of his works had already shown a tendency towards ecstatic vocal utterance, although closer parallels may be found in the music of other Polish composers, in Bujarski's *Gardens* or Augustyn's earlier *A Life's Parallels* for high voice and orchestra (1983). Augustyn's seductive and resonant setting of nineteenth- and twentieth-century British and American poetry breaks ranks with much of what was being composed in Poland at that time. This is especially noticeable in the second movement, a setting of Whitman's 'Apostrophe: Continuities', which Augustyn has acknowledged is indebted both to Mahler and to Knapik's *La flûte de jade*.[6]

The results of Knapik's paradigm shift have been an operatic trilogy, *The Minds of Helena Troubleyn* (1987–96), three ballet scores premiered in Frankfurt, Brussels and Amsterdam, and *Up into the Silence* (1996–2000), a seventy-minute song cycle for soprano, baritone and orchestra to texts by e. e. cummings and Fabre. The scale of these pieces is stunning, as is their wholehearted embrace of a post-romantic idiom with which Scriabin and, to a lesser extent, Karłowicz and Szymanowski would have identified. Knapik's mastery of harmonic and melodic ebb and flow, and of the huge orchestral canvases upon which he paints these luxuriant pictures, is breathtaking. The music remains deeply and unconcernedly anachronistic, however; it has no interest in contemporary referencing, be it the irony espoused by his postmodern contemporaries or the laborious expressivity of Penderecki's recent large-scale scores. Knapik is not the first composer for whom being so deliberately out of time has not been a long-term hindrance, but in these rich and powerfully persuasive scores he has cast back further than most.

Krzanowski and Lasoń have less controversial profiles. Leszek Polony called Krzanowski, who died aged thirty-nine in 1990, 'the bard' of his generation:

> The term 'new romanticism' was used for the first time in Poland in reference to Krzanowski's music . . . Primarily romantic was Krzanowski's accordion – a common, lowly, provincial instrument, with stronger links to small towns than to folk music of the villages . . . [it] was an aesthetic provocation.[7]

In addition to his sizeable contribution to accordion literature, as in Study II (1974) (Ex. 15.2), in both solo and group repertoire, Krzanowski made use of the instrument in mixed ensembles.[8] Among his most individual works were *Programmes* I–VI (*Audycja* I–VI, 1973–82), a sequence of radio-style pieces in which contemporary Polish poetry was recited alongside highly unusual ensembles (the first is scored for flute, siren, whistle,

Example 15.2. Krzanowski, Study II (1974), start of first movement.

tam-tam and two tapes). In *Programme* III for actor, soprano, two accordions, trumpet, baritone saxophone, electric guitar, percussion and slides (1974), he gives an early example of his tendency towards collage by quoting part of Górecki's Second Symphony on tape. His early dependency on his teacher is understandable, but a citation from a recent piece was unusual and not necessarily ironic. *Programme* IV (1975) cites Bach and Szymanowski's Stabat Mater; the latter piece is also quoted on tape in the First String Quartet, version B (1976), a work directly inspired by Crumb's *Black Angels*. The final *Programme*, for soprano and string quartet (1982), was written to commemorate the hundredth anniversary of the birth of Szymanowski (and shortly after the imposition of martial law) and is another work which incorporates the opening phrase of 'Mother of God'. Throughout these semi-staged pieces, there is less a sense of irony and detachment, more a simmering rebellion whose counterparts in popular culture were the student theatre and underground cabaret venues which thrived in the 1970s – like the famous 'Cellar under the Sign of the Rams' ('Piwnica pod baranami') in Kraków.

Krzanowski also added his voice to the trend towards archaisms and Baroque structural techniques while retaining a strongly modernist attitude to his material. *Alkagran* for accordion quintet (1980) is 'a one-movement composition with a polyphonic texture, dominated by the technique of canon-like leading of voices and uninterrupted, densely entangled melodic lines and sound planes . . . aleatoric polymetry of planes with characteristic rhythmical shifts'.[9] Of his more conventionally scored works, the early orchestral *Canti di Wratislavia* (1976) and Second Symphony for thirteen strings (1984) stand out. The former is his equivalent of *Scontri* and is appropriately dedicated to Górecki. It is a brash, rough, teeming cityscape, with vivid and unusual sonorities, a latter-day homage to both Gershwin and Varèse. The Second Symphony is more considered, almost Lutosławskian in tone; indeed, the latter's *Preludes and Fugue* seems to be an immediate ancestor. Here a more traditional romanticism is at work, even though its harmonic language and static heterophony often recall accordion textures. The third movement provides the lyrical focus, with bundled canonic imitation (Ex. 15.3) developing into a genuine twelve-part polyphony towards the close. Its delicacy of timbre is carried over into later works, such as *Relief X* for string quartet and computer-generated tape (1988), whose understated, introspective sighs and tremolandi contrast strongly with the more extrovert compositions of his youth.

While Krzanowski only rarely turned towards sacred music – for example, the unaccompanied and Góreckian *Salve regina* (1981) – Lasoń has on a number of occasions made great play of religious associations. As a student, he participated three times in 'Sacrosong', a competitive ecumenical festival organised by Cardinal Wojtyła (the first and second of these pieces, *To Father Kolbe*, 1972, and *Nicolaus Copernicus*, 1973, wear their patriotic dedications on their sleeve). More recently, he has begun to put together, not unlike Penderecki's piecemeal accumulation of his *Polish Requiem*, a monumental *Mass-Symphony*, 'Apocalipse' (1999–2001), culled in large part from recent works, including *Concerto festivo* for violin and orchestra (1995 – the Agnus Dei), the Third Symphony (1997 – the Gloria and other movements), the orchestral *Credo* (1997) and *Musica sacra* (1998 – the Sanctus). Lasoń is better known for his series of six compositions called *Chamber Music* (1975–2000), six works for string quartet, and several vibrant orchestral pieces. His affinities lie with earlier twentieth-century, non-Polish idioms, such as pre-war French music, Bartók and Stravinsky, with his own native folk traditions, and with Lutosławski and Górecki (*Chamber Music* no. 3, 1978).

Lasoń made his orchestral mark with the First Symphony for wind instruments, percussion and two pianos (1975), whose take on Polish sonorism – plus elements of diatonicism, rhythmic panache and timbral concerns – owes much to the harmonic and orchestral sound worlds of Stravinsky and

Example 15.3. Krzanowski, Second Symphony (1984), figs. 60–1.

Messiaen. The Stravinskian connection resurfaces on many occasions – the ghost of *Petrushka* hangs over both *Chamber Music* no. 3 and the Wind Quintet 'Spring' (previously *Chamber Music* no. 4, 1980) – and a sense of the burlesque is never far from the surface. Gamelan-type sonorities, sometimes linked with early American minimalism, are another resource. The full thrust of Lasoń's exuberance is felt in three orchestral scores: Symphony no. 2 'Concertante' (1979), *Mountains* (*Góry*, 1980) and *Cathedral* (1989). The Second Symphony – originally conceived as a piano concerto – follows in an established line (its rumbustious end, for example, recalls the *oberek* finale of Szymanowski's *Symphonie concertante*); it has a vigorous rhythmic drive, an obsessive motivic character and a textural discourse which revels in diatonic and pentatonic associations. Lasoń's heterophonic roulades are given a folk twist in *Mountains*, which taps into the tradition of Polish evocations of landscape stretching back through Kilar, Krauze and Karłowicz as far as Noskowski's concert overture *The Eye of the Sea* (*Morskie Oko*, 1875). Nevertheless, *Mountains* achieves a degree of abstractness to the extent that its title seems as much a side issue as that of his other symphonic poem, *Cathedral*. The most striking aspect of both works is their sense of dignity and pathos, their resonant harmonic language and richly layered orchestration, features that align him in the 1980s with Lutosławski. Lasoń's debt to Lutosławski is particularly apparent in *Cathedral*'s neo-romantic cantilenas, which expand to proportions and levels of complexity approaching, in spirit if not in idiom, those being explored by Knapik.

Lasoń has been the prime contributor of his generation to the extensive repertoire of the post-war Polish string quartet and his development of new musical ideas is especially apparent in these more intimate pieces. The Second Quartet (1987) is an intense, sometimes folk-inflected web of contrapuntal and heterophonic textures, recalling Krauze's *Aus alle Welt stammende*, although without the latter's monolithic consistency. Lasoń regards the Third String Quartet (1992) as 'another stage of my work on new tonality and – more importantly – on [a] new approach towards melody construction'.[10] Even more than in the Second Quartet, certain pitch-classes are accorded structural significance, such as the punctuations in the first movement on G sharp and C sharp, pitches which form the basis for restricted harmonic or melodic constructs in the second movement (Ex. 15.4). Despite its leaner, tauter language, the music is still rooted in the decorative roulades that have long been one of his most identifiable characteristics. Nevertheless, there are moments of heightened enigma, such as the severe understatement of the brief third movement and the profligate reiterations of commonplace material in the finale, with its postmodern echoes of Bacewicz and Górecki's string quartets. While *Relief for Andrzej* (1995),

Example 15.4. Lasoń, Third String Quartet (1992), start of second movement.

written in memory of Krzanowski, continues the pared-down polyphony of the Third Quartet, the Fourth Quartet (2000) is notable for its return to a more folkloric content.

Warsaw

If Górecki played a significant role in the shaping of several young composers from Katowice and Wrocław, Penderecki seems, despite his senior role at the Kraków Music Academy for many years, to have had a less noticeable compositional influence in the same period. In Warsaw, the main teachers included Baird and Kotoński. Among the latter's many pupils are Jacek Grudzień (b. 1961), Krupowicz, Hanna Kulenty (b. 1961), Szymański and

Wielecki. None of these, however, displays the sort of stylistic or aesthetic rapport with Kotoński that has been observed between Górecki and his students. These Warsaw-based composers evince a more marked sense of ironic detachment and an attitude towards the creative act which stems as much from their responses to contemporary Polish musical and socio-political history as it does from the growth of postmodern outlooks both to the East (polystylism) and to the West (American or Dutch minimalism).

The trend towards archaism already noted in Krzanowski's music is a particular feature of certain composers. Krzysztof Baculewski (b. 1950), also known as a critic and author, has made plain his fascination with Baroque idioms and procedures. His *The Whole and Broken Consort* (1986) is written for period instruments, *Antitheton* I (1989) makes use of Baroque musical–rhetorical figures, Purcell is referenced in *The Profane Anthem* (1993), while *Antitheton* II (1996), written for a Baroque instrumental ensemble, makes no secret of its origins in the finale of Bach's Third Brandenburg Concerto. Other levels of intertextuality – different in virtually every respect from the iconographical intentions of the previous generation – are apparent in the music of Szymański and Krupowicz.

Of the post-war generation, Szymański is the best known both at home and abroad and has one of the most interesting pedigrees, having studied not only with Baird and Kotoński but also with Haubenstock-Ramati in Vienna; he is the only one to have a contract with a major Western publisher. Like his music, he remains something of an enigma, choosing a reclusive existence in preference to a sustained organisational or educational role in Polish musical life. He developed his distinctive compositional idiom and technique with the aphoristic *Limerics* for violin and harpsichord (1975), *Partita* II for orchestra (1978) and *Gloria* for female chorus and orchestra (1979). At the root of his music lies the concept of what Szymański has called a 'basic structure' which, although disguised by transformation and a deliberately intermittent audibility, is normally derived from Renaissance or Baroque polyphonic procedures.[11] His favourite device is the canon, which can vary from two-part, in *Two Illusory Constructions* for clarinet, cello and piano (1984), to multiple voices, such as the eight-part canon in *Lux aeterna* for chorus and ensemble (1984).

The reiterative character of Szymański's music is tempered by an aware-ness of the balance between repetition and change: the continuum is fre-quently interrupted or fractured. This is apparent even in his earliest acknowledged work, *Epitaph* for two pianos (1974), which still bears traces of sonoristic textures as well as hints of Tomasz Sikorski's tritone-based idiom. Szymański established his mature persona with Sonata for violins, double bass and percussion (1982) and *Appendix* for piccolo and mixed ensemble

(1983), which draw on three-part and four-part canonic structures respectively and which are both intercut by distinctive 'stop-time' punctuation. In Sonata, this consists of a string pizzicato combined with a stifled strike on cymbal and marimba, whose timbres, joined by those of tubular bells and gong, proceed to give the work a very particular character (Ex. 15.5). Sonata is his first instrumental work in which the 'basic structure' is given an extended workout. In this case, it is a six-bar phrase (never stated in its entirety) in which alternating tonic and dominant harmonies are implied; G minor is the underlying tonic key, although other key centres are set up in the work in ritornello fashion. Sonata's Baroque turns of phrase 'cannon' into one another harmoniously if somewhat unpredictably in a generally tonal environment; it is as if, in visual terms, the complete image is not directly perceptible but may be viewed only in a constantly shifting mobile of tiny mirrors. Szymański's 'trick' is to exchange notes or motifs for rests in different places as the canon circulates, thereby implying continuity but denying the full actuality at any one moment. It is a wry aural tease that is clearly sustained, in the fast sections, by the regular pulse and the passacaglia role of the pizzicato double bass.

The adherence to tonal elements is integral to Szymański's technique because it facilitates the distinction between the basic structure and its transformations. His stance on the notion of 'new tonality', however, is dismissive: 'In my opinion this is not an adequate term as there is no new tonal system, but just elements of the tonality from earlier music.'[12] Augustyn's pithy observation that Sonata was 'a mixture of Telemann and gamelan',[13] might be true of the surface of the piece, but the underlying process is more fundamentally unified. Nevertheless, Szymański understands the notion of 'a set of elements belonging to a certain convention governed by rules which have nothing to do with this convention [as being like] elements of reality which appear in surrealistic paintings as an extraneous order to this reality'.[14] He might have added that Sonata is not based on an existing Baroque model but on Szymanowski's last mazurka, op. 62/2 (it had been commissioned to celebrate the centenary of Szymanowski's birth). The correspondences with the mazurka highlight diatonic motivic patterns which happen to fit into an eighteenth-century idiom. Szymański is therefore able, alongside the curious timbral–gestural idiom, to suggest a multi-layered intertextuality that is far removed in its elusive subtlety from the compositional concerns of many other Polish composers in the politically charged atmosphere of the early 1980s. While the term 'surconventional music', which Szymański and Krupowicz coined in 1984 for such pieces, has not enjoyed wide currency, the processes it embodies have remained central to the music of both composers. It is also worth remarking that it was not an entirely new phenomenon in

Example 15.5. Szymański, Sonata (1982), bb. 37–47.

Example 15.5. (*cont.*)

Example 15.5. (*cont.*)

Polish music: their concept of the 'sur'-relationship between material and treatment is clearly anticipated by Krauze's approach to found melodies and objects in the 1970s.

Szymański has not been averse to more archaic source material. *Lux aeterna*, for example, like Krupowicz's Concerto for tenor saxophone and computers (1987), returns to the much-parodied medieval tune, 'L'homme armé'. Usually, however, he prefers to sublimate his sources and to create more generalised stylistic allusions, whether to Renaissance fantasia textures in slow tempi or eighteenth-century figuration at faster speeds. Occasionally, he strays further afield, as in the post-minimal Americanisms of *Partita* IV for orchestra (1986), the impressionistic abstraction of *A Study of Shade* for orchestra (1989), or the more playful homophonic 'cut-and-pastiche' of *Recalling a Serenade* for clarinet quintet (1996). His well-developed sense of irony has not kept him from developing a powerful if idiosyncratic sense of structural balance in many of his pieces. He is fond of offsetting an exuberant first movement, as in *Partita* III for harpsichord and orchestra (1986) or the Piano Concerto (1994), with a challengingly attenuated slow movement which often overlaps with the end of the first. This bipartite structure – in which the animated first section is far outweighed by the second – creates a strong dialectical model that gives new life to a concept that has also been explored in different ways by Lutosławski, Górecki, Knapik and others. The Piano Concerto is a particularly memorable example: in the toccata-style first movement, the soloist launches out on waves of rising canonic imitation, in jazzily syncopated rhythms, but is rather abruptly silenced by orchestral interruptions before the movement has much chance to develop. This disruptive move places it – rather like the 'Hésitant' first movement of Lutosławski's Second Symphony – in a subservient position to the second movement, which lasts three times as long. Unlike Lutosławski's 'Direct' finale, Szymański renounces the need for an overt cumulative drama, instead providing a slow-motion complement to the first movement in which veiled orchestral polyphony is reinforced and gilded by a seemingly improvised piano monody (Ex. 15.6). The movement bears traces of a climax and resolution, but so unemphatic are they, and so distant from traditional concerto or symphonic gestures, that the overall compositional intent remains enigmatic.

This degree of coolness towards conventional expressivity reaches its zenith in *Miserere* (1993), a successor to several non-functional sacred pieces Szymański composed in his late twenties. It is also one of a number of contemporaneous Polish works with this title, although its degree of structural artifice implies a remoteness from any other model, ancient or modern. If it has any precedents, they lie in Renaissance compositional applications.

Example 15.6. Szymański, Piano Concerto (1994), second movement, bb. 41–3.

The process of abstraction has reached an extreme, and the text is realised in music that accentuates its theme of abject penance. Scored, characteristically, for an ensemble of mixed heritage (seven male voices including two counter-tenors, four cellos, harp and bowed vibraphone), Szymański's setting of Psalm 50 (51) is constructed as a sequence of interlocking, but independent arcs and planes. Sombre vocal iterations of a combination of C major and D minor triads (cf. Sikorski's *Homophony*) are decorated by isolated notes on harp and vibraphone and traversed by drawn-out cello glissandi (the tension between static chording and a rising string glissando would be further explored in the Piano Concerto). Intercut with these ideas, in alternate psalm verses, are appearances of an invariant Gregorian chant intoned by the solo bass. *Miserere* is powerful because of its taut, constructivist control: the shifting of focus between constancy and change, stasis and motion, harmony and dissonance, has an expressive intensity reminiscent of Stravinsky or Varèse. It achieves a fine balance between the modern and the postmodern.

Krupowicz's *Miserere* (1997) is indicative of his greater willingness to embrace strong polystylistic contrasts (here, an excerpt of Allegri's *Miserere* is quoted towards the end of a work marked by extremes of consonance and dissonance). Krupowicz's early work is also more flamboyant and open to collage than Szymański's. Rather like Krzanowski's *Canti di Wratislaviae*, Krupowicz's Symphony (1980) exudes youthful brashness, calling upon a wide range of idioms, from quasi-Arabic melodic ideas and gritty fugato textures reminiscent of Ruggles to late nineteenth-century stylisations. Canonic techniques loom large but their application seems more impulsive than in Szymański's music. While the modal heterophony of *Tempo 72* for harpsichord and strings (1981) recalls Krauze's approach, *A Certain Case of a Certain Generalised Canon at the Fourth and the Fifth* for nine players (1983) highlights Krupowicz's polystylistic impulses. Many of Krupowicz's titles set up expectations of humorous or quizzical treatment of his material, like *Unquestioned Answer* for chamber orchestra (1984) or *Farewell Variations on a Theme by Mozart* for string quartet and pre-recorded tape (1986). A tenser tone is struck in *Only Beatrice* (*Tylko Beatricze*, 1988) for amplified string quartet and tape (Ex. 15.7). The gravitation towards complex heterophony is realised with particular sophistication in the orchestral *Fin de siècle* (1993), where he employs a pre-composed canon at the fourth and at the seventh, a folk tune, elements of twelve-note manipulation, all of which are worked over and disguised by what he calls 'a collage of twelve compositional techniques, selected arbitrarily by the composer'.[15] Krupowicz's recent turn towards music with sacred themes, especially in *Christmas Oratorio* (1997), reveals a darker side – the clown's mask has slipped and the music is prepared to confront 'a catastrophic vision of the world immersed in chaos and darkness'.[16]

Wielecki, too, veers between the jokey (*Misterioso* for actor-percussionist, 1980) and the existential (*Id* for orchestra, 1996). He is adept at postmodern collage (*Tango*, 1980, written for Krauze's Music Workshop) and has followed Krauze's example in treating folk materials heterophonically (Trio for violin, double bass and piano, 1985). And while much of his music displays a concern with combatting the centrifugal force of tonal centres (the unusually severe *Metaphysical Ballad* for orchestra, 1990), his musical outlook is based less on the primacy of form and more on the sensuality of live performance. His career as a professional double bassist has imbued his music with a virtuosity that highlights both his own capabilities (*Opened*

Example 15.7. Krupowicz, *Only Beatrice* (*Tylko Beatricze*, 1988), 3'54"–4'10".

Series for solo double bass, 1982–91) and those of other soloists (*A Thread is Spinning . . . – Przędzie się nić . . .* – for solo cello, 1991). In his concertante works, this approach frequently leads him into areas bordering on music theatre or social commentary. In *He Breathed Upon Him . . .* (*Tchnął nan . . .*) for bassoon, strings and mime (1992), inspired by Michelangelo's *The Creation of Adam*, Wielecki envisages the soloist as the demiurge, the strings as a chorus of old men, and the mime as Man. *Concerto à rebours* for violin and orchestra (1998) is conceived both as a commentary on the relationship between the individual and society (an interpretation sometimes mapped onto Lutosławski's Cello Concerto) and as a continuation of his explorations in technical virtuosity, especially glissandi and harmonics. In both of these works, Wielecki avoids tonal implications, preferring to employ the full chromatic in a manner that perhaps reflects his postgraduate studies in the late 1980s with Isang Yun in Berlin and Klaus Huber in Freiburg. The timbral and dissonant intensity of his music also suggests a consolidated return to the kinds of modernist aesthetic espoused in earlier times by Baird and Serocki.

The significance of studying abroad in the 1980s and 1990s is also apparent when considering the output of the last, and youngest composer of this selection, Hanna Kulenty. Like Grudzień and Jerzy Kornowicz (b. 1959),

Kulenty took advantage of the increased flexibility of travelling to and from Poland. In her case, as in that of Kornowicz, she went to study with Louis Andriessen (Grudzień chose to study in London). Given her existing aesthetic, this was a natural move, and she has kept a strong presence in Holland since she first went there in the late 1980s. Her earliest works, like the orchestral *Ad unum* (1985), already possessed an elemental character, percussive, energetic and sharply etched; combined with the hard-edged pulsations of Dutch minimalism (*Ride* for six percussionists, 1987), her output is distinctive in the context of contemporary Polish music, even though others, like Grudzień and Kornowicz, have also absorbed many features of minimalism. In a manner reminiscent of some of Szymański's concerns, Kulenty controls both structure and musical momentum by a strategy called the 'polyphony of arcs'. These are applied to a range of parameters, including textural strata, chordal progressions and intensities of expression; *Trigon* for chamber orchestra (1989) is a fine early example, with its overlapped sequence of three arches, each characterised by instrumentation, register and texture (Ex. 15.8). Sometimes, phenomena such as spectral harmony and processes of inhalation and exhalation inform such procedures, for example *Breathe* for strings (1987), *Perpetuus* for chamber orchestra without strings (1989) and *Air* for orchestra (1991). *Breathe* has a brooding, relentless tread and a dense chordal idiom that recalls Górecki's blocked harmonies, although the heterophonic flurries in the upper registers and her command of symphonic argument and momentum owe more to Lutosławski's example. The First Violin Concerto (1992) is a more deliberately intimate work and maintains moderate tempi throughout. Somewhat conventionally, it centres on the soloist, whose initial trills, glissandi and ostinati provoke the orchestra into exploring its own colliding cycles of repetitions, each layer or arc pursuing a seemingly independent trajectory but simultaneously contributing to a structurally expressive design.

As the 1990s progressed, so Kulenty modified the tensile nature of her music and either emphasised a more intimate mode – *Cradle Song* for piano trio (1993) has an almost romantic fervour – or gave freer rein to her interest in minimal or popular idioms. *Sinequan Forte B* for amplified cello, orchestra and electronic delay (1994) returns to the continuum of a fast metrical pulse, although Kulenty's modernist leanings led her to subvert the initial phasing and pitch patterns in order to create more complex layering and to intensify the sense of cumulative exhilaration. Even though her chamber-music output is relatively small, she has produced some memorably relaxed pieces: *Going Up 2*, written for De Ereprijs (1995), updates the funky riffs that were Bernstein's stock in trade, while *Drive*

Example 15.8. Kulenty, *Trigon* (1989), p. 37.

Blues for piano (2000) is an amiable jazz improvisation with no modernist pretensions.

It should also be noted that Kulenty is one of the few Polish composers of her generation to have had the opportunity, or the inclination, to write an opera; her one-act *The Mother of Black-Winged Dreams* (1995) was premiered in Munich in 1996. With the exception of Knapik's Belgian output, other Polish operas by her near-contemporaries have been rare. Baculewski's *New Deliverance* (*Nowe wyzwolenie*, 1974) was an isolated early occurrence, although *An Ignoramus and a Madman* (*Ignorant i Szaleniec*, 2001) by Paweł Mykietyn (b. 1971) was recently produced in Warsaw and operas are awaited from Krupowicz and Szymański. Older composers have contributed to the genre in greater numbers: Meyer's *Cyberiada* (1970, rev. 1985), Ptaszyńska's *Oscar from Alva* (1971) and a children's opera *Mr Marimba* (1995), Krauze's *The Star* (*Gwiazda*, 1981), Zbigniew Rudziński's *The Mannequins* (1981) and *Antigone* (1982), and two operas by Elżbieta Sikora (b. 1943) – *Ariadne* (1977) and *L'arrache-coeur* (1986, rev. 1995). Nevertheless, it remains true that, despite Penderecki's four large-scale operas, Polish interest in the genre has never been high, not least because institutional support for new opera has been at best episodic since the failed attempt to kick-start production in the early 1950s. On the other hand, the post-war generation is closely involved in the more practicable branches of instrumental and music theatre, as its activities in experimental music demonstrate.

Experimental and electronic music

The post-war generation began to come of age as Cagean happenings, Stockhausen's text compositions, Schaeffer's instrumental theatre pieces and Krauze's spatial compositions were grabbing the headlines. It was understandable, therefore, that young composers should gravitate towards creative outlets which were accessible (and anti-establishment) when conventional commissions were not always plentiful. The situation in terms of orchestral and large-scale chamber opportunities deteriorated even further during the confined circumstances of the early 1980s, while the birth of popular democracy at the end of the decade introduced market forces and a reduction of public subsidy for the arts and hence fewer orchestral commissions. It is typical, therefore, to find that most composers of this generation have a more diversified output than their elders and have contributed – as has already emerged – to the linked areas of music theatre, electronic music and the wider experimental tradition.

Music theatre has the lowest profile, partly because its end-product is comparatively ephemeral. Krzanowski and Wielecki both engaged with theatrical elements through their use of actors or mime, as has Zielińska, whose *Eh Joe* for mime, tape and orchestra (1978) and *Cascando* for actor and double chorus (1983) are based on the work of Samuel Beckett. In addition to her music-theatre pieces, such as *Huit heures de la vie des femmes* (1988) and *The Snare of Time* (1994), Zielińska has followed the example of Krauze and others in writing works that straddle the divide between multi-media and art installation (*Artificial Cult* for audio and video tapes, neon signs and visual objects, 1985). Other contributors include Augustyn, who in Wrocław in 1992 mounted a twenty-four-hour sound installation, *SPHAE.RA*, the third of his *Cyclic Pieces*, in which each hour was characterised by different combinations of live performance and taped material.

Arguably the most dedicated contributor to these several genres has been Krzysztof Knittel (b. 1947). Since establishing the improvisation group KEW in the early 1970s, with Sikora and Wojciech Michniewski (b. 1947), he has co-founded several live electronic and intuitive music groups, notably Independent Electroacoustic Music Studio (1982–4), which contributed to underground musical activities during martial law, Freight Train (1986) and the CH&K Studio (1989) with Marek Chołoniewski (b. 1953). As a trained sound engineer and computer programmer, Knittel assigns a significant role to electronic technology in his extensive music-theatre and installation repertoire, which ranges in scope from *Glückpavillon for Cathy* for tuba and tape (1979) to a laser installation, *The Legs* (*Nogi*, 1993), in which mirrors, optical sensors and sine-wave generators are activated by the interrupting action of the perambulating audience. His most unusual venture has been the so-called 'double opera', *HeartPiece* (1999), an hour-long sequence of scenes based upon a surreal short play by Heiner Müller. It unfolds in an improvised sequence based upon music that has been composed separately and without consultation by Knittel and the American composer John King. A third 'unknown' dimension in the premiere at the 1999 'Warsaw Autumn' was the improvised input of the set designer – the performance artist Krzysztof Zarębski – and his team.

The improvised, multi-media events which have been single-mindedly created by Knittel and others have too often been regarded, like their counterparts in other countries, as being on the periphery of contemporary music. It might alternatively be argued, at a time when conservatism and commercialism are dominant, that such experimentation is vital and that comparable work in other art forms is capable of arousing considerable interest if not controversy. The inescapable fact is that most of those who are active in this field are no longer 'young' composers and there are few signs that Polish musicians in their twenties and thirties want to get involved in something which seems like a throwback to the 1960s and 1970s.

There is, however, a great deal of interest in the more closely defined world of modern music technology, both on its own and in partnership with live performance. This is the one area in which the situation improved markedly in the 1990s. During the worst moments of the 1980s, Polish Radio's Experimental Studio had been starved of funds, even running out of blank tapes, and gradually high-quality centres developed in the music academies, notably in Warsaw and Kraków, as well as in a few private studios. Some composers have studied music technology abroad; Krupowicz, for example, worked at CCRMA in Stanford (1984–9) and later at Glasgow University. With the increased availability of computers in Poland in the 1990s, composers in this field have been able to regain the initiative, producing a new wave of electronic music as significant in its way as the pioneering work begun in the late 1950s (Kotoński, now in his late seventies, has continued to contribute regularly to the genre).

Among Szymański's few tape pieces is ... *under the plane tree* ... (1980), which, following on from Krauze's *Idyll*, gently mocks its opening bird-song soundscape and effectively deconstructs the bucolic aesthetic of Karłowicz's song (1897) of the same name. One of the most striking electronic works of the early 1980s was by Andrzej Bieżan (1945–83). *Isn't It?* (1983) is also one of a number of tape pieces to resonate with the trauma of martial law: while Bieżan includes gunshots from the Gdańsk shipyards in his composition, Sikora, living in France, was able to make direct reference to one fatality in the title of *Janek Wiśniewski, December, Poland* (1982). A short while later, Krupowicz made a veiled reference to Solidarity in *Music for S* (1982–4) by using the vowel sounds of the trade union's name towards the end. *Music for S*, like Knittel's *Norcet* (1980), belongs to the group of early computer-generated pieces that laid the groundwork for later developments.

In addition to the many composers who have contributed periodically to the impressive corpus of Polish electronic music (often created in foreign studios), there are several who have developed specialist expertise in the manipulation of computer programmes, digital synthesis, the interface between electronic and live sound sources, and the use of audio-visual technology. These include Magdalena Długosz (b. 1954) and Chołoniewski, who both work at the studios of the Kraków Music Academy, and Ryszard Szeremeta (b. 1952), who was Patkowski's successor as head of Polish Radio's Experimental Studio in Warsaw from 1985 to 1999. Długosz is a 'classic' composer in the sense that her primary focus is on the purely musical relationship between the creative idea and the technical means of production. In her works for tape, such as *Pulsations* (1983) and *Lenyon* (1995), and even more dramatically in the works that incorporate live performance, such as *Mictlan* II with accordion (1988) and *TaBar* for 'electronically transformed double bass and computer sound layer' (2000), composed in close collaboration with Wielecki, the clarity of her thought and the dynamic structural profiles are unusually persuasive.

Szeremeta, in contrast, has long been fascinated by the possibilities of synthesising his compositional career with his activities as a jazz vocal performer. The tape pieces *Points* I and II (1981) explore what he has called a 'borderline' language, whose crossover aesthetic was developed further in *Amphora* for saxophone and tape (1984) and *Agent Orange* (1986), his first essay in digital synthesis. Later works, including *Trickstar* for saxophone, piano, percussion and synthesizer (1989) and *Belief* for jazz vocal quartet and tape (1999), retain many jazz impulses but embrace a more lyrical expressiveness. Chołoniewski is one of the most distinguished explorers of audio-visual technology, using algorithmic computational processes. In *WYSYG* (What You See You Get) for light and computer (1989), changes of light from a 'luminous baton' as it falls upon the face of the performer alter a pre-programmed score stored in the computer's memory. Chołoniewski's more recent explorations into the interplay of live performance and electronics include *Passage* for an octet of woodwind and string instruments (2001):

> The first two movements [Introduction, Theatre of Gestures] are 'performance', in which the musicians through paratheatrical action steer the musical computer system creating a 'live' multi-layered sound structure. Each of the musicians performs an independent part. The computer system simultaneously creates the score, which forms the basic notational material for the performance of movements III and IV of the work [Score, Film] . . . Additionally, the moving of the instruments and the change of the musicians' positions in movement III influences the processing of the acoustic sounds of the instruments. Finally, movement IV assumes the form of an audio-visual spectacle, in which a film projection (computer animation), guided by the musicians and their gestures, combines with the interactive transformations of the instrumental sounds . . . The composition is multiversional. The material 'composes by itself' in a somewhat different way each time the composition is performed. The musicians thus perform movements III and IV extemporaneously, 'a vistà'.[17]

Chołoniewski is bringing Polish instrumental theatre up to date while preserving the delicate thread of creative risk that is the essence of the extemporiser's art. His work, as a symbol of one of the most forward-looking areas of contemporary Polish music, exudes a quiet and justifiable confidence.

PART V

Postscript

16 After Lutosławski

In more ways than one, Lutosławski's death in February 1994 marked the end of an era. He symbolised for many the travails and triumphs of Polish music since the death of Szymanowski fifty-seven years earlier. He had lived through Nazi occupation, Stalinist socialist realism, the vibrancy of the early years of the 'Warsaw Autumn', the increasing international profile of Polish music, the periodic waves of political insurgency and repression, the rise and fall of Solidarity, and, finally, the establishment of a truly democratic state. A new cultural future beckoned and it fell to new, younger figures to secure it. And, as has already been implied, the compositional initiative has largely passed to those born after the war.

With the melting away of regular state subsidies, all institutions have struggled financially – including PWM (still managing to maintain a high profile and beating off takeover bids from venture capitalists) and Polish Radio 2, which faces commercial competition. The shift from state monopoly to private enterprise is nowhere more apparent than in the recording industry, which has capitalised on CD technology to expand enormously the recorded repertoire of Polish music. This has been only partly beneficial to contemporary music, the dissemination of which is as likely to take place via privately burned CD-Rs as by the annual chronicle of the 'Warsaw Autumn'.

Since the dark days of the early 1980s (the 1982 festival was cancelled during the first year of martial law), the finances of the 'Warsaw Autumn' have seemed especially precarious. And it took some time to regain its momentum. But particularly under the guidance of two composers as Festival Directors – Knittel (1995–8) and Wielecki (1998–) – it has discovered a new energy and innovative spirit. In support, the Repertoire Committee continues to adhere to its original pluralist and modernist principles, constantly bringing forward music that otherwise would not be heard in Poland. The festival's impressive tally of foreign works since it began is headed by Xenakis, followed by Stockhausen, Cage, Ligeti, Messiaen and Kagel. Carter was highlighted in 1986 and the 1998 festival had a Nordic theme, although it is symptomatic of the continuing backlog of post-war masterworks that the long-planned Polish premiere of Stockhausen's *Gruppen* took place only in 2000. The festival's selection of Polish compositions reflects the changing circumstances of the past decade, with fewer big names and fewer orchestral concerts, with, as always, insufficient time and space to accommodate all the composers who aspire to be included in its programmes.

A reconfiguration of Polish musical life has also been signalled by regional initiatives, such as the development of new festivals and ensembles, giving additional opportunities for the performance of new music. By and large, these activities remain well co-ordinated nationally, but the centuries-old rivalry between Kraków and Warsaw has led to interesting recent developments. These tend to have focussed on Penderecki, who has been closely involved in boosting the musical profile of his home city. One result has been that some of Kraków's new festivals have clashed directly with the 'Warsaw Autumn' and have been more successful at garnering commercial and state sponsorship. Matters have not been improved by an extraordinarily prolonged public argument involving composers, performers and administrators following the European premiere of Penderecki's Piano Concerto at the 2002 'Warsaw Autumn'. Even though its reception was decidedly mixed, the real polarisation of opinion was caused by a review in the main Polish broadsheet daily newspaper provocatively headlined 'Socialist-Realist Penderecki'.[1] Whatever the long-term outcome of this debate, the controversy may be indicative of a willingness to critique contemporary Polish music and its contexts more openly than has sometimes been the case.

Such matters may be incidental to the future of Polish music, particularly as viewed from the perspective of composers in the early stages of their careers. While it is too early to predict whether any of those in their twenties or thirties will still be the subject of praise or criticism in a decade's time (when the centenary of Lutosławski's birth will no doubt be cause for major celebration), many of them have already begun to make their mark. Some of the most accomplished work has emerged from electronic studios, including that by three graduates of the Kraków Academy of Music: Mateusz Bień (b. 1968), Bartłomiej Gliniak (b. 1973) and Magdalena Klapper (b. 1973). At the other end of the stylistic spectrum is Paweł Łukaszewski (b. 1968), best known for his resolutely anti-modernist sacred choral music. Of those with mixed portfolios, three (all with an element of music technology) are particularly worth highlighting. Michał Talma-Sutt (b. 1969), who has studied at the Łódź Music Academy, IRCAM and at Stuttgart, has specialised since the mid-1990s in electronic music (live and on tape) and in multimedia projects. His works for instrument and computer manipulation, such as *Avalon's Gate* for flute (1997) and *Cellotronicum* for cello (2002), are impressive additions to this developing genre. Marzena Komsta (b. 1970), a graduate of the Gdańsk and Warsaw Music Academies, has since studied in Lyons and at IRCAM. Her music is characterised by its pursuit of tension and relaxation; two works from 1993, the tape miniature *Oqivian* and the orchestral *Agmen*, show propulsive energy and instrumental flair.

Paweł Mykietyn, who studied with Kotoński in Warsaw and then with Bargielski in Vienna, has the highest profile of his generation in Poland. Initially, he pursued a dual career as composer and clarinettist; in 1991 he founded the ensemble Nonstrom, the direct successor to Music Workshop, and he has, like Krauze before him, encouraged new repertoire for this unusual complement of instruments, including his own composition, *At Radek's* (*U Radka*, 1993). Mykietyn's ability to bring fresh insights to found materials, be they Messiaen or jazz, Bach or Lutosławski, gives his instinct for humour, parody and deconstruction an extra edge. The Piano Concerto (1997) manages to be both carefree and artful in its intercutting of disparate materials, especially in the finale's compendium of quotes and allusions (Franck's Symphonic Variations among them). In contrast, *Shakespeare's Sonnets* for male soprano and piano (2000) and the Harpsichord Concerto (2002) have developed a more acid, sinewy language that is less reliant on tonal underpinning and easy-going intertextuality. Furthermore, Mykietyn seems intent on exploiting disjunctions between compositional elements as if to cancel out any suggestion of simple reliance on past symbols, traditions and values. Like many of his contemporaries, he displays a challenging combination of loyalty to his heritage and the determination to move beyond it when its relevance is questionable. Szymanowski and Lutosławski would have understood.

Appendix 1 Cultural events in Poland, 1953–6

1953	Sept.	The Polish Primate, Cardinal Stefan Wyszyński, is put under house arrest and is not released until October 1956
1954	July	Teatr Polski visits Paris; in October 1954, Gerard Philippe and Theatre National Populaire reciprocate with a visit to Warsaw
1954	July	Panufnik defects to England via Switzerland
1955	June	Poland rejoins UNESCO, having left the organisation in 1949
1955	Aug.	The arrival of 30,000 young people in Warsaw from over 100 countries for the Fifth World Festival of Youth and Students for Peace and Friendship
1955	Aug.	The publication in *Nowa Kultura* of 'Poem for Adults' ('Poemat dla dorosłych'), by the propagandist poet, Adam Ważyk, in which the author turns on the Party by lambasting the reality of life in contemporary Poland
1955	Sept.	The previously loyal propagandist outlet of the Polish Youth Union, the weekly *Directly* (*Po Prostu*), becomes an organ for change among students and young intellectuals
1955	Nov.	The first post-war performance, in Warsaw, of Mickiewicz's play *Forefathers' Eve* (*Dziady*) to mark centenary of his death (270 performances follow)
1956	Jan.	The first post-war performance, in Łódź, of Wyspiański's drama, *November Night* (*Noc listopadowa*)
1956	Feb.	The Blue (Błękitny) Jazz ensemble performs at the Palace of Culture and Science in Warsaw, the first official post-Stalin jazz concert
1956	April	Sokorski is replaced as Minister of Culture and becomes chair of the Committee for Radio Affairs
1956	April	Polish Television inaugurated with $13\frac{1}{2}$ hours' broadcasting each week
1956	May	Inauguration of Cricot II theatre in Kraków by the experimental writer and director, Tadeusz Kantor
1956	Aug.	Over one and a half million people make a pilgrimage to the shrine of the Black Madonna in Częstochowa in south-central Poland to honour the 300th anniversary of her crowning as Queen of Poland because she saved the country from being overrun by the Swedish invasion of 1656

Appendix 2 'Warsaw Autumn' repertoire, 10–21 October 1956

**World premiere   *Polish premiere

Non-Polish

Apostel	1949	*Variations on a Theme by Joseph Haydn**
Auric	1938	Overture*
Barraud	1942	*Offrande à une ombre**
Bartók	1931	44 Duets for two violins (37, 28, 44, 33, 39, 29, 41)
	1934	String Quartet no. 5*
	1943	Concerto for Orchestra
Berg	1926	*Lyric Suite**
Berger, T.	1955	*La parola**
Brahms	1885	Symphony no. 4
Britten	1949	*Spring Symphony**
Capdevielle	1943	Overture to Bergerac's *Le pédant joue**
Dutilleux	1951	Symphony no. 1*
Enescu	1903	Suite no. 1
Honegger	1920	Sonatine for two violins
	1923	*Pacific 231*
	1941	Symphony no. 2, 'Symphonie pour cordes'
	1946	Symphony no. 3, 'Symphonie liturgique'
Janáček	1926	Sinfonietta
Jolivet	1953	Symphony no. 1*
Khachaturian	1944	Symphony no. 2, 'Symphony with a Bell'
Lajtha	1950	String Quartet no. 7*
Martinet	1946	Variations for String Quartet*
Martinon	1946	String Quartet no. 1*
Martinů	1930	Sonatina for two violins and piano
	1944	Symphony no. 3*
Messiaen	1930	*Les offrandes oubliées*
Miaskovsky	1950	Symphony no. 27*
Milhaud	1934	*Concertino de printemps**
Novak, J.	1955	Concerto for Two Pianos and Orchestra*
Prokofiev	1936	*Romeo and Juliet* (Suite no. 2)
Ravel	1926	*Chansons madécasses*
Rogalski	1950	*Three Rumanian Dances**
Schoenberg	1942	Piano Concerto*

Shostakovich	1948	Violin Concerto no. 1*
	1953	Symphony no. 10
Strauss, R.	1895	*Till Eulenspiegels lustige Streiche*
Stravinsky	1908	*Fireworks*
	1909	*The Firebird* (suite)
	1911	*Petrushka* (suite)
	1913	*The Rite of Spring*
	1937	*Jeu de cartes*
	1945	*Ebony Concerto**
Tchaikovsky	1888	Symphony no. 5
Zafred	1950	Symphony no. 4, 'In onore della resistenza'*

Polish

Bacewicz	1943	Overture
	1948	Concerto for String Orchestra
	1951	String Quartet no. 4
Baird	1951	*Colas Breugnon*
	1956	*Cassazione per orchestra***
Dobrowolski	1955	Symphony no. 1
Kilar	1953	*Little Overture*
Kisielewski	1949	Concerto for Chamber Orchestra
Lutosławski	1951	*Little Suite*
	1954	Concerto for Orchestra
Malawski	1937	Variations
	1955	Symphony no. 2, 'Dramatic'
Mycielski	1951	Symphony no. 1, 'Polish'
Perkowski	1954	*Warsaw Overture*
Serocki	1956	Sinfonietta
Sikorski, K.	1953	Symphony no. 3, 'In the Form of a Concerto Grosso'
Skrowaczewski	1950	Symphony for Strings
	1952	*Night Music* (*Muzyka noca*)
Spisak	1944	Bassoon Concerto
	1945	Suite for String Orchestra
Szabelski	1951	Symphony no. 3
	1954	Concerto Grosso
Szałowski	1936	Overture for Strings
Szeligowski	1934	*The Angels Sang Sweetly* (*Angeli słodko śpiewali*)
	1937	*Epitaph in memoriam Karol Szymanowski*
	1938	*Sailor's Song* (*Pieśń żeglarza*)
Szymanowski	1916	Symphony no. 3, 'Song of the Night'
	1926	Stabat Mater
	1929	*Six Kurpian Songs* (*Sześć pieśni kurpiowskie*)
Turski	1951	Violin Concerto

Wiechowicz	1922	*From the Other Side of the River* (*Z tamtej strony rzeki*)
	1943	*The Little Eyes Want* (*Pragna oczki*)
	1947	*Harvest Cantata* (*Kantata zniwna*)
Wisłocki	1951	Piano Concerto
Woytowicz	1945	Symphony no. 2, 'Warsaw'
	1953	String Quartet no. 2

Appendix 3 'Warsaw Autumn' repertoire, 1958–61

** World premiere   * Polish premiere

1958 (27 September – 5 October)

Non-Polish

Bartók	1927	*The Miraculous Mandarin* (suite)*
	1928	String Quartet no. 4
Berg	1910	Four Songs, op. 2 (nos. 2, 3 and 4)
	1915	Three Orchestral Pieces*
	1935	Violin Concerto
Berio	1957	*Perspectives* for tape*
Bozza		Scherzo for piano*
Britten	1945	*Peter Grimes** (staged)
Burkhard	1925	*Frage* (nos. 1, 2 and 8)
	1943	*Neun Lieder*, op. 70 (nos. 2 and 8)
Cage	1951	*Music of Changes**
Cilenšek		Symphony no. 4 for strings*
Dessau	1952	*Die Erziehung der Hirse**
Eimert	1956	Five Pieces for tape (nos. 4 and 5)*
Eisler	1940	Septet no. 1*
Françaix	1946	*Cinq poèmes**
Gausec		*Four Pieces* for wind instruments*
Hindemith	1923	*Kleine Kammermusik*, op. 24/2*
	1936	Flute Sonata
Honegger	1941	*Petit cours de morale**
	1945	*Quatre chansons pour voix grave**
Ibert	1930	*Trois pièces brèves**
	1935	*Cinq pièces en trio**
Ivanovs	1949	Symphony no. 6, 'Latgales'
Kabeláč		*Improvisation* for flute*
Liebermann	1945	*Chinesische Liebeslieder**
Ligeti	1958	*Artikulation* for tape*
Maderna	1958	*Continuo* for tape*
Martin	1944	*Sechs Monologe aus Jedermann**
Milhaud	1939	*La Cheminée du Roi René**

Nilsson		*Quantitäten* for piano*
Ponce	1943	Violin Concerto*
Poulenc	1926	Trio for oboe, bassoon and piano
		Three Improvisations for piano
Pousseur	1957	*Scambi* for tape*
Prokofiev	1932	Piano Concerto no. 5*
	1935	Violin Concerto no. 2
	1936	*Romeo and Juliet* (Suite no. 2)
Ravel	1912	*Daphnis et Chloé* (staged)
Schoenberg	1933	Three Songs, op. 48 (nos. 2 and 3)
	1947	*A Survivor from Warsaw*￼*
	1950	*Moderner Psalm*￼*
Schuman	1939	String Quartet no. 3*
Searle	1957	Suite for clarinet and piano*
Shostakovich	1957	Symphony no. 11, '1905'*
Stockhausen	1956	*Klavierstück* XI*
	1956	*Gesang der Jünglinge* for tape*
Taktakishvili	1951	Piano Concerto no. 1*
Webern	1909	Five Pieces for string quartet, op. 5*
	1913	Five Pieces for orchestra, op. 10*
	1935	*Das Augenlicht*
Wolff	1955	*For Piano with Preparations***

Polish

Bacewicz	1956	Ten Concert Studies
	1957	Variations for Orchestra**
Baird	1957	String Quartet
	1958	*Four Essays***
Górecki	1958	*Epitaph***
Kotoński	1958	*Chamber Music***
Lutosławski	1958	*Funeral Music*
Malawski	1956	*Hungaria*
Palester	1952	Symphony no. 4*
Perkowski	1955	Nocturne
Serocki	1956	*Heart of the Night*
	1958	*Musica concertante**
Sikorski, K.	1957	Flute Concerto
Spisak	1957	*Concerto giocoso**
Szabelski	1938	Study
Szeligowski	1954	*Krakatuk* (staged)
Turski	1955	*Little Overture*

1959 (12–20 September)

Non-Polish

Amy	1958	*Mouvements pour 17 instruments solistes**
Bartók	1943	Concerto for Orchestra
Berio	1958	*Sequenza* I for flute*
Boulez	1946	Flute Sonatine*
	1948	Piano Sonata no. 2*
	1949	*Livre pour quatuor* (Ia and Ib)*
Britten	1945	Passacaglia from *Peter Grimes*
Bruns		*New Odyssey* (staged)
Cincadze		String Quartet no. 2*
Dallapiccola	1954	*Piccola musica notturna**
Dessau	1928	*Lustige Variationen**
Ferrari		*Visage* V for tape**
Finke	1946	Horn Sonata*
Geissler		*Heitere Suite**
Gerster	1928	*Heitere Musik**
Henze	1947	Flute Sonatine*
Hindemith	1942	Sonata for two pianos
	1951	Symphony, 'Die Harmonie der Welt'*
Honegger	1917	String Quartet no. 1*
Jolivet	1949	Concerto for Flute and Strings*
Kochan		Divertimento for wind trio*
Mâche	1959	*Prélude* for tape*
Maros	1959	*Ricercare (in memoriam 1918)**
Martin	1951	Violin Concerto*
Martinů	1937	*Quatre madrigaux**
Messiaen	1951	*Le merle noir**
Miaskovsky	1949	String Quartet no. 13
Nono	1951	Composizione no. 1*
Philippot		*Ambiance* I for tape*
Pousseur	1957	Exercices pour piano: Impromptu et Variations II*
Rawsthorne	1937	Theme and Variations for two violins
Regamey	1956	*Cinq Études pour soprano et orchestre**
Roussel	1932	String Quartet*
Schaeffer, P.	1949	*Variations sur une flûte mexicaine* for tape*
	1959	*Études aux objets* for tape*
Schaeffer, P. &	1950	*Bidule en ut* for tape*
Henry	1950	*Symphonie pour un homme seul* for tape*
Schoenberg	1936	String Quartet no. 4*

Shostakovich	1933	Piano Concerto no. 1
	1956	String Quartet no. 6
Silvestri		Prelude and Fugue*
Stravinsky	1945	*Symphony in Three Movements**
Suchoň	1941	*Krútňava* (staged)
Szokolay	1957	Violin Concerto*
Varèse	1936	Density 21.5*
Webern	1909	Six Pieces for orchestra, op. 6*
	1928	Symphony*
Xenakis	1958	*Diamorphoses* for tape*

Polish

Bacewicz	1958	*Music for Strings, Trumpets and Percussion***
Baird	1959	*Espressioni varianti***
Górecki	1959	Symphony no. 1, '1959'***
Krenz	1949	Symphony no. 1
	1958	*Music for Clarinet Solo***
Malawski	1949	Overture
Penderecki	1959	*Strophes*
Spisak	1947	Sonatina for oboe, clarinet and bassoon
	1956	Symphonie concertante no. 2
	1958	Suite for two violins
Szabelski	1936	Toccata
	1959	*Improvisations***
Szalonek	1960	*Confessions* (*Wyznania*)**
Szałowski	1936	Wind Trio
Szymanowski	1916	Symphony no. 3, 'Song of the Night'
	1932	Symphony no. 4, 'Sinfonia concertante'

1960 (17–25 September)

Non-Polish

Badings	1959	*Electromagnetic Sound Figures* for tape*
Bartók	1924	*The Miraculous Mandarin* (staged)
	1931	Piano Concerto no. 2
	1936	*Music for Strings, Percussion and Celesta*
Bennett	1960	*This Worldes Joie**
Berio	1958	*Thema (Omaggio a Joyce)* for tape*
Bořkovec	1931	Piano Concerto*
Boulez	1957	*Improvisation sur Mallarmé* I*
Cage	1958	*Fontana Mix* for tape*

Cardew	1957	*Why Cannot The Ear Be Closed To Its Own Destruction?**
Carter	1951	String Quartet no. 1*
Dallapiccola	1941	*Canti di prigionia**
Evangelisti	1957	*Incontri de fasce sonore* for tape*
Goehr		*Narration**
Hindemith	1922	*Kammermusik no. 1*, op. 24/1*
Hopkins	1948	*Carillon**
Karajev	1957	*In the Path of Thunder* (staged)
Křenek	1957	*Pentagram**
Mamiya		*Enburi**
Martinet	1952	*Trois textes du XVIème siècle**
Martinu	1953	Symphony no. 6, 'Fantasies symphoniques'*
Maw		*Six Chinese Songs* (no. 2)
Mayuzumi	1960	*Mandala Symphony**
Messiaen	1928	*Le banquet céleste*
	1930	*Diptyque*
	1939	*Les corps glorieux* (no. 4)
	1956	*Oiseaux exotiques**
Milhaud	1923	*La création du monde*
	1946	String Quartet no. 13
Nilsson	1961	*Mädchentotenlieder***
Petrassi	1958	*Serenata**
Pijper	1929	Wind Quintet*
Schaeffer, P.	1959	*Étude aux objets* for tape
Schoenberg	1909	Five Orchestral Pieces, op. 16
	1910?	*Drei kleine Stücke für Kammerorchester**
	1924	Wind Quintet
Shostakovich	1959	Cello Concerto no. 1*
Sokola	1952	*Variations on a Theme by Vítězslava Kaprálová**
Stockhausen	1956	*Zeitmasze**
Stravinsky	1927	*Oedipus rex*
	1954	*In memoriam Dylan Thomas**
Toyama		*Berceuse Itsugi**
		Japanese Rhapsody*
Varèse	1923	*Octandre**
Webern	1918	Four Songs, op. 13
	1924	Five Canons, op. 16*
	1934	Three Songs, op. 23*
	1934	*Concerto for Nine Instruments**
Yashiro		Violin Concerto*
Zumbach		*Étude* for tape*

plus a recital of Soviet songs (Miaskovsky, Kotchurov, Frid, Dolukhanian, Prokofiev)

Polish

Bacewicz	1959	*The Adventure of King Arthur*
	1960	String Quartet no. 6**
Baird	1956	Divertimento
	1960	*Exhortation (Egzorta)***
Górecki	1960	*Scontri***
Kotoński	1959	*Study on One Cymbal Stroke*
	1959	*Musique en relief**
Lutosławski	1957	Five Songs
Maciejewski	1959	Requiem**
Malawski	1947	Toccata
Penderecki	1960	*Dimensions of Time and Silence***
Schaeffer, B.	1958	*Tertium datur***
Serocki	1957	*Eyes of the Air*
	1959	*Episodes***
Szabelski	1958	*Sonnets*
Szeligowski	1960	*Psalm CXVI – Laudate Dominum omnes gentes***
Szymanowski	1931	*Mountain Robbers* (staged)
Tansman	1954	Concerto for Orchestra*
Wiechowicz	1960	Passacaglia and Fugue**
Wiszniewski	1959	*Neffru*

1961 (16–24 September)

Non-Polish

Bartók	1911	*Bluebeard's Castle* (concert performance)
	1937	*Sonata for Two Pianos and Percussion*
Berg	1908	*Sieben frühe Lieder* (nos. 1, 5 and 3)
	1934	*Lulu* (suite)
Berio	1956	String Quartet*
	1958	*Thema (Omaggio a Joyce)* for voice and tape
Boulez	1961	*Structures* II (Chapitre I)*
Britten	1940	*Seven Sonnets of Michelangelo**
	1958	*Six Hölderlin Fragments*
Bussotti	1961	*Torso**
Cage	1958	*Fontana Mix* for tape with *Aria* for voice*
Castiglioni	1960	*Gymel**
Čerha	1957	*Relazioni fragili**
Debussy	1915	*En blanc et noir*
Evangelisti	1958	*Proporzioni**
Fribec	1961	*Mouvements cosmiques***
Goleminov	1942	*Variations on a Theme of Dobri Khristov**

Janáček	1928	String Quartet no. 2, 'Intimate Letters'
Kagel	1959	*Transición* II for piano, percussion and tape*
Kayn	1960	*Vectors* I
Klusák		*Studies According to Kafka**
Liang		*Pagoda Lei Fung* (staged)
Lidholm		*Motto**
	1956	*Canto* LXXXI*
Macchi	1960	*Composizione* III*
Maderna	1960	*Dimensioni* II for voice and tape*
Martinů	1938	String Quartet no. 5*
Matsudaira		Piece for flute*
Nono	1956	*Il canto sospeso**
Petrassi	1960	Flute Concerto*
Poulenc	1937	*Tel jour, telle nuit**
Prokofiev	1941	String Quartet no. 2
Raichev	1958	Symphony no. 2, 'The New Prometheus'*
Ravel	1913	*Trois poèmes de Stéphane Mallarmé*
Schoenberg	1912	*Pierrot lunaire*
	1930	*Begleitungsmusik zu einer Lichtspielszene**
Shostakovich	1960	String Quartet no. 7*
	1960	String Quartet no. 8*
Stainov		*Symphonic Scherzo**
Stockhausen	1959	*Zyklus**
Stravinsky	1913	*Three Japanese Lyrics*
	1914	Three Pieces for string quartet
Tippett	1943	*Boyhood's End**
Tormis	1959	Overture no. 2*
Vladigerov	1942	*Improvisation and Toccata**
Varèse	1921	*Offrandes**
	1923	*Hyperprism**
	1923	*Octandre* [cf. 1960]
	1925	*Intégrales**
Webern	1938	String Quartet

Polish

Bacewicz	1961	*Pensieri notturni*
Baird	1961	*Love Poems***
Bloch	1959	*Espressioni*
Dobrowolski	1959	Eight Studies
Górecki	1959	*Three Diagrams***
Haubenstock-Ramati	1957	*Interpolation-Mobile* for flute and tape*
Kilar	1960	*Herbsttag***

Koszewski	1960	*Muzyka fa-re-mi-do-si***
Kotoński	1960	*Concerto per quattro**
	1960	Trio for flute, guitar and percussion
Łuciuk	1960	*Floral Dream (Sen kwietny)**
Lutosławski	1961	*Venetian Games* (rev. vers.)**
Paciorkiewicz	1961	*The Weight of the Earth (Ciężar ziemi)***
Penderecki	1960	*Threnody to the Victims of Hiroshima***
Rudziński, W.	1958	*Musique concertante***
Schaeffer, B.	1961	*Codes***
Spisak	1957	*Allegro de Voiron**
Szabelski	1961	*Verses***
Szymanowski	1924	*King Roger* (concert performance)
	1927	String Quartet no. 2
Turski	1947	*Sinfonia da camera*
Wiechowicz	1961	*Letter to Marc Chagall*

Appendix 4 Selected Polish chronology (1966–90)

1966 Church and State are at loggerheads and celebrate the Polish Millennium separately, mainly because the State refuses to acknowledge the date as the anniversary of the founding of Christianity in the country. Cardinal Wyszyński is denied a visa to visit Rome and Pope Paul VI is not allowed to come to Poland.

   3 May: the Church marks the Millennium at the shrine of the Black Madonna in Częstochowa. A pontifical mass is celebrated by the then metropolitan bishop of Kraków, Karol Wojtyła. The papal throne is empty apart from a framed photograph of the Pope.

1967 6–12 September: French President Charles de Gaulle visits Poland.

1968 30 January: Warsaw National Theatre production of Mickiewicz's *Forefathers' Eve* (*Dziady*), which had opened on 25 November 1967, is banned amid anti-Soviet protests. The controversy leads to a purge of intellectuals, staff and students ('March Events') and to a politically engineered period of renewed anti-Zionism in the Party and the country. In the coming months, over 60% of the remaining post-war Jewish population emigrate.

   20 August: Poland joins the USSR and other socialist countries in invading Czechoslovakia to crush Alexander Dubček's liberalising 'Prague Spring'.

1970 7 December: West German Chancellor Willy Brandt signs a treaty recognising Poland's Western border (the Oder–Neisse line) and pays homage to the Jewish victims of Nazi oppression at the Ghetto Memorial in Warsaw.

   13 December: a sudden increase in the price of basic foodstuffs leads to riots and many deaths in the Baltic ports (Gdańsk, Gdynia and Szczecin). Party leader Władysław Gomułka is replaced by Edward Gierek, who rescinds the price rises. During the 1970s, Gierek funds higher living standards in Poland by taking out enormous credit loans in the West.

1973 A monument to Lenin is unveiled in Nowa Huta, near Kraków.

1974 Cardinal Wyszyński demands 'fidelity to Polish national culture as the country's highest value after God'.

1976   24 June: price rises of up to 100% on food are immediately withdrawn
        after nationwide strikes and riots. Hundreds of protesters are jailed
        without due legal process.

        September: formation of the openly active KOR (Workers' Defence
        Committee), including intellectuals, writers and workers.

1977   May: consecration of first church to be built in Nowa Huta, over twenty
        years since the town and its foundry were created.

1978   16 October: Cardinal Karol Wojtyła from Kraków is elected Pope, taking
        the name John Paul II.

1979   2–10 June: first visit of Pope John Paul II to Poland.

        19 July: Gierek unveils monument to former Party leader, Bolesław Bierut,
        in Lublin.

1980   1 July: unannounced price rises in food, resulting in a wave of strikes.

        31 August: Lech Wałęsa, who leads the strike at the Lenin shipyard in
        Gdańsk, compels the government to sign an agreement permitting the
        establishment of an independent trade union. 'Solidarity' (*Solidarność*) is
        born and soon over 10 million citizens, nearly one third of the population,
        become members of the union and its partner, Rural Solidarity (including
        a million members of the Party). Gierek is replaced as Party leader by
        Stanisław Kania, who is succeeded by General Wojciech Jaruzelski in
        September 1981.

        9 October: Polish emigré writer Czesław Miłosz awarded the Nobel Prize
        for Literature.

        16 December: monument to shipyard workers killed in December 1970 is
        unveiled in Gdańsk. Penderecki's specially commissioned *Lacrimosa* is
        relayed at the ceremony.

1981   19 March: police brutality against Solidarity members in northern town of
        Bydgoszcz.

        28 May: Cardinal Wyszyński dies.

        28 June: monument to those killed in the 'Bread' riots in Poznań in June
        1956 is unveiled. The monument bears other significant dates: 1968, 1970,
        1976 and 1980 (1981 was added later).

        Widespread shortages and the growing militancy of Solidarity threaten
        the position of the Party.

        11–12 December: Lutosławski addresses the opening session of a Congress
        of Polish Culture in Warsaw. Its programme is cut short by the events of
        13 December.

13 December: eleven years to the day after the Baltic riots, the new Party First Secretary, General Wojciech Jaruzelski, declares a 'State of War' (*stan wojenny*). All communications are cut, and Solidarity leaders and other activists, including Wałęsa, are imprisoned. In the following years, much of the more radical Polish culture goes underground and the Church becomes a home for performances of subversive plays, poetry and music.

1982   The 'Warsaw Autumn' festival is cancelled for the first and only time.

8 October: Solidarity is officially outlawed.

31 December: martial law is 'suspended' though many of its provisions become enshrined in law until the late 1980s.

1983   16–23 June: the Pope pays a second visit to Poland.

Lech Wałęsa is awarded the Nobel Peace Prize but is unable to receive it in person.

Lutosławski is awarded the Solidarity Prize for his Third Symphony.

1984   19–20 October: Father Jerzy Popiełuszko, who had conducted a monthly 'Mass for the Fatherland' at his church in North Warsaw since October 1981, is murdered by the security forces. His grave at the church becomes a place of pilgrimage.

1985   10 March: Mikhail Gorbachev becomes Party Secretary in the USSR and promotes the policies of 'openness' (*glasnost*) and 'reconstruction' (*perestroĭka*).

1987   8–14 June: the Pope's third visit to Poland.

1988   1 January: jamming of Radio Free Europe is stopped.

Lutosławski conducts his Third Symphony and Piano Concerto at the 'Warsaw Autumn', thus ending his boycott on public appearances in Poland since the imposition of martial law in 1981.

1989   February–April: 'Round Table' political negotiations take place involving representatives from Solidarity, the Church and the Party. Solidarity is re-legalised and wins a stunning victory in the ensuing parliamentary elections in June. The crown on the head of the White Eagle, the symbol of Poland, is restored after over forty years of communist rule.

1990   September: Panufnik returns to Poland for the first and only time since he left in 1954. Eleven of his works are performed at the 'Warsaw Autumn'.

9 December: Wałęsa is elected President of Poland.

Notes

1 Szymanowski and his legacy

1. A group photograph, including Szymanowski and Lutosławski, taken on 4 May 1935 in Riga, surfaced recently and was reproduced in *Ruch Muzyczny* 40/7 (7 Apr. 1996), p. 26.
2. Polish Radio interview (1981), reprinted in Elżbieta Markowska and Michał Kubicki (eds.), *Szymanowski and the Europe of His Time* (Warsaw: Polish Radio, 1997), p. 108.
3. Karol Szymanowski, letter to Jan Smeterlin (Zakopane, 14 Sept. 1934), translated by and included in B. M. Maciejewski and Felix Aprahamian (eds.), *Karol Szymanowski and Jan Smeterlin: Correspondence and Essays* (London: Allegro Press, 1970), pp. 70–1.
4. Markowska and Kubicki (eds.), *Szymanowski*, p. 107.
5. Witold Szeliga [Piotr Rytel], *Warszawski Dziennik Narodowy* (9 May 1937), quoted in Roman Jasiński (ed.), *Koniec epoki: Muzyka w Warszawie (1927–1939)* (Warsaw: PIW, 1986), p. 424.
6. Karol Szymanowski, letter to Stefan Spiess (Tymoszówka, 14 Oct. 1913), in Teresa Chylińska (ed.), *Karol Szymanowski: Korespondencja, Tom 1 (1903–1919)* (Kraków: PWM, 1982), p. 394.
7. Andrzej Panufnik, in his autobiography *Composing Myself* (London: Methuen, 1987), pp. 42–3, conversely recollected that Szymanowski neglected his academic duties by concentrating on his own career.
8. Alistair Wightman (trans. and ed.), *Szymanowski on Music* (London: Toccata Press, 1999), p. 269.
9. Karol Szymanowski, 'On the Work of Wagner, Strauss and Schoenberg' (c.1925–6, unpublished in his lifetime), in Wightman (ed.), *Szymanowski on Music*, pp. 211–22.
10. Karol Szymanowski, 'Igor Stravinsky', in Wightman (ed.), *Szymanowski on Music*, pp. 223–7.
11. Karol Szymanowski, 'Maurice Ravel on the Occasion of his Fiftieth Birthday', in Wightman (ed.), *Szymanowski on Music*, pp. 237–40.
12. Karol Szymanowski, 'On the Musical Life of Paris', in Wightman (ed.), *Szymanowski on Music*, p. 235.
13. *Ibid.*, p. 234.
14. Karol Szymanowski, 'The Ethnic Question in Relation to Contemporary Music', in Wightman (ed.), *Szymanowski on Music*, p. 128.
15. Karol Szymanowski, 'Fryderyk Chopin' (1923), in Wightman (ed.), *Szymanowski on Music*, pp. 192–3, 195.

16. Much of this information has been gleaned from Jasiński (ed.), *Koniec epoki.*

17. Cf. the careers of Michał Kondracki (1902–84) who moved from Paris to New York after the Second World War, and of Michał Spisak (1914–65), whose brilliant Stravinsky-inspired neo-classical works – for example, the Concerto for Two Pianos (1942) and the Symphonie concertante no. 1 (1947) – deserve wider recognition.

18. Panufnik, *Composing Myself*, p. 72.

19. Quoted in Zofia Helman, *Roman Palester: Twórca i dzieło* (Kraków: Musica Iagellonica, 1999), p. 35.

20. Roman Palester, 'Kryzys modernizmu muzycznego' [The crisis of musical modernism], *Kwartalnik Muzyczny* 14–15 (1932), pp. 489–503; 'W obronie nowej muzyki' [In defence of new music], *Muzyka* 11/5 (1934), pp. 200–3.

21. Józef Koffler, 'Muzyka awangardowa z lotu ptaka' [A bird's eye view of avant-garde music], *Muzyka* 12/1–2 (1935), pp. 20–1.

22. Maciej Gołąb, *Józef Koffler* (Kraków: Musica Iagellonica, 1995), p. 81.

23. Leon Markiewicz, 'II Symfonia Bolesława Szabelskiego. Inspiracje – warsztat – stylistyka', *Górnośląski Almanach Muzyczny* 2 (Katowice: Śląsk, 1995), pp. 9–20.

2 The Second World War

1. Constantin Regamey, quoted in N. Loutan-Charbon, *Constantin Regamey: Compositeur* (Yverdon: Revue Musicale de Suisse Romande et les Editions de Thièle, 1978), p. 22.

2. Adam Zamoyski, *The Polish Way: A Thousand-Year History of the Poles and Their Culture* (London: John Murray, 1987), p. 360.

3. G. Michalski, 'New Music', in Tadeusz Ochlewski (ed.), *An Outline History of Polish Music* (Warsaw: Interpress, 1979), p. 140.

4. *Ibid.*, p. 142.

5. Jarosław Iwaszkiewicz, *Notatki 1939–1945* (Wrocław, 1991), quoted in Piotr Matusak, *Edukacja i kultura Polski podziemnej 1939–1945* (Siedlce: Instytut Historii Wyższej Szkoły Rolniczo-Pedagogicznej w Siedlcach, Muzeum Historii Polskiego Ruchu Ludowego w Warszawie, Siedleckie Towarzystwo Naukowe, 1997), pp. 340–1.

6. *Ibid.*, p. 439.

7. J. Piotrowska: 'Śmierć Romana Padlewskiego' [The death of Roman Padlewski], *Ruch Muzyczny* 1/4 (15 Nov. 1945), pp. 14–15; among the many accounts of those who survived the concentration camps, ghettos and the Warsaw Uprising are two compelling accounts by composers – Szymon Laks (1901–83), *Music of Another World* (Evanston: Northwestern University Press, 1989) and Władysław Szpilman (1911–2000), *The Pianist* (London: Gollancz, 1999). In 2002, Szpilman's book became an award-winning film, directed by Roman Polanski.

8. Michalski, 'New Music', p. 144.

9. Loutan-Charbon, *Constantin Regamey*, pp. 21–2.

10. A. J. Domański, 'Sztuka i Moda' [Art and fashion], *Ruch Muzyczny* 4/8 (1–15 May 1960), pp. 10–11.

11. [no author], 'Ci, co odeszli . . .' [Those, who departed . . .], *Ruch Muzyczny* 1/1 (1 Oct. 1945), pp. 3–5.

12. For a summary of the facts and probabilities surrounding Koffler's death, see Gołąb, *Józef Koffler*, pp. 235–8.

13. Józef Koffler: 'Rik niewtomnoj roboti', *Radiańska Muzyka* 5 (1940), pp. 9–10, quoted in Gołąb, *Józef Koffler*, p. 234.

14. *Ibid.*, p. 101.

15. Witold Lutosławski, 'Une création fascinante – Souvenir de l'an 1944', *Revue Musicale Suisse* 2 (1977), pp. 69–70.

16. Alicja Jarzębska, 'Synteza neoklasycznego i dodekafonicznego idiomu kompozytorskiego w "Kwintecie" Konstantego Regameya', in Krystyna Tarnawska-Kaczorowska (ed.), *Konstanty Regamey: Oblicza polistylizmu* (Warsaw: ZKP, 1988), pp. 112–36.

17. A photograph of the composer conducting a rehearsal for the premiere is included in Panufnik, *Composing Myself.*

18. *Ibid.*, p. 72.

19. *Ibid.*, p. 74.

20. Stephen Walsh, 'The Music of Andrzej Panufnik', *Tempo* 111 (Dec. 1974), p. 8.

21. Krzysztof Stasiak, 'An Analytical Study of the Music of Andrzej Panufnik', Ph.D. thesis, The Queen's University of Belfast (1990), pp. 29–33.

3 Post-war reconstruction

1. Stefan Kisielewski, 'Festival Polskiej Muzyki Współczesnej w Krakowie (1–4 XI 1945)', *Ruch Muzyczny* 1/1 (1 Oct. 1945), p. 24.

2. Nadia Boulanger, *Spectateur* (17 Dec. 1946), quoted in Helman, *Roman Palester*, p. 122.

3. Witold Lutosławski, quoted in Charles Bodman Rae, *The Music of Lutosławski* 3rd edn (London: Omnibus, 1999), p. 28.

4. Steven Stucky, *Lutosławski and his Music* (Cambridge: Cambridge University Press, 1981), p. 30.

5. Panufnik, *Composing Myself*, p. 166.

6. Zygmunt Mycielski, 'I Symfonia Panufnika', *Ruch Muzyczny* 1/6 (Dec. 1945), pp. 7–8.

4 Socialist realism I: its onset and genres

1. Interview with the author, Warsaw, 1 July 1999.

2. Witold Rudziński, 'Nowe czasy – nowe zadania' [New times – new tasks], *Ruch Muzyczny* 1/1 (1 Oct. 1945), p. 8.

3. The most extensive account of the conference in English, including transcripts and background information, is to be found in Alexander Werth, *Musical Uproar in Moscow* (London: Turnstile, 1949).

4. Quoted in Jakub Karpiński, *Poland since 1944: A Portrait in Years* (Boulder: Westview Press, 1995), p. 13.

5. Quoted in Werth, *Musical Uproar*, p. 9; Marta Fik, *Kultura polska po Jałcie: kronika lat 1944–1981* [Polish culture after Yalta] (London: Polonia, 1989), p. 103, believes that the attack was on Sartre.

6. Roman Haubenstock, 'Z zagadnień "atonalizmu"' [Issues of 'atonalism'], *Ruch Muzyczny* 4/1 (1 Jan. 1948), pp. 9–11; 4/2 (15 Jan. 1948), pp. 8–10; NB, Haubenstock added '-Ramati' to his name after he emigrated from Poland (see Chapter 14).

7. Tikhon Khrennikov, 'O nowe drogi twórczości muzycznej' [On the new path of musical creativity], *Ruch Muzyczny* 4/18 (15 Sept. 1948), pp. 2–4; Józef Chomiński, 'Zagadnienia formalizmu i tendencje ideologiczne w polskiej muzyce na tle rozwoju muzyki światowej' [Issues of formalism and ideological bias in Polish music against the background of developing music around the world], *Ruch Muzyczny* 4/20 (15 Oct. 1948), pp. 2–6; Stefan Kisielewski, 'Czy w muzyce istnieje formalizm?' [Can formalism exist in music?], *Ruch Muzyczny* 4/22 (15 Nov. 1948), pp. 2–6; Włodzimierz Sokorski, 'Formalizm i realizm w muzyce' [Formalism and realism in music], *Ruch Muzyczny* 4/23–4 (Dec. 1948), pp. 2–5.

8. A. Moszalukówna, '*Kołysanka* Andrzeja Panufnika', *Ruch Muzyczny* 5/13 (Sept. 1949), pp. 25–6.

9. J. Ryżkin, 'Arnold Schönberg, likwidator muzyki', *Ruch Muzyczny* 5/15 (Oct.–Nov. 1949), pp. 24–31 (reprinted from *Sovetskaya Muzika* 8 (1949)).

10. Łagów issue, *Ruch Muzyczny* 5/14 (Oct. 1949), pp. 1–10, 12–31.

11. *Ibid.*, p. 1.

12. Włodzimierz Sokorski, 'Ku realizmowi socjalistycznemu w muzyce', *Ibid.*, pp. 3–5.

13. *Ibid.*, p. 3.

14. *Ibid.*, pp. 3–4.

15. Zygmunt Mycielski, 'O zadaniach Związku Kompozytorów Polskich' [On the Tasks facing the Polish Composers' Union], *Ibid.*, pp. 9–10.

16. 'Protokół', *Ibid.*, p. 14.

17. *Ibid.*

18. *Ibid.*, p. 28; the original transcript is given in the present tense as reported speech, hence the use of 'he' rather than 'I'.

19. *Ibid.*

20. *Ibid.*, p. 24.

21. *Ibid.*, p. 19.

22. *Ibid.*, p. 23.

23. *Ibid.*, p. 18.

24. *Ibid.*; Stanisław Wisłocki had conducted the symphony earlier that afternoon.

25. *Ibid.*

26. *Ibid.*, p. 19.

27. *Ibid.*

28. *Ibid.*, p. 27.

29. In one of many ironic twists to its history, the fanfare from the third movement appeared on one of Poland's philatelic stamps to celebrate the Rome Olympics

in 1960, by which time socialist realism in Poland had been consigned to history.

30. Krzysztof Meyer, 'Symfonia sprzed półwiecza (o I Symfonii Witolda Lutosławskiego)' [A symphony fifty years on (about Witold Lutosławski's First Symphony)], *Zeszyty Literackie* 16/3 (63) (1998), pp. 96–105.

31. Panufnik, *Composing Myself*, p. 194; despite this verbal 'ban', the symphony was published a few months later by PWM and received several Polish performances in the next few years, some conducted by the composer.

32. Zofia Lissa, 'O polską pieśń masową' [The case for the Polish mass song], *Odrodzenie* 3/29 (20 July 1947), p. 3.

33. Zygmunt Mycielski, 'O drugim zjeździe poetów i kompozytorów' [The Second Conference of Poets and Composers], *Odrodzenie* 4/13–14 (29 Mar. – 5 Apr. 1948), p. 7.

34. 'Kronika', *Ruch Muzyczny* 5/8 (15 Apr. 1948), p. 20.

35. Witold Rudziński (ed.), *Pieśni żołnierskie* [Soldiers' Songs] (Warsaw: Czytelnik, 1953).

36. This and other mass songs are discussed at greater length in Adrian Thomas, 'Your Song Is Mine', *Musical Times* 136/1830 (Aug. 1995), pp. 403–9, and 'Mobilising Our Man: Politics and Music in Poland during the Decade after the Second World War', in Wyndham Thomas (ed.), *Composition–Performance–Reception: Studies in the Creative Process in Music* (Aldershot: Ashgate, 1998), pp. 145–68.

37. Released on video by Agencja Producentów Filmowych as no. 161 in its series, *Filmy Polskie*.

38. Mieczysław Tomaszewski, 'O muzyce panegirycznej', *ViVO* 2 (1992), pp. 16–18.

39. *Ibid.*

40. Quoted in Irina Nikolska, *Conversations with Witold Lutosławski* (Stockholm: Melos, 1994), pp. 41–2.

41. Letter to ZKP, item 56, file 750 (Warsaw: Archiwum Akt Nowych); it is interesting to note that Lutosławski used the same forces, though not the same poet, for his song *Towarszysz* in 1952; for further details on this work and the 1951 Festival of Polish Music, see Adrian Thomas, 'File 750: Composers, Politics, and the Festival of Polish Music (1951)', *Polish Music Journal* 5/1 (Summer 2002): http://www.usc.edu/dept/polish music/PMJ/issues.html.

42. [no author], *22 VII 1944–22 VII 1949 Pięc lat Polski Ludowej* (Five years of People's Poland) (Warsaw: PZPR, 1949), pp. 245–6.

43. It was exported to Moscow and Dresden in 1952; the only other Polish socialist-realist opera of any note is Rudziński's *Janko Muzykant* (Janko the musician, 1951, premiered 1953).

5 Socialist realism II: concert music

1. Roman Palester, 'Konflikt Marsyas', *Kultura* 7–8 (1951), pp. 3–16.

2. Czesław Miłosz, *The Captive Mind* (London, 1953; Penguin edition, 1980), p. 5.

3. Nevertheless, those in the know could readily identify Alpha, the Moralist, as Jerzy Andrzejewski, Beta, the Disappointed Lover, as Tadeusz Borowski, Gamma,

the Slave of History, as Konstanty Ildefons Gałczynski (the author of the text for Lutosławski's *Lipcowy wieniec*), and Delta, the Troubadour, as Jerzy Putrament.

4. Łagów 'Protokoł', *Ruch Muzyczny* 5/14 (Oct. 1949), p. 28.

5. Baird many years later dismissed the Piano Concerto as 'the worst stain on my compositional honour', quoted in Izabella Grzenkowicz, *Tadeusz Baird: Rozmowy, szkice, refleksje* (Kraków: PWM, 1982), p. 88.

6. Antoni Prosnak, 'Koncert na orkiestrę Tadeusza Bairda jako przejaw archaizacji', *Muzyka* 2 (1956), p. 25.

7. Krystyna Tarnawska-Kaczorowska, *Tadeusz Baird. Glosy do biografii* (Kraków: Musica Iagellonica, 1997), p. 59.

8. Szymanowski's cousin and librettist for *King Roger*, Jarosław Iwaszkiewicz, was a comparable case in Polish literature, although unlike Panufnik he weathered the socialist-realism storm to maintain a high profile and reputation within Poland.

9. Panufnik, *Composing Myself*, p. 245.

10. Details from the ZKP *Biuletyn Informacyjny* 3 (1953).

11. Panufnik, *Composing Myself*, p. 200.

12. Letter to ZKP, item 67, file 750 (Warsaw: Archiwum Akt Nowych).

13. Information from the American conductor and musicologist, Joseph Herter.

14. (ibis), interview with Panufnik, 'Treść narzuciła formę' [The Contents Imposed the Form), *Życie Warszawy* 143 (25 May 1951).

15. Panufnik later insisted that *Heroic Overture* was connected with the courage of the Poles in 1939, when he first sketched the piece, although he can hardly have been unaware that its composition and performances in the 1950s, under such a title, would have been construed as supporting the political goals of the post-war regime.

16. Recent research by David Tompkins has revealed, however, that she did participate in the closed competition for mass songs, won by Panufnik, to celebrate the creation of the PZPR in late 1948.

17. There are wind quintets by Szeligowski (1950) and Kilar (1952) as well as Panufnik, flute sonatas by Woytowicz (1952), Szeligowski (1953) and Perkowski (1954), Lutosławski's Dance Preludes (1954), an organ sonata by Bloch (1954), a horn sonata by Kilar (1954) and a piano sonata by Serocki (1955).

18. During the post-war decade, only the Kwartet Krakowski was a stable unit, giving periodic recitals.

19. Andrzej Chłopecki, CD notes for 'Lutosławski Orchestral Works Vol. 2', Naxos 8.553169.

20. [no author], 'Sprawozdanie z obrąd z Walnego Zgromadzenia Związku Kompozytorów Polskich', *Muzyka* 5 (Aug. 1950), pp. 46–59.

21. Zofia Lissa, 'Mała Suita i Tryptyk Witolda Lutosławskiego', *Muzyka* 3/5–6 (May–June, 1952), pp. 7–56; Stefania Łobaczewska, 'Realizm socjalistyczny w muzyce', *Studia Muzykologiczne* 5 (1956), pp. 114–32 (section on '*Mala suita* Lutosławskiego').

22. Zofia Lissa, 'Koncert na orkiestrę Witolda Lutosławskiego', *Studia Muzykologiczne* 5 (1956), pp. 196–299.

23. Arguably, the only weakness in the score is Lutosławski's reluctance to bring the piece to an end. Its coda has sometimes been regarded as over-extended. For example, both Rolf Kleinert with the Berlin Radio SO (1967?) on Berlin CLASSICS and Paul Kletzki with the Suisse Romande (1968) on Decca cut out bb. 852–902 incl. The programme booklet for Václav Smetáček's 1970 recording on Le Chant du Monde (Praga Productions) refers to this same cut as appearing on 'the revised score', but no cuts are actually made on his recording.

24. Cf. also the opening passacaglia of Szabelski's Third Symphony (1951) and his Concerto Grosso (1954).

25. Quoted in Irina Nikolska, *Conversations*, pp. 39–40; 'rough stuff' is probably a poor translation – 'raw material' is a more likely phrase.

26. Stucky, *Lutosławski*, pp. 53–5.

27. *Ibid.*, p. 49.

28. *Ibid.*, p. 130.

29. It is worth noting in passing that there are striking correspondences between the opening texture and the upward trajectory of the theme during the Passacaglia with their parallels in the first movement of the First Symphony (1951) by the French composer Henri Dutilleux, with whose music some of Lutosławski's later output has sometimes been compared.

30. This structural dilemma resurfaced over thirty years later, in the finale of the Piano Concerto (see Chapter 11).

31. James Harley, 'Considerations of Symphonic Form', in Zbigniew Skowron (ed.), *Lutosławski Studies*, p. 166.

32. Stucky, *Lutosławski*, p. 49.

6 The 'Warsaw Autumn'

1. Zygmunt Mycielski, 'Od samego mieszania herbata nie będzie słodka' [Stirring the tea will not make it sweet], *Przegląd Kulturalny* 3/16 (22–8 Apr. 1954), p. 4, quoted in Jan Patrick Lee, 'Musical Life and Sociopolitical Change in Warsaw, Poland: 1944–1960', Ph.D. thesis, University of North Carolina, Chapel Hill (1979), p. 336.

2. Panufnik, *Composing Myself*, pp. 223–4.

3. Włodzimierz Sokorski, 'O rzeczywisty zwrot w naszej polityce kulturalnej' [On a decisive turn in our cultural politics], *Nowa Kultura* 17 (25 Apr. 1954), pp. 1–2; quoted in Richard Hiscocks, *Poland. Bridge for the Abyss? An Interpretation of Developments in Post-War Poland* (Oxford: Oxford University Press, 1963), p. 175.

4. Zofia Lissa, 'Z perspektywy dziesięciolecia' [From the perspective of ten years], *Muzyka* 5/7–8 (July–Aug. 1954), p. 7.

5. *Ibid.*, p. 13.

6. *Ibid.*, p. 22.

7. As a measure of its acceptability, jazz and twelve-note patterns notwithstanding, it won first prize in January 1953 in a competition organised by ZKP with the

Polish Committee for the Defence of Peace, in the category of small-scale vocal or instrumental works; in the same competition, Serocki also won a prize for his mass songs.

8. Hiscocks, 'The Thaw, 1954–6', in *Poland. Bridge for the Abyss?*, pp. 170–209.

9. Lucjan Kydryński, '8 odpowiedzi Andrzeja Panufnika' [8 answers from Andrzej Panufnik], *Dziennik Polski* 140 (13–14 June 1954).

10. Cynthia Bylander, 'The Warsaw Autumn International Festival of Contemporary Music 1956–1961: Its Goals, Structures, Programs, and People', Ph.D. thesis, Ohio State University (1989), pp. 87–100.

11. [no author], *Program I-ego Międzynarodowego Festiwalu Muzyki Współczesnej* (Warsaw: ZKP, 1956), pp. 27–8.

12. 'Filharmonia Krakowska w sezonie 1953/1954', in the programme of the first concert of the 1954–5 season, pp. 15–22.

13. [no author], 'Dodekafonia seryjna', *Radio i Świat* 43 (October 1956), p. 8; this was followed in like manner, but with annotated examples, by 'Utwory seryjne Albana Berga' [Alban Berg's serial works], *Radio i Świat* 52 (Dec. 1956), p. 13; 'Opera Albana Berga "Lulu"', *Radio i Świat* 13 (Mar.–Apr. 1957), p. 2; and 'Anton Webern', *Radio i Świat* 17 (Apr.–May 1957), p. 2.

14. Patkowski went on to become one of the major figures in Polish contemporary music, especially in the Polish Composers' Union and the 'Warsaw Autumn'. He still coaches students in electronic music, at the Kraków Music Academy.

15. The Fourth Symphony (1952) by his fellow exile, Roman Palester, did, however, appear on the programme of the 1958 festival, but his name was then absent from the 'Warsaw Autumn' until 1979.

16. [no author], *Program*, p. 48.

17. Zygmunt Mycielski, 'Kryteria i gusty' [Criteria and tastes], *Przegląd Kulturalny* 5 (8–14 Nov. 1956), p. 6.

18. The success of the 'Warsaw Autumn' spurred musicians in the former Yugoslavia to establish the Zagreb Music Biennale in 1961, and for many years these two festivals provided the main opportunity for East–West exchanges of contemporary music.

19. Sources: Ludwik Erhardt (ed.), *50 lat Związku Kompozytorów Polskich* [50 years of the Polish Composers' Union] (Warsaw: ZKP, 1995), p. 81, and Klaudia Podobińska and Leszek Polony (eds.), *Kilar: Cieszę się darem życia* [I enjoy the gift of life] (Kraków: PWM, 1997), p. 94; Tadeusz A. Zieliński, *O twórczosci Kazimierza Serockiego* [The works of Kazimierz Serocki] (Kraków: PWM, 1985), p. 58, includes Schaeffer in his list of those who also attended Darmstadt in 1957, but not the other four.

20. Stucky, *Lutosławski*, p. 64.

7 Engaging with the avant-garde

1. Other festivals, concentrating on contemporary Polish music, shortly sprang up elsewhere, notably in Poznań (from 1961) and in Wrocław (from 1962).

2. Witold Lutosławski, 'Zagajenie dyskusji na walnym zjeździe Związku Kompozytorów Polskich' [Opening address of the discussion on the General Assembly
   of the Polish Composers' Union], *Ruch Muzyczny* 1 (1 May 1957), pp. 2–3; this
   was the first issue since the end of 1949 of a periodical that had been liquidated
   at the height of the Party drive for *socrealizm*.

3. Adrian Thomas, *Bacewicz: Chamber and Orchestral Music* (Los Angeles: Polish
   Music Reference Center, 1985), pp. 89–90.

4. Witold Lutosławski, interview with Bohdan Pilarski, *Ruch Muzyczny* 2/9 (1957),
   pp. 2–7, quoted in the programme book for the Fifth Polish Radio Music Festival
   (Warsaw: Polish Radio, May 2001), pp. 86–7.

5. Martina Homma, 'Lutosławski's Studies in Twelve-Tone Rows', in Zbigniew
   Skowron (ed.), *Lutosławski Studies*, pp. 194–210.

6. Grzenkowicz, *Tadeusz Baird*, p. 30.

7. *Four Essays* won joint first prize alongside Lutosławski's *Funeral Music* at the 1959
   UNESCO Composers' Tribune, the first time Polish music had been honoured
   in this way.

8. Antoni Prosnak, 'Cztery Eseje Bairda i perspektywy techniki serialnej', *Muzyka*
   9/3–4 (1964), p. 26.

9. Bogusław Schaeffer, 'Serocki', in Stanley Sadie (ed.), *The New Grove Dictionary
   of Music and Musicians* (London: Macmillan, 1980), vol. XVII, p. 177.

10. Serocki may also have been aware of the existence of Xenakis's recent works like
    Pithoprakta (1956) which explored the movement of sound masses within an
    ensemble of strings, although the stylistic gap between the two composers at
    this time was considerable. *Pithoprakta* received its Polish premiere three years
    later, at the 1962 'Warsaw Autumn', and Xenakis remained the most performed
    foreign composer to appear in subsequent festival programmes.

11. As a further sign of relaxation, the 1960 'Warsaw Autumn' mounted the Polish
    premiere of the monumental *Missa pro defunctis, Requiem* (1946–59), by the pre-
    war emigré composer Roman Maciejewski (1910–98). The Requiem's eclectic
    reliance on nineteenth- and early twentieth-century sources was particularly
    anachronistic in 1960s Poland.

12. In *Strophes*, Penderecki introduced to Polish music a practice, already adopted
    by Stockhausen and others, whereby tempo changes are indicated by means of
    a thick black line moving between different levels (cf. also Serocki's *Episodes*,
    1959, Górecki's *Scontri*, 1960, and his own *Anaklasis*, 1959–60).

13. Both Dobrowolski and Lutosławski had attended a public concert in February
    1958 in Katowice devoted solely to Górecki's music, and it is highly likely that
    this was the spur for the commission.

8 The pull of tradition

1. Grażyna Bacewicz, interview (1960), reprinted in Stefan Kisielewski, *Z muzycznej międzyepoki* (Kraków: PWM, 1966), pp. 205–6.

2. Grażyna Bacewicz, letter (12 (?) September 1960) to her brother, Witold, quoted
   in Małgorzata Gąsiorowska, *Bacewicz* (Kraków: PWM, 1999), p. 325.

3. Tadeusz Baird (1979), in Grzenkowicz, *Tadeusz Baird*, p. 92.

4. The Trio for oboe, harp and percussion (1965) is almost identical to *Inkrustacje* for horn and ensemble (1965), while the first two movements of the Concerto for Two Pianos (1966) come from their equivalents in the Second Piano Quartet (1965) and the finale is based on the main material from the last movement of the Seventh String Quartet (1965).

5. Bohdan Pociej, 'Świt awangardy', *Ruch Muzyczny* 1 (1960), pp. 4–10, quoted in Leon Markiewicz, *Bolesław Szabelski: Życie i twórczość* (Kraków: PWM, 1995), p. 81.

6. *Ibid.*, p. 77.

7. Tadeusz Baird, in Tadeusz Sznajderski, 'Ostatni wywiad Tadeusza Bairda' [Tadeusz Baird's last interview], *Życie Literackie* 39 (27 September 1981), pp. 1, 12, quoted in Tarnawska-Kaczorowska, *Tadeusz Baird*, p. 50.

8. Tadeusz Baird, note in programme book of the 7th 'Warsaw Autumn' (Warsaw: ZKP, 1963), p. 110, quoted in Tarnawska-Kaczorowska, *Tadeusz Baird*, p. 33.

9. Jerzy S. Sito, programme book for the premiere at Teatr Wielki, Warsaw (18 September 1966), quoted in *Polish Opera and Ballet of the Twentieth Century* (Kraków: PWM, 1985), p. 20.

10. Tarnawska-Kaczorowska, 'Jutro', in *Tadeusz Baird*, pp. 125–60.

11. Tadeusz Baird, in Ewa Kofin, 'Ponad codzienność' [Beyond the common place], *Odra* 4 (1973), p. 91, quoted in Tarnawska-Kaczorowska, *Tadeusz Baird*, p. 30.

12. *Ibid.*

13. Nikolska, *Conversations*, p. 137.

14. Witold Lutosławski, *Notebook of Ideas* (9 Aug. 1961, unpublished), quoted in *Lutosławski: homagium* (Warsaw: Galeria Zachęta, 1996), p. 38.

15. Witold Lutosławski, 'About the Element of Chance in Music', in *Three Aspects of New Music* (Stockholm: Nordiska Musikförlaget, 1968), p. 52.

16. Stucky: *Lutosławski*, pp. 113–23; Rae, *The Music of Lutosławski*, pp. 49–57; Homma, *Witold Lutosławski: Zwölfton-Harmonik – Formbildung – 'aleatorischer Kontrapunkt'* (Cologne: Bela Verlag, 1995), pp. 445–63.

17. Lutosławski would almost certainly have been aware of earlier Polish artistic experiments in this area, notably in the work of Witkacy, whose numerous portraits of friends (including Szymanowski) are annotated with the precise details of which drugs he had taken at the time.

18. Lutosławski was referring to the internal movement of motifs within blocks, rather than the relationship between the blocks themselves, which remain in a fixed order. Unlike Serocki's *A piacere* (1963), the String Quartet does not play with the order of its larger constituent forms.

19. Maja Trochimczyk, 'The Themes of Death and Night', in Skowron (ed.), *Lutosławski Studies*, pp. 111, 118.

20. John Casken, 'The Visionary and the Dramatic', in *ibid.*, p. 50.

21. *Ibid.*, p. 37.

22. Stucky, *Lutosławski*, p. 162.

23. There are of course some tangential antecedents, such as Mozart's Piano Concerto in E flat, K271 and Brahms's Second Piano Concerto, even Elgar's Cello Concerto, although Beethoven's Fourth Piano Concerto remains the most relevant comparison, not least because of the contrasts and conflicts which follow from the soloist's opening meditation.

24. Tadeusz Kaczyński, *Conversations with Witold Lutosławski* (London: Chester, 1984), p. 61.

25. *Ibid.*, p. 62.

26. Arnold Whittall, 'Between Polarity and Synthesis', in Skowron (ed.), *Lutosławski Studies*, p. 247.

27. Kaczyński, *Conversations*, p. 63.

28. There are other pieces by Lutosławski (e.g. *Funeral Music* and the Third Symphony) which circumstantially seem connected to the position of the individual or artist and the authoritarian state at or shortly before the time of their composition.

29. Kaczyński, *Conversations*, p. 61.

30. *Ibid.*, p. 65.

31. *Ibid.*, p. 64.

32. Rae, *The Music of Lutosławski*, p. 123.

33. Stucky, *Lutosławski*, p. 186.

34. Jean-Louis Bedouin (ed.), *La poésie Surréaliste* (Paris: Seghers, 1970), pp. 146–7.

35. Cf. Górecki's *Three Diagrams* (1959) and *Diagram* IV (1961) for flute and Schaeffer's early piano studies.

36. Kazimierz Serocki, note for the world premiere by Frederic Rzewski, programme book of 7th 'Warsaw Autumn' (Warsaw: ZKP, 1963), p. 52.

37. It was premiered at Darmstadt in July 1964.

38. Tadeusz A. Zieliński, *O twórczości Kazimierza Serockiego* (Kraków: PWM, 1985), p. 93.

9 Sonorism and experimentalism

1. Mycielski, 'O zadaniach Związku Kompozytorów Polskich', p. 10 (see Chapter 4).

2. [no author], *Program*, p. 27.

3. Michalski, 'New Music', p. 165.

4. Danuta Mirka, *The Sonoristic Structuralism of Krzysztof Penderecki* (Katowice: Akademia Muzyczna, 1997), pp. 4–5.

5. Zbigniew Skowron, 'Lutosławski's Aesthetics: A Reconstruction of the Composer's Outlook', in Skowron (ed.), *Lutosławski Studies*, p. 5; see also Stucky, *Lutosławski*, pp. 105–6.

6. There have been some important milestones in the CD market, notably Olympia's reissues in the 1990s of music by Bacewicz, Baird, Górecki and Szabelski but, in the absence of other recording initiatives, the repertoire of these and

many other composers (and not just that from the 1960s) still languishes in obscurity, as it does in Poland.

7. Józef Chomiński, 'Z zagadnień techniki kompozytorskiej XX wieku' [Some problems of twentieth-century compositional technique], *Muzyka* 1/3 (1956), pp. 23–48; some of his younger colleagues soon applied the new idea to music by Chopin, Liszt and Szymanowski.

8. Józef Chomiński, 'Wkład kompozytorów polskich do rozwoju języka sono-rystycznego' [The contribution of Polish composers to the development of a sonoristic language], in Elżbieta Dziębowska (ed.), *Polska współczesna kultura muzyczna 1944–1964* (Kraków: PWM, 1968), pp. 96–112; a different version of the same essay – 'Udział polskich kompozytorów w kształtowaniu nowoczes-nego języka muzycznego' – was published in Józef Chomiński, *Muzyka Polski Ludowej* [The music of People's Poland] (Warsaw: PWN, 1968), pp. 127–71, and reprinted in English, as 'The Contribution of Polish Composers to the Shaping of a Modern Language in Music', in Zofia Chechlińska and Jan Stęszewski (eds.), *Polish Musicological Studies* 1 (Kraków: PWM, 1977), pp. 167–215.

9. Tadeusz A. Zieliński, 'Neue Klangästhetik', *Melos* 7/8 (1966), p. 212, quoted in Mirka, *Sonoristic Structuralism*, p. 326.

10. Ludwik Erhard, *Music in Poland* (Warsaw: Interpress, 1975) and Michalski, 'New Music'.

11. Teresa Malecka, 'I Symfonia Krzysztofa Pendereckiego', in Regina Chłopicka and Krzysztof Szwajgier (eds.), *Współczesność i tradycja w muzyce Krzysztofa Pendereckiego* (Kraków: Akademia Muzyczna, 1983), p. 176.

12. Mirka, *Sonoristic Structuralism*.

13. Several of Dobrowolski's later works for tape and live performers were also published by PWM, with an accompanying recording of the electronic part, an imaginative move to facilitate further performances.

14. Early Polish examples of tape in live performance include Penderecki's use of live playback in *Canon* (1962), Tomasz Sikorski's exploration of spatial echoes and reverberation via pre-recorded versions of some material in *Echoes* II (1961–3), a procedure extended to his *Antiphons* (1963), and Krystyna Moszumańska-Nazar's intermittent use of pre-recorded tape (no specific spatial dimensions) in her orchestral *Exodus* (1964).

15. *Instrumenty perkusyjne we współczesnej orkiestrze* (Kraków: PWM, 1963), subse-quently translated into Hungarian and German. Kotoński later wrote a massive tome, *Muzyka elektroniczna* (Kraków: PWM, 1989).

16. Włodzimierz Kotoński, note in programme book of 40th 'Warsaw Autumn' (Warsaw: ZKP, 1997), p. 56.

17. Włodzimierz Kotoński, technical and compositional foreword to the score (Kraków: PWM, 1975).

18. Joanna Mroczek and Maria Wilczek, interview with Penderecki, 'Inspiracja – kompozycja – cytat', *ViVO* 1 (15 Jan. 1994), p. 24.

19. Izabela Grzenkowicz, 'Bogactwo świata' [The riches of the world], *Kultura* 6 (1981), p. 12; quoted in Mirka, *Sonoristic Structuralism*, p. 338.

20. Jerzy Hordyński, 'Kompozytorzy współcześni. Krzysztof Penderecki' [Contemporary composers. Krzysztof Penderecki], *Życie Literackie* 44 (1960), p. 8; quoted in Mirka, *Sonoristic Structuralism*, p. 329.

21. Krzysztof Penderecki, note for premiere of first version of *Dimensions of Time and Silence*, in programme book of 4th 'Warsaw Autumn' (Warsaw: ZKP, 1960), p. 32.

22. Wolfram Schwinger, *Krzysztof Penderecki. His Life and Work*, p. 140. Schwinger also lists the notational symbols for *Fluorescences*, pp. 141–2.

23. Mieczysław Tomaszewski, 'Listening to Penderecki', in Regina Chłopicka, *Krzysztof Penderecki. The Black Mask. Contemporary Dance of Death* (Kraków: GMCK, 1998), p. 25.

24. In fact, there are only six discrete types of sound production (cf. the role of comparable compendia in *Polymorphia*, figs. 38–44 incl., and *Fluorescences*, figs. 45–53).

25. According to Ray Robinson and Allen Winold, *A Study of the Penderecki St Luke Passion* (Celle: Moeck Verlag, 1983), pp. 14–15, Penderecki worked as a volunteer in a medical centre in Kraków in 1961 and took the opportunity 'to record the brain waves of mental patients while they listened to a tape recording of *Threnody*. The resultant encephalographs were used as the basis of the glissando-like melodic material in *Polymorphia*.'

26. Krzysztof Bilica, 'Pozaekspresyjne porządki w Kwartecie Smyczkowym nr. 1' [Non-expressive systems in the String Quartet no. 1], in Regina Chłopicka and Krzysztof Szwajgier (eds.), *Współczesność i tradycja w muzyce Krzysztofa Pendereckiego* (Kraków: Akademia Muzyczna, 1983), pp. 72–7.

27. Jerzy Hordyński, 'Kompozytorzy współcześni. Krzysztof Penderecki', p. 8; quoted in Mirka, *Sonoristic Expressionism*, p. 329.

28. Cf. the triadic end of Turski's Second Symphony.

29. Cf. the views expressed in The *Musical Times* after the first two British performances, by Robert Henderson, 108/1491 (May 1967), pp. 422–3 and 108/1493 (July 1967), pp. 624 and by Stanley Sadie (editorial), 108/1495 (Sept. 1967), p. 793.

30. Alan Rich, 'The Music Critic as Sex Symbol', *New York Magazine* (31 Mar. 1969), quoted in Ray Robinson, 'Penderecki's Reception in the United States of America', in Mieczysław Tomaszewski (ed.), *The Music of Krzysztof Penderecki. Poetics and Reception* (Kraków: Akademia Muzyczna, 1995), p. 21.

31. Harold Schonberg, 'Romanticism Coming Up', *The New York Times* (16 Mar. 1969), *ibid.*, pp. 176–7.

32. Krysztof Penderecki, in conversation with Marek Stachowski during 'Spotkanie muzyczne w Baranowie' [Musical meeting in Baranów] (1976), in Leszek Polony (ed.), *Muzyka w kontekście kultury* (Kraków: PWM, 1978), p. 62.

33. Krzysztof Penderecki, 'Dyskusja na seminarium poświęconym twórczości Krzysztofa Pendereckiego' [Discussion at the seminar dedicated to the works of Krzysztof Penderecki], *Muzyka* 2 (1981), p. 32; quoted in Mirka, *Sonoristic Structuralism*, p. 346.

34. Maciejewski's work, for example, is dedicated 'to the victims of human igno-rance, the victims of the wars of all time, the victims tortured by tyrants, the victims of human lawlessness, the victims of the violation of God's natural order'.

35. *Utrenia* follows Szymanowski's opera *King Roger* in drawing upon the exoticism of Orthodox church traditions.

36. Józef Patkowski, 'Premieres at the 1962 "Warsaw Autumn"', Polish Radio, 4 Oct. 1962, reprinted in *Horyzonty muzyki* 26 (Kraków: PWM, 1970), p. 3.

37. Tadeusz Marek and David Drew, 'Górecki in Interview (1968) – and 20 Years After', *Tempo* 168 (Mar. 1989), p. 26. *Muzyczka* II and III are, in a sense, reworkings of ideas expounded in *Elementi* and *Canti strumentali* res-pectively.

38. Karol Szymanowski, 'On Contemporary Musical Opinion in Poland', *Nowy Przegląd Literatury i Sztuki* (July 1920), in Wightman (ed.), *Szymanowski on Music*, p. 93.

39. Tadeusz Marek and David Drew, 'Górecki in Interview', pp. 28–9.

40. Andrzej Chłopecki, note in programme book of 42nd 'Warsaw Autumn' (Warsaw: ZKP, 1999), p. 20.

41. Witold Szalonek, 'O nie wykorzystanych walorach sonorystycznych instru-mentów dętych drewnianych' [On the unexploited sonoristic qualities of wood-wind instruments] (1968–70), *Res Facta* 7 (1973), pp. 110–19.

42. Bruno Bartolozzi, *New Sounds for Woodwind*, trans. and ed. Reginald Smith Brindle (Oxford: Oxford University Press, 1967).

43. Carl Humphries, note in programme book of 42nd 'Warsaw Autumn' (Warsaw: ZKP, 1999), p. 62.

44. Witold Szalonek, note in programme book of 15th 'Warsaw Autumn' (Warsaw: ZKP, 1971), p. 115.

45. Carl Humphries, note, p. 62.

46. An interesting comparison can be made with two short, earlier pieces by Szalonek's exact contemporary, Juliusz Łuciuk (b. 1927), *Lirica di timbri* (1963) and *Pacem in terris* (1964), in both of which the pianist plays inside the instrument with a range of percussion sticks.

47. Bogusław Schaeffer, preface to the score (his second 'compositional treatise'), *Equivalenze sonore* (Kraków: PWM, 1959), p. 4.

48. Bogusław Schaeffer, preface to the score of *Montaggio* (Kraków: PWM, 1962).

49. Jadwiga Hodor, note in programme book of 32nd 'Warsaw Autumn' (Warsaw: ZKP, 1989), p. 199.

50. Commentary in Bogusław Schaeffer, *Musica per pianoforte* (Kraków: PWM, 1964), p. 10.

51. Joanna Zając, *Muzyka, teatr i filozofia Bogusława Schaeffera. Trzy rozmowy* (Salzburg: Collsch, 1992), p. 12.

52. Kathleen M. Cioffi, *Alternative Theatre in Poland 1954–1989* (Amsterdam: Harwood, 1996), p. 46.

53. Stefan Kisielewski, 'Schäffer – samobójca' [Schaeffer – suicide], *Ruch muzyczny* 15/9 (1 May 1971), pp. 10–11; Bogusław Schaeffer, 'Kisielewski – nożownik' [Kisielewski – Cut-Throat], *Ruch muzyczny* 15/13 (1 July 1971), pp. 13–18.
54. TIS = Teatr Instrumentalny Schaeffera [Schaeffer's Instrumental Theatre].
55. Bogusław Schaeffer, in note to the score of *TIS MW 2* (Kraków: PWM, 1972).
56. Stefan Kisielewski, 'Schäffer – samobójca', 10.

10 A significant hinterland

1. Janusz Zagrodzki, *Constructivism in Poland 1923 to 1936* (Cambridge: Kettle's Yard, n.d.), p. 58.
2. Władysław Strzemiński, 'An Account of the Exhibition at IPS' (1934), quoted in Janusz Zagrodzki, *Constructivism in Poland*, p. 41.
3. Zygmunt Krauze, note for *Piece for Orchestra* no. 1 in programme book of 14th 'Warsaw Autumn' (Warsaw: ZKP, 1970), p. 13.
4. Zygmunt Krauze, preface to published score of *Voices* (Kraków: PWM, 1976).
5. Tomasz Sikorski, note in programme book of 11th 'Warsaw Autumn' (Warsaw: ZKP, 1967), pp. 89–90.
6. Tomasz Sikorski, note in programme book of 14th 'Warsaw Autumn' (Warsaw: ZKP, 1970), p. 19.

11 Pursuing the abstract

1. Andrzej Dobrowolski, note in programme book of 19th 'Warsaw Autumn' (Warsaw: ZKP, 1975), p. 191.
2. Zbigniew Bargielski, note on *Trigonalia* (1994) in programme book of 41st 'Warsaw Autumn' (Warsaw: ZKP, 1998), p. 179.
3. Bujarski, note on *Similis Greco* I in programme book of 23rd 'Warsaw Autumn' (Warsaw: ZKP, 1979), p. 201.
4. Steven Stucky, 'Change and Constancy: The Essential Lutosławski', in Skowron (ed.), *Lutosławski Studies*, pp. 127–62.
5. Lutosławski's programme note for the Third Symphony, subsequently elaborated by Rae, *The Music of Lutosławski*, pp. 166–8.
6. Lutosławski, note in the preface to the score of *Chain 2* (London: Chester).
7. Irina Nikolska, *Conversations*, p. 101.
8. Arnold Whittall, 'Between Polarity and Synthesis', pp. 244–68.
9. *Ibid.*, p. 267.
10. Cf. Stucky's criticism of the end of *Preludes and Fugue*, in Stucky, *Lutosławski*, p. 184.
11. Krzysztof Penderecki, *The Labyrinth of Time. Five Addresses for the End of the Millennium* (Chapel Hill: Hinshaw, 1998), p. 16.
12. In the 1980s and 90s, Penderecki decided to reissue a number of these six concertos in other guises. Thus it is that the Viola Concerto (1983) reappears as a concerto for violin (1985), cello (1989) and clarinet (1997), the last not

to be confused with the clarinet version (1996) of the Flute Concerto (1992). He also made a version of the Clarinet Quartet (1993) for clarinet and strings (1994).

13. Other examples of tritonal openings include the Second Cello Concerto (B–F), the Fifth Symphony (F–B) and the Second Violin Concerto (A–E flat).

14. Tomaszewski (ed.), *The Music of Krzysztof Penderecki*, p. 121.

15. This may arise from Penderecki's working methods, which in this case included the abandonment of his original intention of writing a multi-movement work when the first movement grew too large. The subtitle of the Fourth Symphony (1989), 'Adagio', tells a similar tale, though in this case the original intention had been to compose an oratorio to celebrate the bicentennial of the French Revolution.

16. Schwinger, *Krzysztof Penderecki*, p. 181.

17. Andrzej Chłopecki, note in CD booklet for Accord ACD 096–2, p. 18.

18. Ryszard Stanisławski (ed.), *Krysztof Penderecki Itinerarium: Exhibition of Musical Sketches* (Kraków: Modulus, 1998), p. 72.

19. Anne-Sophie Mutter, note in CD booklet for Deutsche Grammophon DG 453 507–2, p. 2.

20. Mieczysław Tomaszewski, note in CD booklet for Wergo, WER 6270–2, pp. 5–6.

21. Schwinger, *Krzysztof Penderecki*, p. 158.

22. Penderecki, *The Labyrinth of Time*, p. 59.

23. *Ibid.*, p. 78.

24. Krzysztof Penderecki, 'In the Labyrinth', foreword to Stanislawski (ed.), *Krzysztof Penderecki Itinerarium*.

25. *Ibid.*

12 Music and Symbolism I

1. Meyer included references to the medieval hymn 'Mother of God' ('Bogurodzica'), to the nineteenth-century hymn 'God, Who has Protected Poland' ('Boże, coś Polskę'), and to 'Hymn of 1910' ('Rota'), a song by Feliks Nowowiejski (1877–1946), which, since its premiere at the unveiling of the monument in Kraków to the battle of Grunwald (a monument largely paid for by Paderewski), has become a patriotic song second in popular significance only to the national anthem.

2. Lutosławski admitted in Kaczyński, *Conversations*, p. 145, that 'the idea of composing a Requiem has stayed with me all my life', but it never engaged him sufficiently apart from the two fragments he composed for his student diploma in 1937.

3. Schwinger, *Krzysztof Penderecki*, p. 41, gives the venue as St Catherine's Church in Kraków.

4. Robinson and Winold, *A Study of the Penderecki St Luke Passion*, p. 19.

5. At this stage, the Soviet Union still claimed that the murders had been carried out by the Nazis.

6. Penderecki, in an interview conducted by Marek Zwyrzykowski (1996), quoted in CD booklet for *Seven Gates of Jerusalem*, Accord ACD 036, p. 19.

7. *Ibid.*

8. The *Requiem of Reconciliation* was gathered together by Helmuth Rilling for Süddeutscher Rundfunk and recorded on Hänssler 2-CD 98.931. The other composers who contributed were Berio, Cerha, Dittrich, Kopelent, Harbison, Nordheim, Rands, Dalbavie, Weir, Rihm, Schnittke, Yuasa and Kurtág.

9. Regina Chłopicka, note in CD booklet 'Stabat Mater' for Finlandia 4509–98999–2, p. 6.

10. Górecki's main source has been Father Jan Siedlecki (ed.), *Śpiewnik kościelny* [Church Songbook] (39th edn, Kraków: 1990).

11. Ivan Moody, 'Górecki: The Path to the *Miserere*', *Musical Times* 133/1792 (June 1992), p. 284.

12. It won First Prize at the UNESCO Composers' Rostrum in Paris (1973), but a measure of its obscurity is that its UK premiere took place thirty years after its premiere at the 1972 'Warsaw Autumn' (Manchester, December 2002, conducted by John Casken).

13. Cf. Penderecki's *Cosmogony* and Szabelski's *Mikołaj Kopernik*.

14. Adrian Thomas, *Górecki* (Oxford: Oxford University Press, 1997), p. 75.

15. Psalms 135 (136), vv. 8–9.

16. After at least one leading conductor resigned from the preparations for the first performance, which was to take place during the Pope's visit to Kraków the following year, Górecki conducted the premiere himself, making considerable detours around the southern Polish countryside to avoid the militia road blocks set up to prevent as many people as possible from attending the papal events.

17. For an account of the reception of the Third Symphony in the United States and United Kingdom, see Luke B. Howard, 'Motherhood, *Billboard*, and the Holocaust: Perceptions and Receptions of Górecki's Symphony no. 3', *Musical Quarterly* 82/1 (Spring 1998), pp. 131–59.

18. For a detailed account of the Third Symphony, see Thomas, *Górecki*, pp. 81–93.

19. The subject matter and the composer's compositional intent are therefore totally unconnected with other Polish atrocities, such as the Nazi genocides in Auschwitz and elsewhere.

20. Andrzej Chłopecki, foreword to catalogue of Kilar's works (Kraków: PWM, 1996), p. 7. Kilar distanced himself from such interpretative commentaries.

13 Music and symbolism II

1. Song and dance troupes such Mazowsze (founded 1949) and Śląsk (1953) continued to be extremely popular after the 1950s.

2. Wojciech Kilar, note in programme book of 21st 'Warsaw Autumn' (Warsaw: ZKP, 1977), p. 15.

3. Chłopecki, foreword to PWM catalogue, p. 6.

4. Zygmunt Krauze, preface to score of *Aus aller Welt stammende* (Kraków: PWM, 1974).

5. Zygmunt Krauze, note in CD booklet, Polskie Nagrania PNCD 113, p. 6.
6. Tarnawska-Kaczorowska, *Zygmunt Krauze. Między intelektem, fantazją, powin-nością i zabawa* (Warsaw: PWN, 2001), pp. 212–14.
7. Teresa Malecka, 'O Koncercie klawesynowym Góreckiego' [On Górecki's Harp-sichord Concerto], in Teresa Malecka (ed.), *Mieczysławowi Tomaszewskiemu w 60-lecie urodzin* (Kraków: Akademia Muzyczna, 1985), p. 111.

14 Emigré composers

1. Humphries, note, p. 63.
2. Witold Szalonek, note in programme book of 36th 'Warsaw Autumn' (Warsaw: ZKP, 1993), p. 134.
3. Adrian Thomas, 'Panufnik', in Stanley Sadie and John Tyrrell (eds.), *The New Grove Dictionary of Music and Musicians*, 2nd edn, vol. XIX, p. 47.
4. It would not have been possible in the 1960s for composers living in Poland to present such an overtly political work in public. Penderecki's tribute, the 'Libera me' in the *Polish Requiem*, was not written until 1984.

15 Young Poland

1. MMMM's activities were paralleled by ground-breaking meetings between com-posers and musicologists in the nearby castle of Baranów Sandomierskie (1976–81). With themes such as 'Music in the Context of Culture', 'Music in Music' and 'Music and Literature', these meetings probed deep into the aesthetics and reality of musical creativity. Their inspirational concept brought together not only senior composers (such as Lutosławski, Penderecki and Górecki), musi-cologists from many different disciplines and writers (like Iwaszkiewicz and Szymborska), but also younger composers and critics, many with close involve-ment in MMMM. The proceedings of the first two meetings were published by PWM in 1978 and 1980.
2. Nikolska, *Conversations*, p. 112.
3. Knapik was the first Polish pianist to perform the complete *Vingt regards sur l'enfant Jésus*, in 1976; a commercial recording followed three years later.
4. Quoted in Iwona Bias, *Eugeniusz Knapik. Kompozytor i pianista* (Katowice: Akademia Muzyczna, 2001), p. 102.
5. *Ibid.*, p. 54.
6. Rafał Augustyn, note in programme book of 28th 'Warsaw Autumn' (Warsaw: ZKP, 1985), p. 220.
7. Andrzej Chłopecki, note in programme book of 43rd 'Warsaw Autumn' (Warsaw: ZKP, 2000), pp. 126–7; cf. Krauze's approach to rusticity.
8. Bargielski was another major contributor to Polish accordion literature.
9. Andrzej Krzanowski, note in programme book of 25th 'Warsaw Autumn' (Warsaw: ZKP, 1981), pp. 217–18.

10. Aleksander Lasoń, note in programme book of 36th 'Warsaw Autumn' (Warsaw: ZKP, 1993), p. 30.

11. Paweł Szymański, 'From Idea to Sound: A Few Remarks on My Way of Composing', in Miloš Velimirovič (ed.), *From Idea to Sound*, conference proceedings (Nieborów, 1985) (Kraków: FZE, 1993), p. 135.

12. *Ibid.*

13. *Ibid.*, p. 136.

14. *Ibid.*

15. Stanisław Krupowicz, note in programme book of 37th 'Warsaw Autumn' (Warsaw: ZKP, 1994), p. 114.

16. Stanisław Krupowicz, note in programme book of 40th 'Warsaw Autumn' (Warsaw: ZKP, 1997), p. 99.

17. Marek Chołoniewski, note in programme book of 44th 'Warsaw Autumn' (Warsaw: ZKP, 2001), pp. 127–8.

16 After Lutosławski

1. Andrzej Chłopecki, 'Socrealistyczny Penderecki', *Gazeta Wyborcza* (12–13 Oct. 2002); see also Nicholas Reyland, 'Warsaw Autumn 2002', *Tempo* 57/223 (January 2003), pp. 76–8.

Select bibliography

Apart from footnotes to the text, this bibliography consists primarily of books, with occasional individual book chapters, journal articles or journal issues devoted to a particular composer. As much Polish-language literature is inaccessible to non-Polish readers, non-cited sources have been kept to a minimum. Readers will also find detailed information, including bibliographies and work-lists, in recent editions of *The New Grove Dictionary of Music and Musicians*, in DGG, in the Polish *Encyklopedia Muzyczna* and on the website of the Polish Music Center in Los Angeles.

General literature (non-musical)

[no author], *22 VII 1944–22 VII 1949 Pięć lat Polski Ludowej* (Five Years of People's Poland), Warsaw: PZPR, 1949.

Alvarez, A., *Under Pressure: the Writer in Society – Eastern Europe and the USA*, London: Penguin, 1965.

Bedouin, Jean-Louis (ed.), *La poésie Surréaliste*, Paris: Seghers, 1970.

Cioffi, Kathleen M., *Alternative Theatre in Poland 1954–1989*, Amsterdam: Harwood, 1996.

Davies, Norman, *God's Playground: A History of Poland* (2 vols.), Oxford: Oxford University Press, 1981.

  Heart of Europe: A Short History of Poland, Oxford: Oxford University Press, 1984.

Fik, Marta, *Kultura polska po Jałcie: kronika lat 1944–1981* [Polish Culture after Yalta], London: Polonia, 1989.

Hiscocks, Richard, *Poland. Bridge for the Abyss? An Interpretation of Developments in Post-War Poland*, Oxford: Oxford University Press, 1963.

Karpiński, Jakub, *Poland since 1944: A Portrait in Years*, Boulder: Westview Press, 1995.

Klimaszewski, Bolesław (ed.), *An Outline History of Polish Culture*, Warsaw: Interpress, 1984.

Matusak, Piotr, *Edukacja i kultura Polski podziemnej 1939–1945*, Siedlce: Instytut Historii Wyższej Szkoły Rolniczo-Pedagogicznej w Siedlcach, Muzeum Historii Polskiego Ruchu Ludowego w Warszawie, Siedleckie Towarzystwo Naukowe, 1997.

Miłosz, Czesław, *The Captive Mind*, London, 1953 (Penguin edition, 1980).

Zagrodzki, Janusz, *Constructivism in Poland 1923 to 1936*, Cambridge: Kettle's Yard, n.d.

Zamoyski, Adam, *The Polish Way: A Thousand-year History of the Poles and their Culture*, London: John Murray, 1987.

General literature (musical)

[no author], 'Ci, co odeszli . . .' [Those, who departed . . .], *Ruch Muzyczny* 1/1 (1 Oct. 1945), 3–5.

'Kronika', *Ruch Muzyczny* 5/8 (15 Apr. 1948), 20.

Łagów issue, *Ruch Muzyczny* 5/14 (Oct. 1949), 1–10, 12–31.

'Sprawozdanie z obrąd z Walnego Zgromadzenia Związku Kompozytorów Polskich', *Muzyka* 5 (Aug. 1950), 46–59.

ZKP *Biuletyn Informacyjny* 3 (1953).

Program I-ego Międzynarodowego Festiwalu Muzyki Współczesnej, Warsaw: ZKP, 1956.

Programme books for 'Warsaw Autumn' festivals, Warsaw: ZKP, 1958–81, 82–.

'Dodekafonia seryjna', *Radio i Świat* 43 (Oct. 1956), 8.

'Utwory seryjne Albana Berga' [Alban Berg's serial works], *Radio i Świat* 52 (Dec. 1956), 13.

'Opera Albana Berga "Lulu"', *Radio i Świat* 13 (Mar.–Apr. 1957), 2.

'Anton Webern', *Radio i Świat* 17 (Apr.–May 1957), 2.

Polish Opera and Ballet of the Twentieth Century, Kraków: PWM, 1985.

photo of Lutosławski and Szymanowski, *Ruch Muzyczny* 40/7 (7 April 1996), 26.

Baculewski, Krzysztof, *Polska twórczość kompozytorska 1945–1984* [Polish Composition 1945–1984], Kraków: PWM, 1987.

Historia Muzyki Polskiej, tom VII: Współczesność 1: 1939–1974 [History of Polish Music, vol. VII: Contemporary, part 1: 1939–1974], Warsaw: Sutkowski, 1997.

Bartolozzi, Bruno, *New Sounds for Woodwind*, trans. and ed. Reginald Smith Brindle, Oxford: Oxford University Press, 1967.

Bychawska, Maria and Schiller, Henryk (eds.), *100 lat Filharmonii w Warszawie 1901–2001*, Warsaw: Filharmonia Narodowa, 2001.

Bylander, Cynthia E., 'The Warsaw Autumn International Festival of Contemporary Music, 1956–1961: Its Goals, Structures, Programs, and People', Ph.D. thesis, Ohio State University, 1989.

Chłopecki, Andrzej, 'Socrealistyczny Penderecki', *Gazeta Wyborcza* (12–13 Oct. 2002).

Chomiński, Józef, 'Zagadnienia formalizmu i tendencje ideologiczne w polskiej muzyce na tle rozwoju muzyki światowej' [Issues of formalism and ideological bias in Polish music against the background of developing music around the world], *Ruch Muzyczny* 4/20 (15 Oct. 1948), 2–6.

'Z zagadnień techniki kompozytorskiej XX wieku' [Some problems of 20th-century compositional technique], *Muzyka* 1/3 (1956), 23–48.

Muzyka Polski Ludowej [Music of People's Poland], Warsaw: PWN, 1968.

'The Contribution of Polish Composers to the Shaping of a Modern Language in Music', *Polish Musicological Studies* 1 (1977), 167–215.

Chomiński, Józef and Lissa, Zofia (eds.), *Kultura muzyczna Polski Ludowej 1944–1955* [The musical culture of People's Poland], Kraków: PWM, 1957.

Dąbek, Stanisław, *Twórczość mszalna kompozytorów polskich XX wieku* [Twentieth-century Polish composers and the Mass], Warsaw: PWN, 1996.

Domański, A.J., 'Sztuka i moda' [Art and fashion], *Ruch Muzyczny* 4/8 (1–15 May 1960), 10–11.

Droba, Krzysztof, Malecka, Teresa and Szwajgier, Krzysztof (eds.), *Muzyka polska 1945–95*, Kraków: Akademia Muzyczna, 1996.

Dziadek, Magdalena, Mika, Bogumiła and Kochańska, Anna, *Musica polonica nova na Śląsku 1945–2003*, Katowice: ZKP, 2003.

Dziębowska, Elżbieta (ed.), *Polska współczesna kultura muzyczna 1944–1964* [Contemporary Polish musical culture 1944–1964], Kraków: PWM, 1968.

Encyklopedia muzyczna PWM, Kraków: PWM, 1979–.

Erhardt, Ludwik, *Music in Poland*, Warsaw: Interpress, 1975 (also in French, German, Italian, Polish and Spanish).

(ed.), *50 lat Związku Kompozytorów Polskich* [50 years of the Polish Composers' Union], Warsaw: ZKP, 1995.

Gwizdalanka, Danuta, *Muzyka i polityka*, Kraków: PWM, 1999.

Haubenstock, Roman, 'Z zagadnień "atonalizmu"' [Issues of 'atonalism'], *Ruch Muzyczny* 4/1 (1 Jan. 1948), 9–11; 4/2 (15 Jan. 1948), 8–10.

Helman, Zofia, *Neoklasycyzm w muzyce polskiej XX wieku* [Neo-classicism in twentieth-century Polish music] Kraków: PWM, 1985.

'The Dilemma of Polish Music in the 20th Century: National Style or Universal Values', in Trochimczyk, Maja (ed.), *After Chopin: Essays in Polish Music*, Los Angeles: PMC, 2000, pp. 205–42.

Jabłoński, Maciej and Tatarska, Janina (eds.), *Muzyka i totalitaryzm*, Poznań: Ars Nova, 1996.

Jacobson, Bernard, *A Polish Renaissance*, London: Phaidon, 1996.

Jasiński, Roman (ed.), *Koniec epoki: Muzyka w Warszawie (1927–1939)*, Warsaw: PIW, 1986.

Kaczyński, Tadeusz and Zborski, Andrzej, *Warszawska Jesień – Warsaw Autumn*, Kraków: PWM, 1983.

Khrennikov, Tikhon, 'O nowe drogi twórczości muzycznej' [On the new path of musical creativity], *Ruch Muzyczny* 4/18 (15 Sept. 1948), 2–4.

Kisielewski, Stefan, 'Festival Polskiej Muzyki Współczesnej w Krakowie (1–4 XI 1945), *Ruch Muzyczny* 1/1 (Oct. 1945), 24–5.

'Czy w muzyce istnieje formalizm?' [Can formalism exist in music?], *Ruch Muzyczny* 4/22 (15 Nov. 1948), 2–6.

Z muzyka przez lata [With music through the years], Kraków: WL, 1957.

Z muzycznej międzyepoki [Between musical epochs], Kraków: PWM, 1966.

Dzienniki [Diaries], Warsaw: Iskry, 1997.

Koffler, Józef, 'Muzyka awangardowa z lotu ptaka' [A bird's eye view of avant-garde music], *Muzyka* 12/1–2 (1935), 20–1.

Kotoński, Włodzimierz, *Instrumenty perkusyjne we współczesnej orkiestrze*, Kraków: PWM, 1963.

Muzyka elektroniczna, Kraków: PWM, 1989.

Laks, Szymon, *Music of Another World*, Evanston: Northwestern University Press, 1989.

Lee, Jan Patrick, 'Musical Life and Sociopolitical Change in Warsaw, Poland: 1944–1960', Ph.D. thesis, University of North Carolina, Chapel Hill, 1979.

Lindstedt, Iwona, *Dodekafonia i serializm w twórczości kompozytorów polskich XX wieku*, Lublin: Polihymnia, 2001.

Lissa, Zofia, 'O polską pieśń masową' [The case for the Polish mass song], *Odrodzenie* 3/29 (20 Jul. 1947), 3.

   'Z perspektywy dziesięciolecia' [From the perspective of ten years], *Muzyka* 5/7–8 (July–August 1954), 7.

   Music in Poland 1945–1955. Ten Years of People's Poland, Warsaw: Polonia, 1955.

Malecka, Teresa (ed.), *Mieczysławowi Tomaszewskiemu w 60-lecie urodzin*, Kraków: Akademia Muzyczna, 1985.

   Krakowska szkoła kompozytorska 1888–1988 [The Kraków Composition School 1888–1988], Kraków: Akademia Muzyczna, 1992.

Matracka-Kościelny, Alicja (ed.), *Inspiracje w muzyce XX wieku* [Inspiration in 20th-century music], Warsaw: ZKP, 1993.

Michałowski, Kornel, rev. with additions by Gillian Olechno-Huszcza, *Polish Music Literature*, Los Angeles: PMRC, 1991.

Michalski, Grzegorz, 'New Music', in Ochlewski, Tadeusz, *An Outline History of Polish Music*, Warsaw: Interpress, 1979, pp. 134–86.

Mycielski, Zygmunt, 'O drugim zjeździe poetów i kompozytorów' [The Second Conference of Poets and Composers], *Odrodzenie* 4/13–14 (29 Mar.–5 Apr. 1948), 7.

   'Od samego mieszania herbata nie będzie słodka' [Stirring the tea will not make it sweet], *Przegląd Kulturalny* 3/16 (22–28 Apr. 1954), 4.

   'Kryteria i gusty' [Criteria and tastes], *Przegląd Kulturalny* 5 (8–14 Nov. 1956), 6.

   Ucieczki z pięciolinii, Warsaw: PIW, 1957.

   Dziennik 1950–1959, Warsaw: Iskry, 1999.

Nikolska, Irena, *From Szymanowski to Lutosławski and Penderecki* [in Russian], Moscow: Soviet Composers, 1990.

Oberc, Anna (ed.), *Muzyka, słowo, sens: Mieczysławowi Tomaszewskiemu w 70 rocznice urodzin*, Kraków: Akademia Muzyczna, 1994.

Ochlewski, Tadeusz, *An Outline History of Polish Music*, Warsaw: Interpress, 1979.

Oleschko, Herbert (ed.), *Muzyka polska 1945–1995*, Kraków: Akademia Muzyczna, 1996.

Palester, Roman, 'Kryzys modernizmu muzycznego' [The crisis of musical modernism], *Kwartalnik Muzyczny* 14–15 (1932), 489–503.

   'W obronie nowej muzyki' [In defence of new music], *Muzyka* 11/5 (1934), 200–3.

Patkowski, Józef and Skrzyńska, Anna (eds.), *Horyzonty muzyki* 'Biblioteka Res Facta 1', Kraków: PWM, 1970.

Polony, Leszek (ed.), *Przemiany techniki dźwiękowej, stylu i estetyki w Polskiej muzyce lat 70* [Changes in sound technique, style and aesthetic in Polish music in the 70s], Kraków: Akademia Muzyczna, 1986.

Polony, Leszek (ed.), *Spotkania muzyczne w Baranowie 1976: Muzyka w kontekście kultury* [Musical meeting at Baranów 1976: music in the context of culture], Kraków: PWM, 1978.

Polony, Leszek and Malecka, Teresa (eds.), *Spotkania muzyczna w Baranowie 1977: Muzyka w muzyce* [Musical meeting at Baranów 1977: music within music], Kraków: PWM, 1980.

Prosnak, Jan, *Kantata w Polsce*, Bydgoszcz: Pomorze, 1988.

Rappoport-Gelfand, Lydia, *Musical Life in Poland: The Postwar Years 1945–1977*, New York: Gordon and Breach, 1991.

Reyland, Nicholas, 'Warsaw Autumn 2002', *Tempo* 57/223 (Jan. 2003), 76–8.

Rogała, Jacek, *Polish Music in the Twentieth Century*, Kraków: PWM, 2001.

Rudziński, Witold, 'Nowe czasy – nowe zadania' [New Times – New Tasks], *Ruch Muzyczny* 1/1 (1 Oct. 1945), 7–9.

(ed.), *Pieśni żołnierskie* [Soldiers' songs], Warsaw: Czytelnik, 1953.

Ryżkin, J., 'Arnold Schönberg, likwidator muzyki', *Ruch Muzyczny* 5/15 (Oct.–Nov. 1949), 24–31 (reprinted from *Sovetskaya Muzika*, 8 (1949)).

Schaeffer, Bogusław, *Almanach polskich kompozytorów współczesnych* [Almanac of contemporary Polish composers], Kraków: PWM, 1956; with M. Hanuszewska, rev. 2/1966, rev. 3/1982.

Mały informator muzyki XX wieku, Kraków: PWM, 1958.

Nowa muzyka: problemy współczesnej techniki i kompozytorskiej, Kraków: PWM, 1958.

Klasycy dodekafonii, Kraków: PWM, 1964.

Wstęp do kompozycji, Kraków: PWM, 1976.

Siedlecki, Father Jan (ed.), *Śpiewnik kościelny* [Church songbook], Kraków: 39/ 1990.

Slędziński, Stefan, *Muzyka polska: informator*, Kraków: PWM, 1968.

Smialek, William, *Polish Music: A Research and Information Guide*, New York: Garland, 1989.

Sokorski, Włodzimierz, 'Formalizm i realizm w muzyce' [Formalism and realism in music], *Ruch Muzyczny* 4/23–4 (Dec. 1948), 2–5.

'O rzeczywisty zwrot w naszej polityce kulturalnej' [On a decisive turn in our cultural politics], *Nowa Kultura* 17 (25 Apr. 1954), 1–2.

Tarnawska-Kaczorowska, Krystyna (ed.), *Melos, Logos, Etos*, Warsaw: ZKP, 1987 [conference proceedings on the music of Dąbrowski, Kisielewski and Mycielski].

Muzyka źle obecna (2 vols.), Warsaw: ZKP, 1989 [conference proceedings on the music of Berger, Haubenstock-Ramati, Kassern, Kondracki, Laks, Maciejewski, Palester, Panufnik and Spisak].

Thomas, Adrian, 'Your Song Is Mine', *Musical Times* 136/1830 (Aug. 1995), 403–9.

'Mobilising Our Man: Politics and Music in Poland during the Decade after the Second World War', in Thomas, Wyndham (ed.), *Composition–Performance–Reception*, Aldershot: Ashgate, 1998.

'File 750: Composers, Politics, and the Festival of Polish Music (1951)', *Polish Music Journal*, 5/1 (Summer 2002): http://www.usc.edu/dept/polish_music/PMJ/issues.html.

Tomaszewski, Mieczysław, *Nasze muzyczne dwudziestolecie: reportaż fotograficzny 1944–1964* [Our twenty years of music: photo-reportage 1944–1964], Kraków: PWM, 1965.

'O muzyce panegirycznej', *ViVO* 2 (1992), 16–18.

Velimirovič, Miloš (ed.), *From Idea to Sound*, conference proceedings (Nieborów, 1985), Kraków: FZE, 1993.

Werth, Alexander, *Musical Uproar in Moscow*, London: Turnstile, 1949.

Wysocka, Barbara (ed.), *Muzyka polska a modernizm*, Kraków: PWM, 1981.

Individual Composers

Bacewicz, Grażyna

Bacewicz issue, *Ruch Muzyczny* 13/7 (1969).

Gąsiorowska, Małgorzata (ed.), *O Grażynie Bacewicz*, Poznań: Brevis, 1998.

Bacewicz, Kraków: PWM, 1999.

Szoka, Marta (ed.), *Rodzeństwo Bacewiczów*, Łódź, Akademia Muzyczna, 1996.

Thomas, Adrian, *Bacewicz: Chamber and Orchestral Music*, Los Angeles: PMRC, 1985.

Wittig, Stefan, 'Die Kompositionstechnik der letzten Schaffensperiode Grażyna Bacewiczs (1960–1969)', *Jeder nach seiner Fasson*, Saarbrücken, PFAU, Rheinsberg Academy of Music, 1997, 65–104.

Baird, Tadeusz

Grzenkowicz, Izabella, *Tadeusz Baird: rozmowy, szkice, refleksje*, Kraków: PWM, 1982.

Prosnak, Antoni, 'Koncert na orkiestrę Tadeusza Bairda jako przejaw archaizacji', *Muzyka* 2 (1956), 3–25.

'Cztery Eseje Bairda i perspektywy techniki serialnej', *Muzyka* 9/3–4 (1964), 26–43.

Tarnawska-Kaczorowska, Krystyna, *Świat liryki wokalno-instrumentalnej Tadeusza Bairda*, Kraków: PWM, 1982.

Tadeusz Baird: sztuka dźwięku, sztuka słowa, Warsaw: ZKP, 1984.

Tadeusz Baird: Glosy do biografii, Kraków: Musica Iagellonica, 1997.

Górecki, Henryk Mikołaj

Górecki issue, *Musical Quarterly* 82/1 (Spring 1998).

Harley, James, 'Charting the Extremes: Performance issues in Górecki', *Tempo* 211 (Jan. 2000), 2–7.

Homma, Martina, 'Das Minimale und das Absolute: Die Musik Henryk Mikołaj Góreckis von der Mitte der sechziger Jahre bis 1985', *MusikTexte* (1992).

Howard, Luke, 'A Reluctant Requiem: the History and Reception of Henryk M. Górecki's Symphony no. 3 in Britain and the United States', Ph.D. thesis, University of Michigan, Ann Arbor, 1997.

Malecka, Teresa, 'O Koncercie klawesynowym Góreckiego' (On Górecki's Harpsichord Concerto) in Malecka, Teresa (ed.), *Mieczysławowi Tomaszewskiemu w 60-lecie urodzin*, Kraków: Akademia Muzyczna, 1985, pp. 108–13.

Marek, Tadeusz and Drew, David, 'Górecki in Interview (1968) – and 20 Years After', *Tempo* 168 (Mar. 1989), 25–9.

Moody, Ivan, 'Górecki: The Path to the *Miserere*', *Musical Times*, 133/1792 (June 1992), 283–4.

Thomas, Adrian, *Górecki*, Oxford: Oxford University Press, 1997.

Kilar, Wojciech

Podobińska, Klaudia and Polony, Leszek (eds.), *Kilar: Cieszę się darem życia* [I enjoy the gift of life], Kraków: PWM, 1997.

Knapik, Eugeniusz

Bias, Iwona, *Eugeniusz Knapik. Kompozytor i pianista*, Katowice: Akademia Muzyczna, 2001.

Koffler, Józef

Gołąb, Maciej, *Józef Koffler*, Kraków: Musica Iagellonica, 1995.

Gołąb, Maciej (ed.), Koffler issue, *Muzyka* 41/2 (161) (1996).

Kotoński, Włodzimierz

Jaraczewska-Mockałło, Krystyna, *Katalog twórczości i bibliografia*, Warsaw: Akademia Muzyczna, 1995.

Krauze, Zygmunt

Krauze, Zygmunt, note in CD booklet, Polskie Nagrania PNCD 113, p. 6.

Tarnawska-Kaczorowska, Krystyna, *Zygmunt Krauze. Między intelektem, fantazją, powinnością i zabawą*, Warsaw: PWN, 2001.

Krzanowski, Andrzej

Wachowska, Sonia, *Andrzej Krzanowski: katalog tematyczny dzieł/kalendarium życia i twórczości 1951–1990*, Katowice: Akademia Muzyczna, 2000.

Lasoń, Aleksander

Bias, Iwona, *Aleksander Lasoń. Portret kompozytora*, Katowice: Akademia Muzyczna, 2001.

Lutosławski, Witold

Lutosławski issue, *Muzyka* 40/1–2 (156–7) (1995).

Lutosławski: homagium, Warsaw: Galeria Zachęta, 1996.

Będkowski, Stanisław and Hrabia, Stanisław, *Witold Lutosławski. A Bio-Bibliography*, Westport: Greenwood, 2001.

Chłopecki, Andrzej, CD notes for 'Lutosławski Orchestral Works vol. 2', Naxos 8.553169.

Couchoud, Jean-Paul, *La musique polonaise et Witold Lutosławski*, Paris: Stock, 1981.

Gwizdalanka, Danuta, 'Witolda Lutosławskiego czas utracony?', *Zeszyty Literackie* 17/1 (65) (Winter 1999), 132–8.

Gwizdalanka, Danuta and Meyer, Krzysztof, *Lutosławski*, vol. I: 'Droga dojrzłości' [The road to maturity], Kraków: PWM, 2003.

Homma, Martina, *Witold Lutosławski: Zwölfton-Harmonik – Formbildung – 'aleatorischer kontrapunkt' Studien zum Gesamtwerk unter Einbeziehung der Skizzen*, Köln: Bela Verlag, 1995.

Jarociński, Stefan, *Witold Lutosławski*, Kraków: PWM, 1967.

Kaczyński, Tadeusz, *Conversations with Witold Lutosławski*, London: Chester, 1984.

Historia Muzyki Polskiej, tom IX: Lutosławski, życie i muzyka, Warsaw: Sutkowski, 1994.

Klein, Michael, 'A Theoretical Study of the Late Music of Witold Lutosławski: New Interactions of Pitch, Rhythm, and Form', Ph.D. thesis, State University of New York, Buffalo, 1995.

Lissa, Zofia, 'Mała Suita i Tryptyk Witolda Lutosławskiego', *Muzyka* 3/5–6 (May–June 1952), 7–56.

'Koncert na orkiestrę Witolda Lutosławskiego', *Studia Muzykologiczne* 5 (1956), 196–299.

Łobaczewska, Stefania, 'Realizm socjalistyczny w muzyce', *Studia Muzykologiczne* 5 (1956), 114–132 [section on '*Mala suita* Lutosławskiego'].

Lutosławski, Witold, letter to ZKP (8 Apr. 1950), item 56, file 750, Warsaw: Archiwum Akt Nowych.

'Zagajenie dyskusji na walnym zjeździe Związku Kompozytorów Polskich' [Opening Address of the Discussion on the General Assembly of the Polish Composers' Union], *Ruch Muzyczny* 1 (1 May 1957), 2–3.

'Rhythm and the Organization of Pitch in Composing Techniques Employing a Limited Element of Chance', *Polish Musicological Studies* 2, Kraków: PWM, 1986, 37–53 (exx. 304–35).

Postcriptum, Warsaw: Zeszyty Literackie, 1999.

Metzger, Heinz-Klaus and Riehn, Reiner (eds.), 'Witold Lutosławski', *Musik-Konzepte* 71/72/73 (1991).

Meyer, Krzysztof, 'Symfonia sprzed półwiecza (o I Symfonii Witolda Lutosławskiego) [A symphony fifty years on (about Witold Lutosławski's First Symphony)], *Zeszyty Literackie* 16/3 (63) (Summer 1998), 96–105.

Nikolska, Irina, *Conversations with Witold Lutosławski*, Stockholm: Melos, 1994.

Nordwall, Ove (ed.), *Lutosławski*, Stockholm: Wilhelm Hansen, 1968.

Paja-Stach, Jadwiga, *Witold Lutosławski*, Kraków: Musica Iagellonica, 1996.

   Lutosławski i jego styl muzyczny, Kraków: Musica Iagellonica, 1997.

Pociej, Bohdan, *Lutosławski a wartość muzyki*, Kraków: PWM, 1976.

Polony, Leszek (ed.), *Witold Lutosławski*, Kraków: Akademia Muzyczna, 1985.

Rae, Charles Bodman, *The Music of Lutosławski*, 3rd edn, London: Omnibus, 1999.

Rappoport, Lydia, *Vitol'd Liutoslavskii*, Moscow: Muzyka, 1976.

Skowron, Zbigniew (ed.), *Lutosławski Studies*, Oxford: Oxford University Press, 2001.

Stucky, Steven, *Lutosławski and His Music*, Cambridge: Cambridge University Press, 1981.

Tarnawska-Kaczorowska, Krystyna (ed.), *Witold Lutosławski: prezentacje, interpretacje, konfrontacje*, Warsaw: ZKP, 1985.

Thomas, Adrian, *Lutosławski. Cello Concerto*, Aldershot: Ashgate, forthcoming.

Varga, Balint Andras, *Lutosławski Profile*, London: Chester, 1976.

Malawski, Artur

Schaeffer, Bogusław (ed.), *Artur Malawski: życie i twórczość* [Artur Malawski: Life and Work], Kraków: PWM, 1969.

Meyer, Krzysztof

Weselmann, Thomas, *Musica incrostata. Szkice o muzyce Krzysztofa Meyera*, Poznań: PTPN, 2003.

Padlewski, Roman

Piotrowska, J., 'Śmierć Romana Padlewskiego' [The death of Roman Padlewski], *Ruch Muzyczny* 1/4 (15 Nov. 1945), 14–15.

Palester, Roman

Helman, Zofia, *Roman Palester: Twórca i dzieło*, Kraków: Musica Iagellonica, 1999.

Palester, Roman, 'Konflikt Marsyas', *Kultura* 7–8 (1951), 3–16.

Tarnawska-Kaczorowska, Krystyna (ed.), *Muzyka źle obecna* (2 vols.), Warsaw: ZKP, 1990.

Panufnik, Andrzej

Bolesławska, Beata, *Panufnik*, Kraków: PWM, 2001.

Hall, Barrie, 'Andrzej Panufnik and his Sinfonia Sacra', *Tempo* 71 (1964–5), 14–22.

(ibis), interview with Panufnik, 'Treść narzuciła formę' [The contents imposed the form), *Życie Warszawy* 143 (25 May 1951).

Jaraczewska-Mockałło, Krystyna, *Andrzej Panufnik: katalog dzieł i bibliografia*, Warsaw: Akademia Muzyczna, 1997.

Kaczyński, Tadeusz, *Andrzej Panufnik i jego muzyka*, Warsaw: PWN, 1994.

Kydryński, Lucjan, '8 odpowiedzi Andrzeja Panufnika' [8 answers from Andrzej Panufnik], *Dziennik Polski* 140 (13–14 June 1954).

Moszalukówna, A., '*Kołysanka* Andrzeja Panufnika', *Ruch Muzyczny* 5/13 (Sept. 1949), 25–6.

Mycielski, Zygmunt, 'I Symfonia Panufnika', *Ruch Muzyczny* 1/6 (Dec. 1945), 7–8.

Paja-Stach, Jadwiga (ed.), *The Music of Andrzej Panufnik and Its Reception*, Kraków: Musica Iagellonica, 2003.

Panufnik, Andrzej, letter to ZKP (21 April 1950), item 67, file 750, Warsaw: Archiwum Akt Nowych.

   Impulse and Design in My Music, London: Boosey & Hawkes, 1974.

   Composing Myself, London: Methuen, 1987.

Stasiak, Krzysztof, 'An Analytical Study of the Music of Andrzej Panufnik', Ph.D. thesis, The Queen's University of Belfast, 1990.

Thomas, Adrian, 'Panufnik', in Stanley Sadie and John Tyrrell (eds.), *The New Grove Dictionary of Music and Musicians*, 2nd edn, vol. XIX, pp. 45–8.

Walsh, Stephen, 'The Music of Andrzej Panufnik', *Tempo* 111 (Dec. 1974), 7–14.

Penderecki, Krzysztof

Chłopicka, Regina, *Krzysztof Penderecki między sacrum a profanum*, Kraków: Akademia Muzyczna, 2000.

Chłopicka, Regina and Szwajgier, Krzysztof (eds.), *Współczesność i tradycja w muzyce Krzysztofa Pendereckiego*, Kraków: Akademia Muzyczna, 1983.

Ćwikliński, Przemysław and Ziarno, Jacek (eds.), *Pasja o Kryzysztofie Pendereckim*, Warsaw: Polska Oficyna Wydawnicza BGW, 1993.

Erhardt, Ludwik, *Spotkania z Krzysztofem Pendereckim*, Kraków: PWM, 1975.

Henderson, Robert, reviews in *Musical Times* 108/1491 (May 1967), 422–3 and 108/1493 (July, 1967), 624.

Lisicki, Krzysztof, *Szkice o Krzysztofie Pendereckim*, Warsaw: PAX, 1973.

Malecka, Teresa (ed.), *Krzysztof Penderecki's Music in the Context of 20th-Century Theatre*, Kraków: Akademia Muzyczna, 1999.

Mertens, Uw, *Ein 'Schaf im Wolfspetz' Krzysztof Penderecki: 'Anaklasis' (1959/60)*, Saarbrücken: PFAU, 1995.

Minear, Paul S., *Death Set to Music*, Atlanta: John Knox, 1987.

Mirka, Danuta, *The Sonoristic Structuralism of Krzysztof Penderecki*, Katowice: Akademia Muzyczna, 1997.

Mroczek, Joanna and Wilczek, Maria, interview with Penderecki, 'Inspiracja – kompozycja – cytat', *ViVO* 1 (15 Jan. 1994), pp. 23–7.

Müller, Karl-Josef, *Informationen zu Pendereckis Lukas-Passion*, Frankfurt: Moritz Diesterwef, 1973.

Mutter, Anne-Sophie, note in CD booklet for Deutsche Grammophon DG 453 507–2, p. 2.

Penderecki, Krzysztof, *Labyrinth of Time. Five Addresses for the End of the Millennium*, Chapel Hill: Hinshaw, 1998.

Robinson, Ray (ed.), *Studies in Penderecki*, vol. 1, Princeton: Prestige, 1998.

Robinson, Ray and Winold, Allen, *A Study of the Penderecki St Luke Passion*, Celle: Moeck, 1983.

Sadie, Stanley (editorial), *Musical Times* 108/1495 (Sept. 1967), 793.

Schwinger, Wolfram, *Krzysztof Penderecki: His Life and Works*, trans. William Mann, London: Schott, 1989.

Stanisławski, Ryszard, *Krysztof Penderecki Itinerarium: Exhibition of Musical Sketches*, Kraków: Modulus, 1998.

Tomaszewski, Mieczysław, *Krzysztof Penderecki i jego muzyka: ctery eseje*, Kraków: Akademia Muzyczna, 1994.

   The Music of Krzysztof Penderecki. Poetics and Reception: Kraków: Akademia Muzyczna, 1995.

   note in CD booklet for Wergo, WER 6270–2.

Zwyrzykowski, Marek, note in CD booklet for *Seven Gates of Jerusalem*, Accord ACD 036.

Regamey, Constantin (Konstanty)

Loutan-Charbon, Nicole, *Constantin Regamey: compositeur*, Yverdon: Revue Musicale de Suisse Romande et les Editions de Thièle, 1978.

Tarnawska-Kaczorowska, Krystyna (ed.), *Konstanty Regamey: oblicza, polistylismu*, Warsaw: ZKP, 1988.

Schaeffer, Bogusław

Kisielewski, Stefan, 'Schäffer – samobójca' [Schaeffer – suicide], *Ruch muzyczny* 15/9 (1 May 1971), 10–11.

Schaeffer, Bogusław, 'Kisielewski – nożownik' [Kisielewski – cut-throat], *Ruch muzyczny* 15/13 (1 July 1971), 13–18.

   50 Jahre Schaffen – Musik und Theater, Salzburg: Collsch, 1994.

Stawowy, Ludomira, *Bogusław Schäffer: Leben, Werk, Bedeutung*, Innsbruck: Helbling, 1991.

Synowiec, Ewa, *Teatr Instrumentalny Bogusława Schäffera*, Gdańsk: Akademia Muzyczna, 1983.

Zając, Joanna, *Muzyka, teatr i filozofia Bogusława Schaeffera: trzy rozmowy*, Salzburg: Collsch, 1992.

Serocki, Kazimierz

Schaeffer, Bogusław, 'Serocki', in Stanley Sadie (ed.), *The New Grove Dictionary of Music and Musicians* (London: Macmillan, 1980), vol. XVII, p. 177.

Zieliński, Tadeusz A., *O twórczości Kazimierza Serockiego*, Kraków: PWM, 1985.

Szabelski, Bolesław

Markiewicz, Leon, 'II Symfonia Bolesława Szabelskiego. Inspiracje – warsztat – stylistyka', *Górnośląski Almanach Muzyczny*, vol. II (Katowice: Śląsk, 1995), pp. 7–32.

Bolesław Szabelski: życie i twórczość, Kraków: PWM, 1995.

Szalonek, Witold

Moll, Lilianna M., *Witold Szalonek. Katalog tematyczny dzieł. Teksty o muzyce*, Katowice: Akademia Muzyczna, 2002.

Szalonek, Witold, 'O nie wykorzystanych walorach sonorystycznych instrumentów dętych drewnianych' [On the unexploited sonoristic qualities of woodwind instruments] (1968–70), *Res Facta* 7 (1973), 110–19.

Szpilman, Władysław

Szpilman, Władysław, *The Pianist*, London: Gollancz, 1999.

Szymanowski, Karol

Chylińska, Teresa (ed.), *Karol Szymanowski: Korespondencja, Tom* I *(1903–1919)*, Kraków: PWM, 1982.

Szymanowski, Los Angeles: PMRC, 1993.

Maciejewski, B. M. and Aprahamian, Felix (eds.), *Karol Szymanowski and Jan Smeterlin: Correspondence and Essays*, London: Allegro Press, 1970.

Markowska, Elżbieta and Kubicki, Michał (eds.), *Szymanowski and the Europe of His Time*, Warsaw: Polish Radio, 1997.

Palmer, Christopher, *Szymanowski*, London: BBC, 1983.

Samson, Jim, *The Music of Szymanowski*, London: Kahn & Averill, 1980.

Wightman, Alistair (trans. and ed.), *Szymanowski on Music: Selected Writings*, London: Toccata, 1999.

Karol Szymanowski: His Life and Work, Aldershot: Ashgate, 1999.

Index